STUDIES IN BAPTIST HISTORY
VOLUME 37

Dance or Die

The Shaping of Estonian Baptist Identity under Communism

STUDIES IN BAPTIST HISTORY AND THOUGHT
VOLUME 37

A full listing of titles in this series
appears at the end of this book

This volume is published in cooperation with the
International Baptist Theological Seminary, Prague, Czech Republic,
where the original studies that comprise this volume were researched.

STUDIES IN BAPTIST HISTORY AND THOUGHT
VOLUME 37

Dance or Die

The Shaping of Estonian Baptist Identity under Communism

Toivo Pilli

Foreword by Ian M. Randall

Paternoster:
thinking faith

MILTON KEYNES · COLORADO SPRINGS · HYDERABAD

Copyright © Toivo Pilli 2008

First published 2008 by Paternoster

Paternoster is an imprint of Authentic Media
9 Holdom Avenue, Bletchley, Milton Keynes, MK1 1QR, UK
1820 Jet Stream Drive, Colorado Springs, CO 80921, USA
OM Authentic Media, Medchal Road, Jeedimetla Village,
Secunderabad 500 055, A.P., India

www.authenticmedia.co.uk
Authentic Media is a Division of IBS-STL UK, a company limited by guarantee
(registered charity no. 270162)

14 13 12 11 10 09 08   7 6 5 4 3 2 1

The right of Toivo Pilli to be identified as the Author of this Work
has been asserted by him in accordance with the Copyright, Designs
and Patents Act 1988.

British Library Cataloguing in Publication Data
A catalogue record for this book is available from the British Library

ISBN 978–1–84227–596–2

Typeset by Helle Liht
Printed and bound in Great Britain
by AlphaGraphics Nottingham

Series Preface

Baptists form one of the largest Christian communities in the world, and while they hold the historic faith in common with other mainstream Christian traditions, they nevertheless have important insights which they can offer to the worldwide church. *Studies in Baptist History and Thought* will be one means towards this end. It is an international series of academic studies which includes original monographs, revised dissertations, collections of essays and conference papers, and aims to cover any aspect of Baptist history and thought. While not all the authors are themselves Baptists, they nevertheless share an interest in relating Baptist history and thought to the other branches of the Christian church and to the wider life of the world.

The series includes studies in various aspects of Baptist history from the seventeenth century down to the present day, including biographical works, and Baptist thought is understood as covering the subject-matter of theology (including interdisciplinary studies embracing biblical studies, philosophy, sociology, practical theology, liturgy and women's studies). The diverse streams of Baptist life throughout the world are all within the scope of these volumes.

The series editors and consultants believe that the academic disciplines of history and theology are of vital importance to the spiritual vitality of the churches of the Baptist faith and order. The series sets out to discuss, examine and explore the many dimensions of their tradition and so to contribute to their on-going intellectual vigour.

A brief word of explanation is due for the series identifier on the front cover. The fountains, taken from heraldry, represent the Baptist distinctive of believer's baptism and, at the same time, the source of the water of life. There are three of them because they symbolize the Trinitarian basis of Baptist life and faith. Those who are redeemed by the Lamb, the book of Revelation reminds us, will be led to 'fountains of living waters' (Rev. 7.17).

Contents

Chapter 7
Word and Spirit: A Creative Tension 165

Chapter 8
A Common Goal: Evangelism and Mission 191

Chapter 9
Bearing Fruit: Challenges in Ethics 219

Chapter 10
Conclusion 249

FOREWORD

I am delighted to have the opportunity to write the foreword to this fine study by Toivo Pilli of the story of the development of Baptists and other evangelical traditions in Estonia during the Soviet period, 1945-1991. There are several features of this study which make it particularly significant. It is valuable for the analysis it offers of the way in which external factors, notably Soviet atheistic influences, had an impact on evangelical life. Although some studies of this phenomenon in the Soviet period have been undertaken, Toivo Pilli shows how material which is now becoming available and which was not open to researchers in the past can illuminate what was actually taking place in the interface between the state and the churches in the communist period.

Along with this, there is probing exploration, using a remarkable range of primary sources from the churches, of the inner dynamics of the life of four Estonian evangelical traditions – Baptists, Evangelical Christians, Pentecostals and Revivalist Free churches – which under the directions of the state were put together into one union of churches. Although this process of forced union took place across the USSR, the effect on the theological and spiritual identity of the bodies involved has not previously been subjected to rigorous investigation. This is what has been done here. Toivo Pilli shows how the Union of Evangelical Christians-Baptists in Estonia (UECBE), which was the result of the merger of the four traditions, took on a shared identity and how the leaders grappled with the tensions that were involved in that process.

It is fascinating to be led into an understanding of the areas of the new birth and ecclesiology, the dynamics of Word and Spirit, the concept and practice of evangelism and mission, and ethical reasoning and the understanding of sanctification as these were worked out in an Eastern European evangelical context. As Toivo Pilli points out, much attention has been paid to these themes as they have been discussed among evangelicals in Western Europe and America. However, we are introduced here to important figures who shaped thinking among evangelical communities in eastern Europe.

On the question of ecclesiology, the study uncovers the internal debates that took place over issues such as open membership and open communion. Another area of tension was the understanding of the roles of the Bible and the Spirit. To some extent this had to do with the differing stories of the four traditions, but there is also illuminating description and assessment here of the way the charismatic tendencies of the 1970s and 1980s affected Estonia. The Effataa movement, which advocated the direct guidance of the Spirit and miraculous powers, and which had as its base the huge (approximately 2,000 member) Evangelical Christian-Baptist congregation in Tallinn, challenged the identity of the UECBE. In the wider evangelical world the influence of leaders such as Paul Yonggi Cho, from South Korea, is well known, and this study shows that his influence reached behind the 'Iron Curtain'.

Other important themes that are dealt with here include the out-working of the missional calling of the church during communism, and the understanding of the place of the Holy Spirit in sanctification, with the study exploring especially some of the ethical issues that were addressed and the desire among Estonian evangelicals for deeper Christ-likeness. In these ways, the study contributes to work being done on mission and on spirituality.

In recent decades there has been sustained historical examination, by scholars such as David Bebbington and Mark Noll, of evangelical experiences in the English-speaking world. Relatively little has yet been done – certainly that has been made more widely available – on the identity of evangelicals in Eastern Europe. Toivo Pilli has demonstrated that the Estonian Baptists during the Soviet years developed their own unique identity and he shows how this was formed. While this identity had certain similarities with that of Western and Slavic Baptists and other evangelicals, the specific historical and theological context shaped Estonian evangelicals in distinctive ways.

By its detailed and stimulating examination of an Eastern European Baptist community, using a very wide range of primary sources available in Estonia, this study opens up new dimensions in the area of scholarly study of the world-wide evangelical movement. It is a ground-breaking piece of work, and will undoubtedly be a bench-mark for others writing in similar fields.

Ian M. Randall
International Baptist Theological Seminary
Prague
Czech Republic

Acknowledgements

This book is a slightly modified version of my PhD dissertation, and a result of my research into how Estonian Evangelical Christian-Baptist history and identity was shaped in the Soviet context. I am deeply indebted to many people who have encouraged me in various ways during the research and writing of this volume. Dr. Ian M. Randall has offered invaluable insights. His critical questions were as valuable as his suggestions. Prof. John H.Y. Briggs also read the text and his comments helped me to clarify my argument at several points. For all of this – I am sincerely grateful.

I am thankful to two theological seminaries, which have been my academic homes. The International Baptist Theological Seminary in Prague, Czech Republic, offered an academic and communal atmosphere, a learning community, as well as an excellent library. My colleagues at the Baptist Theological Seminary in Tartu, Estonia, helped me to understand the need for this research, and their questions and interest in my work gave me a new boost to continue – sometimes at the low points of my 'research journey'.

I feel that words are inadequate to express my gratitude to my family: my wife Einike (I am thankful both for her love and academic comments) and our three boys – Iisak, Siimeon and Timoteos – who with patience endured the reality that their father was too often and for too long in his office, instead of playing football or reading a book with them.

The materials for this research would have been much narrower if friendly people had not helped me. The Estonian Evangelical Christian and Baptist leadership gave me access to work held in the union's archive, as well as in the archive of the theological seminary in Tartu. I always found helpful support in the Estonian State Archives and in the archive of the Ministry of Internal Affairs. I am also deeply indebted to many friends who opened their personal libraries for me. Of these, I would specially want to thank pastor Üllas Linder, whose full collection of the *samizdat* publication *Logos* proved a very important source regarding Soviet Estonian Baptist theological views. I am also thankful to pastor Uudu Rips, whose lecture notes and oral comments helped me to have a better understanding of Baptist life in the context of Soviet reality. The language of this volume has been improved – at different stages of writing – by Cheryl Smith, Nancy Lively as well as Dave Cupery. Thank you!

Toivo Pilli

Abbreviations

AUCECB All-Union Council of Evangelical Christians-Baptists

AÜ1971-1990 Aruanded ja ülevaated kirikute tegevuse kohta ENSV-s 1971-1990 (Reports and surveys about the activities of churches in the ESSR 1971-1990)

BWA Baptist World Alliance

CARC Council for the Affairs of Religious Cults

CCECB Council of Churches of the ECB

CRA Council for Religious Affairs (until 1965 Council for the Affairs of Religious Cults)

EBF European Baptist Federation

EBUKirj1945 Eesti Baptisti Usuühingu kirjavahetus 1945 (Estonian Baptist Union correspondence 1945)

ECB Evangelical Christian(s)-Baptist(s)

EEKBLA Eesti Evangeeliumi Kristlaste ja Baptistide Koguduste Liidu Arhiiv (Archive of the Union of the Evangelical Christian and Baptist Churches of Estonia)

ERA Eesti Riigiarhiiv (Estonian State Archive)

ESSR Estonian Soviet Socialist Republic

JKP Juhatuse koosolekute protokollid (Minutes of the UECBE Executive Board) (30.01.1981-12.12.1987)

JKPLis Juhatuse koosolekute protokollid koos lisadega (Minutes of the UECBE Executive Board, with attachments) (11.01.1988-02.03.1992)

KUSA Kõrgema Usuteadusliku Seminari Arhiiv (Archive of the Theological Seminary in Tartu)

PNProt1969-1985 Presbüterite nõukogu protokollid 1969-1985 (Minutes of the Presbyters' Council 1969-1985)

SSR Soviet Socialist Republic

TPL Toivo Pilli's personal library

USSR Union of Soviet Socialist Republics

UECBE The Union of Evangelical Christians-Baptists of Estonia (1945-1989)

UECBCE The Union of Evangelical Christian-Baptist Churches of Estonia (since 1989)

UNVA Usuasjade Nõukogu Voliniku Arhiiv (Archive of the Commissioner of the Council for Religious Affairs)

VpUvk1945-1966 Vanempresbüteri ja usuasjade voliniku kirjavahetus 1945-1966 (Correspondence of the Senior Presbyter and the Commissioner of the CARC 1945-1966)

CHAPTER 1

Introduction

This study analyses the development of Baptists (and other evangelical traditions) in Estonia, which is the northernmost of the Baltic states, during the period of Soviet domination, 1945-1991. The self-understanding of these groups – their values, theological emphases and religious practices – was shaped by two sets of factors: external and internal. External factors, principally Soviet religious legislation, the attitude of local state authorities and the influence of different forms of atheistic propaganda, constantly moulded Baptist life. Internal factors were constituted by the inner relationships of four free churches which were forcibly – under directions from the state – put together in this period into one union of churches. This new ecclesial structure, the Union of Evangelical Christians-Baptists in Estonia (UECBE), became predominantly Baptist in ecclesiology and belonged organisationally to the wider All-Union Council of Evangelical Christians-Baptists of the Soviet Union (AUCECB). Nevertheless, all of these four traditions – Baptists, Evangelical Christians, Pentecostals and Revivalist Free churches – had their own historical identities, and their own theological and worship preferences. Their coming together caused tensions, produced the need for adjustments but also resulted in mutual enrichment. The Estonian Baptist identity during the Soviet period was shaped 'between the hammer and the anvil'.

THE BEGINNINGS OF ESTONIAN FREE CHURCHES

The origins of the Estonian free churches date back to the second half of the nineteenth century and to the first decades of the twentieth century.[1] The first

---

[1] This study does not cover the Methodists and the Seventh Day Adventists, as they were not merged into the UECBE. For a good survey of Methodist history in Estonia, see Heigo Ritsbek, *The Mission of Methodism in Estonia,* project thesis (Boston: Boston University, 1996); see also S.T. Kimbrough, ed., *Methodism in Russia and the Baltic States: History and Renewal* (Nashville, Tennessee: Abingdon Press, 1995); Priit Tamm, 'Eesti Metodisti Kirik 1940-1980: Vaatlusi olulisematele arengut mõjutanud protsessidele ja probleemidele' [Estonian Methodist Church 1940-1980: Observations about Major Problems and Processes which Influenced its Development], BTh thesis (Tartu: Tartu University, 1998). For Seventh Day Adventist history in Estonia, see V.

Baptist church in Estonia was founded in Haapsalu, a seaside town in western Estonia, in 1884. In those days Estonia was a part of Tsarist Russia. Soon other Baptist churches were started, and by 1939 there were fifty-one local churches in the Estonian Baptist Union.[2] The new churches had their roots in the pietistic revival initiated by Swedish Lutheran missionaries in the 1870s on the western coast of Estonia[3] (often called the 'West-Coast Revival'), as well as in the mission of German Baptists who were then 'crossing over into other language groups'.[4] The Baptists emphasised repentance and 'new birth', baptised believers upon their personal profession of faith and formed their ecclesiastical structures on a voluntary basis. In 1904, the monthly publication *Teekäija* (Pilgrim) began to be published on a regular basis.[5] A Baptist theological seminary was founded in 1922. Estonian Baptists created a significant preaching tradition, published Christian literature, had strong youth work, and valued theological education.

Beside Baptists, Revivalist Free churches (Est. 'priikogudused') were born in the same wave of spiritual awakening in the 1870s and 1880s. The Revivalist Free churches emphasised aspects of faith and theology similar to those emphasised by the Baptists. They believed that the New Testament was a guideline for their faith and behaviour. However, the Revivalist Free Church believers put more emphasis on spontaneous faith experience, on the work of the Spirit, and on expressions of joy.[6] As was said: 'Children of joy are … better equipped in their inner life than others who [only] listen to a good sermon.'[7] The initial stages of this revivalist movement were influenced by

Viirsalu, *Loojangu eel/Hämarus laskub maale* [Before Sunset/Dusk Falls on the Earth] (n. p., n. d., 2001).
[2] Toivo Pilli, 'Baptists in Estonia 1884-1940', *The Baptist Quarterly*, vol. XXXIX, no. 1 (January 2001), pp. 27-28.
[3] See Riho Saard, 'Baptismi Viron ja Pohjois-Liivinmaan kuvernementeissa 1865-1920' [The Baptist Movement in the Provinces of Estonia and Northern-Livonia 1865-1920], pro gradu thesis (Helsinki: Helsinki University, 1994).
[4] Ian Randall, 'Every Apostolic Church a Mission Society: European Baptist Origins and Identity', in Anthony R. Cross, ed., *Ecumenism and History, Studies in Honour of John H.Y. Briggs* (Carlisle: Paternoster, 2002), p. 300.
[5] For more about this publication, see Toivo Pilli, 'The Role of the Monthly Publication "Teekäija" in the Estonian Baptist Church 1904-1940', in Siret Rutiku and Reinhart Staats, eds., *Estland, Lettland und Westliches Christentum* (Kiel: Friedrich Wittig Verlag, 1998), pp. 211-218.
[6] Ernst Ader, *Eesti usuajalugu, VIII: Läänemaa ärkamine ja selle tagajärgi* [Estonian Faith History, VIII: West Coast Revival and its Consequences], typewritten manuscript (n. p., n. d.), pp. 152-155. TPL.
[7] A. Seppur, *Jees. Krist. Evg. Priikoguduse tekkimine ja levinemine Läänemaa ärkamises* [The Beginning and Development of Jesus Christ's Evangelical Free Church in the Revival in Western Estonia] (Toronto, 1970), p. 19.

Moravian piety.[8] According to Karl Kaups, an Estonian Baptist leader in the 1930s, Moravians emphasised 'personal religious experience, free commitment and voluntary offerings as well as internal fellowship – thus adhering to beliefs similar to those of the free churches.'[9] Early Revivalist Free Church organisational structures were weaker when compared to those of the Baptists, but their evangelistic enthusiasm was remarkable.[10] Both Estonian Baptist and Revivalist Free churches originated from the same religious context. Some revivalist churches joined the Baptists, but full unification – though considered seriously in the 1930s – never took place until it was forced on believers by the Soviet government.

Evangelical Christian Free churches in Estonia also had their roots in local pietistic revivalism. Religious yearning for a more lively faith experience led to a spiritual awakening in Tallinn in 1905. In 1910 the movement was officially registered as a 'religious society' under the name 'Evangelical Christians'.[11] The name was taken from Russian Evangelical Christians who were a registered community in Tsarist Russia. However, Russian Evangelical Christians had a different history, though some similarities in theology cannot be denied.[12] In the 1920s and 1930s, under the leadership of Karl Leopold Marley, the Estonian Evangelical Christians became a lively and mission-minded movement. Their identity has been characterised by the following convictions: the church consisted of 'newborn' Christians; Christian lifestyle and sanctification was essential for discipleship; it was up to every believer's conscience to decide if he or she was satisfied with infant baptism or would liked to be baptised as an adult believer; all 'God's children', including those

[8] For a wide-ranging study of Estonian Moravians, though basically limited to the eighteenth century, see Voldermar Ilja, *Vennastekoguduse (herrnhutluse) ajalugu Eestimaal (Põhja-Eesti) 1730-1743* [The History of the Fraternity of the Moravian Brethren (Herrnhuter) in Estonia (North-Estonia) 1730-1743], vol. 1 (Tallinn: Logos, 1995); volume 2 (Tallinn: Logos, 2000) expands Ilja's research up to 1764, and volume 3 (Tallinn: Logos, 2002) deals with Moravian history in Livonia (South-Estonia) 1729-1750. Volume 4 (Tallinn: Logos, 2005) and volume 5 (Tallinn: Logos, 2006) continue the story of Moravians in Livonia up to the year 1817. For a free church view of Moravians, see Ernst Ader, *Eesti usuajalugu*, pp. 156-220.
[9] Karl Kaups, *Riigikirik ja vabakogudus* [State Church and Free Church] (Keila: Külvaja trükk ja kirjastus, 1934), p. 105.
[10] Herman Mäemets, 'Priikoguduste tekkimine Eestis ja nende evangeelse tegevuse algus' [Origins of the Revivalist Free Churches in Estonia and the Beginning of their Evangelistic Activity], *Logos*, no. 4 (1982), pp. 24-25.
[11] Johannes Laks, *Kakskümmendviis aastat vabakoguduslist liikumist Eestis 1905-1930* [Twenty-Five Years of a Free Church Movement in Estonia 1905-1930] (Tallinn, 1930), p. 24.
[12] Oskar Olvik, 'Ülevaade Evangeeliumi Kristlaste ajaloost' [Overview of the History of Evangelical Christians], in *Eesti Evangeeliumi Kristlaste juubel 50: 1905-1955* [The 50th Jubilee of Estonian Evangelical Christians: 1905-1955], typewritten manuscript (1955), p. 47. KUSA.

who were not yet church members, were invited to the Lord's Supper; and a
tolerant attitude toward believers of other traditions was to be encouraged.[13] At
the end of the 1930s, with changes in religious legislation in Estonia, a number
of Pentecostals joined the Evangelical Christian union.

Pentecostals were the fourth free church which later was brought into the
Union of Evangelical Christians-Baptists in Estonia. The first influences of
proto-Pentecostalism in Estonia can be traced back to the turn of the twentieth
century. Influenced by European evangelical ideals and having found a
renewed focus on the Holy Spirit, a noblewoman named Margarethe von
Brasch began to organise worship services in Tartu, Southern Estonia. She had
experienced a 'filling with the Spirit' during an evangelistic 'alliance service'
in Germany.[14] On her invitation, guest preachers from Germany, Switzerland
and Britain visited Estonia.[15] At approximately the same time, a similar
movement, with a message about a Spirit-filled life, began in Tallinn. Some of
these groups later joined with Baptists. However, there was also a Scandinavian
branch of Pentecostalism, with American influences, that reached Estonia.[16]
Before the First World War, Finnish Pentecostals visited Narva, a town in
North-East Estonia, and established a congregation there. Swedish Pentecostal
missionaries arrived in Estonia in 1922-23.[17] In the 1920s and the 1930s
Pentecostal groups established their mission stations in different locations in
Estonia. The early Estonian Pentecostals longed for the gifts of the Spirit,
including speaking in tongues, emphasised sanctification and were active in
evangelism. They gave prominence to belief in God's immediate intervention
in human affairs.

The pre-war realities and the ideals of these free churches remained latent
during the years of state-coerced union until well after the Second World War.
However, all four of these Estonian free churches, put together in one union by
the atheistic Soviet government in 1945-1947, underwent considerable changes
and had to adjust to the new political and religious situation. These churches
came to be intertwined in the united church body – the Union of Evangelical
Christians-Baptists in Estonia. Their identities gradually merged, and a new
mosaic of beliefs and practices emerged. The self-understanding of the Soviet
Estonian Evangelical Christians-Baptists, as we will see, contained elements
from all these pre-war free churches, but was not absolutely identical with any
one of the prior movements. Rather a fresh expression of Baptist evangelical
identity emerged.[18]

[13] Olvik, 'Ülevaade Evangeeliumi Kristlaste ajaloost', pp. 49, 51.

[14] Evald Kiil, *Meenutusi nelipühi ärkamisest Eestis* [Memories of the Pentecostal
Revival in Estonia] (Tallinn: Logos, 1997), p. 11.

[15] Kiil, *Meenutusi nelipühi ärkamisest Eestis*, p. 11.

[16] For a general study of Pentecostal history and views, see Walter J. Hollenweger, *The
Pentecostals* (Peabody, Massachusetts: Hendrickson, 1988).

[17] Kiil, *Meenutusi nelipühi ärkamisest Eestis*, p. 17.

[18] For a study of the wider evangelical identity, see Derek J. Tidball, *Who are the
Evangelicals?* (London: Marshall/Pickering, 1994).

THE FOCUS OF THIS STUDY

Except for chapters in monographs dealing with the wider story of Estonian churches,[19] and also some more specific articles and Master's or other post-graduate theses,[20] the Estonian free church story has not been explored to any significant extent. In 2005, I edited a collection of articles concentrating on the history of Estonian free churches, especially Baptists.[21] However, all this has covered only a small area of Estonian Baptist history. So far, a comprehensive and critical narrative of Baptists in Soviet Estonia has been lacking. The theological identity of Estonian Baptists has not been a focus of research. The present work attempts at least partly to fill this gap. In order to obtain a full picture of Estonian church history and cultural identity, attention has to be given not only to the mainline churches, but also to churches which have had a minority position in Estonian religious culture.

By contrast with the Baptists and other free churches, the Estonian Lutherans have been studied more fully. A monograph by Riho Altnurme, researching the relationships of the Estonian Evangelical Lutheran Church and the Soviet state in the period 1944-1949, has offered valuable insights for scholars focusing on church-state relations.[22] There are other monographs or doctoral dissertations dealing with the Estonian Lutheran Church, such as those by Riho Saard and Michael Viise.[23]

---

[19] For example, Jaanus Plaat, *Saaremaa kirikud, usuliikumised ja prohvetid 18.-20. sajandil* [Churches, Religious Movements and Prophets in Saaremaa Island in the 18th-20th Centuries] (Tartu: Eesti Rahva Muuseum, 2003); Jaanus Plaat, *Usuliikumised, kirikud ja vabakogudused Lääne- ja Hiiumaal: usuühenduste muutumisprotsessid 18. sajandi keskpaigast kuni 20. sajandi lõpuni* [Religious Movements, Churches and Free Churches in West-Estonia and Hiiumaa Island: Transformational Processes of Religious Entities from the mid-18th Century to the End of the 20th Century] (Tartu: Eesti Rahva Muuseum, 2001).

[20] For example, Riho Saard, 'Baptismi Viron ja Pohjois-Liivinmaan kuvernementeissa 1865-1920' [Baptist Movement in the Provinces of Estonia and Northern-Livonia 1865-1920], pro gradu thesis (Helsinki: Helsinki University, 1994); Toivo Pilli, 'Eesti baptistid ja nende teoloogilise mõtte kajastumine ajakirjas *Teekäija* kuni 1940' [Estonian Baptists and Their Theology as Reflected in *Teekäija* until 1940], ThM thesis (Tartu: Tartu University, 1996); Toivo Pilli, 'Union of Evangelical Christians-Baptists of Estonia 1945-1989: Survival Techniques, Outreach Efforts, Search for Identity', *Baptist History and Heritage*, vol. XXXVI, nos. 1 and 2 (Winter/Spring 2001), pp. 113-135.

[21] Toivo Pilli, ed., *Teekond teisenevas ajas: peatükke Eesti vabakoguduste ajaloost* [A Journey in Changing Time: Chapters from the History of Estonian Free Churches] (Tartu: Kõrgem Usuteaduslik Seminar ja Sõnasepp OÜ, 2005).

[22] Riho Altnurme, *Eesti Evangeeliumi Luteriusu Kirik ja Nõukogude riik 1944-1949* [The Estonian Evangelical Lutheran Church and the Soviet State 1944-1949] (Tartu: Tartu Ülikooli Kirjastus, 2001).

[23] Michael Viise, *The Estonian Evangelical Lutheran Church During the Soviet Period 1940-1991*, PhD dissertation (University of Virginia, 1995); Riho Saard, *Eesti rahvusest*

The present study looks at Estonian Baptists during a significant period in the religious life of the country, 1945-1991. There is a personal dimension to this study. I have been a part of Estonian Baptist life since my childhood and experienced first-hand the communist environment. Born in a Baptist family in Pärnu, Estonia, I became a member of the 'Immanuel' Baptist church in my home town, and later pastor in two churches and involved in different ministries of the Union of Evangelical Christians-Baptists in Estonia. I am aware of the danger that being too closely related to a research topic can be a hindrance for scholarly analysis. However, it can also be an advantage. In my case, it was easier for me as an 'insider' to find materials which during the Soviet years were not often widely circulated. This 'participatory experience' offered a knowledge of 'free church language' and a better understanding of internal theological dynamics and identity which might go unnoticed by a person who approached the topic as an 'outsider'.

In this work, 'identity' is a focus. This is understood as a set of beliefs, values and practices which give to a religious movement or denomination its own 'face' and its own distinct character when compared to other religious movements or denominations. Some facets of identity change over time, while others remain the same, even over long periods of time. Lieven Boeve has argued that 'every shift in context constitutes a challenge to the Christian tradition to reformulate itself in dialogue with the relevant context'.[24] This is important in researching specific denominational 'traditions'. In the present study the term 'identity' rather than 'tradition' has been used, since – to my mind – identity helpfully indicates the dynamic of a religious movement's process of interpretation of its context and its ongoing search for self-understanding. The identity of a religious movement is not only passively shaped by external factors, but is also shaped by its active attempt to consolidate or to transform its values and practices.

Some other terminology also needs explanation. In this book 'Estonian Baptists' and 'Estonian Evangelical Christians-Baptists' are used as synonyms when referring to the members of the UECBE in Soviet years. The evangelical believers belonging to the Union of Evangelical Christians-Baptists in Estonia were known in the wider society simply as Baptists. In addition, in the Evangelical Christian-Baptist (ECB) union Baptist ecclesiology became gradually predominant. However, this study attempts to show that the 'new' Baptist identity contained elements from all four free churches – communities which before the Second World War operated independently. If specific

---

luterliku pastorkonna väljakujunemine ja vaba rahvakiriku projekti loomine, 1870-1917 [The Formation of a Lutheran Clergy of Estonian Descent and the Establishment of a Programme for a Free People's Church, 1870-1917] (Helsinki: Societas Historiae Ecclesiasticae Fennica, 2000).

[24] Lieven Boeve, *Interrupting Tradition: An Essay on Christian Faith in a Postmodern Context* (Louvain-Dudley, MA: Peeters Press, 2003), p. 22.

theological traditions are referred to, traditions which continued and had their inner dynamic and influence in the union, then usually 'Baptist tradition' or 'Evangelical Christian tradition' or 'Pentecostal tradition' is used. At times it is clear from the context that a specific aspect of historical identity is in focus. Also, the study uses the term 'presbyter' to denote a church leader, now usually referred to as 'pastor'.

SOURCES AND METHOD

Estonian Baptists are analysed here using archive documents as well as typewritten illegal (so called *samizdat*) brochures and books. According to my knowledge there is virtually no other research so far which has made such extensive use of archive materials and *samizdat* literature on Estonian Baptists during the Soviet years. Use has been made of the UECBE archives (EEKBLA), which contain important sources (such as minutes of the Presbyters' Council meetings), and which help to understand Estonian Baptist identity 'from within'. The archives were moved from Tallinn to Tartu in 2004. Some materials were found also in the Baptist Theological Seminary archives in Tartu (KUSA). Semi-illegal typewritten literature and publications, such as *Logos*, reflect the faith and convictions of the UECBE churches and believers. I have also conducted several oral interviews. Though subjective, oral interviews add a dimension of human experience to the whole discussion, either confirming or adding new aspects to the written sources.

However, this emphasis on the place of 'church materials' is not meant to downplay other sources. Valuable information can be found in the State Archives of Estonia in Tallinn (ERA), particularly in the files of the Commissioner of the Council for Religious Affairs (CRA) (part of this collection is located in the Estonian Ministry of Internal Affairs, also in Tallinn, UNVA). These materials offer important insights especially for understanding church-state relationships in the Soviet years. Clearly these materials were collected by an organisation which was hostile to the churches, and they should be interpreted in the light of that reality.

The UECBE archives, and the Baptist Theological Seminary archives, were not filed in a systematic way, and in order to help other researchers this study has made an effort to give as much information as possible (in the footnotes) about the documents used. Usually the title or description of the document is given, the date (if available), and, when appropriate, the heading of the file or the sub-collection where it was found. A similarly detailed method is used in referring to materials found in the Department of the CRA archive in the Ministry of Internal Affairs of Estonia and elsewhere. As typewritten *samizdat* manuscripts can be found in several personal libraries and other places, information about the location of the *samizdat* document is given when the source is first mentioned. Also in relation to typewritten publications the bibliography contains information about the locations where particular copies were found.

As to secondary sources, important background information can be found in a number of books. A classic source is Walter Sawatsky's *Soviet Evangelicals Since World War II* and there are also useful volumes published about Evangelical Christians-Baptists in Russian.[25] The volume *Religious Policy in the Soviet Union*, edited by Sabrina P. Ramet, offers helpful data about church and state relationships in the former Soviet Union.[26] On the question of church-state relations and Baptist dissent in the 1960s and 1970s, *Religious Ferment in Russia* by Michael Bourdeaux is valuable.[27]

Estonian Evangelical Christians-Baptists themselves made determined attempts to produce historical surveys, though often these lacked an analytical dimension. The focus was the descriptive task. Also, during the Soviet years these materials remained in the form of typewritten manuscripts.[28] Estonians abroad also published some volumes; however, these tended to focus on the past and usually had rather limited knowledge of Soviet years in Estonian Baptist life.[29] Also the memoirs of some ECB leaders contain valuable data and analysis, both in relation to the history and the theological identity of Estonian Baptists.[30]

During the Soviet years Estonian Baptists developed what Stanton Norman has called a 'Baptist distinctives genre', an effort to define one's

---

[25] Walter Sawatsky, *Soviet Evangelicals Since World War II* (Kitchener, Ontario: Herald Press, 1981); *Istorija evangel'skih hristjan-baptistov v SSSR* [History of Evangelical Christians-Baptists in the USSR] (Moskva: Izdanije VSEHB, 1989); Sergei Savinskii, *Istorija evangel'skih hristjan-baptistov Ukrainy, Rossii, Belorussii, 1917-1967* [History of Evangelical Christians-Baptists in Ukraine, Russia and Byelorussia, 1917-1967], vol. 2 (Sankt Peterburg: Biblija dlja vseh, 2001), the first volume of Savinskii's book, covering the years 1867-1917, was published in 1999.

[26] Sabrina P. Ramet, ed., *Religious Policy in the Soviet Union* (Cambridge: Cambridge University Press, 1993).

[27] Michael Bourdeaux, *Religious Ferment in Russia. Protestant Opposition to Soviet Religious Policy* (London and New York: Macmillan and St. Martin's Press, 1968).

[28] Ernst Ader, *Eesti usuajalugu*; see also a typewritten collection of articles *Baptismi ajalugu* [History of Baptists] (n. p., n. d.), in the Baptist Theological Seminary Archive in Tartu; several historical surveys and memoirs were 'published' in 1984 in the typewritten publication *Logos*; historical awareness was also to be found at presbyters' conferences, since leaders such as Robert Võsu, Osvald Tärk and others often gave papers or lectures on the topic of Estonian Baptist history.

[29] For example, Richard Kaups, *Hea Sõnum ja Eesti Baptisti Kogudused* [A Good Message and Estonian Baptist Churches] (Santa Barbara, California, 1974).

[30] Johannes Laks, *Mälestusi eluteelt ja töömaalt* [Memoirs from Life and Work] (Toronto: Toronto Vabakoguduse Kirjastus, 1965); Oskar Olvik, *Mälestused* [Memoirs], part 1-2, typewritten manuscript (Tallinn, 1966). Oleviste ECB Church library, Tallinn; Arpad Arder, *Kus on Arpadi kuningas* [Where is Arpad's King?] (Tallinn: [Logos,] 1992). The manuscript of Arder's memoirs was written in the 1960s.

identity from theological, even doctrinal perspectives.[31] Norman prefers to argue for universal Baptist principles. Using a different approach to that of Norman, this dissertation argues that Baptist identity should be seen in its context, and suggests that theology is not the only characteristic of Baptist distinctives. However, theology is important, and Estonian ECB leaders made more than one attempt to define Baptist 'principles'. In the 1945, Johannes Lipstok, as chairman of the Estonian Baptist Union, described Baptist beliefs and practices to the Commissioner of the Council of Religious Cults in Estonia.[32] In 1966, Robert Võsu, an influential Baptist leader, wrote an apologetic treatise, which included basic information about Baptist history, faith and ethics.[33] In 1981-1982, Osvald Tärk, another shaping figure, who worried that 'the education in dogmatical issues in our churches has become very weak', wrote a systematic overview of the principles of the Evangelical Christians-Baptists.[34] These treatises, in typewritten form, offered important information about how Estonian Baptists viewed themselves theologically and these texts – especially the texts by Võsu and Tärk – served as a type of 'Baptist catechism' giving guidance to younger generations.

I have kept in mind some questions which help in the analysis of the dynamics of Estonian Baptist identity. For example: In what ways and for what reasons did the theological positions and religious practices of Estonian Baptists change during the Soviet years? What elements helped to create unity in the ECB union and what influences caused tensions? How did Baptist believers react to external atheistic pressures and what resulted from their stance? In what ways did Estonian Baptists respond to theological influences coming from the wider evangelical world or from Russian Baptists and what were the consequences of these responses? Though concentrating on Baptists in Estonia, the research fits into wider studies of Baptists and other evangelicals, and can add to the broader picture of evangelicalism that is being painted.[35] The

---

[31] See Stanton Norman, *More Than Just a Name: Preserving our Baptist Identity* (Nashville, Tennessee: Broadman and Holman, 2001).

[32] Johannes Lipstok to the Commissioner of the CARC (10.07.1945). Eesti Baptisti Usuühingu kirjavahetus 1945 [Estonian Baptist Union correspondence 1945], KUSA.

[33] [Robert Võsu,] *Baptistide arengust ja põhimõtetest* [About the Development and Principles of Baptists], typewritten manuscript [1966]. Merike Uudam's personal library.

[34] Osvald Tärk, 'Meie vendluse põhimõtted' [Principles of Our Brotherhood], *Logos*, no. 1 (1981), no. 1-4 (1982), no. 1-2 (1983).

[35] Paternoster Press has published a number of academically rich volumes on the history and identity of world Baptists and Evangelicals. For example, see Ian Randall, *Evangelical Experiences* (Carlisle: Paternoster, 1999); David Bebbington, ed., *The Gospel in the World: International Baptist Studies* (Carlisle: Paternoster, 2002); Paul Fiddes, *Tracks and Traces: Baptist Identity in Church and Theology* (Carlisle: Paternoster, 2003); Philip E. Thompson and Anthony R. Cross, *Recycling the Past or Researching History? Studies in Baptist Historiography and Myths* (Milton Keynes:

picture of the development of Estonian Baptist identity proves to be dynamic and multifaceted rather than static or monochrome. The identity of Estonian Baptists was shaped by external influences, but it had its inner logic and texture in the face of these influences which yielded or resisted, and thus it played its own role in the process of 'shaping identity', rather like 'material' playing a role in the process of creating a sculpture.

THE STRUCTURE OF THIS STUDY

This book consists of two parts and eight main chapters. The first part can be characterised as 'historical narrative and analysis', the second part as 'historical-theological analysis', though both approaches belong together; they are two sides of one and the same coin.

Chapters 2-5 focus on church-state relationships and the influence of the external pressures on the ECB churches in Estonia. These chapters explore how the atheistic state forced Estonian Evangelical Christians-Baptists to 're-contextualize' their existence. In order to highlight this reality, each of the chapters looks at a distinct period in the story of Estonian Baptist history during which specific external (rather than internal) factors had a powerful effect: a period of adjustment to a new political situation (1945-1959); reaction to Khrushchev's atheistic campaign which took the UECBE into a period of 'lethargy' (1959-1972); a renewed sense of activity among local churches, especially in the field of evangelism (1972-1985); and lastly, a period of 'finding oneself' in the setting of increasing religious freedom (1985-1991).

In chapters 6-9, the discussion concentrates on the internal – mainly theological – development of the UECBE. These chapters attempt to offer insights in the dynamics of theological identity of Estonian Baptists. A helpful framework for these chapters has been found in the writings of Joosep Tammo, an Estonian ECB leader, who has characterised Estonian Evangelical Christian-Baptist churches as believers' communities that focus on the local church, on the Bible, on mission and on sanctification.[36] The chapters are arranged according to these general themes. These rather broad features, however, must be understood in terms of their historical development and must be interpreted in the light of documentary evidence. Otherwise, these characteristics remain 'empty'.

Parts of this research have been published earlier. Sections from the second chapter appeared in 2003 in *Teologinen Aikakauskirja* (Finnish Journal

Paternoster, 2005); Ian Randall, Toivo Pilli and Anthony R. Cross, eds., *Baptist Identities: International Studies from the Seventeenth to the Twentieth Centuries* (Milton Keynes: Paternoster, 2006).
[36] Joosep Tammo, 'Evangeeliumi Kristlaste ja Baptistide Koguduste Liidu põhimõtted ja töösuunad' [Principles and Visions for the Work of the Union of the Churches of Evangelical Christians and Baptists], *Teekäija* (July-August, 1994), pp. 12-15.

of Theology). A version of the third chapter was published in 2005 in the *Baptist Quarterly*. The main ideas of chapter four were presented in a paper at an international conference at the International Baptist Theological Seminary, Prague, in May 2005, and the paper was published in the proceedings of that conference in 2007. Some of the ideas developed in this volume have indirectly found their way into my book in Estonian, *Usu värvid ja varjundid* (Shades and Colours of Faith), which explores some aspects of Estonian Baptist history and identity that could be only briefly touched upon here, such as Estonian Baptist practices in the area of spirituality, and their understanding of worship.[37]

CONCLUSION

Estonian Baptist life and thought in the Soviet era were refashioned by external forces, as the Soviet state exerted pressure on the churches, and by the changing internal sense of identity. If they wanted to survive in the communist context and continue to operate legally, believers were to learn a new 'dance'. The alternative could have been that as a body Baptists ceased to exist. 'Dance or die.' The outlook was not promising. However, they approached the new situation creatively. A key factor in this re-moulding was the pre-war theological identities of the four Estonian free churches that came together in one union. As a result of this process, as well as because of other factors, Estonian Baptist identity was subject to re-evaluation. Some traditional characteristics remained intact, others were expressed in new ways, still others were reshaped by absorbing the emphases of other traditions, and some features seem to have virtually disappeared. At the same time aspects of the identity of some of the other former free churches were either reinforced or downplayed. This study offers insights into the way in which particular religious communities showed themselves to be capable of adaptation and survival in the face of strong external and internal forces that have the potential to destroy Christian identity. This has arguably happened elsewhere. In *The Death of Christian Britain*, Callum Brown has argued that in Britain the 1960s was the decade in which the Christian-centred culture that had conferred identity on Britain was rejected.[38] But identity in terms of religious movements is a more

---

[37] Toivo Pilli, 'The Forced Blessing of Unity: Formation of the Union of Evangelical Christians-Baptists in Estonia', *Teologinen Aikakauskirja*, no. 6 (2003), pp. 548-562; Toivo Pilli, 'From a Thunderstorm to a Settled Still Life, Estonian Baptists 1959-1972', part 1, *The Baptist Quarterly*, vol. 41, no. 3 (July 2005), pp. 158-174; part 2, vol. 41, no. 4 (October 2005), pp. 206-223; Sharyl Corrado and Toivo Pilli, eds., *Eastern European Baptist History: New Perspectives* (Prague: IBTS, 2007); Toivo Pilli, *Usu värvid ja varjundid: Eesti vabakoguduste ajaloost ja identiteedist* [Shades and Colours of Faith: About Estonian Free Church History and Identity] (Tallinn: Allika, 2007).

[38] Callum G. Brown, *The Death of Christian Britain* (London: Routledge, 2001), pp. 1, 193.

complex phenomenon. Thus in Britain the 1960s, as well as being a decade in which religious decline was evident, was also, David Bebbington argues, notable for the way in which the charismatic movement became a force in British Christianity; a force which has contributed to church growth and emergence of new features of evangelical identity.[39] Much attention has been paid to these developments in Western Europe. This study looks at an aspect of European church life that also merits attention: the different ways in which living under communism affected the identity of Baptists and other evangelicals in Eastern Europe.

---

[39] David W. Bebbington, *Evangelicalism in Modern Britain. A History from the 1730s to the 1980s* (Grand Rapids, Michigan: Baker Book House, 1992), pp. 229-230.

PART ONE

External Pressures on Identity

CHAPTER 2

Adjusting to New Patterns: 1945-1959

During the Second World War, Soviet religious policy towards believers within the USSR became more tolerant. After approximately two decades of severe repression, the Orthodox Patriarchate was re-established, and evangelicals were also allowed to revive their work. The 'friendlier' attitude was motivated by pragmatic considerations. Stalin rewarded churches with some freedoms for supporting the Soviet government in its fight against Nazi Germany. In addition to this, as Sergei Savinskii has pointed out, Stalin wanted to give a positive signal to the western Allies before the Teheran conference that took place at the end of 1943.[1] As questions of opening the Second Front in France, as well as questions related to the future of Iran and Poland were discussed in Teheran,[2] much was at stake for the Soviet Union. The religious concessions were related to foreign policy and Stalin's drive for power. 'Power for him was its own justification, no matter how it had been attained…'[3]

However, the official atheistic line did not change. During Stalin's reign there was 'no point at which propaganda directed against religious faith ceased altogether'.[4] This was certainly true of the whole Soviet period. H. Leon McBeth noted in 1987, in his wide-ranging survey of Baptist life, that through the twentieth century the communist government changed its tactics many times but 'never swerved from its announced goal to stamp out all religion and to create an atheistic society'.[5] In all the Soviet republics the anti-religious stance of the government provided the context in which the 'stories' of the churches and religious communities were developed. After the Second World War, this context began to shape the religious identity of Estonian Baptists. The

---

[1] Sergei Savinskii, *Istorija evangel'skih hristjan-baptistov Ukrainy, Rossii, Belorussii, 1917-1967* [History of Evangelical Christians-Baptists in Ukraine, Russia and Byelorussia, 1917-1967], vol. 2 (Sankt Peterburg: Biblija dlja vseh, 2001), pp. 151-152.

[2] Norman Davies, *Europe. A History* (London: Pimlico, 1997), pp. 1037-1038.

[3] G.R. Urban, ed., *Stalinism, Its Impact on Russia and the World* (Aldershot: Wildwood House, 1985), p. 219.

[4] Philip Walters, 'A Survey of Soviet religious policy', in Sabrina P. Ramet, ed., *Religious Policy in the Soviet Union* (Cambridge and New York: Cambridge University Press, 1993), p. 16.

[5] H. Leon McBeth, *The Baptist Heritage* (Nashville: Broadman Press, 1987), pp. 809-810.

decade after the war was a time among Estonian Baptists and other evangelicals for defining their relationship with the atheistic state, adjusting to organisational changes, and learning to operate in a situation of harshly limited religious freedom.

A PRELUDE TO 1945

It was in the turmoil of the Second World War and its aftermath that Estonian Baptists – as well as other Estonian free churches – became part of the wider family of Soviet evangelicals. However, the political 'dance' under Soviet direction began in Estonia as early as 1939. After the Estonian Republic accepted a pact of defence and mutual assistance with the Soviet Union, the proposed Soviet garrisons in Estonian territory soon surpassed the Estonian army in size.[6] In the summer of 1940, Estonia lost its independence and was incorporated into the Soviet Union.[7] The communist occupation inevitably brought changes for the churches. For example, a Baptist church in Paldiski, on the north-coast of Estonia, ceased to exist, as the whole town was evacuated before the Soviet army established its military base there.[8] Christian publications, including the Baptist monthly *Teekäija* (Pilgrim) and the Evangelical Christian Free Church publication *Evangeeliumi Kristlane* (Evangelical Christian), were closed. Churches became subject to heavy taxation and were excluded from educational and social work.[9] The Baptist Theological Seminary in Tallinn was closed because of state orders and because the British and American Baptist financial support was cut off by the new political powers.[10] In the following summer, the effects of the Second World War swept over the territory of the Soviet Union and reached Estonia. Soviet occupation was followed by German invasion.

For the Estonian Baptist Union, as for other churches, the communist occupation, the war itself, and the anti-religious activities of the Soviet authorities, meant unprecedented losses. In 1959 Robert Võsu, who later became the Senior Presbyter of the UECBE, stated that 'the time of war had had a devastating effect' on all free churches in Estonia. He reported: 'Many prayer houses were destroyed in the fires of war and several preachers were

---

[6] Rein Taagepera, *Estonia. Return to Independence* (San Francisco and Oxford: Westview Press, 1993), p. 60.

[7] For a short survey of these events in English, see Toivo U. Raun, *Estonia and the Estonians* (Stanford, California: Hoover Institution Press, 1991), pp. 142-146.

[8] Richard Kaups, *Hea Sõnum ja Eesti Baptisti Kogudused* [A Good Message and Estonian Baptist Churches] (Santa Barbara, 1974), p. 118.

[9] Taagepera, *Estonia. Return to Independence*, p. 66.

[10] Minutes, no. 89 (02.08.1940). Eesti Baptisti Usuteaduse Seminari protokolliraamat 1920-1940 [Baptist Theological Seminary minute book 1920-1940], KUSA.

killed or taken away from their homeland in the confusions of war.'[11] Võsu's statement summarises the two major problems that the UECBE had to face in 1945 and afterwards: the lack of human and material resources. What Võsu does not mention explicitly is the emotional harm that was done to believers, and the struggle to find new courage after the chaos of 1940-1945. Estonian ECB churches had to rebuild their identity from scattered pieces.

In 1940 there were approximately 15,000 members in total in the four Estonian free churches which later formed the UECBE. Baptists, the largest of the four denominations, made up about half of the members.[12] From 1940 to 1945, these churches lost approximately one third of their membership. According to Aleksander Sildos, then head of the UECBE office, at the beginning of 1946 there were 9,875 members in the union.[13]

There were several reasons for the human losses in Estonian churches during 1940-1945. 'Given their highly visible ideological position, church officials and clergymen were ... ready targets of persecution,' states Toivo U. Raun, referring to the deportation of the bishops and several clergymen of the Estonian Lutheran and Orthodox churches in June 1941.[14] The wave of arrests and deportations to Siberia also touched the minority churches. The Baptist Union secretary, Harald Victor Dahl, was arrested in June 1941, and the union's records and documents were confiscated. A preacher in Narva, Viling Varalaid, was also arrested.[15] In addition, a number of male church members

---

[11] Robert Võsu, *EKB koguduste ajalugu* [A History of ECB Churches], typewritten manuscript (1959), p. 154. KUSA.

[12] At the end of the period of Estonian political independence there were 7,549 full members in Estonian Baptist churches. According to I. Kurg there were 4,438 members in Evangelical Christian Free churches. This figure seems to reflect both Pentecostal and Evangelical Christian statistics, as many Pentecostals joined the Evangelical Christian movement in Estonia at the end of the 1930s. In addition to this there were Revivalist Free Church members that according to Osvald Tärk could reach 3,000. According to Jaanus Plaat there were over 2,000 Revivalist Free Church members, excluding some independent groups, in 1938. See Toivo Pilli, 'Baptists in Estonia, 1884-1940', *The Baptist Quarterly*, vol. XXXIX, no.1 (January 2001), p. 28; Ingmar Kurg, 'Kristlikud uskkonnad ja organisatsioonid tänapäeva Eestis' [Christian Denominations and Organisations in Present Day Estonia], in J. Gnadenteich, *Kodumaa kirikulugu* [Church History of the Home Country] (Tallinn: Logos, 1995), p. 118; Evangeeliumi Kristlaste Baptisti koguduste aruanne 1945 [Report of the Evangelical Christian Baptist Churches of 1945]. Osvald Tärgi materjalid [Materials of Osvald Tärk], EEKBLA; Jaanus Plaat, *Saaremaa kirikud, usuliikumised ja prohvetid 18.-20. sajandil* [Churches, Religious Movements and Prophets in Saaremaa Island in the 18th-20th Centuries] (Tartu: Eesti Rahva Muuseum, 2003), p. 144.

[13] A. Sildos to the Commissioner of the CARC (18.4.1947). Vanempresbüteri ja usuasjade voliniku kirjavahetus 1945-1966 (VpUvk1945-1966) [Correspondence of the Senior Presbyter and the Commissioner of the CARC 1945-1966], KUSA.

[14] Raun, *Estonia and the Estonians*, p. 156.

[15] Kaups, *Hea Sõnum ja Eesti Baptisti Kogudused*, pp. 118-119.

were mobilized into the army, either by the Russians or later by the Germans; many of them were killed in the war.

A further blow to the Estonian free churches was the loss of many of their leaders, and many active church members, who left Estonia for Sweden in autumn 1944, due to the German troops withdrawing from Estonia and the Soviet army once again invading. Estonia was re-annexed in autumn 1944 and again became a part of the Soviet Union. Evald Mänd, a member of the Estonian Baptist Union board, left Estonia with the union's president, Karl Kaups. Mänd has vividly described this sea-journey across the stormy Baltic sea in a small yacht.[16] Also, the leader of the Evangelical Christians, Karl Leopold Marley, left the country. A further reason for decline in membership was the excommunication of 'fallen members'. A short handwritten report describes the year 1941 in Kehra Baptist Church: 'One brother and 4 sisters let themselves become trapped by the net of communism, in addition to them 1 brother and 3 sisters have fallen from the ways of God by other reasons, and two sisters have been erased from the membership list for being away from the congregation for too long a time...'[17] In these times of social and political insecurity, the faith and Christian identity of the believers was tested.

Several congregations of Estonian Evangelical Christians-Baptists had quickly to find new leaders. The number of free churches that had applied in 1945 for registration, and consequently were ready to join into one union, was 119.[18] At the end of 1946 there were 114 churches in the UECBE,[19] some of which were still not officially registered. The UECBE leadership encouraged local churches to register 'deputy presbyters'.[20] This was probably wise. The Commissioner's report of 1946 refers to 30 ECB presbyters, including the Senior Presbyter, and 75 deputy presbyters.[21]

The war also caused material losses. The largest and most beautiful church building of the Evangelical Christian Free Church, the 'Immaanuel' Church in

---

[16] Ain Kalmus [Evald Mänd], *Päästa meid ära kurjast* [Save Us from Evil] (Lund: Eesti Kirjanike Kooperatiiv, 1979), pp. 127-148.

[17] Joh. Lepp, 'Lühike ülevaade 1941 aastast Kehra Baptisti koguduses' [A Short Overview of the Year 1941 in Kehra Baptist Church], handwritten manuscript. Osvald Tärgi materjalid, EEKBLA.

[18] The Commissioner of the CARC report (01.07.1946). ERA, f. R-1989, n. 2, s. 3, p. 64.

[19] J. Lipstok to the Commissioner of the CARC (26.02.1947). VpUvk1945-1966, KUSA. Lipstok reports on 112 churches; reports on Puka and Harmi ECB churches are missing.

[20] In a situation in which there was an urgent need for pastors, the Estonian Evangelical Lutheran Church also created a new office of ministry, that of 'vice pastor' (Est. 'abiõpetaja'). See Michael Viise, 'The Estonian Evangelical Lutheran Church During the Soviet Period 1940-1991', PhD dissertation (University of Virginia, 1995), p. 118.

[21] The Commissioner of the CARC report as of 31.12.1946. ERA, f. R-1989, n. 2, s. 3, p. 102.

Tallinn, was hit by a bomb in March 1944.[22] The expressionistic 'Immaanuel' Church was one of the few purpose-built congregational centres in pre-war Estonia.[23] Also the Revivalist Free Church building in Villard Street in Tallinn was destroyed,[24] as well as a Baptist church building in Iisraeli Street.[25] In several cases church documents were destroyed or lost by 1945. There were churches that had to create membership lists afresh.[26]

Though this wartime chaos left deep scars in the body of the Estonian free churches, both organisationally and psychologically, these experiences also paved the way for the new union. Though fellowship had always been a part of the Estonian free church identity, the need to receive encouragement through Christian fellowship was even more acute during the war. In spite of difficulties, attempts were made by the churches to support each other. Baptist churches in Tallinn organized a week for spiritual encouragement from 7 to 11 December 1943 under the title 'Warnings and blessings from the last year'. The themes of sermons reflected the everyday experiences of church members and attempts being made to provide pastoral care: how to avoid giving way to hopelessness; how God had helped to meet everyday needs; how to value the fellowship within the church; and, how to evaluate and use the opportunities for Christian work.[27] On 27 February 1944, Estonian Baptists celebrated their 60th anniversary with a special service.[28] As the programme of the service reveals, the worshippers sang (in Estonian) the famous hymn by the English Baptist, J. Fawcett, 'Blest be the tie that binds, our hearts in Christian love.' The song must have helped to express the emotions of the day and to remind those present of their historic identity.

Estonian free churches had an existing tradition of working together in organising annual conferences for prayer and mutual encouragement - 'alliance work', as it was called. The idea originated with Karl Kaups and Karl Leopold

---

[22] Johannes Laks, *Mälestusi eluteelt ja töömaalt* [Memoirs from Life and Work] (Toronto: Toronto Vabakoguduse Kirjastus, 1965), p. 73.
[23] Egle Tamm, *Moodsad kirikud: Eesti 1920.-1930. aastate sakraalarhitektuur* [Modern Churches: Church Architecture in Estonia in the 1920s and 1930s] (Tallinn: Eesti Arhitektuurimuuseum, 2001), pp. 20, 42-43.
[24] A. Seppur, *Jees. Krist. Evg. Priikoguduse tekkimine ja levinemine Läänemaa ärkamises* [The Beginning and Development of Jesus Christ's Evangelical Free Church in the Revival in Western Estonia] (Toronto, 1970), pp. 96-97.
[25] Tamm, *Moodsad kirikud: Eesti 1920.-1930. aastate sakraalarhitektuur*, p. 82.
[26] The Senior Presbyter to the Commissioner of the CARC (10.04.1946). VpUvk1945-1966, KUSA.
[27] 'Hoiatusi ja õnnistusi möödunud aastast, 7-11. dets. 1943' [Warnings and Blessings from the Last Year, 7-11 December, 1943], printed programme. Osvald Tärgi materjalid, EEKBLA.
[28] 'Eesti Baptismi 60 aasta juubeli jumalateenistuse kava-laululeht' [The Estonian Baptists' 60th Anniversary Programme and Songs], printed programme. Osvald Tärgi materjalid, EEKBLA.

Marley, and the first such event, initially as a youth conference, took place in 1918.[29] The alliance conferences gained momentum and soon 'embraced all the believers' churches'.[30] The conferences concentrated mostly on the devotional aspects of the Christian life, but the themes of mission and evangelism were also represented. Karl Kaups, who was the president of the Estonian Baptist Union 1933-1944,[31] wanted to go further, and made serious efforts to merge Estonian Baptists and the Revivalist Free Church. However, the Revivalist Free Church leaders withdrew from the conversations at the last moment.[32] Work towards deepening the unity of the free churches in Estonia dates back to the First World War. It was in this context that common grounds for cooperation – the conversion experience and an emphasis on sanctification – began to be highlighted. In a similar way, the social and political turmoil of the Second World War increased the free churches' openness to cooperation with one another.

The wartime losses as well as the pre-war experiences of cooperation drew free church Christians in Estonia closer to each other. These events prepared them for the subsequent years of 'life together', offering the psychological tools to interpret and accept the process of ecclesiastical unification that was initiated by the Soviet state in 1945. In times of shared difficulties the common elements of evangelical identity were highlighted instead of those elements leading to diversity. However, it was the pressure from the state authorities on the churches that proved to be crucial in the events that followed the Second World War.

THE FORMATION OF THE UNION OF EVANGELICAL CHRISTIANS-BAPTISTS IN ESTONIA

The process of the formation of the Union of Evangelical Christians-Baptists in Estonia began in spring-summer 1945. This process brought together into a unified body the Estonian Baptists, the Evangelical Christian Free Church (often known as the Evangelical Christians), Pentecostals and the Revivalist Free Church. This unification of free churches was certainly not a local Estonian phenomenon, but took place throughout the Soviet Union. State

---

[29] Karl Kaups, 'Mineviku teedel' [On the Ways of the Past], in *Põllu Vagudel* [On the Furrows of the Fields], no. 28 (1965), p. 91. Taimi Proos, when referring to 1917, is probably mistaken. Taimi Proos, *Südametunnistuse pärast: Henrik Kokamägi elust ja tööst* [For the Sake of Conscience: About the Life and Work of Henrik Kokamägi] (Tallinn: Eesti Piibliselts, 2002), pp. 157-158.

[30] Evald Mänd, 'Mälumatk mineviku radadele' [A Journey of Memory in the Paths of the Past], *Usurändur*, no. 1 (1984), p. 32.

[31] Riho Saard, 'Eesti kirikute juhtivvaimulikkond läbi aegade' [Estonian Church Leaders through the Centuries], part 2, *Akadeemia*, no. 3 (1998), p. 612.

[32] Artur Proos, oral information (20.08.2002).

authorities were anxious to reduce the number of religious organisations they needed to control. The Stalinist church policy and Soviet religious laws began gradually to shape the religious sphere of life in Estonia. Two decisions made by the Soviet government had far reaching effects for Estonian free church believers.

First, there was the formation of the Council for the Affairs of Religious Cults (CARC) in 1944. This was designed to control the life of all religious communities, except Orthodoxy, which had its own controlling structure. The CARC had to provide smooth communication between the state and the churches, thereby 'securing the execution of the state's policies of religion'.[33] Johannes Kivi, a former secret service officer, was appointed the Commissioner of CARC in the Estonian SSR in January 1945.[34] Registration of churches and church leaders was one of his first tasks, as well as supervising the unification of the free churches according to the detailed instructions given from Moscow.[35]

Second, the life of Estonian evangelical churches was affected by the formation of the All-Union Council of Evangelical Christians and Baptists (AUCECB) which was established in the so-called unification meeting (26-29 October 1944) held in Moscow. In spite of wartime restrictions, forty-five delegates from both Evangelical Christian and Baptist Churches in Russia and Ukraine arrived in Moscow in military transport vehicles. The state provided food and hotel accommodation, but also ensured that the meeting would make the proper decisions.[36] The name of the All-Union Council was slightly modified from 1 January 1946. It became the All-Union Council of Evangelical Christians-Baptists.[37] The AUCECB was to be expanded by the addition of other movements such as the Pentecostals and later the Mennonites, and also by unions in the Soviet republics joining with the AUCECB. As a general policy

---

[33] Otto Luchterhandt, 'The Council for Religious Affairs', in Ramet, ed., *Religious Policy in the Soviet Union*, p. 57.

[34] Riho Altnurme, *Eesti Evangeeliumi Luteriusu Kirik ja Nõukogude riik 1944-1949* [The Estonian Evangelical Lutheran Church and the Soviet State 1944-1949] (Tartu: Tartu Ülikooli Kirjastus, 2001),
p. 36.

[35] For example, see a secret letter of instruction sent by I. Polianski to the Commissioners in Estonia, Latvia, Lithuania, Ukraine and Byelorussia (21.09.1945). ERA, f. R-1989, n. 2, s. 2, pp. 36-39. The letter deals especially with questions related to Pentecostals joining the All-Union Council of Evangelical Christians and Baptists (AUCECB).

[36] Walter Sawatsky, *Soviet Evangelicals Since World War II* (Kitchener, Ontario: Herald Press, 1981), p. 78.

[37] *Istorija evangel'skih hristjan-baptistov v SSSR* [History of Evangelical Christians-Baptists in the USSR] (Moskva: Izdanije VSEHB, 1989), p. 233. The replacement of 'and' with '-' was to emphasize not just partnership but the fusion that was hoped would result.

the Soviet state allowed one national structure for Orthodoxy and one national structure for Protestant churches.[38] However, there were notable exceptions. For example, the Lutheran Church as well as the Methodist Church in Estonia continued to have independent existence. Indeed, the possibility of merging the Estonian Methodists with Evangelical Christians-Baptists was explored in 1945-1946, but without result.[39]

To explain the situation, two representatives of the AUCECB, Aleksander Karev and Nikolai Levindanto, visited Estonia. They met with the Estonian Baptist leadership on 30 April 1945.[40] Their argument, referred to by Johannes Lipstok, the chairman of the Estonian Baptist Union, was as follows: it is self-evident that in the Soviet Union there cannot be two Baptist unions and two unions of Evangelical Christians. 'This kind of union already exists in Moscow, and the only natural solution would be to cooperate with it.'[41] The leading Estonian Baptist figures (Johannes Lipstok, Osvald Tärk, Robert Võsu and Arthur Eiman) expressed their positive attitude towards joining the AUCECB - 'taking into account the present situation' - but they also pointed out that the Estonian Baptist Union conference had to make the final decision.[42] As it turned out, the Soviet authorities did not support the holding of a conference. The Commissioner withheld permission: the conference was not advisable 'until the Baptist churches are registered by the Council for the Affairs of Religious Cults'.[43] As later history showed, the first ECB conference in Soviet Estonia, with delegates from local churches, did not take place until 1966. In 1945 the Soviet authorities preferred to solve the unification questions at the level of church leadership and to avoid democratic decision-making processes in the churches. Already traditional Baptist identity was being modified.

Instead of a conference bringing together delegates from local churches, a further step for Estonians in the way of unification was a meeting with an Estonian ECB delegation and representatives of the AUCECB, in Moscow, 20-25 August 1945.[44] In the Estonian delegation, Johannes Lipstok and Osvald

---

[38] Walter Sawatsky, 'Protestantism in the USSR', in Ramet, ed., *Religious Policy in the Soviet Union*, p. 323.

[39] The Deputy Chairman of the CARC to Commissioner J. Kivi (22.02.1946). ERA, f. R-1989, n. 2, s. 4, p. 18a. See also J. Kivi to I. Polianski (09.02.1946). ERA, f. R-1989, n. 2, s. 4, p. 17.

[40] Excerpt from minutes, no. 5 (30.04.1945). Eesti Baptisti Usuühingu kirjavahetus 1945 (EBUKirj1945) [Estonian Baptist Union correspondence 1945], KUSA.

[41] Circular letter no. 1 of the UECBE Senior Presbyter (01.12.1945). EKB Oleviste kogudus [The ECB Oleviste Church], UNVA.

[42] Excerpt from minutes, no. 5 (30.04.1945). EBUKirj1945, KUSA.

[43] The Commissioner, J. Kivi, to the Baptist Union (14.06.1945). EBUKirj1945, KUSA.

[44] Märkmeid Evangeeliumi Kristlaste ja Baptistide ülevenemaalise liidu ja Eesti NSV Evang. Kristl. ja Baptistide esindajate nõupidamiselt [Notes from the meeting of the representatives of the AUCECB and the Evangelical Christians and Baptists of the Estonian SSR]. EBUKirj1945, KUSA.

Tärk represented the Baptists, Voldemar Nurk represented the Pentecostals, and Johannes Laks represented the Evangelical Christians.[45] The Estonians gained the impression that Yakov Zhidkov, Aleksander Karev and others from Moscow attempted to deal with the different views of the Estonian free churches with understanding.[46] According to Johannes Laks, the method of treatment of problems during the negotiations was 'without any blame'.[47] The Estonian delegation gave a report of church life in Estonia. Then, as a response to the AUCECB proposal, the decision was made to carry out the unification of Estonian 'spiritually alive movements' and join them to the AUCECB – 'for the glory of God and for the benefit of His kingdom work in the Estonian SSR'.[48] Extensive discussion took place over the issues of baptism, the Lord's Supper and church membership. The decision was made to nominate Johannes Lipstok to the post of the Senior Presbyter in Estonia (with the right to open an office) and to invite Johannes Laks, Voldemar Nurk, and Joosep Leisberg to become his assistants.[49] In this way, all the uniting denominations were represented at the leadership level, at least formally. In reality the roles of Leisberg and Nurk proved to be less significant than those of Lipstok and Laks. The latter two represented the two stronger unions, Baptists and Evangelical Christians.

In his circular letter of 1 December 1945, Lipstok informed the local churches that he was now leading the work of the united Estonian free churches and that his official title was 'the Senior Presbyter'.[50] It was made clear that local churches should contact the new office from then on.[51] It is evident that by the end of 1945 the new ecclesiastical structure – the Union of Evangelical Christians-Baptists of Estonia – was taking shape. According to the Commissioner's statistics, by the beginning of 1946 there were 10,107 members in the UECBE.[52] At that point the new body was still in the process

---

[45] According to a personal letter sent by A. Karev to O. Tärk, J. Leisberg, the leader of the Revivalist Free Church, and A. Rajandi, a Baptist, were also initially invited to Moscow. A. Karev to O. Tärk (01.08.1945). EBUKirj1945, KUSA.

[46] Laks, *Mälestusi eluteelt ja töömaalt*, p. 82.

[47] Ibid., p. 81.

[48] Märkmeid Evangeeliumi Kristlaste ja Baptistide ülevenemaalise liidu ja Eesti NSV Evang. Kristl. ja Baptistide esindajate nõupidamiselt. EBUKirj1945, KUSA.

[49] Märkmeid Evangeeliumi Kristlaste ja Baptistide ülevenemaalise liidu ja Eesti NSV Evang. Kristl. ja Baptistide esindajate nõupidamiselt. EBUKirj1945, KUSA. See also The Decree of the Senior Presbyter J. Lipstok, no. 1 (01.11.1945). ERA, f. R-1989, n. 1, s. 2, p. 108.

[50] Circular letter no. 1 of the UECBE Senior Presbyter (01.12.1945). EKB Oleviste kogudus, UNVA.

[51] Circular letter no. 1 of the UECBE Senior Presbyter (01.12.1945). EKB Oleviste kogudus, UNVA.

[52] The Commissioner of the CARC report (01.07.1946). ERA, f. R-1989, n. 2, s. 3, p. 65. The Commissioner's statistics roughly correlate with the 1945 report of the UECBE

of formation. The registration of local ECB churches was still not completed; at the beginning of 1947 there were 9 applications waiting for a final decision.[53]

The Estonian free churches as a whole did not accept the idea of merger as happily as the official documents tended to show. There was a fear of losing one's denominational identity and also losing the possibility of independent work. In July 1945, the Commissioner Johannes Kivi informed the CARC in Moscow that local leaders had accepted the offer of unification, but they did not have much sympathy with the idea.[54] Joosep Leisberg, from the Revivalist Free Church, said to the Commissioner: 'As a believer, I do not have anything against merger with Baptists or with the All-Union Council of Evangelical Christians and Baptists, but we have worked independently for more than 65 years, and we would like to see a continuation of our functioning in the former mode…'[55] Also questions related to theology and worship were raised. The Revivalist Free Church requested that 'jumping under the power of the Spirit' would not be prohibited, and the Pentecostals wanted to continue to teach 'speaking in tongues'.[56] Johannes Lipstok made an appeal to the Commissioner that baptisms would be allowed to be carried out in rivers and lakes, not only in baptisteries inside church buildings.[57] Though all Estonian free churches had to learn to cooperate with each other and were forced to give up some of their cherished religious heritage, the smaller denominations seem to have perceived this process as making concessions to the Baptists. '[W]e all have to become Baptists,' concluded Johannes Laks, the leader of the Evangelical Christians.[58]

However, it was made clear by the state authorities that registration of churches depended on their willingness to work within the state's given framework. The Estonian free churches understood the message: dance or die. Robert Võsu, the Senior Presbyter of the UECBE 1970-1985, said: 'In the changed situation there remained only this possibility to work: to operate in the framework of the All-Union ECB brotherhood.'[59] The Estonian Revivalist Free churches were registered only after their leader, Joosep Leisberg, informed the

---

that counts 10,173 members and lists 116 churches. Evangeeliumi Kristlaste Baptisti koguduste aruanne 1945. Osvald Tärgi materjalid, EEKBLA.

[53] The Commissioner of the CARC report as of 31.12.1946. ERA, f. R-1989, n. 2, s. 3, p. 98.

[54] J. Kivi to the chairman of the CARC, I. Polianski (15.07.1945). ERA, f. R-1989, n. 2, s. 2, p. 18.

[55] J. Kivi to the chairman of the CARC, I. Polianski (15.07.1945). ERA, f. R-1989, n. 2, s. 2, p. 20.

[56] Doklad o poezdke v Pribaltiku [Report of the trip to the Baltics]. ERA, f. R-1989, n. 1, s. 1, p. 74.

[57] Johannes Lipstok to the Commissioner of the CARC (10.07.1945). EBUKirj1945, KUSA.

[58] J. Kivi to the chairman of the CARC, I. Polianski (15.07.1945). ERA, f. R-1989, n. 2, s. 2, p. 19.

[59] Võsu, *EKB koguduste ajalugu*, p. 154.

Commissioner that 11 Revivalist free churches out of 13 were ready to merge with the ECB structures.[60] The authorities were especially careful about Pentecostals. The instructions from Moscow ordered that those Pentecostal churches that opposed the idea of unification should not be registered. The state was not satisfied with merely a nominal approval of the merger; registration was refused when these churches were not ready to adjust to ECB theology and practice, and 'in essence continue[d] to be Pentecostal congregations as before'.[61] It seems that Pentecostals were under particular pressure to adjust to the new patterns. It is probably not by accident that out of twelve churches of Pentecostal background that joined the ECB union in 1945, there were only four left by the end of 1951.[62]

The unification, therefore, was controversial. Lack of democratic patterns and painful concessions made by the churches under state pressure constituted the obvious drawbacks of this process. Some elements of Pentecostal and Revivalist Free Church identity, such as speaking in tongues or spontaneous expressions of religious experiences, were clearly not favoured by the state. This is why the 'religious-enthusiastic input' of Pentecostal and Revivalist churches in the formation of the spirituality of the new union remained relatively modest. Paradoxically, by forcing the unification, the Soviet state made Estonian free church organisational structures stronger, though the churches had to learn how to adjust in a situation of restricted opportunities for spiritual work and how to live in an atheistic society. These new relationships with the state, as well as with the ECB headquarters in Moscow, had an impact on UECBE self-understanding.

ESTONIAN EVANGELICAL CHRISTIANS-BAPTISTS
AND THE ATHEISTIC STATE

Reflecting retrospectively, some Estonian church leaders have concluded that the unification of the free churches in Estonia was invented by the state in order to destroy the evangelical identity. This is how one Baptist pastor expressed it: '...their idea was to put them [free churches] all together, then they [free churches] will start fighting with each other, and we [the state] can liquidate all the sectarians more effectively...'[63] However, things were not so straightforward. Stalin's persecution of churches in the 1930s is a chapter of its

---

[60] J. Leisberg to the Commissioner of the CARC (14.01.1946). ERA, f. R-1989, n. 1, s. 2, pp. 4-4b.

[61] The chairman of the CARC, I. Polianski, to the Commissioner, J. Kivi (21.09.1945). ERA, f. R-1989, n. 2, s. 2, p. 37.

[62] The UECBE statistical reports 1945, 1951. Evangeeliumi Kristlaste-Baptistide koguduste statistilised aruanded 1945-1963 [The UECBE statistical reports 1945-1963], EEKBLA.

[63] Uudu Rips, recorded interview (20.04.2000).

own in the history of persecutions. But later, at least during 1945-47, the Soviet government was not interested primarily in destroying religion, but rather in using it for its own purposes. During and after the Second World War, the Soviet Union used the contacts of religious organisations in seeking to reach its goals in foreign policy.[64] Certainly, the state wanted firmly to direct these processes. Making the churches 'as centralised as possible'[65] enabled the state 'to place the free churches under government control'.[66] When the first winds of the cold war began to blow in 1947-48, the focus moved from political to ideological aspects in Soviet policy towards religion, and further restrictions were put on churches.[67]

Any evaluation made of the post-war period in Estonia depends on taking the immediate prehistory of the churches into account. Comparison with the situation in Russia is instructive in gaining a wider perspective. Russian Baptists came from a dark decade of severe persecution, and welcomed new, though limited, opportunities for Christian work. Estonian believers came from a different background, and their memories of the free exercise of their faith before the war were still very much alive. Adjustment to new restrictive laws and regulations was for them a test of their faith and identity.

In 1945, the Estonian free churches had to join 'the game', the rules of which had already been set up in Moscow. By contrast with Russian evangelicals, the Estonian believers had never experienced such systematic persecution as that in Russia in the 1930s which almost wiped out the Baptist and Evangelical Christian unions.[68] Nevertheless, Estonians remembered vividly the Soviet repressions in 1940-41 and had some knowledge of the persecutions that had taken place in the Soviet Union. During the Baptist Union semi-official conference in Ridala in 1943 some war refugees from an evangelical church in Pljussa, on the Russian side of the border, told delegates about deportations and other repressions before the war. 'In Russia we were not allowed to pray to God even in our own homes,' said the elder of the Pljussa church to the delegates.[69] It was this kind of government that Estonian believers now had to contemplate.

For the Estonian Evangelical Christians-Baptists, the first Soviet years required several painful concessions. On 5 July 1945, the Council of People's

---

[64] Altnurme, *Eesti Evangeeliumi Luteriusu Kirik ja Nõukogude riik*, p. 25.

[65] Walter Kolarz, *Religion in the Soviet Union* (London and New York: Macmillan and St. Martin's Press, 1961), p. 304.

[66] Olaf Sild and Vello Salo, *Lühike Eesti kirikulugu* [A Short Estonian Church History] (Tartu, 1995), p. 152.

[67] Sawatsky, *Soviet Evangelicals*, pp. 62-63.

[68] Savinskii, *Istorija evangel'skih hristjan-baptistov Ukrainy, Rossii, Byelorussii*, pp. 131-135.

[69] Baptisti Liidu kogudustepäeva protokoll [Minutes of the meeting of church representatives of the Baptist Union] (14.-16. 10. 1943). Kalju Raidi kirjavahetus ja märkmed [Correspondence and notes of Kalju Raid], KUSA.

Commissaries of the Estonian SSR passed a decree that – when strictly interpreted – allowed only registered presbyters to conduct services. Worship services were allowed only in registered church buildings. Visiting preachers were not permitted. Social work, youth and children's ministries, as well as 'all kinds of groups, courses and trips', were prohibited. In some exceptional cases, the ministers were allowed to conduct 'religious rites', such as funeral services or baptisms, outside church buildings, 'according to the prescribed order'. Churches, now called religious societies, did not possess the rights of a juridical person.[70] The CARC specifically demanded that the Commissioners had to prohibit events with special programmes for youth and children, meetings where special guests were invited, 'love feasts', and 'harvest festivals'.[71] One can only imagine what these restrictions meant for Estonian ECB churches, whose Christian life focused on fellowship and different church ministries.

The Soviet years had a severe impact on evangelism. Concern for outreach was a part of the identity of the Baptist movement. Historically, the German Baptist Johann Gerhard Oncken and his followers, who exhibited great mission enthusiasm in the nineteenth century, had influenced Russian and Ukrainian Baptists, and undoubtedly also Estonian Baptists.[72] Under the Soviet rule, 'most of the evangelicals' techniques for growth were explicitly forbidden by law'.[73] However, the focus of Soviet Evangelical Christians and Baptists on evangelism had never been completely lost. After the war, the number of baptisms increased all over the Soviet Union.[74] Soon the government noted these mission efforts. In 1948, the Deputy Prime Minister, Kliment Voroshilov, suggested that the authorities investigate Baptists carefully, because their 'proselytism is most harmful'.[75] The last years of Stalin's reign were characterised by political terror and intensified pressure on churches, similar to the earlier Stalinist persecutions.[76] The number of baptisms in the Estonian

---

[70] Usuühingute tegevuse korraldamise ajutine juhend [A Temporary Instruction for the Arrangement of the Operation of Religious Societies] (05.07.1945). ERA, f. R-1989, n. 2, s. 1, pp. 12-14.

[71] The instruction letter of the CARC, no. 2 (15.10.1945). ERA, f. R-1989, n. 2, s. 1, p. 24.

[72] Günther Balders, *Theurer Bruder Oncken* (Wuppertal und Kassel: Oncken Verlag, 1984), pp. 127-129, 136-137; Ian M. Randall, 'Every Apostolic Church a Mission Society: European Baptist Origins and Identity', in Anthony R. Cross, ed., *Ecumenism and History, Studies in Honour of John H.Y. Briggs* (Carlisle: Paternoster, 2002), pp. 296-298.

[73] Sawatsky, *Soviet Evangelicals*, p. 50.

[74] For example, see Y. Zhidkov, 'Na poljah raboty nashevo bratstva' [In the Fields of Our Brotherhood], *Bratskii Vestnik*, no. 4 (1946), pp. 31-41; Y. Zhidkov, 'Vzgljad nazad' [A Look Behind], *Bratskii Vestnik*, no. 1 (1948), pp. 5-10.

[75] Altnurme, *Eesti Evangeeliumi Luteriusu Kirik ja Nõukogude riik*, p. 34.

[76] Michael Rowe, *Russian Resurrection. Strength in Suffering – A History of Russia's Evangelical Church* (London: Marshall Pickering, 1994), p. 123.

ECB union in 1945-1959 reflects the approach of the state authorities to religion. Baptisms grew from 110 in 1945 up to 304 in 1948, only to be followed by a period of decrease. There were 129 baptisms in 1952. Then, in the context of Khrushchev's 'thaw', a clear growth in baptisms can be seen again: 174 baptisms in 1954, 252 baptisms in 1957, and 287 baptisms in 1958.[77]

The state also influenced the way statistical data was reported in the UECBE documents. Before the Soviet years the Baptists usually referred both to the number of full members and the 'general number of souls' (i.e. statistics including Sunday school children and youth, who were not yet baptised as believers). The report of 1947 stated that by the end of the year there were 9,762 members in the Estonian ECB union, and in addition to this there were 2,733 members 'without rights',[78] i.e. children and youth who were not full members.[79] This practice in reporting was soon changed. As it was illegal to have any children's activities or youth work in churches, the official reports cease to reflect the data about this group. However, in 1956 and 1957 the Senior Presbyter encouraged the local churches to keep these records for their own use.[80] It was important to seek to preserve their identity.

The All-Union ECB leadership was more inclined than was the Estonian leadership to give messages to local churches that were in accordance with state policies, though such messages were expressed in theological language. Already in 1947 the AUCECB's President Zhidkov criticised the practice of what he described as too hasty baptisms; the new converts, he argued, should be tested and taught before baptism.[81] Christian work does not need to expand, but rather to become deeper, Zhidkov argued.[82] Estonian ECB leaders tried by contrast to avoid statements that could be subject to ambivalent interpretations.

Learning to cope with the oppressive system was not easy for local Estonian presbyters, especially in the countryside. There were complaints in 1948 and 1949 about high taxes that were applied to presbyters. For example, the presbyter of Küdema ECB church in Saaremaa Island, Eduard Heinmets, who was also a farmer, had been taxed at a much higher rate of income tax when compared to other owners of farmhouses of the same size. Aleksander

---

[77] The UECBE statistical reports 1945-1958. Evangeeliumi Kristlaste-Baptistide koguduste statistilised aruanded 1945-1963, EEKBLA.

[78] The UECBE statistical report 1947. Evangeeliumi Kristlaste-Baptistide koguduste statistilised aruanded 1945-1963, EEKBLA.

[79] In 1956, in the inspection report of the Senior Presbyter's visitation to Jõgeva ECB Church, the term 'members without rights' is defined as 'dedicated children of the members of the church' (Est. 'koguduse liikmete õnnistatud lapsed'). Inspection report, no. 16 (10.08.1956). Revideerimisaktid 1956-1957 [Inspection reports 1956-1957], EEKBLA.

[80] Inspection report, no. 16 (10.08.1956), no. 21 (14.08.1956), no. 38 (12.-13.10.1957). Revideerimisaktid 1956-1957, EEKBLA.

[81] Y. Zhidkov, 'Nash otshet' [Our Report], *Bratskii Vestnik*, no. 1 (1947), p. 15.

[82] Zhidkov, 'Vzgljad nazad', p. 6.

Sildos from the UECBE office wrote to the Commissioner requesting that Heinmets should not be taxed according to the higher tax rate designed for religious workers, as Heinmets 'serves the church without a salary'.[83] One ECB preacher, Juhan Hanslep, from Hiiumaa Island, gave up his work as minister, but the local government financial department continued to apply higher taxes on his farmland. The union office asked the Commissioner to send a confirmation to the local government office that Hanslep was no longer a religious worker.[84] It is probable (though not certain) that one of the reasons why Hanslep decided to retire from pastoral work was strong economic pressure from the state.

There is no evidence that there was any large-scale withdrawal from spiritual ministry in the UECBE because of high taxes or atheistic pressure. The spiritual calling was usually taken so seriously that it helped ministers to withstand outward difficulties. Nevertheless, the presbyters had to cope with economic hardships caused by atheistic restrictions. It became more difficult for church members to support their presbyters with food, work or other help, which had been the normal practice in the countryside before Soviet times. Such support could be interpreted by the state as exploitation of church members.

The UECBE and its leaders, as well as local ECB churches, had to live with the new reality of the imposed 'marriage with the state'. Estonian Baptists, who had defined themselves as a freedom movement in the 1930s,[85] now had to redefine what 'freedom' meant for their identity. They faced the danger of 'the confusion of citizenship and discipleship',[86] to use Walter Shurden's expression, although Shurden is dealing with the rather different set of problems faced by the churches in America. Nonetheless, it is the case that Estonian ECB believers had to be both disciples and Soviet citizens. Finding a balance between these two realities was a challenge for many.

While the Communist party defined the general direction of religious policies, the Commissioner of the CARC had wide powers to control church life. The UECBE office had to provide the Commissioner with reports containing data about church personnel and membership, and about church buildings and their inventory. In 1945-47 one of the main tasks of the Commissioner was to direct the registration of the churches and the

---

[83] A. Sildos to the Commissioner of the CARC (16.01.1948). VpUvk1945-1966, KUSA.

[84] A. Sildos to the Commissioner of the CARC (07.09.1948). VpUvk1945-1966, KUSA.

[85] Karl Kaups, 'Eesti Baptismi ideelised põhialused' [The Principles of the Estonian Baptist Movement], in R. Kaups, ed., *50 aastat apostlite radadel* [50 Years in the Ways of the Apostles] (Keila: E.B.K. Liidu kirjastus, 1934), pp. 13-14.

[86] Walter B. Shurden, *The Baptist Identity. Four Fragile Freedoms* (Macon, Georgia: Smyth and Helwys, 1993), p. 52.

implications of that registration.[87] His permission had to be sought for a variety of questions. For example, the ECB had to request permission to organise annual regional presbyters meetings, or even to publish a small church calendar, which remained for many decades the only ECB publication in Estonia.[88] In some cases, the Commissioner directly interfered in the question of finding church leaders. In 1952, Johannes Lipstok informed the Commissioner: 'According to your wish, I have appointed Stepan Rusmanov to be the temporary acting presbyter in Tallinn Russian ECB church.'[89] At every step the ECB churches were reminded of their dependence on government policies, and of the way in which the interpretation of these policies by officials affected their identity.

The Soviet secret service had a special department for collecting information about churches and for exercising influence over Christians. In the 1950s, the presbyter of Oleviste ECB Church, Osvald Tärk, and the presbyter of Rakvere ECB Church, Arpad Arder, were under regular observation by the KGB. Tärk had wide correspondence with believers in the USA, Britain and Sweden. Arder had openly expressed his criticism of atheistic suppressive policies, received religious literature from abroad, and was involved in 'missionary activities' in Karelia.[90] This was enough to make the KGB suspicious. In several cases the KGB tried to recruit agents from among Christians. However, they met some difficulty when dealing with the ECB believers. Estonian historian Indrek Jürjo refers to a KGB report from 1956, where it is said that 'a special psychological approach is needed to recruit sectarians, among whom there are many religious fanatics…'.[91] 'Fanatic' in the language of the KGB meant a person who strongly held his or her beliefs and refused to cooperate. The KGB certainly had agents among Evangelical Christians-Baptists,[92] but it can be argued that emphasis on ethical living and

[87] For a brief summary about the registration of ECB churches in Estonia see Toivo Pilli, 'The Forced Blessing of Unity: Formation of the Union of Evangelical Christians-Baptists in Estonia', *Teologinen Aikakauskirja*, no. 6 (2003), pp. 554-555.
[88] In 1957, the Estonian Evangelical Lutheran Church was allowed to print its first publication since 1944 (besides song-sheets and small calendars), the EELC yearbook. However, most of the copies were sent abroad, to give an impression that it was possible to publish Christian literature in Estonia. The next EELC yearbook was not printed until 1982. Riho Altnurme, 'Die Estnische Evangelisch-Lutherische Kirhce in der Sowjetunion (bis 1964)', in Siret Rutiku and Reinhart Staats, eds., *Estland, Lettland und Westliches Christentum* (Kiel: Friedrich Wittig Verlag, 1998), p. 243.
[89] J. Lipstok to the Commissioner of the CARC (28.07.1952). VpUvk1945-1966, KUSA.
[90] Indrek Jürjo, *Pagulus ja Nõukogude Eesti* [Exile and the Soviet Estonia] (Tallinn: Umara, 1996), p. 175.
[91] Ibid., p. 161.
[92] For example, the 1956 report of the Estonian KGB fourth department mentioned that a KGB agent, a Baptist preacher, helped the KGB to influence a small group of the

the idea of the separation of church and state, which was an integral part of free church self-understanding, made Estonian ECB believers more resistant to these 'temptations'. The report stated that among Orthodox and Lutheran believers there were far fewer 'fanatics' and their recruitment did not differ from recruitment in the population at large.[93] The whole area of the relationships between the KGB and the free churches in Estonia still awaits impartial and detailed research.

The Soviet state, imposing restrictive religious policies in Estonia, forced Estonian evangelicals, not the least Baptists, to re-evaluate their traditional understanding of church-state relationships. It was a new challenge to be a free church in a society where the state interfered in church life. Joining with each other and with the AUCECB, making concessions in democratic decision-making processes and yielding to state control – these were only some consequences of state pressure on ECB churches in the 1940s and 1950s.

THE UECBE AND THE AUCECB

Estonian Baptists had never previously had any headquarters outside Estonia. Even when they were organisationally a subdivision of the Russian Baptist Union at the beginning of the twentieth century,[94] decisions having an impact on the Estonian Baptist life were made locally. Estonian Baptists would have agreed with the definition of a free church as a Christian group of believers who 'are locally free to choose their own affiliations' and are not obliged 'to accept commitments made for them by a collective or hierarchical action'.[95] However, the affiliation with the AUCECB was not freely chosen by the UECBE and the Estonian union had to face the reality that there was a 'higher' structure in Moscow. Estonian Senior Presbyter Johannes Lipstok became a member of the AUCECB leadership body (12 members) in 1945.[96] He served in this capacity until 1959. Later, other Estonians became members or candidate members of the AUCECB leadership, for example: Aleksander Sildos, 1963-1969; Arpad Arder, 1966-1969; and Robert Võsu, 1969-1979. Võsu became a member of the Presidium of the AUCECB in 1979.[97] According to the 'official

---

followers of Andrew Urshan in Estonia to join Baptist or Methodist churches. Jüri Ojamaa and Jaak Hion, eds., *Aruanded Riikliku Julgeoleku Komitee 2. ja 4. osakonna tööst 1956. aastal* [Reports of the Work of the KGB 2. and 4. Department in 1956] (Tallinn: Rahvusarhiiv, 2000), p. 104.

[93] Jürjo, *Pagulus ja Nõukogude Eesti*, p. 162.

[94] Harald Victor Dahl, 'Ülevaade liidust' [A Survey of the Union], in R. Kaups, ed., *50 aastat apostlite radadel*, p. 19.

[95] Donald F. Durnbaugh, *The Believers' Church* (Scottdale, Pennsylvania: Herald Press, 1985), p. 5.

[96] Sawatsky, *Soviet Evangelicals*, p. 488.

[97] Ibid., pp. 488-491.

approach', the Senior Presbyter was considered to represent the AUCECB in Estonia rather than the Estonian ECB churches in the AUCECB. On his letterhead, Lipstok's title had the unfamiliar words, 'the Senior Presbyter of Evangelical Christians-Baptists in the Estonian SSR'. At least it had been possible to avoid the name 'Plenipotentiary of the AUCECB in the Estonian SSR' which would have sounded even stranger to Estonian ears.[98]

Nonetheless, while there was the danger of losing local identity, there were also certain positive opportunities opened up by belonging organizationally to the All-Union 'brotherhood'. The Estonian ECB union was able to see itself as a part of a wider evangelical family in the Soviet Union. Personal contacts developed with many AUCECB leaders. Aleksander Karev, Yakov Zhidkov, and other Russian ECB leaders became well known names in Estonia, at least among ECB presbyters and active church members. The relationship was mutual: Estonian leaders, especially Osvald Tärk, Johannes Lipstok, Aleksander Sildos, and later Robert Võsu were respected for their advice and balanced theological views. The spirituality of Slavic free churches became better known to Estonian believers.[99] The UECBE Senior Presbyter's report of 1965 stated that 'through the person of the Senior Presbyter, the brotherhood in our homeland is connected with the All-Union work'.[100] At the end of the 1940s and at the beginning of the 1950s, when the links to Western believers were practically cut off, this contact served also as a door – though a very narrow door – into the wider Baptist world.

The AUCECB had a representative, Nikolai Levindanto, who served as a plenipotentiary for the Baltic region with permanent residence in Riga. According to Sawatsky, his task was to make sure 'that churches adhered to the AUCECB statutes' in this region.[101] Levindanto was trusted by the state authorities. The Baltic Commissioners of the CARC were ordered in 1945 'not to allow any kind of official meetings related to the decisions of the expanded meeting of AUCECB' (August meeting) until the arrival of Levindanto in autumn 1945.[102] Levindanto served in this post as a plenipotentiary (later called the Senior Presbyter in the Baltics) until his death on 10 January 1966.[103] Estonian free churches were not used to having somebody supervising their work and having almost a bishop's role - though at the end of the nineteenth century the German Baptist pastor, Adam Reinhold Schiewe, had supervised

[98] Excerpt from minutes, no. 5 (30.04.1945). EBUKirj1945, KUSA.
[99] Toivo Pilli, 'Union of Evangelical Christians-Baptists of Estonia 1945-1989: Survival Techniques, Outreach Efforts, Search for Identity', *Baptist History and Heritage*, vol. XXXVI, nos. 1 and 2 (Winter/Spring 2001), p. 116.
[100] The UECBE Senior Presbyter's report of 1965. EKB vanempresbüteri aruanded (VpAruanded) [The UECBE Senior Presbyter's reports], EEKBLA.
[101] Sawatsky, *Soviet Evangelicals*, p. 96.
[102] The chairman of the CARC, I. Polianski, to J. Kivi (21.09.1945). ERA, f. R-1989, n. 2, s. 2, p. 39.
[103] The Senior Presbyter's report of 1965. VpAruanded, EEKBLA.

emerging Estonian Baptist churches.[104] Schiewe's role, however, was not supported by formal hierarchical structures, but rather by spiritual authority and by the fact that he had played a role as an organiser and helper in the beginnings of the Estonian Baptist movement.[105] Levindanto was, by contrast, an official, who was always received in a friendly way by Estonians, but who seems never to have developed very close relationships. At the same time, Levindanto tried to fulfil his supervisory role tactfully, 'not stepping on a hurting blister'.[106]

In their dealings with the 'Moscow brotherhood', Estonians seem to have attempted to maintain good relationships but to keep some distance at the same time. The language barrier also gave Estonians some space for manoeuvring. In the UECBE, the language of worship was Estonian, though some Russian-speaking churches emerged in the course of years. And though Estonian ECB believers were more concerned about the loss of denominational as compared to national identity, in their relations with 'Moscow brotherhood' the language issue always reminded Estonians about their ethnic roots. The AUCECB publication *Bratskii Vestnik* (Brotherly Herald) was not widely read in Estonia. For example, in 1975 Estonian ECB churches got only 60 copies of this publication,[107] which means that not even every Estonian ECB church or church leader was provided with a copy. The influence of the AUCECB's official policies, theology and spirituality would have been much more powerful if the plan to publish an Estonian version of *Bratskii Vestnik* had gained the Commissioner's support in 1946.[108]

However, the Slavic dimension that was added to Estonian ECB life had its long-lasting effects. Some of these were reflected even in the use of language. Until the Second World War Estonian Baptists used the word 'preacher' (Est. 'jutlustaja') to denote the pastor in a local church. This was borrowed directly from the German 'Prediger'. Also, the 'elder of the church' (Est. 'kogudusevanem') was used. During the early stages of the Soviet times, 'preacher' was changed to 'presbyter' (Est. 'presbüter'). The term 'Senior

---

[104] Riho Saard, 'Baptismi Viron ja Pohjois-Liivinmaan kuvernementeissa 1865-1920' [The Baptist Movement in the Provinces of Estonia and Northern-Livonia 1865-1920], pro gradu thesis (Helsinki: Helsinki University, 1994), p. 42; Toivo Pilli, 'Eesti baptistid ja nende teoloogilise mõtte kajastumine ajakirjas *Teekäija* kuni 1940' [Estonian Baptists and Their Theology as Reflected in *Teekäija* until 1940], ThM thesis (Tartu: Tartu University, 1996), p. 12.

[105] Karl Kaups, 'Kojuhüütud ustavaid sulaseid' [Faithful Servants Who Have Been Called Home], in R. Kaups, ed., *50 aastat apostlite radadel*, pp. 111-112.

[106] Savinskii, *Istorija evangel'skih hristjan-baptistov Ukrainy, Rossii, Byelorussii*, p. 191.

[107] The UECBE statistical report 1978, appendix. Evangeeliumi Kristlaste-Baptistide koguduste aruanded 1964-1990 [The UECBE statistical reports 1964-1990], EEKBLA.

[108] Minutes, no 7. Meeting of ECB spiritual workers (09.03.[1946]). ERA, f. R-1989, n. 1, s. 2, p. 43.

Presbyter' (Est. 'vanempresbüter'), denoting the leader of the ECB union, became a generally used term quite quickly, especially in official correspondence, while the term 'preacher' was used in parallel with 'presbyter' even at the beginning of the 1950s. In 1955 Aleksander Sildos, the head of the UECBE office, asked the Commissioner to issue two minister's licences with the title 'presbyter', 'though in previous licences the official name was "preacher" (which was used earlier to denote the spiritual worker)', as Sildos explained to the Commissioner.[109] In addition, the AUCECB circular letters, especially those sent for church festivals, came to be translated into Estonian and read at church meetings. There were other circular letters giving instructions to the union leadership. For example, one circular letter of the AUCECB, translated into Estonian, exhorted presbyters to educate church members not to avoid military service.[110] Also, attempts were made to introduce new traditions, such as the celebration of Unification Day, to remember the Moscow meeting of October 1944. Financial contributions were now made annually to Moscow ECB headquarters. In 1947, the Estonian ECB churches sent to Moscow 30,182 roubles and 60 kopecks, while the UECBE office in Tallinn received 52,026 roubles and 57 kopecks.[111]

In spite of the fact that the relationships with the AUCECB were to a large extent not a free choice made by Estonian ECB believers, this new dimension in their life forced them to rethink and in some cases to reaffirm the basic characteristics of their identity. Belonging to the AUCECB meant for Estonians not only meeting and engaging with representatives of Russian ECB theology and spirituality, but also gave them a greater sense of belonging to a wider Baptist family beyond Estonia.

CHURCH LIFE, THE ROLE OF THE UNION OFFICE AND LEADERSHIP

Estonian Evangelical Christians-Baptists were not merely the passive objects of outside influences. The Estonian ECB leadership and local churches tried to respond to the pressurizing factors which they were experiencing. To continue Christian work, changes were necessarily taking place both in church life and in organisational and leadership patterns. In many cases the steps taken were not pro-active but rather re-active: learning to live with a given situation.

Though officially there was no permission to have a local union board or other collective decision-making body in the 1940s and the 1950s, there were

---

[109] A. Sildos to the Commissioner of the CARC (20.05.1955). VpUvk1945-1966, KUSA.
[110] Circular letter of the AUCECB, no. 278 (23.02.1953), Estonian translation. EEKBLA.
[111] The UECBE statistical report 1947. The UECBE statistical reports 1945-1963, EEKBLA.

attempts to maintain some kind of collective leadership in Estonia. The Senior Presbyter had a good team of workers in the union office, including Osvald Tärk and Aleksander Sildos. From October 1945 Sildos worked as the head of the union office.[112] Being fluent in Russian he helped to keep contact with the AUCECB. The union office became a 'uniting centre', helping to heal the wounds of war and to find new and younger leaders for local churches. From the winter of 1949 the Estonian union leaders used a car to visit local churches. This was unprecedented in the whole Soviet Union.[113] With the emphasis shifting towards the Tallinn office, the local churches' authority and initiatives were gradually played down. However, in the 1940s and the 1950s the Estonian ECB union office certainly had a positive role in building up trust and hope within the ECB union.

Johannes Lipstok, usually together with his co-workers, was active in visiting local churches. The minutes of his visitations of 1956-1957,[114] show that he gave both pastoral and practical advice; checked the financial documents of the local church; was interested in the presbyters' and the deacons' spiritual role; monitored Sunday service attendance; paid attention to the condition of church buildings and their surroundings; and asked questions about the musical activities of the churches. Lipstok often visited smaller churches, as these churches obviously needed more support and sometimes struggled more than the larger churches with meeting the formal requirements of the state. He usually checked if the church had a record book for membership, and if the minutes of the church board meetings and church members meetings were kept in order. These visitations served also to evaluate the spiritual life of the churches: in some cases the spiritual life showed signs of growth (in Jõgeva, Puka, Tõrva and in other places);[115] in other cases the spiritual life of the church was characterized as being at a standstill (in Laius-Tähkvere).[116] In some cases the Senior Presbyter gave clear instructions: in Puka he suggested that the church should raise their young presbyter's salary 'immediately' from 250 roubles up to, at least, 300 roubles per month.[117] Significant central leadership was being offered.

There is evidence that in several churches mission activity grew in 1955-1957, the period of Khrushchev's political liberalisation. By the middle of the 1950s the Estonian ECB churches had regained a certain confidence in doing

---

[112] Elmar Palumäe, comp., *Elusõnu mitmest suust: Eduard Lilienthal ja Aleksander Sildos* [Words of Life from the Lips of Many: Eduard Lilienthal and Aleksander Sildos], book 6, typewritten manuscript (1977), p. 78. KUSA.

[113] Laks, *Mälestusi eluteelt ja töömaalt*, pp. 84-85.

[114] Inspection reports 1956-1957. Revideerimisaktid 1956-1957, EEKBLA.

[115] Inspection report, no. 16 (10.08.1956), no. 19 (13.08.1956), no. 20. (13.-14.08.1956). Revideerimisaktid 1956-1957, EEKBLA.

[116] Inspection report, no. 17 (11.08.1956). Revideerimisaktid 1956-1957, EEKBLA.

[117] Inspection report, no. 19. (13.08.1956). Revideerimisaktid 1956-1957, EEKBLA.

evangelism, though the methods were limited to evangelistic services and
personal witness. In Kuressaare, for instance, in one year 'approximately 60
new members' joined the church.[118] Atheistic writers noted the current of new
life in the churches. Lembit Raid, writing about the history of atheism in
Estonia, called the period of 1952-1957 'years of temporary revival of
ecclesiastical rituals', and pointed out that believers, including Baptists,
'revived their mission work'.[119] Ülo Meriloo mentioned that in 1955 a 'revival'
began among the younger generation in Tallinn and its surroundings.[120] At one
service 42 people responded to the 'altar call' in the Oleviste church; they were
mostly young people, many from Christian families.[121] The membership
statistics of the UECBE showed a slight growth in the 1950s: in 1953 there
were 8,900 members in the 88 churches of the union, whereas in 1959 there
were 9,306 members in 89 churches.[122] According to Sawatsky, the Senior
Presbyter Johannes Lipstok confirmed that the gradual decline in membership
from the 1940s had stopped by 1959.[123] Unfortunately, Lipstok was too
optimistic. There was soon to be an even more rapid decline. Nevertheless, the
positive experience of the mid-1950s, relative as it was, helped to reconfirm the
evangelistic ideals of the Estonian free churches, who were now working
together in one union. The Senior Presbyter, though under pressure from the
state, tried to support local church life and the evangelistic identity of the ECB
churches.

Johannes Lipstok served the UECBE as the Senior Presbyter for the first
15 of the Soviet years. This was a difficult position: a Senior Presbyter was
inevitably between the hammer and the anvil. Senior Presbyters like Lipstok
had information about church-state relationships that others did not possess,[124]
which increased their authority, but they also had to make decisions that
attempted to balance compromise and benefit for the churches. However,
Lipstok's ability to work in a team, his long-term experience with the Estonian
Baptists, and his caution about having too close a relationship with the state
authorities, helped him to fulfil his role in these difficult years. Lipstok came
from a rural background and perhaps his practical rural mindset also had a part
to play in his achievements.

---

[118] Inspection report, no. 11 (09.07.1956). Revideerimisaktid 1956-1957, EEKBLA.
[119] Lembit Raid, *Vabamõtlejate ringidest massilise ateismini* [From the Circles of
Freethinkers to Mass Atheism] (Tallinn: Eesti Raamat, 1978), pp. 162-163.
[120] Ülo Meriloo, 'Ühistöö aastad' [Years of Cooperation], in *Oleviste 50. Oleviste
koguduse juubelikogumik* [Oleviste 50. The Anniversary Collection of Oleviste Church]
(Tallinn: Oleviste kogudus, 2000), p. 9.
[121] Aili Niilo, oral information (21.12.2003).
[122] The UECBE statistical reports 1953, 1959. Evangeeliumi Kristlaste-Baptistide
koguduste statistilised aruanded 1945-1963, EEKBLA.
[123] Sawatsky, *Soviet Evangelicals*, p. 264.
[124] Joosep Tammo, oral information (10.07.2000). Joosep Tammo was the President of
the UECBE 1992-1998.

Johannes Lipstok had been born on 13 September 1883, in Valkla village in northern Estonia. Elmar Palumäe, in a short summary of Lipstok's life, said that the young Lipstok's conversion in 1901 was accompanied with strong emotions. Lipstok experienced speaking in tongues, and felt a calling to preach. As a preacher, Lipstok was a good communicator.[125] It is quite obvious that Lipstok's own conversion and his understanding of early Estonian free church spirituality, which involved certain pneumatological elements, was a good preparation for his work as leader of a union of diverse traditions. In spite of a rather modest elementary education, he was accepted into Lodz Seminary in 1907.[126] In 1921-1922 his name was in the student list of Hamburg Baptist Seminary.[127] In 1911 Lipstok was elected the preacher of Rummu-Valkla Baptist Chuch, but his life's work as a pastor was done in the oldest of Estonian Baptist churches, Haapsalu Baptist Church, where he began his ministry in 1923. He seems to have valued the sermons of the great Victorian Baptist preacher, C.H. Spurgeon; in Lipstok's personal library there were twenty five volumes of Spurgeon, more than any other author.[128] The elements of traditional Baptist identity are clearly to be seen in Lipstok.

Johannes Lipstok had long experience in a wider spiritual leadership role. In 1921, when he was still continuing his studies, he was elected the chairman of the Estonian Baptist Union. In 1933, when Karl Kaups was elected to this post, Johannes Lipstok continued as deputy chairman. He fulfilled these responsibilities until 1945, when, as we have seen, he became Senior Presbyter of the newly formed UECBE. He held this post until 1960, when his health started to decline. Lipstok died on 17 January 1961. His funeral service was conducted by Aleksander Karev from Moscow on 22 January 1961.[129] Robert Võsu said that Lipstok, when he was on his deathbed, sent greetings to the Commissioner of the CARC; these greetings emphasised the goodness and faithfulness of God. According to Võsu, the Commissioner was deeply moved.[130]

It seems that Lipstok in his role as the Senior Presbyter was in most cases

---

[125] Eerik Rahkema, 'Johannes Lipstok kui vaimulik juht' [Johannes Lipstok as a Spiritual Leader], diploma thesis (Tartu: Kõrgem Usuteaduslik Seminar, 2002), pp. 7, 16.

[126] Eduard Kupsch, *Geschichte der Baptisten in Polen, 1852-1932* (Lodz: Im Selbstverlag des Verfassers, s.a. [1932?]), p. 468.

[127] *Festschrift für Feier des 50 jahrigen Jubiläums des Predigerseminars der deutschen Baptisten zu Hamburg-Horn vom 1. Bis 3. Juni 1930* (s. a. [1930?]), pp. 82-85.

[128] Johannes Lipstoki raamatukogu kataloog (1958) [The list of books in Johannes Lipstok's library (1958)]. EEKBLA.

[129] Rahkema, 'Johannes Lipstok kui vaimulik juht', p. 11.

[130] H. Veermets, *Albomi juurde. Haapsalu koguduse 100 aastapäev* [To the Album. The 100th Anniversary of the Haapsalu Church], typewritten manuscript (1984). EEKBLA.

able to avoid becoming the herald of the Soviet state policies,[131] and acted primarily as a spiritual leader. The AUCECB leaders in Moscow were not always as successful in this respect. It has also been argued that in some areas of the Soviet Union, such as Moldavia for example,[132] the Senior Presbyters were actually actively hindering the initiatives of the local churches, and thus not supporting but rather destroying local evangelical identity. Estonian Evangelical Christians-Baptists were fortunate to have leaders whom they knew and respected. Lipstok tried to encourage the common spiritual goals that different Estonian free church traditions had shared even before the merger: evangelism, growing in faith, maintaining fellowship, and living a biblical lifestyle. This is not to say that there were no difficulties or compromises. One test of unity for many local churches was the state policy that tried to carry out mergers not only on the denominational, but also on the local church level. However, under the leadership of Lipstok the basis for the developing sense of identity in the ECB union was sought not so much in the formal merger, but rather in shared spiritual values.

MERGER OF LOCAL CHURCHES

The Soviet Union's religious policies included plans to merge or close local churches. In Estonia, during the registration process in 1945-1947, a number of local churches were closed and the church buildings were taken over for the use of the local government.[133] Believers usually joined some nearby church. For example, in 1946, the Commissioner of the CARC demanded the closure of

---

[131] Certainly, Lipstok was not able absolutely to avoid state politics. For example, Lipstok's name, together with other Baltic Baptist leaders, can be found under a rather patriotic article 'Evangel'skie hristjane-baptisty v sovetskoi Pribaltike' [The Evangelical Christians-Baptists in the Soviet Baltics], *Bratskii Vestnik*, no. 6 (1947), pp. 36-38. In 1951 Lipstok passed on Levindanto's instructions to local churches asking them to celebrate 1 May with a worship service and to turn the attention of church members to the fight for world peace. Lipstok's letter ends with words of wisdom: 'I hope ... that you can do something for the glory of God and for the benefit of the people. Let God give you wisdom.' Johannes Lipstok to Arthur Eiman (24.04.1951). Tartu EKB koguduse sissetulnud kirjad 1945-1950 [Incoming correspondence of Tartu ECB Church 1945-1950], Tartu 'Kolgata' Baptisti koguduse arhiiv [Tartu 'Kolgata' Baptist Church archive].

[132] Irina Bondareva, '"Separation or Cooperation?": Moldavian Baptists, 1940-1965', MTh dissertation (Prague: IBTS, 2004), pp. 34-39.

[133] See also Toivo Pilli and Tõnis Valk, 'Ühest ateistliku töö meetodist: evangeeliumi kristlaste-baptistide palvemajade sulgemine Eestis 1945-1965' [A Method of Atheistic Work: Closures of Evangelical Christian-Baptist Prayer Houses in Estonia, 1945-1965], in Toivo Pilli, ed., *Teekond teisenevas ajas: peatükke Eesti vabakoguduste ajaloost* [A Journey in Changing Time: Chapters from the History of Estonian Free Churches] (Tartu: Kõrgem Usuteaduslik Seminar ja Sõnasepp OÜ, 2005), pp. 89-127.

four ECB prayer houses in Estonia, and asked for clarification about two further prayer houses. One of the churches that was closed had formerly belonged to Pentecostals in Tartu. One prayer house in Nõmme was closed with the explanation that there were only twenty persons who used the building.[134]

One can only partly agree with the statement that in Estonia, unlike in some other parts of the Soviet Union, registration was 'a relatively simple process of reconfirming the registration of existing church communities, although many forcible closures also occurred'.[135] The process was not so simple, as it required paperwork that some smaller churches were not equipped to produce. Osvald Tärk, noting this problem, stated: 'The leader of the church has to be a person for whom the different administrative tasks do not pose much difficulty.'[136] In addition, the registration of the local church and its executive board, registration of the church building or prayer house, and registration of the presbyter, were all linked together, and depended on each other. The registration could be refused if the church did not have a presbyter. Closure could follow if the church building did not meet sanitary requirements, or if the church members were not living in the administrative area where the church building was located.[137] Registrations were also refused when the application documents were inadequate or were handed in after the deadline, 31 December 1945.[138] These were some formal reasons that could lead to refusal of registration and mergers of local congregations. As for the number of closures, it is possible today to discover that while the Commissioner had 119 registration applications from free churches in 1945, there were 107 Estonian ECB churches in 1947 and 102 churches in 1948.[139] At least seventeen churches or mission stations were closed within three years.

Referring to the post-war situation, it has been rightly stated: 'In most cities where there were congregations belonging to the different denominations that had joined the ECB union only one combined congregation was allowed to exist. The union leadership was obliged to present this as a voluntary process of reconciliation and an expression of new Christian brotherhood, but the result was to close neighbourhood churches and reduce the scope for public

---

[134] The chairman of the CARC to the Commissioner, J. Kivi (07.08.1946). ERA, f. R-1989, n. 2, s. 4, pp. 81-81a.

[135] Sawatsky, *Soviet Evangelicals*, p. 61.

[136] Osvald Tärk to Heimar Melsas (16.07.1945). EBUKirj1945, KUSA.

[137] The Commissioner of the CARC report (01.01.1946). ERA f. R-1989, n. 2, s. 3, p. 49b.

[138] The Commissioner of the CARC report (31.03.1946). ERA f. R-1989, n. 2, s. 3, p. 57.

[139] The Commissioner of the CARC report (01.01.1946). ERA f. R-1989, n. 2, s. 3, p. 50. See also The Commissioner of the CARC report (01.07.1946). ERA f. R-1989, n. 2, s. 3, p. 64; The UECBE statistical reports 1947, 1948. Evangeeliumi Kristlaste-Baptistide koguduste statistilised aruanded 1945-1963, EEKBLA.

witness.'[140] In Estonia, the closures that took place in 1945-1947 touched mostly smaller churches. But the later campaign of diminishing the number of ECB churches in 1949-1952 focused mainly on larger congregations. Closures gave a clear message that believers were 'second class' citizens. They were pushed to accept unfavourable conditions and were identified as belonging to the periphery of the society.

Pressures on churches increased during the last years of Stalin's reign. In Kärdla, the administrative centre of Hiiumaa Island, the ECB church building was taken away in 1949 and the believers had to join the Second ECB Church in Kärdla that met in a former Pentecostal building which was much smaller. The believers' application, supported by the Senior Presbyter, that the joint work would continue in the larger building (the former Baptist church),[141] was rejected. In a seaside town, Pärnu, the former Evangelical Christian congregation had to move out of their modern church building to an older and more remotely located building where a former Baptist congregation met. This happened against the believers' wish to continue using the former Evangelical Christian church for their joint services.[142] According to Joosep Tammo, the presbyter Jaan Treufeldt of the former Evangelical Christian Church was threatened and he did not dare to oppose the city government.[143] The 'redundant' building was turned into a sports-hall in 1953.[144] Also, in December 1950, the former prayer house of the Evangelical Christians in Tõrva was taken from the congregation.[145] A month earlier the local government authorities made an attempt to take away the historic limestone building of Tallinn 'Kalju' ECB Church, which had been built with the help of Baron Woldemar von Üxküll. The attempt was not successful and presbyter Robert Võsu stated in his report to the church members: 'God removed the danger.'[146] However, from 1950 the church had to share its building with the Russian speaking ECB congregation.[147]

Tallinn saw the most comprehensive merger take place, when eight ECB churches with different historical backgrounds were put together into the Oleviste cathedral, a medieval building which had hitherto housed a German-

---

[140] Rowe, *Russian Resurrection*, p. 121.

[141] Johannes Lipstok to the Commissioner of the CARC (06.04.1949). VpUvk1945-1966, KUSA.

[142] The head of the Senior Presbyter's office to the Commissioner of the CARC (27.07.1951). VpUvk1945-1966, KUSA.

[143] Joosep Tammo, telephone interview (25.05.2000).

[144] Tamm, *Moodsad kirikud: Eesti 1920.-1930. aastate sakraalarhitektuur*, pp. 55, 94.

[145] Inspection report, no. 20 (13.-14.08.1956). Revideerimisaktid 1956-1957, EEKBLA.

[146] Tallinna Kalju EKB koguduse 1950. a. tegevuse ülevaade. [A survey of Tallinn 'Kalju' ECB Church activities in 1950]. Kirjavahetus ja dokumendid 1950-1974: Kalju kogudus [Correspondence and documents 1950-1970: 'Kalju' Church], EEKBLA.

[147] Tallinna Kalju EKB koguduse 1950. a. tegevuse ülevaade. Kirjavahetus ja dokumendid 1950-1974: Kalju kogudus, EEKBLA.

speaking Lutheran congregation but had been empty since the Second World War. The Oleviste case can serve as a model of the identity issues that local churches had to face when forcefully joined together.

The Commissioner of the CARC informed the Senior Presbyter, J. Lipstok, on 8 June 1950 that a major merger of ECB churches in Tallinn had to take place without delay. The executive committee of Tallinn city was at first not sure which building would be allocated to the combined congregation. The old (and cold) Oleviste cathedral in the centre of the city seemed to be the likely choice, but at the beginning of August 1950 nothing had been decided.[148] The Commissioner himself then asked for permission from Moscow on 25 August.[149] Events then moved swiftly. On 17 September 1950, a festive opening worship service in Oleviste Cathedral was held, with approximately 3,000 people attending. A united choir of 160 singers took part. J. Lipstok led the service and A. Karev from Moscow preached. Based on eight ECB churches in Tallinn and its surroundings, a new church with 1,923 members was created.[150] In spite of the grandeur of the opening day, the presbyters Osvald Tärk and Oskar Olvik already saw possible difficulties in a multifaceted congregation that brought together former Pentecostal, Evangelical Christian, Revivalist Free Church and Baptist traditions. What had happened on the union level in 1945 was now played out at the local church level. One can understand why the presbyters emphasised peace and unity, the need to keep pure hearts, and the central uniting role of Christ.[151]

There were certainly positive aspects about the merger in Tallinn. Michael Rowe even affirmed that 'this solution had advantages for everyone': the city council had an ancient monument restored by the church members; the Council for the Affairs of Religious Cults had only one congregation to deal with; and the congregation had the use of a church building that dominated the city skyline and was easy for everyone who wanted to come to worship to find.[152] But difficulties should not be neglected either. First, the new congregation was put under much pressure, as tremendous resources were needed to restore the building. Second, the buildings of the uniting churches, all these 'prayer houses being in good condition',[153] were lost, and became used for secular purposes. These buildings had conveyed the sense of spiritual home for church members. Ülo Meriloo expressed the feelings of these days: 'People were overwhelmed

---

[148] Jaan Bärenson, 'Oleviste koguduse asutamine', in *Oleviste 50*, p. 7.

[149] The Commissioner to the Chairman of the CARC (25.08.1950). ERA, f. R-1989, n. 1, s. 10, pp. 145-146.

[150] Bärenson, 'Oleviste koguduse asutamine', pp. 7-8; Meriloo, 'Ühistöö aastad', p. 8.

[151] Bärenson, 'Oleviste koguduse asutamine', p. 7.

[152] Rowe, *Russian Resurrection*, p. 121.

[153] The Commissioner of the CARC to the Deputy Chairman of the Council of Ministers of the ESSR (12.08.1950). ERA, f. R-1989, n. 1, s. 10, p. 117.

by confusion, anxiety and grieving.'[154]

If the aim of the authorities was to diminish the ECB churches in Tallinn and elsewhere, they no doubt succeeded. However, this project of mergers did not in fact marginalise Baptist witness in the capital of Estonia, though it did in some other parts of the country. The Oleviste Church soon became 'the mother church' for Estonian ECB churches. It was the biggest church, had a historical and visible building, and was led by two outstanding pastors, Oskar Olvik and Osvald Tärk, who were well known all over the country. During the Soviet years, the Oleviste church was an argument in itself in favour of the vitality of the ECB movement in the country.

In general, the forcible mergers of local churches was accompanied with anxieties and challenges, but also with opportunities, that to a certain extent had already been experienced on the union level. The atheistic state, taking away the prayer houses from several strong ECB churches, caused a sense of inferiority and helplessness among believers. This experience was balanced by some new opportunities that opened up in the mid-1950s, during 'Khrushchev's thaw'. Evangelistic efforts, though restricted, were important. Another important event was the production of distance learning courses in pastoral training, which during the approximately four years of their existence provided a medium through which Baptist theology could be communicated.

THEOLOGICAL DISTANCE LEARNING COURSES: 1956-1960

Baptists were the only free church in Estonia that had attempted to give systematic theological education before the Second World War.[155] The Baptist Theological Seminary operated from 1922 to 1929 in Keila, and from 1931 in Tallinn,[156] until its closure by the Soviet powers in 1940. The benefits of the educational efforts of Estonian Baptists became visible when the 'hard times' began: many of the seminary graduates made their pastoring of ECB churches their life work during the Soviet years.[157] The search for theological knowledge, though often following a self-help model, enabled leaders to focus on new tasks in the changed religious situation. Gatherings for biblical training and discipleship offered the possibility for fellowship, the exchange of information, and the giving of guidance in matters of behaviour and teaching. The unifying role of theological studies and the input it gave in the search for identity in UECBE cannot be underestimated.

---

[154] Meriloo, 'Ühistöö aastad', p. 8.

[155] See also Toivo Pilli, 'Finding a Balance between Church and Academia: Baptist Theological Education in Estonia', *Religion in Eastern Europe*, vol. XXVI, no. 3 (August 2006), pp. 17-43.

[156] Albert Wardin, ed., *Baptists Around the World* (Nashville, Tennessee: Broadman and Holman, 1995), p. 240.

[157] Pilli, 'Baptists in Estonia 1884-1940', p. 31.

In 1950, the Senior Presbyter asked permission to organise a brief training course (planned for 1-10 March 1950) for presbyters.[158] The plan was to teach pastoral work, preaching skills, church administration, the ordering of worship services and spiritual ordinances, biblical knowledge, including the life of Jesus and exegesis of Colossians, and a survey of general Church history and a history of the Evangelical Christians-Baptists in the Soviet Union. Four hours were planned for studying the Soviet Constitution, the teacher being Nikolai Levindanto.[159] There is no evidence that permission was given to hold the training, but the effort itself shows the priorities the UECBE had in these years: in spite of atheistic restrictions, offering training for local church leaders and securing theological unity. The regional meetings of local presbyters, which officially were organised annually for extending the dates of the presbyters' licences, also served partly to achieve these goals.

In the context of 'Khrushchev's thaw', the UECBE took the initiative to start Theological Distance Courses for presbyters. The preparations began in early summer 1956, after the Commissioner had given oral permission.[160] On 14 October 1956 the courses started in Tallinn with 40 students.[161] Several of the students represented the new generation of ECB church leaders or potential leaders who had emerged during the Soviet years: Karl Tutsu, Paldor Teekel, Osvald Talts, Allar Puu, Ilmar Kurg, Arpad Arder, and others. Lecture sessions were organised systematically, but the studies included a great deal of independent work. The amount of study material and textbooks written, typed and rotaprinted during these years was remarkable. Within four years, Oskar Olvik, Osvald Tärk and Robert Võsu wrote more than 20 theological textbooks, each approximately 100-150 pages (A4 format) of single space, typewritten text. When translated materials and the work of some other authors are included, the total number of volumes reached over 30. The courses were intended to be offered in two levels: the basic level required two years of study, and the advanced level required four years of study. Systematic studies and a pastor's work were not easy for most students to combine. Only one person, Paul Himma, was able to fulfil the requirements of the 4-year course.[162]

The distance courses were closed in 1960. It has been argued that the

---

[158] The Senior Presbyter to the Commissioner of the CARC (13.01.1950). VpUvk1945-1966, KUSA.

[159] Schedule for the presbyters' courses. Tallinn, 1-10 March 1950. VpUvk1945-1966, KUSA.

[160] Johannes Lipstok to the Commissioner of the CARC (31.08.1956). VpUvk1945-1966, KUSA.

[161] Decree of the Senior Presbyter, no. 187 (30.10.1956). VpUvk1945-1966, KUSA; Ülo Meriloo, *Ränduri päevik* [A Diary of a Pilgrim] (Tallinn, 2001), pp. 77-78.

[162] Uudu Rips, comp., *Issanda aednik. Märkmeid Paul Himma elust* [A Gardener of the Lord. Notes from the Life of Paul Himma] (Tartu: Saalemi Baptisti Kogudus, 2000), p. 25.

teachers were tired of the heavy workload.[163] However, the more decisive reason was that the authorities were interested in terminating the courses, as Khrushchev's atheistic campaign was gaining strength. The UECBE report of 1960-1962 stated that the closure of the courses took away a valued fellowship opportunity between ECB leaders: 'The courses had enabled the keeping of contact between the workers of the Kingdom of God, but now this [opportunity for fellowship] did not exist any more.'[164] In spite of the short term of its existence, an important effort had been made. The courses functioned as a means of forming spiritual unity. Ülo Meriloo, who took part in the courses as a student, stated: 'During the four years not only our heads, but also our hearts were being educated.'[165] Also, in 1957-1959 distance courses for choir conductors were organised in the Oleviste Church in Tallinn. They were also planned for four years but were finished after two years of activities.[166] These attempts to give theological education not only helped to develop new leaders for local churches but were also important means of unifying theological positions and giving guidance for worship and Christian practice in the context of the post-war years of confusion and state pressure.

CONCLUSION

The Soviet government's anti-religious policy, the forceful merger of the Estonian free churches, and the new hierarchical leadership patterns that were imposed, put the UECBE and the local churches under enormous pressure. Estonian Evangelical Christians-Baptists had to adjust to the new situation: restricted evangelism possibilities; a changed position in the society; the controlling eye of the state structures; and unprecedented ecclesiastical relationships outside Estonia with the AUCECB. This all began to shape the UECBE organisational structures, ministry methods, and even theology. The role of the union leadership became central. In addition to the merger at the union level, some mergers at the local church level took place, causing considerable difficulties. There was, however, some renewal of evangelism efforts in the middle of the 1950s. Estonia was in a better situation than several other Soviet regions, as ECB leaders and the union office took the initiative in the search for a new identity, focusing much more on spiritual values than on formal state or AUCECB requirements. An important chapter in the process of trying to find common theological emphases and common worship practices

---

[163] Ülo Meriloo, telephone interview (08.06.2000). Meriloo was a student who took the courses, and was later (from 1985) the Senior Presbyter of the UECBE.

[164] Eesti EKB vendlus 1960.-1962. a. [Estonian ECB brotherhood 1960-1962]. Kirjavahetus ja dokumendid 1950-1974: 'Kalju' kogudus, EEKBLA.

[165] Meriloo, *Ränduri päevik*, p. 78.

[166] Marika Kahar, *Muusikakursused Oleviste kirikus* [Music Courses at Oleviste Church], manuscript (n. p., n. d.), p. 1. A copy in Toivo Pilli's personal archive.

was an attempt to give theological education to a new generation of presbyters.

In 1959 Robert Võsu, who later became the Senior Presbyter of the Union of Evangelical Christians-Baptists of Estonia, said: 'The work in the united union has developed peacefully. The membership numbers have stayed at more or less the former level during the last 15 years. Differences between congregations have almost entirely disappeared. The spiritual direction has become steadier, deeper and wider. Differences between congregations have mutually strengthened and completed the union.'[167] Võsu's statement shows a considerable degree of wishful thinking, since it glosses over all the difficulties of the times. As a statement that was no doubt intended to reassure the authorities as well as the churches, it should be evaluated critically. Nevertheless, the evidence as a whole suggests that by the end of the 1950s Estonian Evangelical Christians-Baptists, after surviving an era of massive turmoil, had found a certain stability and self-confidence. A new Baptist – or at least 'baptistic' – identity had begun to emerge. The church members had learned how to operate in an atheistic context. But this relatively stable situation was soon to be shaken by a new wave of atheistic campaigns.

---

[167] Võsu, *EKB koguduste ajalugu*, p. 154.

CHAPTER 3

From a Thunderstorm to Still Life: 1959-1972

The end of the 1950s and the beginning of the 1960s were difficult years for all religious communities in the USSR. During this period – Khrushchev's reign - a major atheistic wave swept over the Soviet Union. This atheistic campaign seemed to come as 'a traumatic shock to the religious believers of the Soviet Union'.[1] This judgment, by Philip Walters, holds true for Evangelical Christians-Baptists (resp. 'Baptists') in Estonia. Probably many of them had placed far too much reliance on what was termed 'Khrushchev's thaw', but this turned out to be nothing more than a short-term liberalisation in the political and cultural spheres of life. Due to Khrushchev's anti-religious campaign many Estonian Baptists gradually accepted a position of being marginalised citizens and adopted a 'survival theology', a term used by Karl H. Walter to denote the inward-looking views that characterised Soviet Baptists.[2] After the ousting of Khrushchev in October 1964, it seemed that some easing of the atheistic pressures could be expected.[3] But apart from some tactical manoeuvring, Soviet religious policy remained unaltered. The traditional identity of Estonian Baptists and other evangelicals was in danger. After the end of the Second World War and even after the period of the Stalinist political terror, believers had tried to recover an active approach comparatively quickly. But after Khrushchev's severe atheistic pressure a period of lethargy followed. The Union of Evangelical Christians-Baptists of Estonia moved from an atheistic thunderstorm (1959-1964) into a period of still life (1965-1972).

FROM KHRUSHCHEV TO BREZHNEV

The signs of imminent repression in the religious field could be seen as early as 1954 when the Central Committee of the Communist Party passed a resolution entitled 'Serious Shortcomings in Scientific-Atheistic Propaganda and

---

[1] Philip Walters, 'A survey of Soviet religious policy', in Sabrina P. Ramet, ed., *Religious Policy in the Soviet Union* (Cambridge and New York: Cambridge University Press, 1993), p. 20.

[2] Karl Heinz Walter, 'The Future of Theological Education Within the European Baptist Federation', *Religion in Eastern Europe*, vol. XXI, no. 3 (June 2001), p. 22.

[3] Walter Sawatsky, *Soviet Evangelicals Since World War II* (Kitchener, Ontario: Herald Press, 1981), p. 145.

Measures for Improving This'. The tone of the resolution was aggressive, and it accused believers of opposing the rest of the society, a society which was committed to building communism.[4] However, the extensive and militant atheistic campaign was delayed for several years. This was partly because behind 'the smoke-screen of collective leadership'[5] the Soviet government was experiencing serious power struggles, and partly because Khrushchev was interested in some relaxation in Soviet anti-Western foreign policy. The issues related to churches were pushed, for a while, to the back burner.[6] For a short period in the later 1950s, churches in the Soviet Union even saw a modest renaissance. In Estonia, there was growth in the number of those being confirmed in the Lutheran Church, and the Orthodox Church also expanded its activities.[7] The number of Estonian Evangelical Christians-Baptists grew slightly: from 8,950 in 1955 to 9,322 in 1958.[8] But the climate soon changed. In 1960, the chairman of the CARC, A. Puzin, declared that the task of the council and its local commissioners was 'to help liquidate one of the most vigorous and dangerous remnants of the past, that is the religious beliefs of people'.[9] Anti-religious education was intensified, many churches were closed, and taxation of churches and clergy was made heavier. In 1964, the Senior Presbyter of the UECBE wrote to the Commissioner of the CARC: 'The believers do not understand why the [insurance] rates for churches and prayer houses have suddenly increased by 4 to 13 times...'[10] This was a diplomatic expression; in reality the believers understood the situation very well.

The reasons why Khrushchev gave his support to the 'anti-religious war'

---

[4] Tatiana A. Chumachenko, *Church and State in Soviet Russia: Russian Orthodoxy from World War II to the Khrushchev Years* (New York and London: M. E. Sharpe, 2002), p. 129.

[5] Hugh Seton-Watson, *From Lenin to Khrushchev: The History of World Communism* (New York: Frederick A. Praeger Publications, 1960), p. 357.

[6] Chumachenko, *Church and State in Soviet Russia*, p. 136.

[7] Jaanus Plaat, *Usuliikumised, kirikud ja vabakogudused Lääne- ja Hiiumaal: usuühenduste muutumis-protsessid 18. sajandi keskpaigast kuni 20. sajandi lõpuni* [Religious Movements, Churches and Free Churches in West-Estonia and Hiiumaa Island: Transformational Processes of Religious Entities from the mid-18th Century to the End of the 20th Century] (Tartu: Eesti Rahva Muuseum, 2001), p. 209.

[8] The UECBE statistical reports 1955, 1958. Evangeeliumi Kristlaste-Baptistide koguduste statistilised aruanded 1945-1963 [The UECBE statistical reports 1945-1963], EEKBLA.

[9] O merah po likvidatsii narushenii duhovenstvom sovetskovo zakonodatel'stva o kul'tah [About measures on liquidating the clergy's disobedience to the Soviet legislation on cults] (18.04.1960). ERA, f. R-1989, n. 2, s. 25, p. 44.

[10] The Senior Presbyter to the Commissioner of the CARC (04.03.1964). Vanempresbüteri ja usuasjade voliniku kirjavahetus 1945-1966 (VpUvk1945-1966) [Correspondence of the Senior Presbyter and the Commissioner of the CARC 1945-1966], KUSA.

are not clear. Referring to several unsuccessful reforms that were attempted in Soviet society in the 1950s, Roy and Zhores Medvedev observed: 'Although aware that not only his own popularity but also the prestige of the Party was diminishing, Khrushchev incredibly stepped up anti-religious propaganda.'[11] Was it the old trick of finding a scapegoat - in this case the Christians, who came to be accused of hindering progress in society? The reasons were probably more complex. Tatiana Chumachenko has pointed out that by the end of the 1950s the supporters of a hard-line religious policy, headed by Mikhail Suslov, later to be accompanied by Leonid Ilichev, had improved their positions in Soviet government circles. Those who were more moderate about religious issues were now openly accused of Stalinism.[12] This was a stigma which no one wanted to have in a period which saw the denunciation of Stalin's cult of personality. The deeper roots of the attack against religion were ideological. Khrushchev declared at the Twenty-first Communist Party Congress in 1959 that Soviet society would soon enter a new stage of communism. He seems to have sincerely believed that this dream would come true.[13] But for this to happen the basis for the new era had to be built, and religion as well as other views incompatible with communism had to be destroyed.[14]

The strict atheistic policy that had been freshly formulated was applied through oral instructions and written decrees, most of which remained secret. However, the political course taken in 1958-59 received juridical formulation. On 16 March 1961 the Council of Ministers of the USSR passed a resolution (no. 263) 'On Strengthening Control over Obeying Legislation on Cults'. This document meant that the churches returned to the situation that had existed at the end of the 1930s in the Soviet Union.[15] In the light of this resolution, the Council for the Affairs of Religious Cults (from 1965 the Council for Religious Affairs, CRA) sent a circular instruction letter to the commissioners. This document emphasised restrictions on the churches. Pastors were not allowed to 'distract believers from Soviet culture and social-political life'. It was stressed again that Christian work was practically limited to worship services inside church buildings: social work, children's and youth activities, even excursions and sports events organised by believers, were all prohibited. Permission from the local government authorities was needed to organise church members meetings convened 'to discuss the leadership issues of the religious society or

---

[11] Roy Medvedev and Zhores Medvedev, *Khrushchev: The Years in Power* (London and Oxford: Oxford University Press, 1977), p. 150.

[12] Chumachenko, *Church and State in Soviet Russia*, p. 148.

[13] Nathaniel Davis, *A Long Walk to Church: A Contemporary History of Russian Orthodoxy* (Boulder and Oxford: Westview Press, 1995), p. 34.

[14] Sergei Sannikov, *Dvadsat' vekov hristjanstva* [Two Thousand Years of Christianity], vol. 2 (Odessa and Sankt Peterburg: Bogomyslie, 2001), pp. 409, 455.

[15] Chumachenko, *Church and State in Soviet Russia*, p. 186.

the use of property'. If churches acted contrary to these prohibitions they risked losing their registration.[16] According to the Russian Criminal Code, passed in 1961, any religious activity which might cause citizens to 'reject socialist activity or performance of their duties as citizens' was regarded as criminal.[17] One can imagine that feelings of fear and desperation spread among believers. One Estonian ECB leader called the years 1960-1962 'the most difficult period after the war'.[18] This was a comparatively mild description.

Church closures added to the feelings of helplessness. During 1960-1963, ECB church buildings in Ühtri, Kaiu, Kuijõe, Vilivalla, Viru-Aruküla, and Suigu were closed. In some cases, the church buildings were turned into community halls.[19] In Suigu the modern cement brick building was used as a grain store for a local collective farm, and later as an apartment building.[20] In Viru-Aruküla, force was used to liquidate the church.[21] These closures were a ritualistic demonstration of atheistic power, a so called anti-liturgy,[22] all of it designed to make clear the state's omnipotence and the impotence of the churches. A dramatic case was that of Viljandi ECB Church. The former church building was torn down according to the new general plan for the town. The believers were not given any other place to meet. In discussions that the church had with the authorities, it was suggested to the believers that they could build a new prayer house, which they did. However, when the new building was ready in 1960, it was immediately taken away. Pastor Aamo Remmel stated: 'This was a deep disappointment for the Viljandi ECB Church, as well as for all our brotherhood. The house that was built according to an agreement,

---

[16] Rasjasnenije o porjadke primenenija zakonodatel'stva o kul'tah [Explanation about the order of applying the legislation on cults] (26.07.1961). ERA, f. R-1989, n. 1, s. 52, pp. 31-35.

[17] Medvedev and Medvedev, *Khrushchev: The Years in Power*, p. 151.

[18] Eesti EKB vendlus 1960-62. a. [Estonian ECB brotherhood, 1960-62]. Kirjavahetus ja dokumendid 1950-1974: Kalju kogudus [Correspondence and Documents 1950-1974: 'Kalju' Church], EEKBLA.

[19] Tõnis Valk, 'Eesti Evangeeliumi Kristlaste-Baptistide Liidu ja riigivõimu suhted aastatel 1953-1964' [The Relationship between the State Authorities and the Union of Evangelical Christians-Baptists of Estonia during 1953-1964], diploma thesis (Tartu: Kõrgem Usuteaduslik Seminar, 2003), pp. 24-30.

[20] Egle Tamm, *Moodsad kirikud: Eesti 1920.-1930. aastate sakraalarhitektuur* [Modern Churches: Church Architecture in Estonia in the 1920s and 1930s] (Tallinn: Eesti Arhitektuurimuuseum, 2001), p. 95.

[21] The Senior Presbyter to the Commissioner of the CARC (27.09.1966). EEKBL kirjavahetus usuasjade volinikuga 1966-1990 (KirjUv1966-1990) [The correspondence of the UECBE with the Commissioner of the CRA 1966-1990], EEKBLA.

[22] William Cavanaugh uses this term in his book *Torture and Eucharist* to interpret the methods of torture used by Latin American military government authorities. Though borrowed from a different context, it helps in understanding the meaning of severe atheistic actions. See William T. Cavanaugh, *Torture and Eucharist* (Oxford: Blackwell Publishing, 1998), p. 30.

and was finished with the congregation's sacrifices and labour with the support from all our brotherhood, was taken away.'[23] The life of the churches seemed to be under severe threat.

In 1968, in all regions of Estonia, supervisory committees (steering commissions),[24] which functioned under the local government's executive committees, were established. Their task, in official language, was to control churches and to ensure that they followed Soviet law.[25] This was in addition to the controlling functions that the KGB, the Commissioner himself and the Communist Party exercised toward individual believers and the churches. All these demonstrations of atheistic power structures gave Estonian Evangelical Christians-Baptists and other churches a clear message that they were dependent on the state's decisions and authority. They were declared outlaws of society, 'remnants of capitalism'. At the same time, any links that churches had abroad were used by the state to further the propagandistic goals of Soviet foreign policy.[26] Freedom for the churches to express their own identity seemed to be diminishing as time went on.

Estonian ECB churches had the impression that the state was especially hostile against 'our brotherhood'.[27] This was probably not true, as all churches in Estonia suffered from atheistic persecution.[28] When the administrative measures were slightly loosened in the middle of the 1960s, with Leonid Brezhnev becoming the leader of the USSR, Estonian ECB churches were slow to regain their strength. In 1967 the Senior Presbyter, Aleksander Sildos (who was Senior Presbyter from 1964 until the end of 1969), said figuratively: 'There are no blossoms of hope to be seen; and those that were there have been cut by blossom weevils. The wine tree of the church has no new fruit.'[29] Hope was in short supply.

During the first half of the Brezhnev era, beginning in 1964, the assumption had to be made by the state authorities 'that religion was not going

---

[23] Aamo Remmel, private letter (26.01.2001). Toivo Pilli's personal archive.

[24] As was typical of the Soviet times, the committee had a long official name: Commission for the Support of the Executive Committees of the Soviets of the People's Deputies in the Observation of the Legislation on Religious Cults.

[25] Raigo Liimann, *Usklikkus muutuvas Eesti ühiskonnas* [Religiosity in the Changing Estonian Society] (Tartu: Tartu Ülikooli Kirjastus, 2001), p. 26. See also Plaat, *Usuliikumised, kirikud ja vabakogudused Lääne- ja Hiiumaal*, pp. 215-220.

[26] Otto Luchterhandt, 'The Council for Religious Affairs', in Sabrina P. Ramet, ed., *Religious Policy in the Soviet Union*, pp. 58-59; Sawatsky, *Soviet Evangelicals*, p. 146.

[27] Eesti EKB vendlus 1960-62. a., KirjDok1950-1974, EEKBLA.

[28] See Liiman, *Usklikkus muutuvas Eesti ühiskonnas*, pp. 20-34; Vello Salo, *Riik ja kirikud 1940-1991* [The State and Churches 1940-1991] (Brampton, Ontario: Maarjamaa, 2000), pp. 27-36.

[29] The UECBE Senior Presbyter's report of 1967. EKB vanempresbüteri aruanded (VpAruanded) [The UECBE Senior Presbyter's reports], EEKBLA.

to die out', despite what Khrushchev had proclaimed.[30] The Communist Party
initiated criticism of Khrushchev's policies, including his religious policies. As
to atheistic propaganda, these years can be described as a transition period from
'administrative methods' to more 'educational methods', including sociological
arguments against religion. Select, 'interpreted' statistical data was often
published to show Christians in an unfavourable light.[31] In addition, the need
was felt to train 'better informed propagandists who might be taken more
seriously by believers themselves'.[32] However, even if officially it was now
declared that 'a socialist state does not use administrative measures to fight
against religious rituals',[33] in practice, churches constantly met administrative
restrictions. The actual applications made by the UECBE in this period to
publish a new hymnal or to give theological education were turned down.
When the new translation of the Estonian Bible was published by the British
and Foreign Bible Society in 1968, an application was made by the UECBE for
a mere two hundred copies to be brought into Estonia,[34] but there is no evidence
the permission was ever given.

    Though the UECBE moved from suffering the attacks of Khrushchev's
atheistic campaign to a comparative still life at the end of the 1960s, it was still
a life, as the image suggests. A quiet, low-profile existence characterised local
churches. They had their own programmes of choirs and meetings in homes.
Churches were inward-looking, but nonetheless maintained warm fellowship
among believers. The energy of local church members was mostly channelled
into congregational activities and efforts were made to witness to the Christian
faith in personal relationships and by lifestyle rather than publicly. A
comparatively passive approach within public spheres of life has continued to
be characteristic of the identity of Evangelical Christians-Baptists in Estonia.
This tendency was evident in the 1980s, but it was largely moulded in the
1960s. The reasons for this way of thinking are partly theological, growing out
of an individualistically understood paradigm of the Christian faith.
Nevertheless, the experience of the churches in Estonia has also to be taken into
account: the shock of the harsh atheistic measures of the 1960s and the
continuing elimination of believers from public spheres of life robbed Estonian
believers of the confidence that they could have an impact on society in
general.

---

[30] Walters, 'A survey of Soviet religious policy', p. 23.

[31] Salo, *Riik ja kirikud*, pp. 29-31.

[32] Michael Rowe, *Russian Resurrection. Strength in Suffering – A History of Russia's
Evangelical Church* (London: Marshall Pickering, 1994), p. 149.

[33] Lembit Raid, *Vabamõtlejate ringidest massilise ateisimini* [From the Circles of
Freethinkers to Mass Atheism] (Tallinn: Eesti Raamat, 1978), p. 26.

[34] Robert Võsu to the Commissioner of the CRA (19.11.1969). KirjUv1966-1990,
EEKBLA.

KEEPING THE POSITIONS

The UECBE did not, however, simply accept the unfolding events with total passivity. There were attempts made by the union leadership to analyse the situation.[35] Local churches also made efforts to maintain the patterns of their religious activities, limited as these were. To use popular Baptist language, the 1960s and the beginning of the 1970s constituted, spiritually, a time of 'desert experience', when no revivals occurred. Robert Võsu defined the task of the UECBE throughout these years in this way: 'During the periods between revivals, which often are rather long, it is necessary to keep the positions.'[36] Indeed, Estonian Evangelical Christians-Baptists experienced several defeats in the decade of the 1960s: the closure of the semi-illegal theological distance learning courses, the Senior Presbyter Johannes Lipstok's death in 1961, and the closure of a number of church buildings.[37] The union leadership, however, made efforts to boost the spirits of local church members, and to call them to faithfulness. In 1968 Aleksander Sildos, the Senior Presbyter, who had spoken of 'no blossoms of hope', said at the presbyters conference: 'We are living in a spiritual winter-time... But winter-time is the right time to prepare for spring. ... Outwardly, there are no reasons for rejoicing, but we want to rejoice in God!'[38]

During the Brezhnev years at the end of the 1960s, the UECBE leaders tried to take some cautious steps to strengthen the union's positions, though the predominant focus was on survival. One gets the impression that the union leaders were trying to see if there were any 'holes' in the atheistic barriers that were surrounding and restricting Christian work and church initiatives. For example, in 1964 the Senior Presbyter tried to convince the Commissioner to increase the number of copies of the 1965 UECBE church calendar to 4,000.[39] This was a very modest request, given that this calendar for ECB churches was not allowed to include texts, but only dates and information about Christian holidays. Attempts were also made to explain to the Commissioner the need for an Estonian evangelical publication, similar to the Russian *Bratskii Vestnik*.[40]

---

[35] In this respect, Robert Võsu's strategic thinking should be noted. The Senior Presbyter's reports show an ability to analyse how the union and the local churches were influenced by atheistic and political as well as by sociological, theological, and spiritual factors.

[36] The UECBE Senior Presbyter's report of 1970-1972. VpAruanded, EEKBLA.

[37] Eesti EKB vendlus 1960-62. a. KirjDok1950-1974, EEKBLA.

[38] Eesti EKB koguduste presbüterite konverents. Tallinnas, 15.-18. veebruaril 1968. [The Estonian ECB Presbyters' Conference in Tallinn, 15-18 February 1968], typewritten manuscript [1968], p. 16. Ülo Meriloo's personal library.

[39] Aleksander Sildos to the Commissioner of the CARC (25.11.1964). VpUvk1945-1966, KUSA

[40] Aleksander Sildos to the Commissioner of the CRA (18.10.1966). KirjUv1966-1990, EEKBLA.

Even if not successful, there were a few efforts to sustain ECB identity in this period of still life.

Usually the union leaders worded their letters very carefully, but sometimes it was difficult to hide the emotions being felt. In 1967, in Saaremaa Island, the administration refused to give permission to the local ECB church to hold an open air memorial service at a cemetery. These services, usually held once a year, used to be a widespread practice in Estonian Protestant churches. Even during the Soviet years this tradition continued, depending on how strictly local authorities interpreted the religious laws. Robert Võsu, in explaining the situation to the Commissioner, referred to the argument of the administration in Saaremaa that these memorial services were not an ECB tradition. He exclaimed: 'How long should one repeat a phenomenon so that it will become a tradition? In our churches the memorial services have been held for 60-70 years. This is approximately two generations. Often a phenomenon that appears only for some years is called a tradition.'[41] The last remark sounds somewhat sarcastic. The Soviet authorities were themselves introducing new traditions. From 1957-58 they made serious attempts (drawing on ideas talked about in the 1920s[42]) to create substitute traditions related to life-cycle rituals, for example non-Christian funeral services or secular wedding ceremonies instead of Christian ones.[43] Special efforts were made to mould young people's minds in the spirit of atheism.[44] The state was quite successful: the number of baptisms, confirmations and Christian wedding ceremonies dropped dramatically in the 1960s – especially in Estonian Lutheran and Orthodox churches.[45] Dedication of children, which traditionally had been a congregational ceremony in Baptist churches, now usually happened at home and was understood in private terms.

Estonian ECB leaders tried to strengthen local church life by applying to register groups of under twenty members with the authorities. This would have given the UECBE more of a presence, especially in the countryside. The wider societal trend was one of rapid urbanisation, so that the countryside was losing its traditional importance. For example, during 1944-1990 the population of the capital city Tallinn grew 260% and the share of its population in Estonia grew from 11.7% in 1930 to 29.3% in 1979.[46] In 1966 the Senior Presbyter sent a list

---

[41] Robert Võsu to the Commissioner of the CRA (25.07.1967). KirjUv1966-1990, EEKBLA.

[42] Moshe Lewin, 'Grappling with Stalinism', in David L. Hoffmann, ed., *Stalinism* (Oxford: Blackwell Publishing, 2003), p. 51.

[43] Liiman, *Usklikkus muutuvas Eesti ühiskonnas*, pp. 27-31.

[44] Riho Altnurme, 'Die Estnishe Evangelish-Lutherische Kirche in der Sovjetunion (bis 1964)', in Siret Rutiku and Reinhart Staats, eds., *Estland, Lettland und Westliches Christentum* (Kiel: Friedrich Wittig Verlag, 1998), pp. 244-245.

[45] Plaat, *Usuliikumised, kirikud ja vabakogudused Lääne- ja Hiiumaal*, pp. 214-215.

[46] Jaak Kliimask, 'Economic Transformation in the Post-Socialist City. The Case of Tallinn', in Martin Aberg and Martin Peterson, eds., *Baltic Cities: Perspectives on*

to the Commissioner of twenty-seven locations where registered groups of Evangelical Christians-Baptists could potentially be formed. The Senior Presbyter used both historical and political arguments to support his application. He stated that the ECB churches in Estonia used to have mission stations before 1945. He also stressed that it would be possible to avoid disorderly events if these believers' groups could be registered.[47] In particular, there were hopes to register four churches: Antsla, Rapla, Selise and Võõpsu.

The UECBE leadership assumed that the government would show more favour toward the registration of ECB groups and churches in order to control the religious situation. However, the process of registration moved very slowly. In March 1967 not a single new ECB group or church had reached the point of registration in Estonia. The Senior Presbyter's 1966 report stated that 'this issue develops with difficulty, because local authorities resist it'.[48] Antsla ECB Church was registered later in 1967,[49] but this was the exception rather than the rule. It was a struggle simply to maintain existing positions.

All these experiences affected the UECBE and within that, had an influence on local ECB churches' self-understanding, their theological emphases and their practices. It can be argued that Khrushchev's anti-religious campaign had the side-effect in Estonia of drawing the historically different free church traditions within the UECBE more closely together. This process intensified in the 1970s, when outstanding spiritual leaders such as Aleksander Sildos and Oskar Olvik, both former Evangelical Christians, died. Their particular tradition was no longer so strongly maintained. For local church members, the present experience of fellowship became more important than the awareness of the historical roots of the individual church traditions in the UECBE.

An Estonian scholar, Jaanus Plaat, has pointed out that Estonian free churches in general, including the Baptists, were better able to resist atheistic pressure than the Lutheran and Orthodox churches. One reason for this, according to Plaat, was their focus on fellowship and 'constant strengthening of the ties [of individual members] with the group'.[50] This emphasis, certainly,

---

Urban and Regional Change in the Baltic Sea Area (Lund: Nordic Academic Press, 1997), pp. 154-155.

[47] The Senior Presbyter to the Commissioner of the CRA (27.09.1966). KirjUv1966-1990, EEKBLA.

[48] The UECBE Senior Presbyter's report of 1966. VpAruanded, EEKBLA.

[49] The UECBE Senior Presbyter's report of 1967. VpAruanded, EEKBLA.

[50] Jaanus Plaat, 'Eesti vabakoguduste vastupanu nõukogude religioonipoliitikale võrreldes luterliku ja õigeusu kirikuga (1944-1987)' [Estonian Free Churches' Resistance to Soviet Religious Policies in Comparison with Lutheran and Orthodox Churches (1944-1987)], in Toivo Pilli, ed., *Teekond teisenevas ajas: Peatükke Eesti vabakoguduste ajaloost* [A Journey in Changing Time: Chapters from the History of Estonian Free Churches] (Tartu: Kõrgem Usuteaduslik Seminar ja Sõnasepp OÜ, 2005), p. 155.

was nothing new for Estonian free churches, but was rather an inherent characteristic of their identity.

Coming together, being a gathered church, was not only a spiritual value, but had practical consequences. In 1964-65 the average attendance at the churches of the UECBE was approximately sixty percent of membership (higher on Sundays, lower at prayer and Bible study meetings during weekdays). In some rural areas the attendance on Sundays was often close to one hundred percent.[51] In 1972 Robert Võsu, who became UECBE Senior Presbyter in 1970, stated that in some places (Kuressaare, Nõmme, Kärdla, Tapa) the numbers attending were higher than the church membership. Special events such as church anniversaries were used for fellowship and encouragement. It was usual at the beginning of the 1970s for local church anniversary celebrations to attract three times more people than were present at the regular worship services.[52] It was normal that a communal meal - a 'love feast' - was organised for all anniversary participants. Many who attended came from other ECB churches. Toward the end of the 1960s and in the 1970s, these anniversary celebrations in Estonia, expressing a kind of 'Baptist pilgrimage tradition', not only offered mutual support but also gave some publicity to local churches in the communities around them. In 1967, the Commissioner complained to the union leadership that local churches were having some 'festive worship services or anniversaries' of which he was not informed. After that the schedule with the dates for local church anniversaries was presented to the Commissioner.[53]

Another characteristic feature of these years was that there was considerable willingness to support church work financially or to offer time to church work without payment. Tallinn Oleviste Church, according to the heavier taxation introduced in 1963, had to pay a building tax and insurance payments amounting to 5,000 roubles per year. This was difficult even for a large church such as Oleviste. However, the church was able to collect 5,700 roubles during a single Sunday collection. The Senior Presbyter, Aleksander Sildos, commented to his fellow presbyters: 'This is something worth calling a 'sacrifice' and this is a leap together with God high over the tax barriers.'[54]

All this supportive activity strengthened mutual relationships between church members and also between local churches in the ECB union. The report of 1967 observed: 'Perhaps we are a people too centred on worship and meetings. But we have to maintain this, too. It is important to keep fellowship with each other and continue the work. When a train has stopped it is very difficult to get it moving again, but when it moves slowly not much energy is

---

[51] The UECBE Senior Presbyter's reports 1964, 1965. VpAruanded, EEKBLA.

[52] The UECBE Senior Presbyter's report of 1970-1972. VpAruanded, EEKBLA.

[53] The UECBE Senior Presbyter's report of 1967. VpAruanded, EEKBLA.

[54] Eesti EKB koguduste presbüterite konverents Tallinnas, 15.-18. veebruaril 1968, p. 9.

needed to speed it up.'[55] However, it was not always easy to keep to traditional evangelical positions. Membership decline continued in the UECBE. Religious indifference among the Estonian population was growing. A new generation, born during or after the war, had no personal experience of political or religious freedom. Generally, they were more easily influenced by atheistic propaganda.[56] There were some examples of spiritual encouragement in this period, but overall it was difficult to do more than conserve Baptist life.

IDENTITY AND THE LOSS OF NUMBERS

Identity was affected by the loss of members. Statistical reports confirm that after 1960 the UECBE entered a time of numerical decline. At the end of 1960 there were 9,141 members in the UECBE, in 1963 there were 8,774 members, in 1965 there were 8,575 members, and in 1970 there were 8,206 members.[57] From 1969-1971 the decline temporarily stopped, because during these years many Russian-speaking believers came from other parts of the Soviet Union and joined ECB churches in Estonia. During 1970-1972 there were 454 such 'immigrants', many of them so called Volga-Germans, who joined the UECBE.[58] Many of them settled in Pärnu, Valga, Kohtla-Järve and other towns, and contributed a great deal of spiritual energy to local – mostly Russian-speaking – ECB churches or groups. As a result, several predominantly Russian-speaking churches in the UECBE, such as in Kohtla-Järve and Kivióli, were started or grew in this period. The church in Narva, near the eastern border of the Estonian SSR, was practically formed on the basis of these immigrant believers.[59] The Commissioner of the CRA pointed out that these Baptists and Mennonites were 'good workers', but did not always have 'right positions'.[60] By this the Commissioner probably referred to a certain tendency among these immigrants to form illegal religious groups. Many of these believers left Estonia for West Germany in the 1980s, but in the 1970s they affected UECBE identity, adding to it a new dimension.

Baptisms in the union generally fluctuated between 115 and 150 persons per year in 1964-1972.[61] The lowest numbers of baptisms were in the years

---

[55] Ibid., p. 6.

[56] Toivo Pilli, 'Union of Evangelical Christians-Baptists of Estonia 1945-1989: Survival Techniques, Outreach Efforts, Search for Identity', *Baptist History and Heritage*, vol. XXXVI, nos. 1 and 2 (Winter/Spring 2001), p. 121.

[57] The UECBE statistical reports 1960, 1963, 1965, 1970. Evangeeliumi Kristlaste-Baptistide koguduste statistilised aruanded 1945-1963, EEKBLA.

[58] The UECBE Senior Presbyter's report of 1970-1972. VpAruanded, EEKBLA.

[59] The UECBE Senior Presbyter's report of 1965. VpAruanded, EEKBLA.

[60] The Commissioner of the CRA report of 1969. ERA, f. R-1989, n. 2, s. 93, p. 75.

[61] The UECBE statistical reports 1964-1972. Evangeeliumi Kristlaste-Baptistide koguduste statistilised aruanded 1964-1990 [The UECBE statistical reports 1964-1990], EEKBLA.

1960 (27 persons) and 1961 (23 persons).[62] This correlation with the peak of Khrushchev's atheistic campaign is no surprise. The union also had to cope with the harsh reality that in many churches the average age of members was high and the death rate was growing. In 1972 there were 286 deaths in the UECBE, out of 8,023 members. This number can be compared with the figures for the Estonian Baptist Union in 1937, when there were only 138 deaths out of approximately 7,500 members.[63] The most significant decline took place in Saaremaa and Hiiumaa islands, the traditional revival areas of the nineteenth century. In 1970-1972 not a single ECB church on these islands was able to grow in membership. During the same period seventeen churches in mainland Estonia were able to grow or keep their membership numbers at the same level.[64] In part this difference can be attributed to urbanisation. During the Soviet years 'the predominantly agrarian Estonian economy was rapidly transformed in an industrial direction'.[65] Another factor was the general secularisation in Europe. The picture was mixed, but in general, all church bodies in Estonia saw a decline in church membership numbers.[66]

Certainly, statistical data cannot be the only criteria for assessing the inner dynamics of church life. This was understood also by the UECBE leaders, who used to say that 'God does not count [church] members; rather he weighs them'.[67] This slogan was of some help in interpreting the situation. Also, there were some signs of hope. In some cases, in spite of overall membership decline, the churches were able to baptize younger and more active people, and in such instances the loss of members was not so dramatic. While many churches diminished, especially in the countryside, there were some churches in the bigger towns and cities that were actually able to grow. Also, there were new presbyters who began to serve local churches. In 1966 there were 84 presbyters in the UECBE, and 40 of them had begun their spiritual ministry after the Second World War.[68] According to the Commissioner, in 1969 there were 77 presbyters in the UECBE, including the Senior Presbyter.[69] Nevertheless, the union's presbyters were aware that the situation was critical and that - as time passed - it was not growing any better.

Robert Võsu, after becoming the Senior Presbyter in 1970, gave some advice as to how larger and stronger churches could help and support smaller and weaker ones. According to Võsu, there were 16 churches in UECBE with a

---

[62] The UECBE Senior Presbyter's report of 1965. VpAruanded, EEKBLA.

[63] The UECBE Senior Presbyter's report of 1970-1972. VpAruanded, EEKBLA.

[64] Ibid.

[65] Kliimask, 'Economic Transformation in the Post-Socialist City: The Case of Tallinn', p. 154.

[66] Plaat, 'Eesti vabakoguduste vastupanu nõukogude religioonipoliitikale', pp. 150-153.

[67] The UECBE Senior Presbyter's report of 1970-1972. VpAruanded, EEKBLA.

[68] The UECBE Senior Presbyter's report of 1965. VpAruanded, EEKBLA.

[69] The Commissioner of the CRA report of 1969. ERA, f. R-1989, n. 2, s. 93, p. 78.

membership of under 25. This was partly the legacy of the Soviet religious policies of 1945, which demanded that every mission station had to be registered as a church with its own presbyter. However, the opportunities for other presbyters to visit nearby churches were severely restricted by the state. Võsu analysed the situation in this way: 'We do not wish', he stated, 'that these work stations would disappear.' He suggested, rather, that the church should either move and meet in a nearby village or a town with a larger population, perhaps becoming a mission station of a bigger church, or ask for registration as a group of believers.[70]

There were mostly two sources for new church members: baptisms of new believers (often children brought up in the churches) and the addition of people who came from other free churches, including ECB churches outside Estonia. In 1966, however, there were baptisms in only 31 local churches,[71] while the total number of churches was over 80. Much emphasis was placed on the children of believers' families, but not all of these remained in the churches. The rise in the average age of church members influenced the ways in which churches engaged in self-reflection. In some cases an idealisation of the past rather than any attempt at serious work for the future came to characterise the churches. There were also conservative currents from outside Estonia. Though a Russian-speaking Baptist church existed in Tallinn before the First World War, this did not have a significant impact on the union. But the growth of Russian-speaking ECB groups and congregations that took place in the 1960s and 1970s did have an effect. This section of the UECBE tended to be more conservative, following the principle of strict adherence to closed communion and having a tradition of married women covering their heads.[72]

Two other aspects must be mentioned regarding the issue of church membership. First, churches found it difficult to attract or retain men. The ratio of women to men in 1945 on Soviet collective farms was 2.7:1, and women 'constituted the great majority of the post-war Soviet population'.[73] But in Estonian ECB churches the situation was even more out of balance. In 1946 there were 2,140 men and 7,611 women in the union,[74] and by 1970 there were 1,649 men and 6,557 women in the UECBE.[75] 'Is there something wrong with

[70] The UECBE Senior Presbyter's report of 1970-1972. VpAruanded, EEKBLA.

[71] The UECBE Senior Presbyter's report of 1966. VpAruanded, EEKBLA.

[72] Oksana Vertšerkovskaja, 'Vene baptisti koguduste teke ja areng Eesti Evangeeliumi Kristlaste ja Baptistide Koguduste Liidu ajaloo taustal' [The Beginnings and Development of Russian Baptist Churches in the Background of UECBE History], diploma thesis (Tartu: Kõrgem Usuteaduslik Seminar, 1999), pp. 51, 69.

[73] Elena Zubkova, 'Russia after the War: Hopes, Illusions and Disappointments', in David L. Hoffmann, ed., *Stalinism* (Oxford: Blackwell Publishing, 2003), p. 281.

[74] The UECBE statistical report 1946. Evangeeliumi Kristlaste-Baptistide koguduste statistilised aruanded 1945-1963, EEKBLA.

[75] The UECBE statistical report 1970. Evangeeliumi Kristlaste-Baptistide koguduste statistilised aruanded 1964-1990, EEKBLA.

our style of proclaiming the Gospel?' the Senior Presbyter asked.[76] Second, in the 1960s some large extended families became influential in Estonian ECB life, and it became almost the norm that every Baptist knew every other Baptist in Estonia. The sense of being a united family, holding together under state pressure, was both the strength and the weakness of the UECBE. Belonging together was encouraging, but a diminishing ability to reach beyond the church walls was a disturbing sign.

In addition to the discouraging statistical realities, Evangelical Christians-Baptists in Estonia had to cope with a distorted image created by atheistic propaganda. The atheistic system deliberately presented a gloomy picture of Christians, especially during the times of intensified atheistic pressure. Besides other means, official periodicals were used to depict believers, including Baptists and other evangelicals, as dangerous sectarians. The propaganda articles were 'directed at the mass market' and 'characterised by crudity and shallowness'. They caricatured the external forms of religion, while being ignorant of its inner significance.[77] The influence of the written word and other forms of media, such as television and radio, was recognised by atheistic theoreticians,[78] and the use of these methods of communication to oppose religion had far-reaching effects in shaping the popular mindset about believers. In Estonia, 13 atheistic propaganda articles were produced in 1952, and in 1962 this figure had risen to 63. In 1960 there were 118 atheistic articles in Estonian periodicals.[79] It should also be noted that a massive number of atheistic booklets and books were published. According to Vello Salo, between 1954 and 1972 there were 91 titles of atheistic literature published in Estonia (the total number of copies produced was 323,315).[80] At the same time, the churches had practically no opportunity to publish literature of their own, which would have helped to deepen their spirituality. The situation looked bleak.

THE ECHOES OF THE ALL-UNION SPLIT IN ESTONIA

Problems within the All-Union Council of Evangelical Christians-Baptists also

---

[76] The UECBE Senior Presbyter's report of 1970-1972. VpAruanded, EEKBLA.

[77] Walters, 'A survey of Soviet religious policy', p. 22. For a study of atheism in Estonia, see Atko Remmel, 'Ateismi ajaloost Eestis (XIX sajandi lõpust kuni aastani 1989)' [The History of Atheism in Estonia (From the End of the Nineteenth Century to 1989)], ThM thesis (Tartu: Tartu University, 2004), especially on Soviet atehistic methods and propaganda, pp. 44-86, 114-125.

[78] Raid, *Vabamõtlejate ringidest massilise ateisimini*, p. 190.

[79] Meelis Süld, 'Ateistlik propaganda Nõukogude Eesti ajalehtedes aastail 1952 ja 1962' [Atheistic Propaganda in the Soviet Estonian Newspapers in 1952 and 1962], unpublished seminar paper (Tartu: Tartu University, 1998), p. 12. TPL. Süld used only these articles that were referred to in the Article and Review Chronicle (*Artiklite ja retsensioonide kroonika*) under the subtitle 'Atheism. Science and religion.'

[80] Salo, *Riik ja kirikud*, p. 31.

affected Estonia. As a result of Khrushchev's atheistic persecutions, a painful and confusing split among the Soviet Baptists occurred at the beginning of the 1960s. As with other major denominations, the AUCECB was put under pressure to modify its own internal statutes in accordance with the intensified atheistic restrictions. In 18 April 1960, the report of A. Puzin, the chairman of the CARC, stated that 'on the demand of the CARC' several religious societies had 'adjusted their statutes to the laws'. As a positive example of this, he made a reference in the report to the statutes of the AUCECB.[81] For the time being, the Soviet state was satisfied. However, this was not to be the case for long.

Under heavy state pressure, the AUCECB leadership in Moscow prepared New Statutes and sent a 'Letter of Instruction' in 1960 to all Senior Presbyters. Ernest A. Payne has summed up the content of these two documents: 'Children ought not to be brought to the worship services ... and it would certainly be unwise to step up evangelistic activities.'[82] In addition, 'baptism of people between the ages of eighteen and thirty was to be discouraged'.[83] Michael Bourdeaux has shown that the message of these documents was one of the formal reasons for a split in the AUCECB; the *initsiativniki*, or Reform Baptists, increasingly began to raise their voices against believers compromising with the atheistic state in this way.[84] In the 1960s there was increasing conflict between these two approaches to the state. Church leaders had to choose between 'discretion' (by which they could 'buy' ongoing pastoral supervision for their people) and 'valour' (by which they avoided compromises, but risked being separated from their pastoral tasks by persecution).[85]

The official body of the AUCECB preferred a moderate, even obedient attitude in their relationships with the atheistic authorities, in order not to undermine the possibility of working legally. They believed, it can be argued, that the concessions had not yet reached a critical level that would be irreversibly dangerous for their identity as believers. For the Reform Baptists, the critical line had been reached; they chose protest and began to operate as underground churches. For them, faithfulness to God came to be measured by disobedience to state requirements. They even tended to glorify the conflict with the atheistic state. They declared that many of their 'brothers and sisters

---

[81] O merah po likvidatsii narushenii duhovenstvom sovetskovo zakonodatel'stva o kul'tah (18.04.1960). ERA, f. R-1989, n. 2, s. 25, pp. 50-51.

[82] Ernest A. Payne, *Out of Great Tribulation. Baptists in the U.S.S.R.* (London: Baptist Union of Great Britain and Ireland, 1974), p. 42.

[83] Trevor Beeson, *Discretion and Valour. Religious Conditions in Russia and Eastern Europe* (Glasgow: Collins Fontana Books, 1974), p. 99.

[84] Michael Bourdeaux, *Religious Ferment in Russia: Protestant Opposition to Soviet Religious Policy* (London and New York: Macmillan and St Martin's Press, 1968), pp. 20-21, 26. From September 1965, the Reform Baptists used the name Council of Churches of the Evangelical Christians and Baptists (CCECB).

[85] Trevor Beeson has explored this thesis in *Discretion and Valour*.

were elevated by God to His glory by imprisonment and prison camps'.[86]
Trevor Beeson has argued that the resistance of the Reform Baptists 'to the
encroachments of the State' was 'almost certainly the explanation of the greater
freedom of action' which was granted to the AUCECB later in the 1960s.[87]

The reality of conflict with the state, which could not be completely
avoided, and the implications of compromise with the state, were both factors
that shaped the life of all Soviet Evangelical Christians-Baptists. The Reform
Baptists, that part of the Soviet Baptist life which was operating illegally,
preferred to take the way of conflict and confrontation. The AUCECB, who
operated legally, had to deal with serious issues that related especially to the
consequences of compromise in their value-systems and practices.
Unfortunately, these two wings of Baptists drifted away from each other. Thus
'illegal' Baptists often considered the 'registered' believers as traitors.[88] On the
other hand, 'legal' Baptists saw 'unregistered' believers as troublemakers. The
tensions that emerged in the 1960s have not been finally resolved even today.[89]

This split in the 1960s in the AUCECB did not entirely by-pass Estonia, as
has sometimes been assumed to be the case. It is true that Estonian Evangelical
Christians-Baptists remained mostly, though not exclusively, observers of these
events. Some Russian-speaking evangelical groups in Estonia, however,
became more involved in the so-called 'underground work', and were also
more apt to become involved in conflict. The Senior Presbyter of the UECBE
referred to the All-Union split in his 1964 report to presbyters. According to
him, the split started with the application of the statutes of 1960 that restricted
the number of preachers in local churches. 'As a result', he said, 'many
preaching brothers were put aside and some of them left the churches together
with their supporters. ... For all the restrictions, the criticism was addressed to
the All-Union Council of ECB...'.[90] In reality, the reasons for this conflict were
deeper.

The Estonian union leadership seems to have decided to adopt a position
of 'neutrality' in the conflict. The report stated that 'because this split did not
touch Estonia' the AUCECB circular letters related to this matter were not
forwarded to local churches in Estonia. In 1971, when the Commissioner of the
CRA demanded that the presbyters conference in Estonia should discuss their
approach to the underground organisation of Reform Baptists (now known as
the Council of Churches of the ECB - the CCECB), and that A. Karev's paper,

[86] *Bratskii Listok* [Fraternal Leaflet], no. 6 (1966), Estonian translation. Robert Võsu
materjalid [Materials of Robert Võsu], EEKBLA.
[87] Beeson, *Discretion and Valour*, p. 101.
[88] Hans Barndenburg, *The Meek and the Mighty: The Emergence of the Evangelical
Movement in Russia* (New York: Oxford University Press, 1977), p. 199.
[89] I.V. Podberezkii, *Byt' Protestantom v Rossii* [To Be a Protestant in Russia] (Moskva:
Institut religii i prava, 1996), pp. 166-167.
[90] The UECBE Senior Presbyter's report of 1964. VpAruanded, EEKBLA.

'A Christian and the Homeland', should be introduced to Estonian ECB presbyters, the UECBE leadership refused politely: 'The problem of the CCECB is mostly related to other republics. It would not be understood by the [Estonian] presbyters why in the meeting of our republic we should discuss the problems of other republics.'[91] There was clearly a separate Estonian identity.

The attempts at 'neutrality' by the Estonian ECB leadership made it possible for them to play something of a balancing role between the Reform Baptists and the AUCECB. Two Estonians, Osvald Tärk and Arpad Arder, were involved in the work of a unity commission elected at the AUCECB congress in Moscow in October 1966.[92] Obviously, by this time reunification had become rather difficult, if not impossible, and the work of the unity commission was not very effective. Nonetheless, Tärk and Arder were sincerely committed to securing reconciliation and they took their task seriously. As their correspondence shows, they were in close contact by phone and mail, planning their positions and statements for the committee meetings. On 16 June 1967 Arder wrote to Tärk: '... the text of the new circular letter of the Commission will be discussed... It was not good that we were not present when the first circular letter was finalised; let us try not to repeat this mistake now.'[93]

The unity commission that was set up was ready to listen to voices coming from local churches. The first circular letter of the commission (26 January 1967) asked respondents to send all suggestions and questions to Arpad Arder in Rakvere, Estonia, or to the chairman of the commission, V. Kovalkov in Moscow.[94] For Tärk and Arder, the work connected with the commission involved a good deal of travelling across Soviet territories. Tärk visited the Tula region (1966), Tbilisi (1967), and Tashkent (1967). 'There is hope for true co-operation in the future,' Tärk stated after a meeting with a non-registered group.[95] In Kazakhstan the registered churches were, he reported, 'unity-friendly'. However, in Semipalatinsk and Alma-Aty the *initsiativniki* refused to meet formally with members of the unity commission. Only some individual contacts were possible.[96] This was to be the more common experience.

The work of the unity commission must have been difficult; and not simply because of the psychological pressures on those involved in this attempt at conflict resolution. Walter Sawatsky has pointed out that the commission

---

[91] Robert Võsu to the Commissioner of the CRA (23.03.1970). KirjUv1966-1990, EEKBLA.

[92] Sawatsky, *Soviet Evangelicals*, p. 228.

[93] A. Arder to O. Tärk (16.06.1967). Osvald Tärgi materjalid [Materials of Osvald Tärk], EEKBLA.

[94] Circular letter of the unity commission, no. 1 (26.01.1967). Osvald Tärgi materjalid, EEKBLA.

[95] O. Tärk to V. Kovalkov (13.11.1967). Osvald Tärgi materjalid, EEKBLA.

[96] Aruanne reisist Taškenti 13. apr.-2. maini 1967 [Report of a trip to Tashkent, from 13 April to 2 May 1967]. Osvald Tärgi materjalid, EEKBLA.

members were often 'trusted by both sides but they did not occupy positions of power' and thus had little to say at the decision-making stages. The commission was working during the time when dialogue between 'registered' and 'unregistered' parties became more and more difficult.[97] Hans Brandenburg has described how among Soviet Christians in the 1930s 'false denunciations were used to play one group off against another',[98] and there were those trying to do that in the 1960s. To improve the possibility of mutual understanding, Tärk suggested that it was necessary to increase the authority of the local presbyters and Senior Presbyters, and to find new ways to work for unity. Tärk, a wise statesman, was aware that the hindrances to unity did not always lie among Reform Baptists. He stated: 'We should possibly pay attention ... to educating the registered churches.'[99] Tärk, representing Estonian Evangelical Christians-Baptists, conveyed an image of a theologically balanced, responsible, comparatively conservative, and peace-seeking spiritual leader.

The local authorities in Estonia hindered the contribution that Tärk and Arder made to the All-Union work. In particular, the Commissioner of the CRA did not favour Osvald Tärk's travels. In spring 1968, Tärk wrote to Vassili Lebedev, another member of the committee: 'As you know, already on 17 October 1967 the Commissioner in the Estonian SSR of the Council for Religious Affairs prohibited me from travelling in connection with the responsibilities of the [unity] commission.'[100] Tärk could not fully participate in the commission's work because of these travel restrictions, which lasted from autumn 1967 until spring 1968, and probably longer. However, the experiences of Tärk and Arder in the unity commission helped Estonians to gain first-hand information about the situation among Russian-speaking evangelicals, and also helped them to analyse the split from both sides. Being involved in conciliatory work on a wider scale was certainly an important lesson for Estonians. They became more appreciative of the sense of unity that existed in Estonia. 'We have good reason to be thankful that we have maintained our unity; we understood that the restrictions applied in 1960 did not depend on our leading brothers,' the Senior Presbyter stated in 1964.[101] However, the split in Russia made Estonian ECB believers alert to the fact that outside pressures could endanger unity. Some years later, the Senior Presbyter's report declared: 'The enemy [Satan] does not sleep ... he makes every effort to sow seeds of hatred and create mistrust.'[102]

---

[97] Sawatsky, *Soviet Evangelicals*, p. 229.

[98] Brandenburg, *The Meek and the Mighty*, p. 192.

[99] Aruanne reisist Taškenti 13. apr.–2. maini 1967. Osvald Tärgi materjalid, EEKBLA.

[100] Osvald Tärk to Vassili Ivanovitsh [Lebedev] (24.04.1968). Osvald Tärgi materjalid, EEKBLA.

[101] The UECBE Senior Presbyter's report of 1964. VpAruanded, EEKBLA.

[102] EKB Eesti NSV vanempresbüteri aruanne EKB konverentsil 19. sept. 1966. a. [The UECBE Senior Presbyter's report at the ECB conference 19 September 1966]. VpAruanded, EEKBLA.

After 1963, the Soviet government made some minor concessions to the churches, probably realising that excessively strict administrative measures against religion led to open conflict and that the situation might slip out of control. In 1964, the Estonian Senior Presbyter informed his co-workers that, according to the 1963 AUCECB statutes, there was no longer any need to ask the Senior Presbyter for permission for baptisms since 'baptism is an inner issue of a local church'. The government ceased to demand that the local governments' executive committee vet candidates for church leadership. Preachers did not encounter restrictions in visiting and preaching in neighbouring churches, though official permission was not given.[103] However, Estonians did not expect much from such laws and statutes. Answering the question of how their church viewed the 1963 statutes of the AUCECB, the local Estonian ECB church leaders said rather vaguely that they were 'good' or 'satisfactory', but they hoped for 'better'. One answer suggested that 'the authority of the statutes has disappeared', and a little church in Pärispea stated that 'we base ourselves on the Word of God and not on the statutes'.[104] Estonians, not only at the union level but also at the local church level, tried to pursue their own way as much as possible. Nevertheless, their identity was inevitably affected by the developments within wider Soviet Baptist life.

The split of the 1960s can be seen as a sign of one of the major challenges for Soviet Baptists, namely, the challenge to maintain an atmosphere of mutual trust in their unions and churches. The AUCECB failed to meet this challenge. Even if the Estonian union was not so deeply shaken by the events of the split as were Evangelical Christians-Baptists in Russia and Ukraine, nevertheless they also had to deal with the issues of trust and unity. Their involvement in seeking reconciliation was valuable to them even if not much was achieved on the wider front. Despite wider Baptist tensions, from the mid-1960s Estonian Evangelical Christians-Baptists were able to maintain, and in some measure to strengthen, the organisational unity and the sense of mutual cooperation in the union that historically included several evangelical traditions. However, there was no reason for optimism.

THE SENIOR PRESBYTER AND HIS TEAM

The state authorities in the 1960s made significant efforts to teach Estonian ECB churches, and other churches as well, that religion belonged to the past and that Christianity had no future in Communist society. At least in part, they succeeded: Estonian ECB members tended to accept the view of themselves as a marginalised community that lived under strict government control. Sometimes heroic or tragic accounts of persecution were added to this picture.

---

[103] The UECBE Senior Presbyter's report of 1964. VpAruanded, EEKBLA.
[104] Küsimused 1964. aasta aruande juurde [Questions attached to the 1964 report]. EEKBLA.

A belief emerged that ECB members could influence their surroundings as individuals at best, but as a union they had little hope of influencing society. However there were some encouraging developments. One of these was that collective leadership patterns, though restricted and strictly observed by the state, began to be restored in the later 1960s. Presbyters' Council and Presbyters' Conferences (meetings), and later conferences with delegates from local churches, conveyed the message that state imposed centralised leadership models could be balanced by some input from local churches.

In 1964, the Senior Presbyter again obtained the right 'to use advisers', as the UECBE report carefully formulated it.[105] In fact, the collective leadership ideal, an important feature of the identity of all Estonian free churches, had never been completely wiped out. Johannes Lipstok had regularly called together 'advisory brothers' in the 1950s,[106] when his office had enjoyed opportunities for work unknown on the All-Union scale.[107] Even in 1960-1963, when for a time Estonia was not allowed to have its own Senior Presbyter, and when Nikolai Levindanto was officially the Senior Presbyter for all three Baltic republics, with his residence in Riga, the centralised model did not work 'perfectly'. Estonian ECB church leaders still tried to keep contact with each other. They were appreciative that 'even brother Levindanto', who represented the AUCECB, consulted Estonian leaders, usually the presbyters of the Tallinn ECB churches.[108] The position of the Senior Presbyter was re-instituted in Estonia in 1964, and under Aleksander Sildos' leadership the office began to assume importance once more. In July 1964, Robert Võsu began to work in the office as an assistant and as secretary for Sildos. By 1966, it was possible to form 'a council of brothers' consisting of ten members, in addition to Sildos.[109] The members represented different geographical regions of Estonia.[110] All the members were well-known and respected church leaders. Nevertheless, at the beginning they were simply named and appointed by the Senior Presbyter, who at the 1966 presbyters meeting asked for the support of other presbyters for this structure, which came to be known as 'Presbyters' Council'.[111]

---

[105] The UECBE Senior Presbyter's report of 1964. VpAruanded, EEKBLA.

[106] The UECBE Senior Presbyter's report of 1965. VpAruanded, EEKBLA.

[107] Johannes Laks, *Mälestusi eluteelt ja töömaalt* [Memoirs from Life and Work] (Toronto: Toronto Vabakoguduse Kirjastus, 1965), pp. 82-83.

[108] The UECBE Senior Presbyter's report of 1964. VpAruanded, EEKBLA.

[109] These members were: Aleksander Sildos (Senior Presbyter), Robert Võsu (Senior Presbyter's assistant and secretary), Osvald Tärk, Oskar Olvik, Gustav Nõlvak, Eduard Heinla, Hermann Mäemets, Albert Tammo, Imant Ridaliste, Arpad Arder, Kalju Raid. Presidiumu VSEHB. Presviterskii sovet u starshevo presvitera po Est. SSR [To the presidium of the AUCECB. Presbyters' Council by the Senior Presbyter of the Est. SSR] (21.11.1966). Kirjavahetus EKBÜN-iga [Correspondence with the AUCECB], EEKBLA.

[110] The UECBE Senior Presbyter's report of 1966. VpAruanded, EEKBLA.

[111] The UECBE Senior Presbyter's report of 1965. VpAruanded, EEKBLA.

The Presbyters' Council was first and foremost a body for spiritual and theological reflection. It discussed issues related to the life and work of presbyters, and analysed situations in local churches.[112] This group was also supposed to help the Senior Presbyter to find new presbyters for churches needing pastors.[113] In some cases the council members assisted in solving conflicts when local churches were not able to find satisfactory solutions. According to the AUCECB statutes of 1966, as interpreted in Estonia, they had the right to visit churches. However, it became an unwritten rule that, first and foremost, it was the Senior Presbyter's responsibility to visit local churches.[114] This added to the authority of the Senior Presbyter and enabled him to get first-hand information about life in the churches. In March 1967, according to the new AUCECB statutes, the Presbyters' Conference elected a twelve-member Presbyters' Council, plus three observers. Also Aleksander Sildos, as Senior Presbyter, received the full support of his fellow-presbyters.[115] He usually acted as chairman of the Presbyters' Council, with Robert Võsu as deputy chairman.[116] The Presbyters' Council of 1967 received approval from the local church leaders, not from church delegates. However, it was an important step forward, and after all, Estonian evangelicals had learned to adjust to changing realities.[117] In 1973, a four-member Ordination Committee (Est. 'Presbüterite Katsekomisjon', literal translation 'Testing Committee for Presbyters') came into being, formed from the members of the council.[118]

At the end of the 1960s and at the beginning of the 1970s, it was repeatedly emphasised in the UECBE reports that a spirit of mutual

---

[112] The UECBE Senior Presbyter's report of 1966. VpAruanded, EEKBLA.

[113] The UECBE Senior Presbyter's report of 1970-1972. VpAruanded, EEKBLA.

[114] Both Aleksander Sildos and Robert Võsu visited churches very frequently. In 1973 Võsu stated that his aim was to visit all the churches of the union at least once a year, and that 'with some exceptions' he had suceeded. The UECBE Senior Presbyter's report of 1970-1972. VpAruanded, EEKBLA. In 1972 there were 82 local churches in the union.

[115] A. Sildos to the Commissioner of the CRA (15.03.1967). KirjUv1966-1990, EEKBLA. In addition to the members of 1966 there were now Allar Puu, Ilmar Kurg, Jaan Hanni. The three observers were Paul Himma, Rein Kiviloo and Paldor Teekel.

[116] Spisok presviterskovo soveta Estonskovo bratstva EHB [List of the members of the Presbyters' Council of the Estonian ECB brotherhood] (21.03.1967). Kirjavahetus EKBÜN-iga, EEKBLA.

[117] A short overview 'Evangeeliumi kristlaste-baptistide põhimõtted, struktuur ja karakteristika' [Evangelical Christian-Baptist Principles, Structure and Characteristics], typewritten document (n.d.), probably written in the middle of the 1960s, still stated the theoretical ideal: conferences or congresses held on a democratic representative basis elect the leaders of the union and discuss issues of general importance. KirjUv1966-1990, EEKBLA.

[118] Members of the Ordination Committee in 1973: Osvald Tärk, Oskar Olvik, Robert Võsu, Kalju Raid. The UECBE Senior Presbyter's report of 1970-1972. VpAruanded, EEKBLA.

understanding and respect reigned in the council meetings. 'There have been absolutely no disputes or conflicts.'[119] There is no reason to think that this was only an empty slogan; the early years of this leadership structure were characterised by thankfulness and even enthusiasm about having this opportunity to meet, discuss and decide, an opportunity that was unprecedented during the Soviet years in Estonia. The existence of the council meant that the local voice being given more weight, over against decisions made in Moscow. Also, outward pressure made the inward fellowship and sense of brotherhood stronger.

The existence of the Presbyters' Council gave the message to local churches that some decisions were being made by their representatives and that they were not totally dependent on an all-powerful state, at least in spiritual matters. In addition, the presbyters meetings, often also called presbyters conferences, began to take place on a more or less regular basis. There had been a possibility of having regional meetings for church leaders before the middle of the 1960s, but these were replaced after 1966 by meetings bringing together presbyters from all over Estonia. However, the Senior Presbyter's wish that the meetings should take place annually[120] was not altogether implemented. Though according to the 1966 statutes of the AUCECB the Senior Presbyter and his associates had the freedom to call conferences - 'for deciding questions that arise, as deemed necessary, the Presbyters' Council calls a conference of church workers'[121] - in reality, every meeting had to have permission from the Commissioner of the CRA. As the correspondence between the UECBE office and the Commissioner shows, permission could not be taken for granted.

A further step was organising conferences that included representatives who were not presbyters. An ECB conference was held in Estonia on 19 September 1966 and the Senior Presbyter noted that this was the first conference in the Estonian SSR that brought together representatives from local churches.[122] It is not clear how these representatives were chosen, or indeed if they were chosen at all. The conference took place in Kalju Baptist Church in Tallinn. One of the reasons why permission was given to hold the conference was probably the forthcoming ECB Congress in Moscow, which took place from 4 to 7 October that year.[123] At the Tallinn conference, the delegation for the Moscow Congress was elected. Estonian representation could consist of up

---

[119] The UECBE Senior Presbyter's report of 1966. VpAruanded, EEKBLA.

[120] The UECBE Senior Presbyter's report at the ECB conference 19 September 1966. VpAruanded, EEKBLA.

[121] 'Constitution of the ECB Church in the USSR', in Sawatsky, *Soviet Evangelicals*, p. 483.

[122] The UECBE Senior Presbyter's report at the ECB conference 19 September 1966. VpAruanded, EEKBLA.

[123] *Istorija evangel'skih hristjan-baptistov v SSSR* [History of Evangelical Christians-Baptists in the USSR] (Moskva: Izdanije VSEHB, 1989), p. 246.

to 17 delegates and 4 observers.[124] During this conference, the UECBE leadership encouraged unregistered groups of believers in Estonia to be hopeful that the door for registration would be opened. In fact the registration process turned out to be much more difficult than expected. The report also referred to 20 years of united ECB work in Estonia, and stated bleakly that during the last years 'heaven has been like copper over our heads, the believers have become lukewarm and passive and there are no conversions.'[125] However, participation in the Moscow Congress gave Estonians more self-confidence; they realised that they had something to offer to the All-Union brotherhood. Estonians learned more about All-Union church life and came to know church leaders from other parts of the Soviet Union. Osvald Tärk preached at the opening Congress service and Oskar Olvik presented one of the two main theological papers.[126] 'We believe that through the Congress, the Estonians' name became known to all our brotherhood,' observed Aleksander Sildos.[127]

Aleksander Sildos (1891-1976) was Senior Presbyter from 1964 until the end of 1969,[128] but he had been working in the leadership of the UECBE for a long time before that. Though ethnically an Estonian, he grew up in a home where Russian was the everyday language.[129] In his early twenties he experienced an evangelical conversion during a worship service at a Moravian prayer house.[130] Sildos became active in Christian Endeavour work and was closely related to the ministries of the Evangelical Christian Church in Narva. In 1945 he started to work in the union office in Tallinn and this proved to be good preparation for the Senior Presbyter's work. He was the only Senior Presbyter in Soviet Estonia who came from an Evangelical Christian rather than

---

[124] The UECBE Senior Presbyter's report at the ECB conference 19 September 1966. VpAruanded, EEKBLA. Probably there were even more Estonians who took part of the congress in Moscow in 1966.

[125] The UECBE Senior Presbyter's report at the ECB conference 19 September 1966. VpAruanded, EEKBLA

[126] The UECBE Senior Presbyter's report at the ECB conference 19 September 1966. VpAruanded, EEKBLA; *Istorija evangel'skih hristjan-baptistov v SSSR*, p. 247.

[127] The UECBE Senior Presbyter's report of 1966. VpAruanded, EEKBLA.

[128] Riho Saard, 'Eesti kirikute juhtivvaimulikkond läbi aegade' [Estonian Church Leaders through the Centuries], part 2, *Akadeemia*, no. 3 (1998), p. 613. For a more recent presentation of this study, see Riho Saard, *Eesti kirikute esivaimulikkond 1165-2006* [Estonian Church Leaders 1165-2006] (Tallinn: Argo, 2006). Already in January 1963, at local presbyters meetings in Tallinn, Haapsalu and Tartu, the Estonian ECB church leaders had expressed their support to A. Sildos. Johannes Laks, *Aleksander Sildos: elulugu* [Aleksander Sildos: A Biography], typewritten manuscript (Tallinn, 1967), p. 117. TPL.

[129] Elmar Palumäe, comp., *Elusõnu mitmest suust: Eduard Lilienthal ja Aleksander Sildos* [Words of Life from the Lips of Many: Eduard Lilienthal and Aleksander Sildos], typewritten manuscript, book 6 (1977), p. 71. KUSA.

[130] Laks, *Aleksander Sildos: elulugu*, pp. 23-25.

a Baptist background. He visited local churches all over Estonia, often together with Johannes Lipstok, in this way developing personal contacts with local church leaders and learning of the spiritual atmosphere of the churches. From 1951-1957, he was acting presbyter of Kiviõli ECB Church in northern Estonia. When Levindanto visited Estonia, Sildos helped as an interpreter.[131] In 1966, Sildos was elected to the AUCECB council, which was expanded from ten to twenty-five persons.[132] His All-Union contribution was modest when compared to that of Tärk and Võsu, but his spiritual personality, his commitment to Christian work, and his good relationships with his co-workers[133] were qualities that helped the UECBE through the difficulties of the 1960s.

Although Sildos was a devoted believer and a leader with pastoral abilities, in the more official aspects of his work, even in preparing annual reports, Sildos seems to have relied heavily on the assistance of Robert Võsu, who began to play a significant role in the union office after 1964 and who was to succeed Sildos as Senior Presbyter in 1970. However, Sildos' faithfulness, his popular and biblical preaching style, and his balanced character,[134] helped to ensure stability in the union. Sildos stood up for the interests of the churches in the union when circumstances demanded. But the methods used were those of 'the poor widow' in the New Testament, who respectfully and persistently presented her cause, until she obtained what she had applied for. An annual report from the mid-1960s stated: 'We do not want to express our wishes in an aggressive or protesting way to the authorities, but in a respectful way, and thereby moderately.'[135] This approach was not only 'common sense wisdom' but it also correlated with Sildos' character and spiritual values.

In spite of the restrictions and pressures they suffered under Khrushchev's atheistic campaign, in its aftermath Estonian ECB churches found an opportunity to restore – though inadequately – some patterns of collective leadership which had earlier been an important element of their church life. Probably due to the split in the AUCECB and the state's attempts to limit the consequences of that split, the state gradually began to give more freedom to registered churches to take local initiatives, though under strict control. In this way, the public protest of the *initsiativniki*, from a long-term perspective, helped to win more opportunities for the AUCECB. In Estonia, the opportunity to have the Senior Presbyter's institution restored, to have the Presbyters'

---

[131] Palumäe, comp., *Elusõnu mitmest suust: Eduard Lilienthal ja Aleksander Sildos*, pp. 77-79.

[132] Sawatsky, *Soviet Evangelicals*, pp. 216, 225.

[133] Robert Võsu, 'Aleksandr Mihailovitsh Sildos' (22.06.1976), typewritten text in Russian. Kirjavahetus EKBÜN-iga, EEKBLA.

[134] See Johannes Vink, comp., *Aleksander Sildose surm* [Death of Aleksander Sildos], typewritten manuscript ([Vancouver], 1977), p. 5. TPL.

[135] The UECBE Senior Presbyter's report at the ECB conference 19 September 1966. VpAruanded, EEKBLA.

Council and even to have wider conferences, was a rare ray of light in the dark sky of the 1960s. In the same period it also became clear that Estonians were able to give theological help to All-Union activities. Aleksander Sildos, Arpad Arder, Osvald Tärk, Oskar Olvik and Robert Võsu became well known among Soviet evangelicals, especially after the 1966 Congress. Estonian ECB believers could see that Soviet atheistic power had not been able to destroy all the elements of their traditional faith and practice – their identity.

SOME INFLUENCES THROUGH THE IRON CURTAIN

The life and beliefs of Estonian Evangelical Christians-Baptists in the 1960s were affected not only by the atheistic state, or by contacts with the Russian-speaking Baptists, nor through the AUCECB, but also by a new factor: increasing contact with evangelical believers from the non-communist world. This happened in the context of a political situation where the general trend in Eastern European countries was to seek international contacts for the benefit of the communist regimes. In some cases this had religious consequences and involved a 'move towards a less restricted toleration', as Eric Ruden (perhaps too optimistically) stated in 1965.[136] In Estonia, the new foreign contacts came to affect ECB and wider Estonian church life, especially in the 1970s and 1980s, but the first signs of this development go back to the 1960s.

The first Baptist delegation from a non-communist country to visit Estonian Baptists came from Sweden in 1956. This was such an exceptional event that even people who were not related to the Baptist community took note of the visit. For example, Elo Tuglas, the wife of the legendary Estonian writer, Friedebert Tuglas, wrote about it in her diary, as the visit was discussed in their home.[137] During Khrushchev's atheistic campaign, the chairman of the CARC, A. Puzin, bluntly pointed out: 'International activity – this is the only area where the church and the servants of cults can bring benefit to the Soviet government.' He specifically mentioned that churches could be used by the Soviet state in the 'struggle for peace' and for 'counter-propaganda abroad'.[138]

After the visit of the Finnish president, Urho Kaleva Kekkonen, to Estonia in March 1964, a ferry began to ply between Tallinn and Helsinki.[139] This ferry, which began in 1965, increased the number of tourists – initially, many of them

---

[136] *The Truth That Makes Men Free. Official Report of the 11ᵗʰ Congress of BWA* (Nashville, Tennessee: BWA and Broadman, 1966), p. 291.

[137] Elo Tuglas, *Elukiri* [A Print of Life] (Tallinn: Faatum, 1993), p. 140.

[138] O merah po likvidatsii narushenii duhovenstvom sovetskovo zakonodatel'stva o kul'tah (18.04.1960). ERA, f. R-1989, n. 2, s. 25, p. 81.

[139] Lauri Vahtre, *Elu-olu viimasel vene ajal* [Living Conditions During the Last Russian Rule] (Tallinn: Kirjastuskeskus, 2002), pp. 62, 64.

were 'vodka tourists' – coming via Helsinki to Tallinn.[140] However, several believers, mostly Finnish evangelicals, also used the opportunity to visit Tallinn. By the end of 1969, a number of close contacts had developed between Estonian ECB churches in Tallinn and the Finnish Christians visiting Estonia, among whom there were many Pentecostals. In 1966, two groups of Finnish Pentecostals visited Tallinn (8-10 May, and 17-19 July).[141] Through personal contacts, and later through literature that was smuggled into Estonia and translated into Estonian, the theological trends that were present among Finnish Pentecostals and the Finnish Free Church began to play an important part in the reshaping of Estonian ECB life and theology.

Relationships with the wider Baptist world were also gradually opened up, even though most of the official contacts were channelled through the AUCECB headquarters in Moscow. From 2 to 4 November 1966, a Baptist World Alliance (BWA) delegation, led by the General Secretary of the BWA, Josef Nordenhaug, visited Estonia. The delegation included John Williams, representing African American Baptist churches in the USA, and the President of the Southern Baptist Convention, Wayne Dehoney.[142] The visit of this Baptist World Alliance delegation to Estonia was important for local believers: 'This was the first experience of this kind', it was noted, 'in the history of our united brotherhood.'[143] In 1971, the General Secretary of the Danish Baptists, Knud Wümpelmann, visited Tallinn in the course of a trip he made to the Soviet Union as a representative of the European Baptist Federation.[144] In the same year, BWA President Carney Hargroves and General Secretary Robert Denny visited Tallinn.[145] 'This type of visit has happened only once before, namely 40 years ago. Then, also, the worship services took place in the Oleviste Church, without even guessing that one day this could be our church,' the Senior Presbyter stated.[146] The BWA, however, was cautious about publicly raising issues of religious freedom, as this might have worsened the situation for many believers. As Denny noted: 'The question is, how much outside pressure will help or hurt when freedom is restricted.'[147]

---

[140] Rein Taagepera, *Estonia. Return to Independence* (San Francisco and Oxford: Westview Press, 1993), p. 105.

[141] The UECBE Senior Presbyter's report of 1966. VpAruanded, EEKBLA.

[142] Aleksander Sildos to the Commissioner of the CRA (22.03.1967). KirjUv1966-1990, EEKBLA.

[143] The UECBE Senior Presbyter's report of 1966. VpAruanded, EEKBLA.

[144] Stanley Crabb, comp. and ed., *Our Favourite Memories. European Baptist Federation 1949-1999* (n. p., n. d.), pp. 37-38.

[145] Minutes of the Presbyters' Council meeting, no. 12 (21.05.1971), no. 13 (28.08.1971). Presbüterite nõukogu protokollid 1969-1985 (PNProt1969-1985) [Minutes of the Presbyters' Council 1969-1985], EEKBLA.

[146] The UECBE Senior Presbyter's report of 1970-1972. VpAruanded, EEKBLA.

[147] *Reconcililation Through Christ. Official report of the 12th Congress of BWA* (Valley Forge: BWA and Judson Press, 1971), p. 180.

The importance of the attention paid by these European and world Baptist leaders to believers in the Soviet Union cannot be over-estimated. In Estonia the Evangelical Christians-Baptists certainly got the message: they were not left to survive alone. Unfortunately, the foreigners visiting Estonia were usually not allowed to travel outside Tallinn, which limited their opportunities to develop contacts with the many believers who did not live in the capital city. In addition, it was a 'publicly known secret' that the KGB observed carefully the steps of foreign visitors. Taimi Vanaselja, an ECB church member from Tallinn, has vividly described in her memoirs some of the experiences she had of being spied upon and followed when having Christian friends from Finland visiting her home.[148]

Contacts were also gradually revived with Estonian expatriates who lived in Sweden, Canada and the USA. Asta Kaups, an active member of the Estonian Baptist Church in Toronto, has described her first visit to Soviet Estonia in 1967.[149] In the early 1970s, Leonhard Heinmets, Artur Proos and other Estonian Baptists who were living abroad visited Estonia.[150] Robert Võsu was able to travel outside Estonia reasonably often. In 1968 he visited Finland, and in 1969 he travelled to Austria, Canada and the USA.[151] In 1971, by which time he was Senior Presbyter, he visited Sweden.[152] Plans for him to take part in the BWA's twelfth congress in Tokyo did not, however, materialise.[153] The state authorities, who tried to use contacts with the non-communist world for their own propagandistic goals, became aware that visits by Christians from abroad to the USSR or visits made by believers from the USSR to other countries strengthened churches in the Soviet Union. Churches tried to use contacts abroad to revive religious life at home and to increase their authority, complained the chairman of the CARC.[154] During his trips, Robert Võsu tried to meet Estonian Baptist expatriates, and tried to analyse what methods of Christian work used abroad could be relevant in Estonia. He often shared information about wider Baptist life with his fellow ECB presbyters and in this way Estonian Baptist identity was strengthened.

---

[148] Taimi Vanaselja, *Kun sydän pelkää* [When the Heart is Frightened] (Hämeenlinna: Päivä Osakeyhtiö, 2000), pp. 114-117.

[149] Asta Kaups, *Pärija* [Inheritor] (Tallinn, 2000), pp. 199-206.

[150] The UECBE Senior Presbyter's report of 1970-1972. VpAruanded, EEKBLA.

[151] The Commissioner of the CRA report of 1969. ERA, f. R-1989, n. 2, s. 93, p. 83.

[152] Salo, *Riik ja kirikud*, p. 35.

[153] The Presbyters' Council encouraged Võsu to take part in the Congress. Minutes of the Presbyters' Council meeting, no. 1 (15.09.1969). PNProt1969-1985, EEKBLA.

[154] O merah po likvidatsii narushenii duhovenstvom sovetskovo zakonodatel'stva o kul'tah (18.04.1960). ERA, f. R-1989, n. 2, s. 25, p. 81.

CONCLUSION

Estonian Evangelical Christians-Baptists went through what can be termed a period of still life in the 1960s, in which relatively little advance was evident. This period began with the experience of severe atheistic pressure under Khrushchev at the end of the 1950s. This pressure was relaxed a little after Brezhnev came to power in 1964, but in spite of some oral promises from the Commissioner for the CRA, the churches gained no significant freedoms. The Estonian ECB leadership defined the task for the union and for local churches in this period: keep the positions! A rather cautious attitude toward involvement in public spheres of life and a relatively passive approach toward social problems was the norm among Estonian ECB members. Some of the attitudes that have continued to characterise Evangelical Christians-Baptists in Estonia were shaped in the experiences of these years. A survival-orientated approach became part of the UECBE's identity and spirituality. A low profile in the society was the price that was paid in order to maintain elements of identity in spirituality and worship. Decline in membership and the effect of atheistic propaganda left their marks on the age-structure of the UECBE – even today there is a generation gap in the UECBE churches, as people in their 50s and 60s are poorly represented among ECB churches in Estonia.

There were, however, some positive features. Estonian Evangelical Christians-Baptists responded to the situation of limited freedoms and lessened atheistic pressure in the later 1960s by paying more attention to Christian fellowship and using every opportunity to come together for worship. Church fellowship – a traditional facet of evangelical identity – was strengthened despite external restrictions. Besides the official worship services, church anniversaries, and activities such as choir rehearsals and meetings in private homes, offered additional opportunities for encouragement. Although this was helpful, many local churches gradually became focussed only on building up the inner life of their communities. The families of believers often sustained churches, with no new outsiders in evidence. This was especially true of several of the churches in the countryside, which were also weakened because of the trend toward urbanisation.

The union's leadership structures were gradually revived after the hard years at the beginning of the 1960s. For three years Estonian ECB churches, at least formally, were not allowed to have their own Senior Presbyter. A change for the better came after 1964, when the Senior Presbyter's post was restored, the collective leadership structure - the Presbyters' Council - was established, and the union was allowed to organise some conferences. The pressures of the period when churches were living largely in isolation from each other were gradually relaxed. An increasing number of contacts with Baptists abroad also encouraged Estonian believers. However, the feelings of fear and the sense of being controlled by the state did not readily disappear. The feelings that little could be done seemed to be widespread, and the union leadership constantly had to inspire churches with a message of hope. As to relationships with the AUCECB, especially with regard to the conflicts between Reform Baptists and the AUCECB, the Estonian brotherhood followed a line of 'polite and constructive distance', trying to act in a way that would foster reconciliation.

The atheistic campaign led by Khrushchev, and the effects that continued to be felt even after it had passed its peak, meant that Estonian ECB churches, like churches within the USSR, had many reasons to move toward a closed, sectarian form of church life. Their identity as a union of churches that sought to reach out to others was threatened. They had good reason to develop an alternative identity – that of a persecuted group of people, characterised by their passivity and their suffering. Still life could lead to a standstill and even to death. As we will see in the next chapter, this did not happen. There was life in the churches that could still be revived. The severe difficulties of the 1960s gave way to a different scenario in the 1970s, the decade which, unexpectedly, saw the emergence of a youth revival in Estonia.

CHAPTER 4

Light at the End of the Tunnel: 1972-1985

In political terms, the second half of Brezhnev's rule, especially the end of the 1970s and beginning of the 1980s, has been called the period of stagnation (or 'Brezhnevian stagnation'), characterised by slowing economic growth, ideological rigidity, an atmosphere of cynicism and corruption, and repressive methods directed toward dissidents.[1] Rein Taagepera, an Estonian scholar in the field of political sciences, has suggested that the period of 1968-1980 in Estonia should, because of its social and political atmosphere, rather be called the 'years of suffocation', because of 'the almost painlessly slow but relentless squeeze on the national psyche'.[2] In the religious sphere, Soviet policy became one of 'divide and rule'. As in the social life of the country, where a division was made between the communist elite, the rulers, and the rest of the people,[3] so also a similar division took place in the state attitude toward churches. The state was 'granting concessions to registered congregations and even whole denominations, while dealing harshly with unregistered and dissident groups'.[4] However, even when giving some opportunities for registered churches the state never treated churches as equal partners; it was always a game of cat and mouse.

In the 1970s, the atheistic propaganda in Estonia became subtler: a psychological approach to influence believers was used more widely. Personal interviews of believers at schools and in work places were part of this approach. Already in the 1960s, sociological data was used for the goals of atheistic propaganda,[5] to show statistically the diminishing number of churches and church members. The power of the Council for Religious Affairs was

---

[1] Nathaniel Davis, *A Long Walk to Church: A Contemporary History of Russian Orthodoxy* (Boulder and Oxford: Westview Press, 1995), p. 46.

[2] Rein Taagepera, *Estonia. Return to Independence* (San Francisco and Oxford: Westview Press, 1993), pp. 97-98.

[3] Paul Johnson, *Modern Times. A History of the World from the 1920s to the 1990s* (London: Orion books, 1994), p. 676.

[4] Philip Walters, 'A survey of Soviet religious policy', in Sabrina P. Ramet, ed., *Religious Policy in the Soviet Union* (Cambridge and New York: Cambridge University Press, 1993), p. 23.

[5] Lembit Raid, *Vabamõtlejate ringidest massilise ateismini* [From the Circles of Freethinkers to Mass Atheism] (Tallinn: Eesti Raamat, 1978), p. 188.

strengthened during the 1970s, especially after 1975 when a revised version of the law regulating religious life in the Soviet Union was published.[6] In the Estonian context the Commissioner for the CRA had tried to play a decisive role even earlier. This sometimes led to tensions between the office of the Commissioner and the local Soviet executive committees.[7] In the 1970s and 1980s, the Commissioner obtained valuable information about church activities from steering commissions which operated within all regional and city executive committees in Estonia.[8] Because some of the commissions' reports were too superficial, the Commissioner sent detailed instructions to the chairmen of the steering commissions on how to prepare their reports.[9] The state carefully observed church life.

All this may give an impression that not much had changed in Estonian ECB church life when compared to the 1960s. However, a closer look at the situation shows light at the end of the tunnel for believers. In the 1970s an evangelical thrust touched almost every Estonian Baptist church. Local churches, acting semi-illegally, made attempts to revive work with children and youth. The number of typewritten publications and books increased. In 1985 the Senior Presbyter's report stated that from 1978-1985 the ECB churches in Estonia had baptized 570 young people between 18-25 years of age, including 220 'brothers' (i.e. males). The report added: 'Youth are active and the working capacity of our brotherhood has increased, though membership numbers have decreased.'[10] The 'evangelistic situation', limited as it was, was partly due to the fact that a new generation of Estonian youth, disillusioned by the hollowness of Marxist propaganda, became increasingly interested in the religious message. This, in turn, was influenced by the Estonian geographical and cultural situation: proximity to Scandinavia and links with European – and thus formally Christian – values. In this chapter the response of Estonian ECB churches to this situation will be analyzed.

PEACEFUL RESISTANCE

In spite of the fact that by the 1960s 'the church had lost its traditional role of

---

[6] Walters, 'A survey of Soviet religious policy', p. 24.

[7] See Riho Altnurme, *Eesti Evangeeliumi Luteriusu kirik ja Nõukogude riik 1944-1949* [The Estonian Evangelical Lutheran Church and the Soviet State 1944-1949] (Tartu: Tartu Ülikooli Kirjastus, 2001), pp. 57-61.

[8] Jaanus Plaat, *Usuliikumised, kirikud ja vabakogudused Lääne- ja Hiiumaal* [Religious Movements, Churches and Free Churches in West-Estonia and Hiiumaa Island] (Eesti Rahva Muuseum: Tartu, 2001), p. 215.

[9] See The Commissioner of CRA to the local executive committees (02.12.1971). Aruanded ja ülevaated kirikute tegevuse kohta ENSV-s (AÜ1971-1990) [Reports and surveys about the activities of churches in the ESSR 1971-1990], UNVA.

[10] *Logos*, no. 2 (1985), p. 29.

maintaining morale and balance in the everyday routine of Estonians',[11] it has been argued by some Estonian historians that the church, nonetheless, 'remained practically the only public institution in the Estonian SSR that was not entirely subjected to the control of the regime in power'.[12] The researchers usually refer to the Lutheran Church, as the majority church in Estonia, but this statement is applicable also to ECB communities and some other free churches, such as the Methodists. Certainly, it can be argued that the church leaders made many concessions to Soviet policies. It can also be argued that inside the Estonian churches there was no strong opposition movement to the Soviet oppressive influence, as was present in Russian Orthodoxy in the wider Soviet Union, for example.[13] Neither can any of the Estonian churches claim to have had a similar influence to that of the Roman Catholic Church in Lithuania.[14] The cases of organised protest emerging from Estonian churches were rather exceptional. Nevertheless, the churches offered 'an intellectual opposition in Soviet society'.[15] As mentioned, the younger generation especially came to see in religion a form of opposition against the superficiality of materialism.

Baptists and other evangelicals added some further aspects to this picture. Fundamentally, traditional Baptist theology and Soviet ideology were irreconcilable. Baptists believed and witnessed to their belief in a transformational process that takes place in the life of a believer through faith, and their conviction was that this inner change is not dependent on the material basis of society. They emphasised that a person needs God's grace, whereas atheistic literature optimistically believed in the human capacity for 'unlimited social and intellectual development'.[16] Baptists opposed the claims of the totalitarian regime to guide and control the minds of its citizens – or at least such opposition was a Baptist ideal. State authorities often perceived freedom of conscience, when put into practice by members of ECB communities, as a rival to the communist worldview. Even if church members did not express

---

[11] Mati Laur, Tõnis Lukas et al., *History of Estonia* (Tallinn: Avita, 2000), p. 304.

[12] Ibid.

[13] See William C. Fletcher, *The Russian Orthodox Church Underground, 1917-1970* (London and New York: Oxford University Press, 1971); Michael Bourdeaux, *Patriarch and Prophets* (London: Macmillan, 1970); Jane Ellis, *The Russian Orthodox Church: A Contemporary History* (London and Sydney: Croom Helm, 1986), pp. 287-447.

[14] See Jaanus Plaat, 'Eesti vabakoguduste vastupanu nõukogude religioonipoliitikale võrreldes luterliku ja õigeusu kirikuga (1944-1987)' [The Resistance of Estonian Free Churches to Soviet Religious Policies, in Comparison with Lutheran and Orthodox Churches (1944-1987)], in Toivo Pilli, ed., *Teekond teisenevas ajas: peatükke Eesti baptismi ajaloost* [A Journey in Changing Time: Chapters from the History of Estonian Free Churches] (Tartu: Kõrgem Usuteaduslik Seminar ja Sõnasepp OÜ, 2005), pp. 128-159.

[15] Laur, Lukas et al., *History of Estonia*, p. 304.

[16] A. Okulov et al., *Teaduslik ateism* [Scientific Atheism] (Tallinn: Eesti Raamat, 1975), p. 209.

their protest publicly against the atheistic-soviet system, their presence, their attempts to maintain their identity and their lived-out convictions, were themselves acts of peaceful resistance, a prophetic criticism of the godless approach to life.

However, in some cases the resistance took more active forms. Some Estonian Evangelical Christians-Baptists were involved in 'underground' activities which defied Soviet restrictive laws. During the Soviet years, the ECB leadership understated this fact, as they tried to distance themselves from the confusion created by the split of the 1960s among Soviet Baptists.[17] 'These questions do not concern us directly,' emphasised the Senior Presbyter in 1974.[18] It is possible that due to this 'policy of neutrality' the evangelical churches in Estonia enjoyed comparatively more freedoms than their counterparts in Russia, Ukraine or Byelorussia. Nevertheless, this does not mean that the 'Baptist underground movement' did not reach Estonia. According to the Commissioner of the CRA, in addition to some small and non-organized groupings (130 persons) of 'underground' evangelicals, there were 5 groups of Pentecostals (350 persons) and 3 groups of 'Baptists-splitters', i.e. Reform Baptists (230 persons) in Estonia in 1977.[19] These groups consisted mostly of Russian or German-speaking people. In 1978, the senior inspector of the CRA, L. Tsybulskii, in a secret report to the chairman of the CRA, Vladimir Kuroedov, pointed out critically that the work with illegal religious groups in Estonia was weak.[20] In soviet rhetoric this meant that 'underground' groups must be liquidated, merged into legally functioning churches or registered officially. Probably, part of the background to this report was that there were an increased number of Russian speaking believers, many of them from underground churches, who visited the Tallinn Oleviste Church evangelistic meetings in the 1970s. Later, in the 1980s, even a few Pentecostal groups – until then operating 'underground' – obtained registration in Estonia.[21]

Enno Tuulik, as well as ECB presbyters Osvald Talts and Udo Veevo,

---

[17] See the discussion in chapter 3 above.

[18] The UECBE Senior Presbyter's report (12.10.1974). EKB vanempresbüteri aruanded (VpAruanded) [The UECBE Senior Presbyter's reports], EEKBLA.

[19] Õiend Eesti NSV-s asuvate usukoondiste tegevusest ja üldisest olukorrast 1977. aastal [A report of the general situation and activities of the churches in the Estonian SSR in the year 1977] (29.03.1978). AÜ1971-1990, UNVA.

[20] *Dokladnaja zapiska o komandirovke v Estonskuju SSR v maje 1978 goda* [Report of an inspection trip to the Estonian SSR in May 1978]. AÜ1971-1990, UNVA. The state officials were concerned about illegal printing activities and emigration ideas that were spread among the 'underground' Christians.

[21] By 1985, two groups of Pentecostals obtained registration in Estonia, and 4-5 were in the process of applying for registration. The Commissioner mentioned this fact as a positive tendency in the work done with unregistered groups. Aruanne usuasjade olukorrast Eesti NSV-s seisuga 31. detsember 1984 [A report of the state of religious affairs in the Estonian SSR as of 31 December 1984]. AÜ1971-1990, UNVA.

were actively involved in helping 'underground brothers and sisters'. Tuulik and some other 'brothers' made preaching trips to Latvia, Ukraine and Byelorussia, which took them also to non-registered churches of Pentecostal leanings. In the small village church of Puka in Southern Estonia, Talts helped to organise a secret meeting of *Orgkomitet* (Reform Baptists) representatives with hundreds of participants from all over the Soviet Union.[22] In the mid-1970s, Tuulik transported a van-load of paper to an underground printing press in Latvia.[23] Bibles and New Testaments in Russian and in German, often smuggled into the Soviet Union via Finland, were forwarded through Estonia to Siberia and other parts of the Soviet Union. Arpad Arder, ECB presbyter in Rakvere and later in Suure-Jaani, developed a large literature ministry. He received thousands of Bibles and other Christian literature in German from the German Democratic Republic, where he had correspondence with approximately 700 persons. As the German Democratic Republic was a socialist country, the literature arrived by mail, and was not confiscated. Arder sent this literature to German speaking evangelicals in Siberia and Central-Asia, and developed many personal contacts with 'underground believers'.[24]

Tuulik has stated that many contacts with 'underground believers' took place secretly, 'our leadership ... did not know or did not want to know' about this.[25] Before he moved to Latvia in 1973, Gennadi Krjuchkov, one of the key leaders of the Russian Reform Baptists, lived secretly in Estonia for some time.[26] This was probably not known by the Estonian ECB leaders. However, issues of 'underground work' could not be entirely avoided even at Presbyters' Council meetings. In April 1977 the Senior Presbyter informed the Presbyters' Council that an underground printing press was found in Ivangorod, a twin town of Narva on the eastern border of Estonia, and a search took place in the home of one Narva ECB church member.[27] In 1982, the KGB organised searches in several church members' homes in Narva, and found literature which had been published by the Council of Churches of the ECB (CCECB),[28] an organisational body of the Reform Baptists.

In the 1970s, some Estonian ECB church members became involved in activities which lay outside restrictive Soviet religious laws. It is possible that Estonian Evangelical Christians-Baptists who helped in the 'underground

---

[22] Enno Tuulik, a private letter (20.02.2005). Toivo Pilli's personal archive.

[23] Ibid.

[24] Arpad Arder, *Kus on Arpadi kuningas?* [Where is Arpad's King?] (Tallinn: Logos, 1992), pp. 110, 118.

[25] Enno Tuulik, a private letter (20.02.2005). T. Pilli's personal archive.

[26] Pentti Heinilä, *Erittäin salainen* [Top Secret] (Helsinki: Uusi Tie, 1995), p. 477.

[27] Minutes of the Presbyters' Council meeting, no. 47 (05.04.1977). Presbüterite nõukogu protokollid 1969-1985 (PNProt1969-1985) [Minutes of the Presbyters' Council 1969-1985], EEKBLA.

[28] Minutes of the Presbyters' Council meeting, no. 85 (17.03.1982). PNProt1969-1985, EEKBLA.

work' were sympathetic to the commitment of the underground believers and to the sufferings which several non-registered churches in the Soviet Union endured. Supporting the 'dissident' movement was a way of expressing their own criticism of the atheistic system. This was a radical way of re-affirming some important facets of traditional Estonian Baptist identity: that the Bible and other Christian literature must be available for those interested in the Christian message; that the state should not interfere in matters of religious conscience; and that Christian education of children and youth was not an option but a responsibility of the church.

Nevertheless in most cases, the members of Estonian ECB churches chose less risky methods of resisting state pressure on their life and identity. For example, resistance to ideological pressure was expressed in attempts to offer informal theological training in spite of this being prohibited, or to organise semi-illegal discussion groups where the way of thinking clearly differed from the 'unifying' Soviet mind-patterns. Though the distance learning courses had been closed in 1960,[29] and the hopes, cherished in the 1960s, to open some sort of officially allowed theological courses in Estonia did not materialise,[30] the Senior Presbyter systematically gathered younger preachers for fellowship, seminars and lectures. The sessions were held in different towns. For example, a group of young men from Tartu and the surrounding area gathered from 1973-1978. According to the lecture notes taken by Uudu Rips, a former presbyter in Võru in Southern Estonia, the themes ranged from exegesis to principles of personal evangelism, from homiletics to doctrine, from Baptist teachings to ecumenical work. Robert Võsu also shared information about Christian life outside Estonia.[31] This was a small window to a wider and freer world.

From 1981-1987, Võsu organised so called 'consultation days' for presbyters and active church members. The topics included evangelism, Christian ethics, homiletics, the work and gifts of the Holy Spirit, pastoral counselling and psychology, religious movements in Estonia, local church issues, and difficult passages from the Bible.[32] The first consultation day was held on 13 October 1981.[33] In addition, from 1983-1987, 'Bible courses' took

---

[29] See chapter 2 above.

[30] This hope was expressed in the Senior Presbyter's reports of 1964 and 1965. In the 1967 report the Senior Presbyter said: 'The attitude toward the matter of [theological training] courses [in Estonia] is negative. We were told that we have far more educated presbyters than in the [other republics of the Soviet] Union and we are not supposed to need any more.' The UECBE Senior Presbyter's report of 1967. VpAruanded, EEKBLA.

[31] Lecture notes 1973-1978, notebook 1-3. Uudu Rips' personal archive.

[32] Konsultatsioonide lindistusi 1981-1987. Nimistu. [Recordings of the consultation days 1981-1987. A list of topics]. KUSA.

[33] Minutes of the Presbyters' Council meeting, no. 79 (09. 09.1981). PNProt1969-1985, EEKBLA.

place. The method was well proven: occasional regional meetings and seminars took place in bigger towns, such as in Tallinn, Tartu, Pärnu and Kuressaare, in support of the self-learning of younger preachers. The basic theological knowledge of students was uneven. In 1983, approximately 60-70 students, including 17-18 presbyters, were involved in this type of supervised self-study.[34] Today, this type of study would probably be called 'continuing theological education'. One may wonder whether these training efforts would have better prepared the participants to reflect on their mission in Estonia if the studies had been more 'problem-orientated' and less 'subject-orientated'. However, these 'courses' and 'consultations' played an important role in consolidating what had been fundamental Baptist teaching, supporting independent thinking, and maintaining theological unity, especially in the 1970s and 1980s when traditional Estonian Baptist approaches met challenges from the charismatic movement.

Theological education continued in various forms. Some Estonians studied through Moscow Distance Bible Courses. At the request of Russians and Latvians several kinds of theological study materials were translated from Estonian into Russian.[35] Some students from Estonia, as exceptional cases, could study abroad. In 1979, Joosep Tammo, Peeter Roosimaa, and Ermo Jürma were sent to study in Buckow Baptist Seminary, in the German Democratic Republic. The Senior Presbyter Robert Võsu, after taking part in the inauguration of the school year in Buckow Seminary, stated: 'Our boys are in good hands.'[36] It seems that Võsu was congratulating himself for managing, after years of effort, to send Estonian students for theological studies abroad. His method of knocking persistently on the door of the unfriendly Soviet bureaucracy had finally worked.

Võsu's example in organising informal study groups was later followed by other, younger leaders. At the end of the 1970s and in the 1980s, the younger generation began to gather in friendship-circles. These 'circles' gathered in Pärnu, Tartu and Tallinn.[37] The atmosphere of these gatherings bears clearer signs of protest against materialist ideology, though direct political statements were seldom made. The group members discussed theological and philosophical issues as well as the relationship between Christian faith and the wider culture. Pierre Teilhard de Chardin's use of the language of 'evolution' in theological thinking inspired the participants, and Hans Küng's *Does God*

---

[34] Minutes of the Presbyters' Council meeting, no. 100 (10.10.1983). PNProt1969-1985, EEKBLA.

[35] The UECBE Senior Presbyter's report of 1965.VpAruanded, EEKBLA.

[36] Postcard from Robert and Leida V[õsu] to R. Kiviloo and A. Kajaste (17.09.1979). EEKBLA.

[37] In Tallinn one of these groups was called 'Club Areopagus' (Est. 'Areopaagi klubi'), in Pärnu it was named 'Haraka Institute' (Est. 'Haraka instituut'), after Haraka Street, where the group usually met.

Exist? helped them to find arguments for Christian faith in God in a godless
society. In 1985, during a retreat of the Pärnu 'circle', several papers focused
on the criticism of atheism, which was described as being 'a worldview of a
person encapsulated into oneself'.[38] Typewritten semi-illegal and illegal
literature circulated in these fellowships. In a society that often depicted
believers as uneducated and unintelligent, these educational efforts had the
character of non-violent protest against this distorted picture.[39]

   All these efforts were peacefully challenging the restrictive atheistic
system. Usually avoiding public criticism of the socialist-atheistic system, the
Estonian ECB churches persistently, even stubbornly, worked at going around
the restrictive laws and attempted to maintain their identity, of which pastoral
training was a part. Christian education had a hidden message: though ECB life
was in many different ways restricted outwardly, compared to what had been
the situation in the pre-communist period, evangelical thinking and ideas were
not as easily limited by the communist mindset.

MAINTAINING IDENTITY THROUGH LITERATURE AND MUSIC

There is no documentary evidence that the Soviet government used a more
relaxed approach to religion in Estonia based on a view that Estonia could be
an experimental zone for such an approach – as one former ECB presbyter
suggested.[40] However, in reality, the Commissioner of the CRA turned a blind
eye to some aspects of the UECBE activity in the country. One of the areas of
traditional Baptist work that was revived during the period discussed in this
chapter was literature: translated books and articles as well as original Estonian
works. These books and articles were typed on mechanical typewriters. This
method of production usually allowed one to produce 6-8 copies at a time.
Additional church music was also developed during these years.

   On a wider front, so called *samizdat* or self-published literature was
not limited to religious themes only. In the Soviet Union, during Khrushchev's
years of relaxed censorship, some heterodox material dealing with issues
relating to general cultural values began to appear in the press and in book
form. When the Soviet approach to literature again became strict, attempts to
achieve freedom in thinking and literary expression continued to live on in the
widespread efforts of *samizdat* literature. In 1966-1967 *samizdat*-type
underground publications were published more freely than ever before.[41] This

---

[38] Ermo Jürma, notes at Metsaküla retreat (07.02.1985). T. Pilli's personal archive.

[39] For more on Baptist educational efforts see also Toivo Pilli, 'Finding a Balance
between Church and Academia: Baptist Theological Education in Estonia', *Religion in
Eastern Europe*, vol. XXVI, no. 3 (August 2006), pp. 17-43.

[40] This has been suggested by Jüri Puusaag, oral information (08.05.2003).

[41] Paul Johnson, *Modern Times. A History of the World from the 1920s to the 1990s*, p.
679.

had its influence also on religious *samizdat* literature in Estonia. It is fair to estimate that the highest peak of typewritten publications in Estonian Evangelical Christian-Baptist circles was reached in the 1970s and early 1980s. However, as early as the 1950s and 1960s several sermon collections,[42] theological treatises,[43] and conference materials[44] were reproduced and copies multiplied by *samizdat* methods.

In addition to sermon collections, translated devotional literature and some theological volumes, books by the American evangelist, Billy Graham, were systematically translated into Estonian and reproduced on mechanical typewriters. Also, from Finland, several books published by the Finnish Free Church publishing house Päivä OY found their way to Estonia, including books by Tapio Nousiainen and Niilo Yli-Vainio,[45] the latter being influential within charismatic circles in the 1970s. Topics and themes in this 'semi-illegal' literature show the general trends of interest within the UECBE during these years: the work of the Holy Spirit, evangelism and sanctification. For those interested in popular apologetics, Paul E. Little's *Miks ma usun* (Know Why You Believe) was a helpful tool. Many translated books like this one came from an Anglo-American background. There is no reliable research on how many titles or how many copies were 'published' in the Estonian language by Baptist *samizdat* efforts, but it is possible to talk about hundreds of titles and probably tens of thousands of copies in total. This was not only an attempt to provide reading material for church members; it was an attempt to maintain one's identity and freedom to be informed about Christian thought.

Besides original works and translated volumes, Estonian ECB leaders made systematic attempts to issue typewritten collections of articles or 'publications' that resembled Christian journals. One of these, entitled *Lectio*, was 'published' in the second half of the 1970s by Joosep Tammo, who had become an outstanding young ECB preacher and youth leader in the 1970s. The

---

[42] For example, Robert Võsu, *Armastusest* [About Love], typewritten manuscript (1965), KUSA; [O. Tärk], *Märkmeid O. Tärgi jutlustest 1965. a.* [Notes from the Sermons of O. Tärk, 1965], typewritten sermon collection (1966?), KUSA. Many sermons were written down by a few dedicated church members while the presbyter was preaching. These sermon notes were typewritten later.
[43] Many volumes of theological literature were 'published' in 1956-1960 in relation to the semi-illegal theological training courses. In the 1960s, Arpad Arder compiled a 2000 A4 typewritten page concordance of the Bible in five volumes.
[44] For example, a collection of materials related to the celebration of the Estonian Evangelical Christian Free Church movement's 50th anniversary, *Eesti Evangeeliumi Kristlaste 50. a. juubel 1955. a.* (1955), as well as two volumes with materials from the presbyters conferences of 1968 and 1969.
[45] Riho Saard, 'Uskonnollisen ja teologisen kirjallisuuden lähettäminen Suomesta Neuvosto-Viroon 1950-1980-luvuilla' [Sending Religious and Theological literature from Finland to Soviet Estonia in the 1950s-1980s], *Teologinen Aikakauskirja*, no. 6 (2003), p. 544.

collection explained that its goal was to 'expand the readers' horizons in every aspect of Christian teaching and life'.[46] Though the volumes covered many traditional evangelical themes such as evangelism, Christian leadership, pneumatology and biblical topics, *Lectio*'s innovation was its courage to engage the critical minds of readers, to initiate discussion and to touch topics which were not traditional for Estonian Baptists: the relationship of Christianity to the wider culture, dialogue between Christianity and other religions, and the role of youth in churches. The reader found articles written by a remarkably wide variety of authors, ranging from American charismatic-conservative preachers and Soviet Baptists to Swiss and German Reformed theologians: Oral Roberts and Jürgen Moltmann, Alexei Bychkov and Derek Prince, Osvald Tärk and Emil Brunner.

Also, a typewritten publication entitled *Logos* appeared – usually six times a year, with 30-40 A4 format pages in each issue – from 1981 until 1988. Most of the articles for *Logos* were written by Estonian ECB presbyters, both from the older generation (Osvald Tärk, Robert Võsu, Kalju Raid, Arpad Arder), and the younger generation (Joosep Tammo, Peeter Roosimaa, Ants Rebane, Jüri Puusaag, Ingmar Kurg). The topics ranged from justification, sanctification and evangelism to questions of church life and to homiletical-exegetical materials that proved helpful aids for preachers. Much space was given to personalia and aspects of Estonian ECB history. Three of the longest treatises were devoted to questions of sanctification,[47] to an exegetical analysis of the book of Revelation,[48] and to the principles of Evangelical Christians-Baptists[49].

Before the Soviet times, Estonian Baptists had already accepted an emphasis on pastoral training and literature which they often linked with the name of the German Baptist pioneer Johann G. Oncken.[50] This was inseparable from their way of being a Baptist community. This traditional emphasis was continually 'breaking through' and being expressed in different modes during Soviet times. However, in the Estonian context, congregational singing and church music must also be seen as contributing alongside literature to the maintenance of identity.

For Estonian Baptists, and for the free churches in general, singing and

---

[46] *Lectio* VII (1978), p. 117.

[47] Ants Rebane, 'Piibellik pühitsus' [Biblical Sanctification], *Logos*, no. 1(1981) – no. 5 (1982).

[48] Peeter Roosimaa, 'Apokalüpsis – Ilmutusraamatu eksegeetilisi probleeme' [Apocalypsis – Exegetical Problems of the Book of Revelation], *Logos*, no. 2 (1982) - no. 5 (1983).

[49] Osvald Tärk, 'Meie vendluse põhimõtted' [Principles of our Brotherhood], *Logos*, no. 1 (1981) – no. 2 (1983).

[50] See Martin Schmidt, 'Eesti baptisti jutlustajate usuteadusliku hariduse ajaloost' [About the History of Estonian Baptist Preachers' Theological Education], in R. Kaups, ed., *50 aastat apostlite radadel* [50 Years in the Ways of the Apostles] (Keila: E.B.K. Liidu kirjastus, 1934), p. 174.

music played an important part in their historic understanding of worship and spiritual life. Even the Revivalist Free Church tradition, though cautious about accepting musical instruments, could not imagine its worship without congregational singing.[51] By Soviet times, the earlier hymnals, such as *Laulud Talle kiituseks* (Songs for the Glory of the Lamb), published in gothic print, or *Võidulaulud* (Songs of Victory), had become outdated both with regard to language and the selection of hymns/songs. This was one reason why Estonian ECB leaders persistently applied to Soviet authorities for permission to publish a new hymnal.

A committee for a new hymnal held its first meeting 1 May 1947 in Tallinn.[52] In the same year the Senior Presbyter asked for permission to publish the hymnal. In 1956 this application was repeated. The Senior Presbyter Johannes Lipstok wrote to the Commissioner: 'According to your wish the manuscript has been shortened and the number of songs has been reduced to 519.'[53] Permission was not granted. In the 1960s, the need for a new songbook was expressed by several local churches. For example, Rakvere ECB church sent a 19-point list of their suggestions to the ECB office in Tallinn, to be forwarded to Moscow to the Presidium of the AUCECB. The first items, besides a plea to reduce the taxes and unjustly high rates for electricity for churches, referred to church music and the need for literature. The hope was that an application could be made 'immediately' for permission to print the Bible in Estonian, to publish Christian songs with notes, and a hymnal.[54] In 1965 and 1966, the leadership of the UECBE hoped that the hymnal project would move forward. The Commissioner had suggested that the hymnal consist of only 300 songs.[55] Expectations rose that permission for printing would be granted in the first half of 1966. 'We live, we see; but we believe and hope,' reported the Senior Presbyter.[56] Later in 1966, with no movement evident, the Senior Presbyter, 'on behalf of all ECB believers in the Estonian SSR', insisted that the Commissioner solve this problem.[57] All seemed in vain. In 1968, there

---

[51] A. Seppur, *Jees. Krist. Evg. Priikoguduse tekkimine ja levinemine Läänemaa ärkamises* [The Beginning and Development of Jesus Christ's Evangelical Free Church in the Revival in Western Estonia] (Toronto, 1970), pp. 15, 20-21.

[52] Ene Rahkema, 'Lauluvaliku kujunemine Eesti vabakiriklikes kogudustes' [Shaping the Choice of Songs in Estonian Free Churches], *Usuteaduslik Ajakiri*, no. 2 (2003), p. 60.

[53] Johannes Lipstok to the Commissioner of CARC (02.03.1956). Vanempresbüteri ja Usuasjade voliniku kirjavahetus 1945-1966 (VpUvk1945-1966) [Correspondence of the Senior Presbyter and the Commissioner of CARC 1945-1966], KUSA.

[54] Rakvere ECB church to the Senior Presbyter A. Sildos (05.01.1965). Küsimused 1964. a. aruande juurde [Questions attached to the 1964 report], EEKBLA.

[55] The UECBE Senior Presbyter's report of 1964. VpAruanded, EEKBLA.

[56] The UECBE Senior Presbyter's report of 1965. VpAruanded, EEKBLA.

[57] Aleksander Sildos and Robert Võsu to the Commissioner of CRA, M. Teder (18.10.1966). EEKBL kirjavahetus usuasjade volinikuga 1966-1990 [The

were 'no signs that the issue of a hymnal would move ahead'.[58]

At last, in 1975, a miracle happened. Official permission was given to publish *Evangeelsed Laulud* (Evangelical Hymns), a songbook with 400 songs but without accompanying music being included in the book. Also the Estonian Methodist Church was interested in using the new hymnal and participated in negotiations with the Commissioner.[59] It was soon realized that the printing process was rather slow. Finally in 1976 the songbooks came from the printer and were distributed to all ECB churches in Estonia.[60] By 1979, musical accompaniment for all the songs was prepared, written by hand.[61] These were multiplied by simple methods, such as making photos of the notes. The hymnal had its limits: some words had been changed because of the censor, children's and youth songs were not allowed, and there were fewer songs than originally planned. Furthermore, because of the small number of printed copies, in some churches only half of the church members were able to buy the hymnal.[62] In spite of this, the role of the hymnal as a contributor to identity should not be underestimated. Congregational singing deepened the worship experience of church members, and songs in contemporary Estonian brought this experience into the present day world. In addition, the hymnal was a visible sign of the vitality of the UECBE: after 28 years of applications the book had at last been printed. In 1973, the Senior Presbyter stated that because of the lack of hymnals the role of congregational singing was declining in Estonian ECB Churches.[63] Now, with the new hymnal, this was no longer an acute problem.

Congregational singing was supported by choir activities. In approximately fifty percent of the ECB churches in Estonia there was at least one choir. The total number of choir members in the Union was approximately one thousand, and in all the churches together there were approximately four hundred musicians,[64] who played various musical instruments: mandolins, violins and brass instruments. For a union with a total membership of 7,963 in 1973,[65] these statistical estimations show a living tradition of choral music.

---

correspondence of the UECBE with the Commissioner of the CRA 1966-1990], EEKBLA.

[58] The UECBE Senior Presbyter's report of 1967. VpAruanded, EEKBLA.

[59] Minutes of the Presbyters' Council meeting, no. 35 (31.01.1975). PNProt1969-1985, EEKBLA.

[60] Minutes of the Presbyters' Council meeting, no. 44 (12.09.1976). PNProt1969-1985, EEKBLA.

[61] Minutes of the Presbyters' Council meeting, no. 56 (16.02.1979). PNProt1969-1985, EEKBLA.

[62] Kaaskirjad koguduste 1976. a. aruandele [Explanatory letters attached to churches' 1976 reports], EEKBLA.

[63] The UECBE Senior Presbyter's report of 1970-1972. VpAruanded, EEKBLA.

[64] The UECBE Senior Presbyter's report of 1970-1972. VpAruanded, EEKBLA.

[65] The UECBE statistical report 1973. The UECBE statistical reports 1964-1990, EEKBLA.

During these years much Christian activity was channelled into music work: singing in choirs or instrumental ensembles. A veteran choir conductor, Viljo Liik, stated that even during the severest atheistic pressure, choirs continued to operate and helped to preserve churches and their work.[66] Estonian ECB believers were 'singing people': they not only preached but also sang their theology and convictions. Many Baptist parents suggested that their children should study music, hoping that these skills would later benefit the church. It was also more difficult for the state authorities to control the effect and impact of music and singing.[67] By the 1970s it had become clear that the attempts of the authorities in the beginning of the 1960s to forbid solo songs and instrumental music in churches, except organ and piano music, had failed. In many cases, the believers' participation in worship was channelled into music ministry. Sometimes music was too dominant. Aita Dahl commented that in these times some younger people who did not sing felt useless and excluded,[68] as choirs functioned often as fellowship groups where friendships developed.

Gradually, young people became more and more involved in music. For example, toward the end of 1967 a youth choir was secretly formed in Oleviste Church in Tallinn. The choir, a kind of Christian discipleship group, met under the fatherly supervision of pastors Oskar Olvik and Osvald Tärk.[69] Music work in the Oleviste Church was rich and multifaceted. In 1974 an ensemble called Ihtys[70] came together, being active until 1979. Another ensemble called Rebecca (formed in the 1970s, later called Sanctus) and a youth choir, Rändur (Pilgrim, from 1985), were also significant.[71] Young people's music groups and choirs became an integral part of ECB life in the 1970s and the 1980s. In addition, new music styles – gospel and Christian 'rock' – arrived on the scene. Effataa,[72] a choir and ensemble, became the symbol of a new music style, which was used for the goal of evangelism.

On 23 February 1980 musicians from 25 ECB churches formed a 'music council',[73] a work-group to coordinate music work in ECB churches and to

---

[66] Rahkema, 'Lauluvaliku kujunemine Eesti vabakiriklikes kogudustes', p. 62.

[67] Toivo Pilli, 'Union of Evangelical Christians-Baptists of Estonia 1945-1989: Survival Techniques, Outreach Efforts, Search for Identity,' *Baptist History and Heritage*, vol. XXXVI, nos. 1 and 2 (Winter/Spring 2001), p. 123.

[68] Aita Dahl, interview notes (15.01.2001). Toivo Pilli's personal archive.

[69] Peeter Roosimaa, oral information (17.07.2002). Peeter Roosimaa was a member of the choir and moderator for its first years of existence.

[70] The Greek 'Ichthus' (fish) – a symbol used by the early church, the initial letters spelling out 'Jesus Christ, Son of God, Saviour'.

[71] Veronika Arder, 'Muusikatöö' [Music Ministry], in *Oleviste 50. Oleviste koguduse juubelikogumik* [Oleviste 50. The Anniversary Collection of Oleviste Church] (Tallinn: Oleviste kogudus, 2000), pp. 17-18.

[72] The Greek 'Ephphatha' (be opened), in Mark 7:34-35.

[73] Minutes of the Presbyters' Council meeting, no. 65 (26.02.1980), no. 68 (13.05.1980), no. 69 (10.06.1980). PNProt1969-1985, EEKBLA

offer advice and training to choir conductors and musicians. There was also a smaller work-group at the ECB office which focused on recording and reproducing the tapes, though this had to take place in secret. In 1980, about 1,000 copies of the first tape with Christmas music was prepared. Recordings took place in the Oleviste Church, and the technical team included Raigo Tammo, Mati Särglepp and Allar Kaasik. Later Tammo recalled: 'The tape was practically hand-made. ... At the same time there was a fear that [the KGB] would come to search. Believers were not permitted to have professional recording and reproduction equipment.'[74] The next year a tape, *Kuldkeeled* (Golden Strings), including Kaljo Raid's music,[75] was prepared with the help of 'the ECB recording choir Gloria'. In 1984, the Nõmme ECB church youth choir and ensemble recorded a tape, *Laula rõõmsalt sa* (Sing Joyfully), with classic spirituals and some songs written by a young Christian composer, Piret Pormeister. The music in the Estonian ECB churches derived its energy from the grass-roots level. It was based on enthusiasm and strengthened by the fact that music helped to combine some important aspects of Christian spirituality: it brought together meditative and emotional dimensions with the language of evangelism. Perhaps music naturally balanced the Baptist preaching tradition which was often rather intellectually orientated. Certainly the role of literature and music shows the ways in which the churches negotiated their way through state restrictions and forged an identity which would take them into the future.

EVANGELISTIC EFFORTS

In 1968, Osvald Tärk had reminded his fellow presbyters that 'the gospel is the power of God even if we have difficulties in our ministry of proclamation'. 'Do not stop doing your work even in the hardest situations,' he encouraged.[76] Tärk's advice was appropriate and timely. Only a few years later new signs of evangelistic opportunities emerged, in Tallinn and in other parts of Estonia. Younger ECB leaders and church members had the courage to experiment with new methods of reaching out with the Christian message: evangelistic youth evenings in churches, personal contacts and discussion groups in homes, and witnessing to people outside church buildings. Robert Võsu, the Senior Presbyter, emphasised the importance of personal evangelism in his book

---

[74] Raigo Tammo, oral information (13.05.2002).

[75] Kaljo Raid was pastor of The Estonian Baptist Church in Toronto. He was also a professional musician and composer.

[76] Osvald Tärk, 'Evangeelium on Jumala vägi' [Gospel is the Power of God], a speech at the presbyters conference in Tallinn (17.02.1968). VpAruanded, EEKBLA; *Eesti EKB koguduste presbüterite konverents Tallinnas, 15.-18. veebruaril 1968. a.* [The Estonian ECB Presbyters' Conference in Tallinn, 15-18 February 1968], typewritten manuscript [1968], pp. 162-163. Ülo Meriloo's personal library.

Isiklik evangelism (Personal Evangelism),[77] which circulated as a typewritten manuscript among church members. He also developed the theme of evangelism in many of his speeches. There was increasing criticism of 'old-style revival weeks' as these had become comparatively ineffective as evangelistic methods. In 1976, commenting on the evangelistic work in the churches, the Senior Presbyter said that ECB churches in Estonia had 'not adjusted themselves to a new situation'.[78] At a Presbyters' Council meeting in 1980 Võsu was more outspoken: 'Our revival weeks are the work-method of our fathers. Shouldn't we change our methods?'[79] However, it was not just a matter of methods. The 1970s saw both renewed motivation for evangelism in churches and a renewed interest in religion among the younger strata in the society.[80]

The centre for this renewed thrust for evangelism became Tallinn Oleviste Church. The Oleviste Church youth ensemble and ministry team, Effataa, which was formed at the beginning of the 1970s and was influenced in its spirituality and style by charismatic tendencies, opened an entirely new era in organising evangelistic services and prayer ministry. Effataa was more than a music group. Haljand Uuemõis, a member of the Oleviste Church board of elders, called the evangelistic movement of the 1970s the 'Effataa revival'.[81] Effataa became a keyword for an evangelistic and charismatic ministry. By the late 1970s, the 'Effataa evenings' included sermons, testimonies, invitation time, and prayers for the sick. To a certain extent the 'evenings' could be described as being along the same lines as the campaigns of American evangelists such as Oral Roberts or Kathryn Kuhlmann. Certain phenomena, such as people falling on the floor during prayers,[82] caused confusion among the ECB leadership, created both supporters and opposition in churches, and provoked criticism from state authorities.

The ECB Presbyters' Council, without condemning the phenomena, called for care: the most important criterion should be 'fruit' - the impact of prayer and spiritual experience on the person's character and behaviour. Besides, the Bible warned against being hasty with the laying on of hands. However, some people, the ECB leadership accepted, had 'received spiritual revival, blessing and joy, and help for their health'.[83] According to one of the leaders of the Effataa movement, Rein Uuemõis, the phenomena manifested God's power and

[77] Robert Võsu, *Isiklik evangelism* (Personal Evangelism) (Tallinn, 1971). EEKBLA.
[78] The UECBE Senior Presbyter's report of 1975. VpAruanded, EEKBLA.
[79] Minutes of the Presbyters' Council meeting, no. 67 (18.04.1980). PNProt1969-1985, EEKBLA.
[80] See also chapter 8.
[81] Haljand Uuemõis, 'Effataa-ärkamine' [Effataa Revival], in *Oleviste 50*, pp. 22.
[82] *Jumala teenistuses: Rein Uuemõis* [In the Service of God: Rein Uuemõis] (Tallinn: Oleviste kogudus, 2001), p. 37.
[83] Minutes of the Presbyters' Council meeting, no. 51 (07.03.1978), no. 52 (18.04.1978). PNProt1969-1985, EEKBLA.

attracted people to church.[84] For the UECBE the 'Effataa revival' was a mixed blessing. It created heated discussions, even controversies. Issues like the baptism of the Holy Spirit, praying for the sick and laying on of hands, falling down in the power of the Spirit, and speaking in tongues – all these themes were debated both in churches and at the meetings of the Presbyters' Council.[85] Nevertheless, the movement had an impact on Oleviste membership statistics. The decline in membership slowed down from 1970, stabilised and turned into a modest growth in the 1980s.[86] Against the background of the continuing decline in the union membership, which dropped from 8,206 members in 1970 to 6,346 members in 1985,[87] there is no doubt that the evangelistic activity in Oleviste had measurable results. Moreover, Albert Wardin has said that the Oleviste Church 'became a dynamic evangelical centre known throughout the Soviet Union'.[88] The charismatic elements in the 'Effataa revival' harmonized with Estonian Pentecostal and Revivalist Free Church Spirit-orientated and enthusiastic identity, which had been suppressed during the Soviet years. This may be one reason why the Effataa revival was well received in Saaremaa and Hiiumaa islands, the traditional Revivalist Free Church areas. For Baptists the revival brought new elements into their congregational life.

The input of the Finnish Pentecostals and the charismatically orientated Finnish Free Church in this 'Effataa revival' is clearly evident. However, the leading figures who preached and prayed for people were Estonians: Rein Uuemõis, Udo Veevo, Ülo Niinemägi and others.[89] The Effataa 'meetings' took place both in Estonian and in Russian, as many people travelled from different places in the Soviet Union to participate in these events. Sometimes 300 people or more came from other Soviet Republics to attend these services. Many came from 'underground churches', arriving in Tallinn by train from as far away as Dushanbe and Vladivostok.[90]

[84] *Jumala teenistuses: Rein Uuemõis*, p. 37.

[85] See Minutes of the Presbyters' Council meeting, no. 30 (20.05.1974), no. 31 (17.09.1974), no. 51 (07.03.1978), no. 52 (18.04.1978), no. 53 (30.05.1978), no. 54 (11.09.1978). PNProt1969-1985, EEKBLA.

[86] In 1965 there were 1613 members, in 1970 there were 1385 members, in 1975 there were 1333, in 1980 there were 1309, in 1985 there were 1310 and in 1990 there were 1383 members. The UECBE statistical reports 1965, 1970, 1975, 1980, 1985, 1990. Evangeeliumi Kristlaste-Baptistide koguduste statistilised aruanded 1964-1990 [The UECBE statistical reports 1964-1990], EEKBLA.

[87] The UECBE statistical reports 1970, 1985. Evangeeliumi Kristlaste-Baptistide koguduste statistilised aruanded 1964-1990, EEKBLA.

[88] Albert Wardin, ed., *Baptists Around the World* (Nashville, Tennessee: Broadman and Holman, 1995), p. 240.

[89] Today, Rein Uuemõis and Ülo Niinemägi are pastors in the Oleviste Church, the late Udo Veevo was a long- time pastor in Palade on Hiiumaa Island.

[90] Minutes of the Presbyters' Council meeting, no. 54 (11.09.1978). PNProt1969-1985, EEKBLA; Enno Tuulik, a private letter (20.02.2005). Toivo Pilli's personal archive.

The worship style at these evangelistic and prayer evenings was generally non-traditional. The music was rhythmical and joyful, and, as Haljand Uuemõis pointed out, 'non-Christian' instruments (as they were perceived at the time) were used, instruments 'that are accepted by all Christians today'.[91] Uuemõis was referring to drums and electric musical instruments. This new music style had become widespread in other churches too. In the Estonian Methodist Church, a youth 'band' called Selah had already been formed in 1968. According to Heigo Ritsbek, this was the first gospel-rock group in the whole Soviet Union.[92] In 1978 and 1979, a 'gospel-band' from the USA called Living Sound gave concerts in the Tallinn Oleviste Church and Merepuiestee Methodist Church.[93] All this encouraged young people to organise music bands with electronic instruments in several ECB churches, though some believers thought that this was a sign of the 'world invading the church' and was something that would undermine their traditional identity.

The flow of visitors from other Soviet Republics to the Tallinn Oleviste Church, the extraordinary worship elements, young people attending the evangelistic evenings, and similar evangelistic patterns spreading to other ECB churches, did not go unnoticed. The State authorities felt uneasy about these tendencies. Under the heavy pressure of government authorities, the 'Effataa evenings' in the Russian language were ended in 1981. 'This decision was hard and painful, and meant – as it soon was realized – a blow to the whole revival process…'.[94] However, the evangelistic evenings in Estonian continued, and constantly troubled the Commissioner of CRA. In January 1987 the Commissioner stated, concerning youth activities, that the Oleviste Church was balancing on 'a critical line'. The Commissioner was worried that young people were 'under Pentecostal influence'.[95]

It is important to note that the Effataa-revival, controversial and inspiring as it was, was not the only evidence of the UECBE's efforts to develop its own evangelistic language in the changing socio-political context. Witnessing and 'winning souls', to use the kind of expression that was derived from C.H. Spurgeon,[96] was a uniting force among the historically different Estonian free churches, even before the Second World War. It could only be expected that under Soviet rule this uniting feature of identity was searching for new ways to be expressed.

---

[91] Uuemõis, 'Effataa-ärkamine', p. 24.

[92] Heigo Ritsbek, 'The Mission of Methodism in Estonia', project thesis (Boston: Boston University, 1996), p. 100.

[93] 'Living Soundist' üldse… [About 'Living Sound'…], *Jäljed II* (1979), pp. 7-13.

[94] Uuemõis, 'Effataa-ärkamine', p. 24.

[95] Statistiline ülevaade usuasjade olukorrast Eesti NSV-s 1986. aastal [A statistical survey of the religious situation in the Estonian SSR in 1986]. AÜ1971-1990, UNVA.

[96] See also Toivo Pilli, 'Eesti baptistid ja nende teoloogilise mõtte kajastumine ajakirjas *Teekäija* kuni 1940' [Estonian Baptists and Their Theology as reflected in *Teekäija* until 1940], ThM thesis (Tartu: Tartu University, 1996), pp. 81-82.

Jüri Puusaag, presbyter of Tallinn 'Kalju' Church who had studied for a short period at McMaster Seminary in Canada in 1980, made serious efforts to encourage every church member to live an 'active spiritual lifestyle'.[97] 'Friendship evangelism' by church members in their everyday life setting and well-planned discipleship training in church were central to Puusaag's vision. He was critical of 'Christian propaganda campaigns',[98] such as traditional revival weeks, and also to an extent of Effataa-style evangelism. Some younger intellectually orientated church members made efforts to provide some readings for culturally alert youth. This was how the typewritten collections *Jäljed* (Footprints [1979-1980]) and *Lugemisvihik* (Reader [1987-1988]) were born. These volumes included, for example, short articles about Federico Fellini's *Orchestra Rehearsal*,[99] comments about Samuel Beckett's play *Waiting for Godot'*,[100] which had been staged by a promising producer Lembit Peterson, as well as a 'meditation' inspired by the pianist Rein Rannap's concert in the Estonia Concert Hall 14 April 1979.[101] *Lugemisvihik* included two choruses from T.S. Eliot's *The Rock,* translated into Estonian by the young philologist, Anne Lange.[102] The idea that music, film and literature that were not directly 'evangelical' could be conversation partners in a process of searching for the relevance of the Christian message in a socialist setting was a fairly uncommon approach among Estonian ECB believers, who, as a rule, tended to create their own 'prayer house subculture' which often had few links to a wider context.

This period included another significant evangelistic episode: Billy Graham's visit to Tallinn. Though a 'one-off event', Billy Graham's visit in 1984 was 'a gift from God' for the Estonian Baptists' Centennial year, as Jüri Puusaag, Graham's interpreter in Estonia, has said.[103] Graham preached in the Lutheran Dome Cathedral, as well as in the Oleviste Church, and met with ECB presbyters in 'Kalju' Baptist Church. In Oleviste his sermon title was 'Hope for the Future'.[104] Though he was advised by the state authorities not to make an invitation or altar call in Oleviste, and he left quickly after he had preached in the church (which was packed with approximately 3,000 people), Graham's

---

[97] Jüri Puusaag, 'Sajandivanune Tallinna "Kalju" kogudus [One century old Tallinn 'Kalju' church], *Logos*, no. 3 (1984), p. 6.
[98] Jüri Puusaag, private letter (16.08.2002). Toivo Pilli's personal archive.
[99] 'Filmikommentaar Moskvast' [Film Comments from Moscow], *Jäljed II* (1979), pp. 3-6.
[100] 'Kui oodatu ei tule...' [When the One Who Has Been Waited for Does Not Come] *Jäljed II* (1979), pp. 27-40.
[101] 'Üles, üles, järve uppunud kellad!' [Up, Up, You Bells That Are Drowned in the Lake], *Jäljed I* (1979), pp. 4-6.
[102] Anne Lange, 'Ühest T.S. Elioti luuletajaisiksuse tahust' [About One Aspect of T.S. Eliot as a Poet], *Lugemisvihik* (1988), pp. 11-18.
[103] Jüri Puusaag, private letter (16.08.2002). Toivo Pilli's personal archive.
[104] Mihail Zhidkov and Jüri Puusaag, 'Billy Graham taas Nõukogude Liidus' [Billy Graham again in the Soviet Union], *Logos*, no. 4 (1984), p. 29.

visit brought Baptists into the Estonian mass media. Perhaps for the first time during Soviet years, Baptists were depicted in a positive light by the press.[105] For the everyday challenges faced by Estonian local churches, Graham's model for evangelism offered little help, though his influence as a Christian example and writer was significant. The Senior Presbyter Robert Võsu admired Billy Graham's evangelistic style, as well as his comparatively conservative and Christ-centred approach to doctrine and preaching. He said that 'the greatest event' of 1984 was Graham's visit to Tallinn.[106] Though less effective in terms of direct evangelistic results, Graham's visit provided spiritual encouragement and was symbolic for Baptist identity in Estonia.

CHRISTIAN YOUTH WORK REVIVED

In the 1970s, in spite of the state's increased efforts to influence the children and young people with atheistic ideology,[107] Estonian ECB churches were able to attract a number of young people. Those who in the midst of political 'stagnation' and 'suffocation' were still seeking ethical values and philosophical ideals often found inspiration from religion. The following quotation, though referring more generally to the Soviet situation, pointedly describes the situation in Estonia, too: 'From the mid-1970s the pace of proliferation of all kinds of unofficial religious activity had been accelerating, particularly in the major cities and amongst educated young people. Some of this activity was part of the continuing search for spiritual values amongst young people disenchanted with the dead official ideology; while an increasing proportion was related to the defence of religious rights and human rights in general, an area of activity which was given a specific boost by the Soviet Union's signing of the Helsinki Final Act in 1975.'[108] In 1979, the ECB Senior Presbyter stated that in the area of mission and evangelism 'the good soil' was no longer the countryside population, as it used to be earlier, but 'the educated youth living in cities'. The ECB churches should direct their attention, prayers and work toward this social group.[109] One gets the impression that this statement was 5-6 years late in being made.

At home, at school and in church 'serious battles took place about the length of hair and width of trouser legs' and 'electric guitar ensembles were

---

[105] Jüri Puusaag, private letter (16.08.2002). T. Pilli's personal archive.

[106] Minutes of the UECBE all-republic conference (23.02.1985). Juhatuse koosolekute protokollid (JKP) [Minutes of the Executive Board] (30.01.1981-12.12.1987), EEKBLA.

[107] Walter Sawatsky, *Soviet Evangelicals Since World War II* (Kitchener, Ontario: Herald Press, 1981), p. 297.

[108] Walters, 'A survey of Soviet religious policy', p. 27.

[109] The UECBE Senior Presbyter's report of 1978 (20.10.1979). VpAruanded, EEKBLA.

mushrooming'[110] – youth culture was gradually influencing ECB self-understanding. Young people who joined ECB churches often came from non-Christian families and had to face opposition at home. Their presence, however, challenged traditional understanding in local churches regarding how a believer should appear or speak. 'The language of Canaan', a 'Baptist dialect' loaded with biblical expressions, was unknown to most of the new converts. However, this new 'wave', when compared to 'the children of believers', was more effective in building relationships and witnessing to their friends. Duane Pederson's *Jeesusrahvas* (Jesus People) was translated into Estonian and reproduced by *samizdat* methods.[111] The Jesus-movement as a counter-culture, though comparatively short-lived in the USA, had its impact on Estonian Christian youth. From the mid-1970s, the Presbyters' Council repeatedly discussed issues related to youth work. Though still semi-illegal, the youth work had come 'above ground'. A younger generation was there and this fact could not be denied. The youth demanded attention.

The leadership of the UECBE attempted to coordinate the new developments in Christian youth work. In 1976, the Presbyters' Council stated that there was an urgent need to find youth leaders both for local churches and at the union level. The council recognised tension between different generations in churches, which some church leaders interpreted as 'a non-brotherly and disobedient mentality' that was spreading among the young people.[112] Such statements reflected traditional ECB thinking about authority as well as the repressive atmosphere of the communist years. By the end of 1976 the council worked out some simple advice: in the churches where young people are present they should be given the opportunity to have separate youth work for 'self-education and evangelism'; youth work should take place in consultation with the congregation in general and with the church board; youth leaders should be persons who are trusted both by the church board and by the youth; and every local church is free to organise its youth work independently, but in order to avoid misunderstandings it is recommended that the work should be coordinated.[113]

However, only in May 1979 was a coordinating body for youth work formed.[114] This 'youth council', expanded to include 18 members in 1980, was

[110] Lauri Vahtre, *Elu-olu viimasel vene ajal* [Living Conditions During the Last Russian Rule] (Tallinn: Kirjastuskeskus, 2002), p. 89.

[111] Duane Pederson, *Jeesus-rahvas* [Jesus People], typewritten Estonian translation (n. p., n. d.). TPL. The Estonian translation was probably made from the Swedish version of the book, which was published in 1972.

[112] Minutes of the Presbyters' Council meeting, no. 44 (12.09.1976). PNProt1969-1985, EEKBLA.

[113] Minutes of the Presbyters' Council meeting, no. 45 (07.12.1976). PNProt1969-1985, EEKBLA.

[114] Members of this initial 'youth council': Ingmar Kurg (Tallinn Oleviste), Jüri Puusaag (Tallinn 'Kalju'), Aamo Remmel (Tallinn Nõmme), Dimitri Lipping (Tapa), Avo

led by Ingmar Kurg. It was supposed to work directly under the supervision of the Senior Presbyter and with the close cooperation of local presbyters.[115] The members represented mostly the larger and stronger ECB churches. The 'youth council' set as its goal to prepare Bible study materials for youth and to support evangelism.[116] In order to maintain closer links with the youth, a 'spiritual advisor Jüri Puusaag' was involved in this work. Later, Joosep Tammo began supervising ECB youth work. Also the Senior Presbyter Võsu often attended the meetings of youth leaders. In 1979 youth work was organised in approximately 20, mostly larger, churches. By 1981 youth work had spread, despite internal and external difficulties, and there were approximately 600 young people actively involved in ECB youth work.[117]

The Presbyters' Council was concerned with avoiding a separatist movement among young people and encouraged youth work to be integrated into the general life of the congregations. An old theme of 'maintaining unity' emerged now from a new direction. In some cases the suggestions of older pastors did not reveal much awareness of the psychology of young people, their gifts and interests. For example, the advice of one member of the Presbyters' Council, that 'an important aspect of youth work should be visiting the sick and elderly, and helping to carry out funeral services',[118] was probably not the best guideline for youth work in general. However, more effective means of integrating youth into church life included attempts that were made to give them more responsibility in evangelism work and worship services, and offer them new Christian training opportunities.

Besides the strengthening of local youth groups, where much of the actual work among youth took place,[119] there were two other wider aspects, which not only showed the growing role of young people, but also served as a means for spiritual development, evangelism and for helping youth to become better informed of the Evangelical Christian-Baptist tradition and spirituality. These developments made a crucial contribution to identity.

First, semi-illegal youth summer camps began. These began to be organized regularly in the 1970s by more active churches. According to Milone Ugam, the first summer camp for the Tallinn Oleviste Church youth was

---

Rosenvald (Tartu 'Kolgata'), Jüri Nõlvak (Haapsalu), Eduard Kakko (Pärnu 'Immaanuel'). Minutes of the Presbyters' Council meeting, no. 57 (23.05.1979). PNProt1969-1985, EEKBLA.

[115] Minutes of the Presbyters' Council meeting, no. 57 (23.05.1979), no. 68 (13.05.1980), no. 69 (10.06.1980). PNProt1969-1985, EEKBLA.

[116] Minutes of the Presbyters' Council meeting, no. 74 (13.01.1981). PNProt1969-1985, EEKBLA.

[117] Minutes of the Presbyters' Council meeting, no. 57 (23.05.1979), no. 74 (13.01.1981). PNProt1969-1985, EEKBLA.

[118] Minutes of the Presbyters' Council meeting, no. 72 (21.10.1980). PNProt1969-1985, EEKBLA.

[119] Minutes of the Presbyters' Council meeting, no. 117 (09.12.1985). JKP, EEKBLA

organized in 1973. Some smaller-scale efforts to organise Christian children and youth camps or hiking trips had already taken place in the 1960s.[120] In the 1970s, a friendship-group, Konsiil (a shortened version of Est. 'konsiilium', Eng. 'council'), which consisted of seven young men, organised several summer camps in Vikipalu, which brought together up to 200 young people.[121] There was never official approval for organising these camps and this form of youth work always had a taste of civil disobedience. Jyrki Raitila stated: 'Usually they were either organized in secret or with an unofficial "silent agreement" with local officials.'[122] In some cases organizers were fined, interviewed by the KGB or harassed in other ways. In other cases, however, the authorities preferred not to take severe measures. Heigo Ritsbek has pointed out that this ambiguity in the approach of the authorities has confused several Soviet church life experts.[123] Nevertheless, the State officials were interested in getting information about this form of activity. Under special observation were symbols like the camp flag and neckerchiefs.[124] The authorities were nervous about the possibility that these symbols might refer to Estonian pre-war independence. For youth, these camps were mostly events for Bible study, prayer, singing around the fire, and building new friendships – all of which strengthened Christian commitment. Still today, the youth camp tradition remains a part of Estonian Evangelical Christian-Baptist life.

Second, Youth Bible Days were initiated. With a growing number of youth in churches, there emerged a need for an event bringing together all the active youth at least once a year. The so-called Youth Bible Days (Est. 'Noorte Piiblipäevad'), usually took place in Tallinn at the end of April or the beginning of May, and began to fulfil this role. 1 May was International Workers' Day and was a holiday, which allowed young people to travel to Tallinn and stay there two or three days. It is paradoxical that when the government made efforts to fill Christian holidays and traditions with atheistic meaning, the youth then used socialist holidays as a suitable time for organising Christian events. The first of these Bible Days took place in 1979.[125] In 1980, there were 411 participants at this youth meeting.[126] It became a major meeting place for ECB

---

[120] Milone Ugam, 'Laste- ja noortetöö' [Youth and Children's Work], in *Oleviste 50*, pp. 13-14.

[121] Einike Pilli and Daily Valk, 'Eesti EKB Liidu haridustöö evangeliseerimise ja eluaegse õppimise dünaamikas' [The UECBE Educational Work in the Dynamics of Evangelism and Lifelong Learning], in Toivo Pilli, ed., *Teekond teisenevas ajas*, p. 60.

[122] Jyrki Raitila, 'History of Evangelicalism and the Present Spiritual Situation in Estonia', MA thesis (Providence Theological Seminary, 1996), p. 45.

[123] Ritsbek, 'The Mission of Methodism in Estonia', p. 96.

[124] Ugam, 'Laste- ja noortetöö', p. 14.

[125] Minutes of the Presbyters' Council meeting, no. 57 (23.05.1979). PNProt1969-1985, EEKBLA.

[126] Minutes of the Presbyters' Council meeting, no. 68 (13.05.1980). PNProt1969-1985, EEKBLA.

youth. The Senior Presbyter often took part in the event, in this way giving more 'weight' to it and keeping contact with the active youth from local churches. In 1983, the Senior Presbyter gave a Bible Day paper dealing with the role of family and home in evangelistic work.[127] In 1984 the logo for Bible Days was 'Life in the Power of Faith'.[128] Usually the programme included both classical and contemporary music, Bible studies and presentations, prayer time and sometimes an evening with a poetry recital or a Bible quiz. Attempts to dramatise some Biblical truths – such as 'a trial over a weak brother' in 1986 – sometimes provoked severe criticism from the older generation, who were worried that God's holiness was being compromised. However, others emphasised the need for the contextualisation of the Christian message. If drama was understood as a parable, it could help young people to reflect upon their role as Christians, the advocates of 'unusual' methods argued.[129] The tradition of Youth Bible Days is still alive in Estonia. These gatherings, which usually took place in a Baptist church in Tallinn, offered fellowship, spiritual guidance and encouragement. They helped Baptist youth to relate to the context of their everyday life as Christians, and understand themselves as part of an older but continuing Estonian Baptist community which had shaped their identity as believers.

According to Liivia Kaustel, though in some churches attempts were made to organise children's work, often under the guise of a birthday party or some other 'legal' umbrella, the first ECB children's camp took place in a rainy summer-season of 1977 in Puka.[130] An actual revival of children's ministry began at the end of the 1980s. In the 1970s, in Estonia, as in other parts of the Soviet Union, much of the Christian education for children had to be done by Christian parents at home.[131] However, the state authorities 'looked through their fingers', as an Estonian saying goes, at some Baptist attempts to live out their convictions. In this situation, the growing youth work turned a new page for Estonian ECB understanding of church dynamics and evangelism. Youth were also challenged to think more deeply about relationships between church and the wider culture. Though not a painless process, the emergence of Christian youth work in the ECB churches showed that the rigid atheistic system could not totally shape the life of churches. There was an inner strength in historic Estonian Baptist identity, which was trying to resist, or by-pass, atheistic restrictions and suppressive rules. Certainly, the atheistic state had not lost its power, and often church leaders, first and foremost the Senior Presbyter,

---

[127] Minutes of the Presbyters' Council meeting, no. 96 (16.05.1983). PNProt1969-1985, EEKBLA.

[128] *Logos*, no. 3 (1984), pp. 30-31.

[129] Minutes of the Presbyters' Council meeting, no. 122 (12.05.1986). JKP, EEKBLA.

[130] Pilli and Valk, 'Eesti EKB Liidu haridustöö', p. 55.

[131] Samuel Nesdoly, *Among the Soviet Evangelicals* (Edinburgh: The Banner of Truth Trust, 1986), p. 43.

had 'to pay' for the attempts of churches to revive their ministries and find appropriate ways to express their identity. The Senior Presbyter's role became especially important in the 1970s. He 'softened' the first attacks of the authorities and tried to present information in a way that enabled churches to operate as 'smoothly' as possible in an officially atheistic state.[132]

BETWEEN STATE AND CHURCH: SENIOR PRESBYTER ROBERT VÕSU

From 1970-1985, Robert Võsu was the Senior Presbyter of the UECBE.[133] Võsu was born in Tartu, on 17 February 1914, into a Christian family. His father had converted to evangelical faith in Pljussa, on the Russian side of Lake Peipsi, where some Estonians had established a Revivalist Free Church.[134] His mother came from a family that had experienced spiritual revival through the work of Moravians (Herrnhuters) in Southern Estonia.[135] His own spiritual journey continued with a conversion experience at the age of 15, after which he began to preach regularly, often in Rõngu (Palupera) Baptist Church, where his father had served as a pastor from 1921.[136] He independently conducted worship services in the nearby town of Puka.[137] In the 1930s, he received theological training at the Estonian Baptist Theological Seminary, which operated from 1922 with British and American Baptist support.[138] Exceptionally, the seminary offered Võsu a scholarship to continue his studies in the philosophy department of Tartu University.[139] His Master's thesis, which he was never able to defend because of the instability that the Second World War brought about, analysed the role of Lutheran Halle pietism in Estonia in the eighteenth century.[140] These early influences – personal faith experience,

[132] Pilli, "Union of Evangelical Christians-Baptists of Estonia 1945-1989', p. 121.

[133] Riho Saard, 'Eesti kirikute juhtivvaimulikkond läbi aegade' [Estonian Church Leaders through the Centuries], part 2, *Akadeemia*, no. 3 (1998), p. 613.

[134] Herman Mäemets, 'Priikoguduste tekkimine Eestis ja nende evangeelse tegevuse algus' [Origins of the Revivalist Free Churches in Estonia and the Beginning of their Evangelistic Activity], *Logos*, no. 4 (1982), pp. 24-25.

[135] Arpad Arder, 'Robert Võsu – 70. aastane' [Robert Võsu – 70 years old], *Logos*, no. 1 (1984), p. 22.

[136] Richard Kaups, 'Kogudused' [Churches], in R. Kaups, ed., *50 aastat apostlite radadel*, pp. 78-79.

[137] Robert Võsu, 'Autobiograafia' [Autobiography], *Kalju Sõnum*, no. 1 (2004), p. 9.

[138] Bernard Green, *Tomorrow's Man: A Biography of James Henry Rushbrooke* (Didcot: The Baptist Historical Society, 1997), pp. 81, 96.

[139] Minutes, no. 64 (19.03.1935), no. 78 (09.06.1938), no. 79 (24.08.1938). Eesti Baptisti Usuteaduse Seminari protokolliraamat 1920-1940 [Baptist Theological Seminary minute book 1920-1940], KUSA.

[140] Robert Võsu, 'Halle pietism Eestimaal XVIII sajandil' [Halle Pietism in Estonia in the 18th Century], handwritten manuscript (1943). Original manuscript at the Estonian Literary Museum in Tartu, a copy available at KUSA.

pietistic ethics and intellectual interests – were all integrated into Võsu's personality.

Though active as a young preacher and youth leader before the war, Võsu's life mission was to be fulfilled in communist and atheistic Estonia. In 1945, he was ordained as the presbyter of Tallinn 'Kalju' Baptist Church. He became involved in the leadership of the ECB union as a close co-worker of the Senior Presbyter. Võsu's energy was phenomenal. Besides pastoral work in his own church, he wrote study materials for presbyters, coordinated preparation of a manuscript of an ECB hymnal, and often visited local churches all over Estonia. After he began to work as Senior Presbyter in 1970, he devoted much of his time to giving informal training to young preachers and encouraging local churches to use appropriate evangelistic methods. During his service as Senior Presbyter, Võsu was able to inaugurate 53 new presbyters. During this period, 43 ECB presbyters died and 12 retired from their job.[141] There was a pressing need in every Estonian church for new spiritual leaders. Remarkably, Võsu was able to maintain the number of presbyters in the UECBE. Some even studied abroad. It is not an overestimation to say that Robert Võsu found and mentored a whole new generation of ECB leaders in Estonia.

Võsu also became more involved in the work of the All-Union Council of Evangelical Christians-Baptists. In 1969 he was elected to the leadership of the AUCECB.[142] At the AUCECB 1979 congress he read 'a major doctrinal paper'.[143] Võsu's reflections on the Sermon on the Mount were published in a Russian translation in *Bratskii Vestnik*,[144] and his contribution within the AUCECB, as well as that of Osvald Tärk, was highly respected by the Russian speaking 'brotherhood'.[145] Being able to make several trips abroad in the 1970s, and being interested as a church historian and a Christian leader in the mission of and challenges for Christianity, he often informed Estonian churches about the life of the Baptists and other churches in the wider world.[146] His little book *Isiklik evangelism* (Personal Evangelism), written in 1971, grew out of his deep conviction that in the atheistic context traditional revival events at churches were less effective than the personal witness of believers. His major works, such as *Evangeelne eetika* (Evangelical Ethics),[147] *Kristluse ajalugu*

---

[141] *Logos*, no. 2 (1985), p. 29.

[142] Meego Remmel, 'Ma lähen koju, ma lähen ära...' [I will go home, I will go away...]. In memoriam Robert Võsu', *Logos* (April 1994), p. 17.

[143] Sawatsky, *Soviet Evangelicals Since World War II*, p. 271.

[144] An Estonian version, Robert Võsu, *Mäejutlus* (The Sermon on the Mount), typewritten manuscript (Tallinn, 1957). EEKBLA.

[145] Alexei Bychkov, oral information (03.07.2000).

[146] Arpad Arder, 'Robert Võsu – 70. aastane' [Robert Võsu – 70 years old], *Logos*, no. 1 (1984), p. 23.

[147] Robert Võsu, *Evangeelne eetika* (Evangelical Ethics) (Tallinn: Logos, 1996). The manuscript was completed in 1978.

(History of Christianity)[148] in four volumes, and *EKB koguduste ajalugu* (History of ECB Churches)[149] continue to be valuable resources for Estonian Baptist students.

An introvert by temperament, Võsu buried many of his emotions within himself. In 1984, Võsu suggested to his co-workers: 'Take everything peacefully, one needs to force oneself to be calm.'[150] In his relationships with the government authorities he followed a simple Estonian rule: better a sparrow in the hand than a dove on the roof. For this diplomatic approach, he has sometimes been accused of having too close a relationship with the Commissioner of the CRA, a modest echo of accusations which 'underground' Baptists in Russia addressed to the AUCECB leadership. However, the Commissioner's archive materials show that the state authorities considered Võsu to be 'an experienced Baptist' who was committed to the cause of the churches. The Commissioner described Võsu as a person with whom it would be possible 'to solve problems' in a way that was necessary for the Soviet authorities, but who would take actions which would be 'beneficial first and foremost only for the church', as soon as 'an opportunity opens up'. The Commissioner did not applaud this stance by Võsu and was specifically critical of the 'missionary activities' of Võsu.[151]

The Commissioner was right. Though the KGB intimidated Võsu at the end of the 1940s, and Võsu was forced to consent outwardly to the KGB's demands, it is clear from his life and ministry that he was a strategically-thinking Baptist leader who did much to shape and consolidate Baptist identity in Estonia during the Soviet years. In the 1970s and 1980s, while trying to keep a doctrinal balance between Word-orientated theology and Spirit-orientated tendencies within the union, Võsu supported the evangelistic youth initiatives that were emerging. This put him in an unfavourable light with the state authorities. In his 1982 report to the chairman of the CRA, the Commissioner criticized Võsu for not being 'up to the level of his responsibilities', for 'not [being] able to keep order in his denomination', and for having 'lost control over a group of young people' in the Oleviste Church. This is an allusion to the Effataa revival. The Commissioner suggested that Võsu be replaced by another person, Ants Rebane. 'We are trying to solve this question in a delicate way for the future,' concluded the Commissioner.[152] However, Võsu continued as Senior Presbyter until 1985, when he retired.

---

[148] Robert Võsu, *Kristluse ajalugu* (A History of Christianity), vols. 1-4, typewritten manuscript (Tallinn, 1957-1960). KUSA.

[149] Robert Võsu, *EKB koguduste ajalugu* (A History of ECB Churches), typewritten manuscript (Tallinn, 1959). KUSA.

[150] H. Veermets, *Albomi juurde. Haapsalu koguduse 100 aastapäev* (1984)) [To the Album. The 100th Anniversary of the Haapsalu Church (1984)], p. 34. EEKBLA.

[151] A report of the Commissioner of CRA of the year 1969. ERA, f. R-1989, n. 2, s. 93, pp. 83-84.

[152] A report of the Commissioner of CRA of the year 1982. AÜ1971-1990, UNVA.

While in office, Võsu also supported several building projects of ECB churches and prayer houses, which were, as an exception, allowed to be built 'with believers' resources'.[153] New prayer houses were erected in Kohtla-Järve, Elva, Palade, and some other places in Estonia. Võsu persistently worked at helping some smaller churches to be registered as 'religious groups' or a 'branch' of some larger church, a possibility which had opened up, at least theoretically, in the second half of the 1960s.[154] In earlier times, churches under 20 in membership would have been closed by the state. Baptist witness had been curtailed, mostly in the countryside. Now it was possible to maintain a Baptist (ECB) presence in these places.

It seems that the decision to retire was not easy for Võsu. But after consulting with Mikhail Zhidkov of the AUCECB, he decided to retire and to give more attention to writing for *Bratskii Vestnik* and to teaching Moscow Distance Bible Courses. In January 1985, at a Presbyters' Council meeting, Võsu informed the members of the council of his plans.[155] The pastor of Oleviste Church, Ülo Meriloo, became the candidate for the post of Senior Presbyter. During his last years, Võsu devoted much time to writing, several of his articles appearing in the typewritten publication *Logos*.[156] From 1989-1991 he edited the ECB publication *Teekäija* (Pilgrim), which in the relaxed atmosphere of Gorbachev's times was now printed officially. Võsu died on 20 March 1994 and was buried in Tallinn Rahumäe Cemetery.[157] With his analytical mind and writing abilities, his focus on evangelism, and his persistent support for churches and for the training of young leaders, Robert Võsu helped to shape Estonian Baptist self-understanding for a new generation and to clarify their mission in the 1970s and 1980s. Standing between the state and the churches, he helped the ECB churches to interpret state pressure and restrictions in ways that helped Estonian Evangelical Christians-Baptists to maintain their basic beliefs and revive, though semi-illegally, some of their ministries.

CONCLUSION

In the 1970s and the first half of the 1980s, the Estonian ECB union was

---

[153] Decree of the Council of Ministers of the ESSR (03.02.1967). ERA, f. R-1989, n. 1, s. 93, p. 3.

[154] See Explanatory letter of the CRA (21.06.1966). ERA, f. R-1989, n. 1, s. 97, pp. 6-7.

[155] Minutes of the Presbyters' Council meeting, no. 108 (14.01.1985). PNProt1969-1985, EEKBLA.

[156] Robert Võsu, 'Armastuse tähendus apostel Johannese kirjades' [The Meaning of Love in the Epistles of Apostle John], *Logos*, no. 3 (1986), pp. 27-34; 'Baptismist' [About Baptist Movement], *Logos*, no. 4 (1986), pp. 19-23; 'Tasadus ja alandus Pauluse käsitluses' [Meekness and Humbleness in Paul], *Logos,* no. 1-2 (1987), pp. 28-32.

[157] Remmel, 'Ma lähen koju, ma lähen ära…', p. 17.

gradually able to take advantage of the situation in society, which in political terms has been characterised as a period of 'stagnation' or 'suffocation', but during which ECB church life saw some new signs of evangelistic efforts. This was a period when a generation of young people in the society began to express their dissatisfaction with superficial Marxist ideology. Some began to look for answers in religion. The UECBE churches, though limited in their work opportunities and in their vision for youth, were able to respond to this situation by reviving and reshaping their worship: Christian youth organised music 'bands', Bible study and prayer groups of young people came to life, and in the Tallinn Oleviste Church charismatic-evangelistic Effataa evenings began to attract people of all generations, both from Estonia and other Soviet republics. These signs of life were like blades of grass sprouting through asphalt. Baptists in Estonia re-confirmed their identity as an evangelistically-orientated ecclesial body, though there were discussions and debates about what were the most effective methods of evangelism.

Surprisingly, in some cases the state authorities did not take severe measures to suppress Estonian ECB activities, such activities as the efforts to reproduce typewritten literature, to revive and organise youth work in churches and on a union level, to organise evangelistic services with youth participation, and to give theological training through informal study groups. Robert Võsu, the Senior Presbyter, with his diplomatic abilities, was able to send some young men to study theology abroad. In 1975, a new hymnal was published, an important help for communal singing in churches. All these phenomena give evidence that Estonian Baptists tried to revive and reconfigure some of their traditional ministries in the 1970s and 1980s, though the general membership numbers in the UECBE continued to decline. Although ECB believers restrained from publicly criticising the socialist-atheistic political system, their presence was a witness to a non-materialistic worldview. They represented an alternative way of life, which was characterised by trust in God, not by human-bound atheistic optimism. This was one way to express peaceful resistance in the context of atheistic suppression. However, in some cases, Estonian Baptists actively helped the 'underground Baptist movement', which openly defied the restrictive religious laws. All this helped to develop and form the UECBE identity in Estonia. During the period of 'Brezhnevian stagnation', Estonian ECB churches were looking for a better understanding of their mission and calling. Searching for their way of life in the socialist-atheistic labyrinth, they saw some rays of light which directed their path: renewed evangelism in several churches, emerging youth groups, and attempts to keep their minds and thinking free.

CHAPTER 5

Opening Doors: 1985-1991

Together with other Soviet Christians, members and leaders of Estonian ECB churches met new challenges in the second half of the 1980s. The political and cultural context was going to be reshaped at an increasing pace and this would profoundly affect all churches. Not only religious legislation and the attitudes of authorities toward Christians changed, but a considerable – even dramatic – change took place in the evaluation being made of religion in the society as a whole, most noticeably in the sphere of popular opinion. Evangelical Christians-Baptists who had survived through many difficult restrictions saw new opportunities for Christian work being undertaken in a public way. The challenge to re-interpret their relationships with society, and with the wider world located outside the clearly and safely defined area of church life, was probably one of the most important factors in these years of rapid transformation for Soviet Baptists in general and for Estonian Baptists in particular. How did Estonian Baptists respond to the social, political and religious turmoil of *perestroika*? What resources did they have? In January 1988, pastor Arpad Arder asked these kinds of questions while making a rather prophetic statement at the Presbyters' Council meeting: 'We have our plans. But our plans must not hinder God's plans. God has a good and powerful plan for us. ... I have a feeling that this year something will happen. ... Doors will be opened, but do we have resources to go in?'[1]

CHANGES IN SOVIET RELIGIOUS POLICY

In summer 1986, Soviet leader Michail Gorbachev announced that a new religious law was in preparation. For many Soviet Christians this was a sign of a change for the better. It was hoped that the law would reflect the 'openness' (*glasnost*) and 'renewal' (*perestroika*) initiated by Gorbachev in the wider society. Some positive, though still cautious, signs also came from the chairman of the CRA, Konstantin Khrachev. In 1985, Alexei Bychkov, the general secretary of the AUCECB, gave the following message to the Estonian

---

[1] Minutes of the Presbyters' Council meeting, no. 137 (11.01.1988). Juhatuse koosolekute protokollid koos lisadega (JKPLis) [Minutes of the Executive Board, with attachments] (11.01.1988-02.03.1992), EEKBLA.

ECB union: 'In church-state relationships there are steps toward more freedoms. Two meetings with the new chairman of the CRA indicate optimism.'[2]

However, the different bodies concerned with the drafting of the religious law were not able to reach agreement; for example, there was a prolonged debate over the religious education of children.[3] It took four years to resolve the issues, until finally in September 1990 the law was passed in the Supreme Soviet of the Soviet Union. At that point, the new law was already largely irrelevant in Tallinn. Estonia was drifting apart from the Soviet Union. In March 1991, all three Baltic countries held referenda 'in which the demand for independence was endorsed by overwhelming majorities'.[4] It has been argued that Estonians, due to their Protestant spirituality, which affirmed the taking of initiatives, were 'especially fit to meet the challenges of *perestroika*'.[5] There may be a grain of truth in this statement, and it is, arguably, relevant to religious life. For example, Baptists were fairly quick to revive some of their traditional activities, such as pastoral training, children's ministries and publishing projects.

Nevertheless, during the years 1985-1988, the ties with Moscow were still strong, and the tendencies in the wider Soviet Union could still be applied in describing the situation in Estonia. However, it became evident that there was an increasing tension between the anachronistic regulations and actual religious life and practice. Many changes first took place *de facto,* and only later did the law adjust itself to the actual situation. The major changes included the restoration of dignity to religious affiliations, the normalisation of the legal status of religious organisations, the restoration of confiscated church facilities, and the granting of permission to construct new churches, expand publication possibilities, and open up contacts with foreign religious organisations and persons.[6]

Substantial shifts in the state's religious policy did not come immediately after Gorbachev came to power in March 1985. At least in the case of unregistered churches, severe restrictions and arrests continued through 1985-

---

[2] Minutes of the Presbyters' Council meeting, no. 111 (01.04.1985). Juhatuse koosolekute protokollid (JKP) [Minutes of the Executive Board] (30.01.1981-12.12.1987), EEKBLA.

[3] Jane Ellis, 'Some reflections about religious policy under Khrachev', in Sabrina P. Ramet, ed., *Religious Policy in the Soviet Union* (Cambridge and New York: Cambridge University Press, 1993), p. 103.

[4] Paul Johnson, *Modern Times. A History of the World from the 1920s to the 1990s* (London: Orion Books, 1994), p. 766.

[5] Kristian Gerner and Stefan Hedlund, *The Baltic States and the End of the Soviet Empire* (London and New York: Routledge, 1993), pp. 100-101.

[6] Sabrina P. Ramet, 'Religious Policy in the era of Gorbachev', in Ramet, ed., *Religious Policy in the Soviet Union*, p. 32.

1986.[7] For many functionaries who controlled the religious organisations, 'loyalty to the law' was still a leading motif; many of them followed the tradition of dealing harshly with unregistered churches. According to this view there was no clear-cut line between the disloyal attitude of the unregistered churches and conspiracy to commit all sorts of crimes; all this was often referred to as 'anti-social activity'.[8]

There is no doubt that the changes during Gorbachev era caused confusion among Soviet functionaries. What was their role now? Was it to restrict and control religious activities, to support them, or to take a 'hands off' approach? In 1990, surprising some observers, Gorbachev himself strongly appealed to spiritual values in his speech to the Global Forum.[9] But in January 1989, the Estonian Commissioner of the CRA, Rein Ristlaan, in his 1988 report to the Council for Religious Affairs in Moscow, stuck to very 'traditional' rhetoric, stating: 'There were no attempts at breaking the laws or any other illegal activities from the side of Baptists in the year under review.'[10] However, in the same report he mentioned certain activities of the Baptists that would have been considered impossible only some years earlier: open-air worship services, public concerts, and religious articles published in the secular press. Baptists had begun to express their historic identity and convictions more publicly.

The year 1988 was crucial in the process, within the Soviet Union, of 'the gradual rehabilitation of religion as a healthy force...'.[11] This 'rehabilitation' drew churches into the focus of media and popular attention. One can agree with Jane Ellis that it was the Russian Orthodox Church that benefited most from the changes in religious policy under Gorbachev, especially in the early phases.[12] But also other churches, including Evangelical Christians-Baptists, gained a degree of publicity, and used new opportunities to renew their church life and ministry. Russian Baptists became active in social work and evangelism. Freedom and democratization also brought problems. As early as 1985, Alexei Bychkov complained that the world was invading the church, that church authorities were being questioned, and that unity in the AUCECB was continuously in danger.[13] In December 1987, the former Estonian Senior Presbyter Robert Võsu said to his co-workers: 'I have the impression that I

---

[7] Michael Rowe, *Russian Resurrection. Strength in Suffering – A History of Russia's Evangelical Church* (London: Marshall Pickering, 1994), p. 199.

[8] Michael Bourdeaux, *Religious Ferment in Russia. Protestant Opposition to Soviet Religious Policy* (London and New York: Macmillan and St. Martin's Press, 1968), p. 143.

[9] Gerner and Hedlund, *The Baltic States and the End of the Soviet Empire*, pp. 158-159.

[10] Report of the Commissioner of the CRA of the year 1988 (03.01.1989). Aruanded ja ülevaated kirikute tegevuse kohta ENSV-s 1971-1990 (AÜ1971-1990) [Reports and surveys about the activities of churches in the ESSR 1971-1990], UNVA.

[11] Ramet, 'Religious Policy', p. 33.

[12] Ellis, 'Some Reflections', p. 86.

[13] Minutes of the Presbyters' Council meeting, no. 111 (01.04.1985). JKP, EEKBLA.

have jumped into a void.'[14] Changing contexts posed a crisis for Evangelical Christians-Baptists: including both dangers and opportunities.

Turning from the general background to the specific situation in Estonia, the push for political independence in the Baltics encouraged Estonian ECB believers to seek their own way and their own identity, gradually distancing themselves from the Moscow headquarters of the AUCECB. In addition, the 1980s saw a growing dissatisfaction with the highly centralised ECB structures at the All-Union level. Not only political, but also religious ties with Moscow became weaker.

ESTONIAN BAPTISTS, THE STATE AND SOCIETY

There seem to have been a few areas where Estonian ECB churches were not immediately able to respond to the new opportunities, or where the resistance of the atheistic state structures was still strong. In February 1988 the Senior Presbyter, Ülo Meriloo, stated that in some other parts of the Soviet Union the believers now had greater freedoms than was the case in Estonia, noting: 'Believers have been asked to help in hospitals and childrens' day care centres.'[15] He also referred to Kyrgyzstan where once a month a Christian programme was broadcast to introduce the ECB movement.[16] According to a researcher Raigo Liiman, the first religious programme in Soviet Estonia was broadcast in 1986,[17] but it is certain that at that time neither Baptists nor other denominations were actively investigating the possibilities offered by the media.

In 1985-1986 the atheistic system was still powerfully at work, though showing evidence of inertia. In spite of some oral and unofficial concessions on the part of the Commissioner of the CRA, the general religious policy was repressive. Special attention was paid to a small number of unregistered religious groups in Estonia. The state made their life difficult and made it clear to them that they were being kept under observation. On 5 September 1985, J. Petrova, who lived in Valga, South-Estonia, was fined 30 roubles because her ten-year-old son Vitali had taken part in a secret meeting of 'underground' Baptists.[18] In 1986 administrative punishments were given to five members of

---

[14] Minutes of the Presbyters' Council meeting, no. 136 (12.12.1987). JKP, EEKBLA.

[15] Minutes of the Presbyters' Council meeting, no. 138 (14.02.1988). JKPLis, EEKBLA.

[16] Ibid.

[17] Raigo Liiman, *Usklikkus muutuvas Eesti ühiskonnas* [Religiosity in the Changing Estonian Society] (Tartu: Tartu Ülikooli Kirjastus, 2001), p. 36.

[18] Minutes of the Commission for Juvenile Issues at Valga District Executive Committee, no. 22 (05.09.1985). AÜ1971-1990, UNVA.

unregistered groups.[19] However, there were some signs that the atheistic grip on Estonian churches was being slightly loosened. The present author's personal experience of this process dates from 1985: he was informed at that time that he could not work as a schoolteacher because of his Christian convictions; four months later he was allowed to become a teacher. The Soviet system was losing its enthusiasm for atheistic work, though without publicly admitting it. In a secret report from the beginning of 1987 the Commissioner complained that atheistic propaganda had become weaker in radio, TV and even in communist newspapers.[20]

The 'new winds' that began to blow in the second half of the 1980s gradually helped to loosen the pressure that the churches had experienced for many decades.[21] In December 1987 Christmas songs could be heard from the Estonian State Radio and for the first time since the Second World War people were wished a Merry Christmas by a Radio broadcaster.[22] From 1988 on, both believers and local state authorities were increasingly ignoring religious laws.[23] In February 1989, the First Secretary of the Estonian Communist Party, Vaino Väljas, received a group of leaders of Estonian Methodists, Evangelical Christians-Baptists and Seventh Day Adventists. Väljas, a former ambassador in Nicaragua, spoke of the positive role of Baptists in society. He referred to the former Estonian Baptist leader, Karl Kaups, as well as to Martin Luther King Jr. and Nicaraguan Baptists.[24] Väljas was given a Bible as a gift by the church leaders. The reception was an important sign to believers and to the society, indicating the changed attitude at the highest level of the political hierarchy. The Baptists realised that they were moving from a position of being a marginalised religious movement towards a new and more respected role in the society. How well were they prepared for this new role? This chapter argues that they tried to confirm and re-interpret their identity through different church ministries, but that their voice and also their self-reflection in the field of socio-political processes remained comparatively weak.

---

[19] Statistical survey of the religious situation in the ESSR in 1986 (30.01.1987). AÜ1971-1990, UNVA.

[20] Ibid.

[21] A short but informative letter written in 1989 by Arpad Arder describes the ECB's revived hopes. See Stanley Crabb, comp. and ed., *Our Favourite Memories. European Baptist Federation 1949-1999* (n. p., n. d.), pp. 53-54.

[22] Jaan Kiivit, 'Eesti Evangeelne Luterlik Kirik pärast Teist maailmasõda' [The Estonian Evangelical Lutheran Church after the Second World War], in J. Gnadenteich, *Kodumaa kirikulugu* [Church History of the Home Country] (Tallinn: Logos, 1995), p. 111.

[23] Jaanus Plaat, *Usuliikumised, kirikud ja vabakoguduses Lääne- ja Hiiumaal: usuühenduste muutumis-protsessid 18. sajandi keskpaigast kuni 20. sajandi lõpuni* [Religious Movements, Churches and Free Churches in West-Estonia and Hiiumaa Island: Transformational Processes of Religious Entities from the Mid-18th Century to the End of the 20th Century] (Tartu: Eesti Rahva Muuseum, 2001), pp. 242.

[24] Minutes of the Presbyters' Council meeting, no. 148 (13.02.1989). JKPLis, EEKBLA.

Not only did the Estonian churches need to find a new self-understanding; the Commissioner of the CRA faced the same challenge. In 1989-1990 the Commissioner's office began to lose its repressive function.[25] The Commissioner admitted in the summer of 1989 that the Christian church in Estonia had suffered 'serious moral repressions'. He added: 'During the period of *perestroika* the main goal is to re-establish the church's moral and material rights.'[26] In August 1989 the Commissioner informed the churches that the government had abolished the special (heavy) taxation rate for clergy, and that the employees of religious organisations would henceforth be taxed at the same rate as factory or office workers.[27] Churches were now allowed to have their own bank accounts.[28] From 1 January 1990 it became possible for churches to have work contracts for ministers and other religious workers, and the state recognised religious work as entitled to social guarantees.

The Commissioner's function had indeed changed. He helped to arrange documents for trips abroad by believers and assisted in obtaining permission to bring large quantities of religious literature into the country free of charge. However, cooperation with the state in these practical matters was a new experience for all Estonian churches, including ECB churches. How could they become partners with state institutions, instead of being subordinate and suppressed organisations? The churches were not prepared for this challenge. Sometimes even correct planning and doing the paperwork posed difficulties. The Commissioner complained in autumn 1989 that both Lutherans and Baptists were slow to inform him beforehand about the literature that was sent to these churches. Sometimes the literature was already in customs when his help was asked. He was willing to help, but getting the necessary permission could take up to two months. The Commissioner stressed: '... I can offer actual help ... only when receiving the information in time.'[29] The practice of responsible and voluntary citizenship, instead of 'friendly obstinacy', was a new skill that Estonian ECB believers slowly began to learn. For example,

---

[25] According to the Estonian government's decree of 10 October 1990 the Commissioner's office was closed and the documentation handed over to the Cultural Ministry of Estonia. A letter of the Commissioner of the CRA (31.10.1990). EEKBL kirjavahetus usuasjade volinikuga 1966-1990 (KirjUv1966-1990) [The correspondence of the UECBE with the Commissioner of the CRA 1966-1990], EEKBLA.

[26] The activities of religious organisations in the Estonian SSR (27.07.1989). Kirjavahetus usukeskustega vabariigis 1977-1990 [Correspondence with religious centres in the Republic 1977-1990], UNVA.

[27] The Commissioner Rein Ristlaan to the members of the Estonian Council of Churches (08.08.1989). Kirjavahetus usukeskustega vabariigis 1977-1990, UNVA. See also Ramet, 'Religious Policy', p. 37.

[28] Rein Ristlaan to the chairman of the Savings Bank in Estonia, R. Dontsov (10.02.1989). Kirjavahetus usukeskustega vabariigis 1977-1990, UNVA.

[29] The Commissioner of the CRA to the president of the Estonian Council of Churches, Kuno Pajula (16.11.1989). Kirjavahetus usukeskustega vabariigis 1977-1990, UNVA.

establishing clear accounting and financial procedures in the union office took several years. In Soviet times many 'financial transactions' took place 'from one pocket to another', partly to avoid unjust taxation.

All these processes in Estonia took place in a context of growing 'sentiments for complete political independence'.[30] Independence was formally declared in August 1991. All this had an effect upon Evangelical Christians-Baptists in Estonia. Like many other believers under the Soviet regime, Estonian Baptists had – at least in part – developed an attitude that they could not significantly influence political and social processes; Christian activity was understood to belong to the private, not to the public sphere of life.[31] Though the declaration approved by the UECBE conference in 1989, and sent to the Prime Minister, stated that the 'present processes' orientated toward Estonian self-government were 'from God',[32] this was an exceptionally bold statement. As a rule, the UECBE tended to be much more cautious in political issues. The Presbyters' Council suggested that a pastor should not join any political movement, although church members had the freedom to take part or not to take part in social and political life as their conscience urged them to do.[33] In summer 1989 Joosep Tammo warned against 'political prophets' in the churches. 'Preach the Word of God!' was his message.[34] In some cases there was confusion about whether it was right to allow a church building to be used for a political meeting. This was the case in Paide, where the newly formed Eesti Kristlik Liit (Estonian Christian Union) had held a meeting.[35] Some church members were supportive, while some strongly opposed it. To fit political interests into the picture of ECB self-understanding caused difficulties.

There was also a kind of common sense realism among the leadership of ECB. Even in 1989, when the excitement about the national awakening was high, there was a warning given by the union leadership: 'Events can be reversed quickly.'[36] The political situation was still unstable. Signs of religious freedom could not yet be taken for granted. However, Evangelical Christians-Baptists shared the nation-wide joy when Estonia became a politically free country. In September 1991, in many ECB churches, there had been thanksgiving services for the political independence that was achieved without

---

[30] Toivo U. Raun, *Estonia and the Estonians* (Stanford, California: Hoover Institution Press, 1991), pp. 227-228.

[31] Anna-Marie Kool, 'A Protestant Perspective on Mission in Eastern and Central Europe', *Religion in Eastern Europe*, vol. XX, no. 6 (December 2000), pp. 6-7.

[32] Declaration of the UECBE (09.12.1989). Aastakonverentsid 1989-1991, EEKBLA; The UECBE President Ülo Meriloo to the Prime Minister Indrek Toome (15.01.1990). Aastakonverentsid 1989-1991 [Annual conferences 1989-1990], EEKBLA.

[33] Minutes of the Presbyters' Council meeting, no. 144 (14.10.1988). JKPLis, EEKBLA.

[34] Minutes of the Presbyters' Council meeting, no. 152 (12.06.1989). JKPLis, EEKBLA.

[35] Minutes of the Presbyters' Council meeting, no. 145 (14.11.1988). JKPLis, EEKBLA.

[36] Minutes of the UECBE conference (09.12.1989). Aastakonverentsid 1989-1991, EEKBLA.

destructive violence and bloodshed.[37] This was a miracle indeed, as political
shifts of such a magnitude and in so short time, as Martin Bailey comments,
'probably never had come before without violence'.[38] However, Estonian
Baptists, in general, continued to be characterized by pietistic restraint from
involvement politics.

While Estonian Baptists preferred to keep a low profile in political
pronouncements they were comparatively active in giving their suggestions in
the field of religious legislation. In 1988, an Estonian Baptist lawyer, Elmar
Lepik, informed the Presbyters' Council about his suggestions regarding such
legislation.[39] After approval by the council the suggestions were sent to the
Council for Religious Affairs in Moscow, though this Estonian contribution
was considered to be too 'radical' by the leadership in the AUCECB
headquarters.[40] In addition, the UECBE Statutes of 1989 expressed the wish to
secure working opportunities for the future, as far as legal aspects were
concerned. Today it may appear surprising that a general document listed such
specific rights and activities as the following: to receive gifts and educate
spiritual workers, to build and repair buildings, to sell religious literature and to
use printing and copying machines, to distribute religious literature, to organise
concerts, to take care of elderly and sick people, to organise trips and camps
both at home and abroad, and to take part in mission work and organise Sunday
schools.[41] But these words must be seen in their contemporary context: this was
more than just a legal document, it was a document of hope and of a renewed
sense of identity, though this identity was expressed in terms of 'doing' rather
than 'being'.

The ECB focus on 'doing' was inspired by new freedoms; 'a religious
resurrection' in society, as an Estonian Lutheran theologian Toomas Paul
stated.[42] The Baptists quickly re-established their educational structures. They
also used the new literature distribution opportunities well and revived their
children's work. They were involved in 'mass-evangelism': they preached at
open-air services and in concert halls. However, they were much slower in
reinterpreting their role in wider society. They were also struggling with
finding effective ways to cooperate with new Christian movements and mission
organisations coming to Estonia. To a large extent Estonian Baptists in the
period of the 'singing revolution', a term used for the years 1988-1991 (because

---

[37] A report at the UECBE annual conferene of 1991. Aastakonverentsid 1989-1991,
EEKBLA.
[38] J. Martin Bailey, *The Spring of Nations: Churches in the Rebirth of Central and
Eastern Europe* (New York: Friendship Press, 1991), p. 118.
[39] Minutes of the Presbyters' Council meeting, no. 140 (11.04.1988). JKPLis, EEKBLA.
[40] Minutes of the Presbyters' Council meeting, no. 143 (12.09.1988). JKPLis, EEKBLA.
[41] Eesti Evangeelsete Kristlaste-Baptistide Koguduste Liidu Põhikiri [Statutes of the
Union of Evangelical Christian-Baptist Churches in Estonia] (09.12.1989). EEKBLA.
[42] Toomas Paul, 'Eesti kirik 1980. aastatel' [The Estonian Church in the 1980s],
Vikerkaar, no. 6 (1991), p. 63.

of the large rallies in the county),[43] re-built their identity through re-establishing the ministry structures which had been typical in the pre-war period. A comparatively successful attempt was made to re-tell the Estonian Baptists' narrative of the past. However, they were less prepared to add new elements to this narrative, for example, to analyse and meaningfully address the deep ethical vacuum in society, to stand against growing individualism and consumerist values, or to express more adequately how their religious identity was related to their Estonian national identity.

THEOLOGICAL EDUCATION

As this study has demonstrated, the desire for theological education had never died out among Estonian Baptists. In 1985 they stated that their goal in giving theological education, then still unofficially, was to pass on trustworthy biblical teaching in the context of a 'new-paganism' and 'new teachings coming from abroad'.[44] In 1987 there were approximately 40 preachers and presbyters in the UECBE who pursued their training, in the form of self-study, under the supervision of more experienced pastors. Though there were some students who did not see clearly in what direction their studies would take them, and some did not have the qualities to become leaders of churches,[45] these educational efforts maintained at least some kind of continuity in the field of Baptist theological education.

Realising the opportunities afforded by the 'opening doors', the question about re-establishing a theological seminary was raised at a Presbyters' Council meeting in September 1988. Ülo Meriloo, the Senior Presbyter, took a cautious approach, suggesting that it would be better to wait one more year.[46] Meanwhile the foreign educational and mission agencies were quick to use the new opportunities of increased religious freedom. In October 1988 Campus Crusade for Christ organised evangelism training in cooperation with the 'study sector' of the UECBE.[47] By March 1989 Biblical Education by Extension (BEE) was working in Estonia. But Estonians saw two problems with BEE

---

[43] Raun, *Estonia and the Estonians*, p. 225. The years 1988-1991 saw the birth of political parties and striving for democracy in Estonia, as well as the rebirth of the civil society. It was a time of mass movements, which 'organized political meetings and demonstrations across Estonia.' 'The number of participants in the largest rallies on the Tallinn Song Festival Grounds reached 300,000 – almost one third of the Estonian population. These rallies inspired the name "Singing Revolution".' Marju Lauristin, Peeter Vihalemm et al., eds., *Return to the Western World: Cultural and Political Perspectives on the Estonian Post-Communist Transition* (Tartu: Tartu University Press, 1997), pp. 82, 88.
[44] Minutes of the Presbyters' Council meeting, no. 114 (16.09.1985). JKP, EEKBLA.
[45] Minutes of the Presbyters' Council meeting, no. 130 (09.03.1987). JKP, EEKBLA.
[46] Minutes of the Presbyters' Council meeting, no. 143 (12.09.1988). JKPLis, EEKBLA.
[47] Minutes of the Presbyters' Council meeting, no. 144 (14.10.1988). JKPLis, EEKBLA.

courses: first, the short-time course model did not allow teachers to have a lasting and deep impact on the students' spiritual formation; and second, it was much more difficult to direct the graduates of this non-affiliated programme into the areas of ministry that were considered crucial for the union.[48] These 'imported' courses, though temporarily helpful, did not greatly assist in the task of the contextualisation of theological reflection, a problem which continues in post-socialist countries.[49] The only solution was to open an Estonian Baptist seminary, and in this way to participate more effectively in the reshaping of the denominational-educational identity.

After a period of preparation, the Estonian Baptist Theological Seminary (Est. Kõrgem Usuteaduslik Seminar) began its work in Tallinn 16 October 1989.[50] Until the last moment it was not certain whether or not the opening ceremony would take place.[51] However, it did, albeit in a modest form. The director of the Seminary, Peeter Roosimaa, who had received his theological education in Buckow (GDR), as well as the Senior Presbyter, Ülo Meriloo, addressed those present. In the reopened school there were five students in the first year: three full-time and two part-time. In addition to these students the seminary regarded as its students three more persons whom the union had sent to study theology abroad, one to Sweden and two to Finland.[52] The seminary was probably the first effort in the vast region of the Soviet Union to start a Baptist theological school with full-time students and a four-year programme. Evangelical seminaries and Bible schools began mushrooming in the former Soviet Union areas only in the 1990s, and 'only a few can date their origins before the nineties'.[53] In 1989 Alexei Bychkov announced that a dream for a seminary in Moscow with a four-year programme could go ahead,[54] but the first group of full-time students in the Moscow Theological Seminary of the ECB began studies only in 1993.[55]

The Conference of the UECBE in 1989 accepted the Estonian Baptist Seminary Statute, though it was sent for registration to the Estonian

[48] Minutes of the Presbyters' Council meeting, no. 149 (12.03.1989). JKPLis, EEKBLA.
[49] Cheryl Brown and Wesley Brown, 'Progress and Challenge in Theological Education in Central and Eastern Europe', *Transformation*, vol. 20, no. 1 (January 2003), pp. 1-3.
[50] Minutes of the UECBE conference (09.12.1989). Aastakonverentsid 1989-1991, EEKBLA.
[51] Peeter Roosimaa, telephone interview (10.05.2003).
[52] Minutes of the Presbyters' Council meeting, no. 154 (16.10.1989). JKPLis, EEKBLA.
[53] Peter Penner, 'Critical evaluation of recent developments in the Commonwealth of Independent States', *Transformation*, vol. 20, no. 1 (January 2003), p. 21.
[54] Bernard Green, *Crossing the boundaries: A history of the European Baptist Federation* (Didcot: The Baptist Historical Society, 1999), p. 114.
[55] *Moskovskaja Bogoslovskaja Seminarija Evange'lskih Hristjan-Baptistov*. A leaflet (n. p., n. d.). Toivo Pilli's personal archive.

government only in June 1990.[56] It seems that the Statute was initially a working document, as the union conference immediately expressed the need to change it.[57] By 1991 there were 18 students at the seminary and the school had moved from the Tallinn union office building to the premises of Tartu 'Kolgata' Baptist Church.[58] It was hoped that Tartu, as a university town, would offer a better context for studies, that it would be possible to use the University library, and that the extra burden for the school caused by a flow of foreign visitors coming to the union office would be smaller in Tartu. The new seminary building in Tartu was completed in 1994. As in all areas of Estonian life, the rising inflation rate caused financial difficulties for the school. The seminary had difficulties even photocopying the study materials.[59] In 1989-1990 a seminary teacher could only buy an ice-cream cone for the pay received for one hour of work. Much work was done on a voluntary basis.[60] Voluntary work or 'love-work', as it was usually called, was still considered the norm rather than the exception among Estonian believers. Along with organisational developments, and the growing ideals of the 'market economy' in society, this was soon going to change.

Without doubt, it was a courageous attempt to start a seminary in times of instability and confusion. A Baptist leader from Ukraine, Grigori Komendant, in his address to the Estonian ECB conference in 1990, emphasised that Slavic Baptists would like to learn from the Estonian experience in this field.[61] This was probably not only a polite way to pay a compliment, but a serious intention. However, as Estonians increasingly began to link their identity with Scandinavia and more widely with Western Europe, their contribution to Slavic Baptists could never be the same as in the 1960s and 1970s.

The further development of the seminary involved both growth and challenges. It was recognised by the state and thus it became a part of the overall educational system in Estonia.[62] The number of students grew. In the 1990s, the seminary programme was comparable to the requirements of a university programme, at the Bachelor's level, in theology. The admission requirements included academic criteria and also a recommendation letter from

---

[56] Ülo Meriloo to the government of the Estonian Republic (08.06.1990). KirjUv1966-1990, EEKBLA.
[57] Minutes of the UECBE conference (09.12.1989). Aastakonverentsid 1989-1991, EEKBLA.
[58] Minutes of the UECBCE annual conference (23.11.1991). Aastakonverentsid 1989-1991, EEKBLA.
[59] Ibid.
[60] Peeter Roosimaa, telephone interview (10.05.2003).
[61] Minutes of the UECBCE annual conference (17.11.1990). Aastakonverentsid 1989-1991, EEKBLA.
[62] Ain Riistan, 'Theological Education in Estonia – a Survival of the Fittest Game or an Opportunity for the Future?', unpublished paper (Pancrac Teologicky Forum, 12 July 2002, Siroky Dul, Czech Republic), pp. 5, 7. A copy in TPL.

a local church. Besides this, a sense of calling for Christian ministry was emphasised.[63] There were also early signs of criticism directed toward the seminary. In 1991 it was stated that there was a need to prepare evangelists, but 'the Seminary draws too narrow a contingent [of students]'.[64] There was another fear: 'Although it was generally understood to be a good thing that the seminary gives an academically recognized education, it was also increasingly felt that this might cause students to become "mere academics".'[65] For well-founded or unfounded reasons, the seminary in Tartu began to be criticised for its inability to prepare enough pastors and evangelists. At least in part, this was a disappointment caused by unrealistically high expectations at the turn of the 1990s.

Unfortunately, Estonian Evangelical Christians-Baptists were largely neglecting the potential of the seminary as a helper in the process of theological reflection. The combination of formal academic requirements, students exploring the borders of their 'intellectual world', and an influx of new books (creating so-called 'book-knowledge'), posed challenges to an established Estonian Baptist view of theological education: learning in fellowship with an emphasis on preaching and spiritual edification, or self-help learning under the supervision of teachers-pastors. The establishment of the seminary, as the fulfilment of a long time dream, increased the self-esteem of Estonian ECB believers and supported their wish to be a respected religious group in society. On the other hand, the seminary began to be a challenge to the identity of the union. There was a growing need to find a new balance between intellectual efforts and grass-roots spirituality, between theological reflection and the urgent needs of churches to engage in appropriate evangelism. Donald Messer has said: 'Seminaries typically experience tension in their relationships with their church constituencies.'[66] Estonian ECB churches expected answers from their seminary, but were not well prepared to meet the questions of identity that the seminary brought along. At the same time, the seminary was preoccupied with offering courses and teaching subjects and had less energy for its prophetic task – for contextually relevant theological reflection and for offering 'tools' for the ECB union churches to reach a better understanding of themselves and their mission in the changing society.

---

[63] Minutes of the UECBCE annual conference (17.11.1990). Aastakonverentsid 1989-1991, EEKBLA.
[64] Minutes of the UECBE conference (09.12.1989). Aastakonverentsid 1989-1991, EEKBLA.
[65] Ain Riistan, 'Theological Education in Estonia', p. 8.
[66] Donald E. Messer, *Calling Church and Seminary into the 21st Century* (Nashville: Abingdon Press, 1995), p. 16.

PUBLISHING ACTIVITIES

At the ECB union conference in December 1989, the Senior Presbyter Ülo Meriloo pointed out two areas of rapid development: theological education and Christian literature.[67] The area of literature, as has been seen, had always been important. Even before Baptists could access a printing press, opportunities were opened to use copying machines. In 1986 the Senior Presbyter asked permission from the Ministry of Internal Affairs to install a copying machine in the UECBE office in Tallinn. The application mentioned that the copying machine was needed for preparing circular letters of the union, but also study materials for presbyters and deacons.[68] Response was slow in coming. At last, permission was given. The copier was placed in a locked room behind a metal door. A careful record was kept about what materials were copied. However, this opened up an opportunity to photocopy some urgent informational materials with less energy and effort, instead of using a typewriter.

But in 1989-1990 a dam burst: ECB believers began their own publishing activities, and there was also a flood of religious literature that reached Estonia from abroad. Instead of the typewritten 'journal' *Logos*, the union revived the tradition of issuing the publication *Teekäija* (Pilgrim), that had played a key role in strengthening Baptist identity and doctrinal unity before the Second World War.[69] In addition, by 1990 the children's magazine *Päikesekiir* (Sunbeam) was well established and highly appreciated in local churches, often as a tool and source of ideas for the growing Sunday school work. Also, an informational letter *Kristlik Kiri* (Christian Letter) was published,[70] though it did not survive long. 'Where is our *Kristlik Kiri*?' exclaimed Joosep Tammo in spring 1991.[71] The irregular appearance as well as the content of *Teekäija* was criticized: 'The publication *Teekäija* should be revived by making it more popular, in order to widen the scope of readership. The issues until now are too theological and attract a narrow scope of readers.'[72] *Teekäija* began to be published regularly only after 1992.

Probably the first book published as a result of the initiative of Estonian Evangelical Christians-Baptists during this period of religious liberalisation was *Esimesed Jõulud* (First Christmas). This book, printed in 50,000 copies,

---

[67] Minutes of the UECBE conference (09.12.1989). Aastakonverentsid 1989-1991, EEKBLA.
[68] Ülo Meriloo to the Ministry of Internal Affairs (14.04.1986). Kirjavahetus usukeskustega vabariigis 1977-1990, UNVA.
[69] Toivo Pilli, 'The Role of the Monthly Publication 'Teekäija' in the Estonian Baptist Church 1904-1940,' in Siret Rutiku and Reinhart Staats, eds., *Estland, Lettland und Westliches Christentum* (Kiel: Friedrich Wittig Verlag, 1998), pp. 215-218.
[70] Circular letter, no. 1 (1991). Eesti EKB koguduste 1990. a. aruanne [Report of the Estonian ECB churches of 1990]. Aastakonverentsid 1989-1991, EEKBLA.
[71] Minutes of the UECBCE board, no. 15 (13.05.1991). JKPLis, EEKBLA.
[72] Minutes of the UECBCE board, no. 1 (08.01.1990). JKPLis, EEKBLA.

was not a theological treatise, but a children's Christmas story. However, it fitted well into a social context where there was general enthusiasm about celebrating Christmas and a wide interest in Christian children's ministries. The money for publishing came from a donation from Sweden.[73] In spite of inflation and lack of printing paper in the period of 1990-1991, Estonian Baptists – with considerable support from abroad – managed to continue their publishing activities.

Though Eesti Kristlik Kirjastus (Estonian Christian Publishing), later the Publishing House Logos, was not exclusively a Baptist enterprise, the initiator of this project, Ingmar Kurg, was an ECB pastor. In 1990, Eesti Kristlik Kirjastus published a small book *Kümme käsku* (Ten Commandments) written by Osvald Tärk. *Kümme käsku*, a kind of Baptist catechetical text, was the UECBE answer to the quest for ethical guidance in a confused society. Tärk stated that the Ten Commandments include elements that are universally important for moral order.[74] In the book, 'the specialists do not find sophisticated theological arguments, but rather moral advice'.[75] Later, Stanley Jones' *Mäejutlus* (The Christ of the Mount) was also published in Estonian. The question remains if Tärk's book, originally written decades earlier, was really able meaningfully to address non-Christian readers or if it was mainly church members who benefited from it. However, an important attempt was made to spread a Baptist biblical-ethical identity in this new era of religious freedom.

Though significant, the first cautious steps in publishing Christian literature in Estonia were almost nothing when compared to the huge amount of Bibles and New Testaments as well as other Christian books and materials published abroad and imported into Estonia. In 1990 local churches were informed that two books in Estonian - Billy Graham's *Rahu Jumalaga* (Peace with God) and Patricia St. John's *Tahad uskuda* (Would You Believe It?) - would be printed abroad.[76] In that period, Billy Graham's *Rahu Jumalaga*, as well as his other books, were widely distributed. *Rahu Jumalaga* was additionally printed in Estonia in 1991. The interdenominational evangelical organisation Campus Crusade for Christ brought into the country a movie about the life of Jesus according to the gospel of Luke. Between 1988 and 1994 a small team of Estonian Baptists showed it approximately 200-250 times in different auditoriums - in churches, schools and public halls.[77] Before Christmas 1990 it was presented in cinemas in Tallinn and Tartu. Also Estonian Television showed the movie several times. This major project gave Estonian

---

[73] Minutes of the UECBCE board, no. 9 (12.11.1990). JKPLis, EEKBLA.

[74] Osvald Tärk, *Kümme käsku* (Tallinn: Eesti Kristlik Kirjastus, 1990), p. 5.

[75] Tarmo Toom, 'Järelsõna', in Osvald Tärk, *Kümme käsku* (Tallinn: Eesti Kristlik Kirjastus, 1990), p. 94.

[76] The UECBCE circular letter, no. 2 (1990). Aastakonverentsid 1989-1991, EEKBLA.

[77] Avo Valk, telephone interview (18.05.2003).

Evangelical Christians-Baptists more publicity, though its mission-effectiveness is difficult to evaluate. No doubt for many people this was the first opportunity to become acquainted with the story of Jesus. The UECBE also commissioned a 30-minute video introducing the principles and practices of ECB churches in Estonia.

Bibles and parts of the Bible, both in Estonian and in Russian, flowed into the country. For example, Estonian Christian Ministries in the USA, led by a Baptist, Endel Meiusi, organised the printing of 20,000 Bibles which arrived in the Tallinn harbour in December 1988.[78] In 1989, the Finnish Bible Society sent to Estonia a gift of 100,000 Bibles. These were distributed through the Estonian Council of Churches. The Bibles were also given to Estonian libraries and educational institutions.[79] The UECBE was entitled to have 10,000 of this consignment. This was far from being the only gift. In spring 1990 Finnish Christians planned to send 15,000 Russian Bibles and New Testaments,[80] though the UECBE had among its membership only approximately 900 Russian speakers. In 1987 permission was given to bring into the Soviet Union 5,000 sets of the William Barclay New Testament Commentary.[81] In 1988-1989 some of these sets became the first full New Testament commentary for Estonian ECB pastors. In 1991 the Finnish Bible Society sent to Estonia a consignment of Children's Bibles *Piibliloold* (Bible Stories),[82] that became popular not only among children but also among adults who were interested in Christianity, but who found the 'real' Bible too difficult to read. The believers' cry for Bibles and New Testaments, which was dramatically expressed in explanatory letters attached to the ECB church reports of 1976,[83] was now abundantly answered.

This is far from being a full account of the literature sent to Estonia in the period 1989-1992. But it shows the huge increase in possibilities for literature distribution. With evangelistic goals, innumerable volumes of the Bible, the New Testament, Billy Graham's books, the American Christian apologist Josh McDowell's *Rohkem kui puussepp* (More Than a Carpenter) and other literature, such as the evangelistic tract *Neli vaimuliku elu tõsiasja* (Four Spiritual Laws), were distributed free of charge or sold for a very reasonable price. Churches and church members were active in 'literature work', and often

---

[78] Minutes of the Presbyters' Council meeting, no. 147 (16.01.1989). JKPLis, EEKBLA.

[79] Rein Ristlaan to the President of the Estonian Council of Churches, Kuno Pajula (05.12.1989). Kirjavahetus usukeskustega vabariigis 1977-1990, UNVA.

[80] Ruudi Leinus to the Commissioner of the CRA (28.03.1990). Kirjavahetus usukeskustega vabariigis 1977-1990, UNVA.

[81] Green, *Crossing the boundaries*, p. 114.

[82] Minutes of the UECBCE board, no. 15 (13.05.1991). JKPLis, EEKBLA.

[83] 'We prayed to both heaven and earth that we would receive New Testaments before we die,' wrote the presbyter in Kohtla-Järve. 'Soon the last Bible we have will be placed on the pulpit,' said the presbyter of Pärnu church. Kaaskirjad koguduste 1976. a. aruandele [Explanatory letters attached to churches' 1976 reports], EEKBLA.

people came to churches to ask for reading material. Literature was seen as a means of preaching the gospel. Baptists believed so much in the written text that they sometimes forgot to build meaningful relationships with the people who received the literature. As early as in 1934 Estonian Baptists had agreed: 'The Baptist movement and mission work through literature are inseparable.'[84] Sixty years later they confirmed this important feature of their identity. However, for those who during Soviet years were alienated from a Christian way of thinking, Baptists were less well prepared to offer help in interpreting Christian texts.

WORK AMONG CHILDREN AND YOUTH

Just as new opportunities in the changing socio-political context pushed Estonian Evangelical Christians-Baptists toward confirming their identity as people who valued theological training and literature, they also developed other ministries. They had been painfully aware for many years that they had been deprived of an organised children's ministry. Now suddenly there was a 'social demand' for this work. Schools asked pastors to teach Bible stories to children, and parents enquired if they could enrol their children in Sunday schools at churches. Estonian ECB children's work grew rapidly after 1988, and became one of the major fields of work at the union level. With young and energetic people involved, this ministry soon became well organised and effective.

Estonia was a step ahead of the wider Soviet Union Baptist scene in its work with children and youth. The foundation *Päikesekiir* (Sunbeam) was established 4 March 1991 in order to coordinate these activities as well as to improve the quality of the magazine for children.[85] The UECBE children's work leaders cooperated with Child Evangelism Fellowship, but defined the aims of their work more broadly. [86] Not only did they focus on leading children to an evangelical conversion experience, but they were also interested in wider aspects of their spiritual, social and personal growth. By the end of 1989 there was organised children's work in 43 Evangelical Christian-Baptist churches in

---

[84] P. Passelmann, 'Ülevaade kirjandusest' [A Survey of Literature], in R. Kaups, ed., *50 aastat apostlite radadel* [50 Years in the Ways of the Apostles] (Keila: E.B.K. Liidu kirjastus, 1934), p. 164.

[85] Einike Pilli and Daily Valk, 'Eesti EKB Liidu haridustöö evangeliseerimise ja eluaegse õppimise dünaamikas' [The UECBE Educational Work in the Dynamics of Evangelism and Lifelong Learning], in Toivo Pilli, ed., *Teekond teisenevas ajas: peatükke Eesti vabakoguduste ajaloost* [A Journey in Changing Time: Chapters from the History of Estonian Free Churches] (Tartu: Kõrgem Usuteaduslik Seminar ja Sõnasepp OÜ, 2005), pp. 55-56.

[86] Daily Valk, 'Eesti Evangeeliumi Kristlaste ja Baptistide Koguduste Liidu laste- ja noortetöö ülevaade' [A Survey of Children's and Youth Work in the Union of Evangelical Christian-Baptist Churches in Estonia], course paper (Tartu: Kõrgem Usuteaduslik Seminar, 2003), p. 29.

Estonia.[87] According to the Commissioner of CRA's report, probably referring to the year 1989, there were 1602 children involved in the UECBE Sunday school work.[88] However, this facet of church life was expanding rapidly. In 1991 Sunday schools were being held in 62 ECB churches bringing together 4693 children.[89] The 7,000 copies of the children's magazine *Päikesekiir* proved to be too few,[90] as many copies were distributed outside the churches.

There was an urgent need for Sunday school teachers in churches. Also, state schools began to ask churches if suitable lay persons, not only pastors, were available to teach basic Christian knowledge – either in literature or in history classes. From 1990 to 1991, the Theological Seminary organised a special training programme that brought together 150-170 lay persons, both Estonian and Russian-speaking, who were interested in developing their knowledge and skills for youth and children's work.[91] This was probably the largest training course which the seminary ever organised. Some Estonians participated in short-term children's and youth work training courses in Finland and in Sweden. In 1991 there were 34 Sunday school teachers in the UECBE who had received special training to work both in churches and as Religious Education teachers in public schools.[92]

In addition to the growing children's ministry, some traditions in youth work, such as Bible Days, a major annual meeting point for ECB youth all over the country, proved to be vital – and were successfully continued. In May 1990, the twelfth of the Bible Days of the ECB took place. The *leitmotif* of this event expressed the sentiments of the time: 'The time has come. The Kingdom of God is near. Repent and believe the good news.' (Mark 1: 15) Most responsive to this call in local churches were youth. Many, actually the majority, of the people who were baptised and joined the ECB churches in these years were young. However, the most significant growth in activity, both statistically and structurally, happened in children's work.[93] In many churches, children's choirs were formed. Sometimes Sunday school functioned as a means of pre-evangelism: it was the first step and a good reason for the parents to come to church. Traditional Baptist concerns for children were being refashioned and expanded.

---

[87] Minutes of the Presbyters' Council meeting, no. 156 (04.12.1989). JKPLis, EEKBLA.

[88] The same report demonstrates that Lutherans had 3568 children in their Sunday schools, Orthodox 46, Seventh Day Adventists 251, and Methodists 157. Õiend konfessionaalsete pühapäevakoolide koha [An explanatory letter about confessional Sunday schools] (1989?). Kirjavahetus usukeskustega vabariigis 1977-1990, UNVA.

[89] Robert Võsu, 'Eesti EKB Liidu tegevusest 1991. a.' [About the Activities of the UECBE in 1991], *Teekäija*, no. 10 (1992), p. 17.

[90] Minutes of the UECBCE board, no. 2 (12.02.1990). JKPLis, EEKBLA.

[91] The UECBCE circular letter, no. 2 (1990). Aastakonverentsid 1989-1991, EEKBLA.

[92] Minutes of the UECBCE annual conference (23.11.1991). Aastakonverentsid 1989-1991, EEKBLA.

[93] The UECBCE circular letter, no. 2 (1990). Aastakonverentsid 1989-1991, EEKBLA.

PROCLAIMING THE WORD

After 1988 the proclaiming of the Word 'stepped outside' of the church buildings. Baptists made attempts to plant new churches and to revive the old ones. By 1991 they were also actively contributing to Christian programmes on the State Radio and Television.[94] It should also be mentioned that in the situation of the 'singing revolution', the Estonian musical traditions were used creatively by Baptists.[95] Music occupied an important role in evangelism. In 1990 there were 76 choirs with a total of 1,400 singers in the churches of UECBE. Also, visiting choirs from the USA, Canada, Finland, Norway and Sweden made successful tours in Estonia.[96] The union's representative choir, Gloria, with singers from more than ten different ECB churches, [97] began a successful ministry. Gloria gave one of its first public concerts in the seaside town of Haapsalu, in the western part of Estonia, in March 1988.[98] The programme included Estonian classical spiritual music by C. Kreek, R. Tobias, and others. As was typical of this time, the programme also included a poetry recital. Use of Estonian music and poetry showed ECB efforts to speak the same 'language' as the audience, to identify with Estonian cultural and ethnic consciousness.

Already at the dawn of *perestroika* in 1985, Dimitri Lipping, the leader of the 'evangelism sector' of the UECBE, a kind of informal department with the task of coordinating evangelistic work, tried to give such work a more systematic pattern. He set a number of goals: preparing a schedule of 'revival weeks' covering Estonian ECB churches, collecting suggestions from local churches, searching for and finding people who had a calling to evangelistic work, and recruiting co-workers for the 'evangelism sector'.[99] However, carrying out the vision for dynamic evangelism proved to be harder than expected. In 1988, the 'evangelism sector' prepared a report with numerous suggestions for improving evangelism in the UECBE.[100] The Presbyters' Council, however, critically remarked that the report paid more attention to negative than to positive evidence, and that the solution for improving evangelism efforts did not lie in increasing formal-administrative measures but rather in motivating and helping local churches to do mission in their own

---

[94] Minutes of the UECBCE annual conference (23.11.1991). Aastakonverentsid 1989-1991, EEKBLA.

[95] See Steven James Pierson, 'We Sang Ourselves Free: Developmental Uses of Music among Estonian Christians from Repression to Independence', PhD dissertation (Deerfield, Illinois: Trinity International University, 1998).

[96] A report of the UECBCE churches of 1990. Aastakonverentsid 1989-1991, EEKBLA.

[97] Minutes of the Presbyters' Council meeting, no. 138 (14.02.1988). JKPLis, EEKBLA.

[98] Minutes of the Presbyters' Council meeting, no. 139 (14.03.1988). JKPLis, EEKBLA.

[99] Minutes of the Presbyters' Council meeting, no. 115 (14.10.1985). JKP, EEKBLA.

[100] Evangeelsest tööst Maarjamaal [About Evangelistic Work in the Land of Mary] (1988). EEKBLA.

context.[101] Dimitri Lipping gained the impression that his suggestions were not taken seriously as a basis for further action.[102]

Obviously, there was a deeper conflict between these two evangelistic strategies: Lipping emphasised the need to increase the union's responsibility in the area of evangelism as well as creating formal structures and engaging in planning, whereas the majority of the Presbyters' Council believed that the responsibility for evangelism was at the local church level, and the union structures could only offer advice, training and literature.[103] 'Every church has to find its own method for evangelistic work,' said Jüri Puusaag, presbyter of Tallinn 'Kalju' Baptist Church. In his church, there was an increase in the number of people who came from non-Christian backgrounds and joined the church.[104] However, the 'opening doors' in Estonian society and 'opening borders' between the small republic and the wider world let in a wave of 'major evangelistic events' which in the long run tended to undermine the sense of responsibility for evangelism in both the local churches and the union itself.

In 1988 a booming development of massive evangelistic campaigns began, mostly organised by foreign mission organisations with preachers from abroad, both from countries in Europe and in America. Estonian ECB believers were actively involved.[105] There was unanimous enthusiasm about the fact that the Gospel was preached in stadiums, concert halls and other public places. But unfortunately, this tendency also took the focus away from the local context and from local responsibility. It was somebody else who was doing the mission; it was somebody else's project. Paradoxically, it was not only the years of socialist state pressure that endangered the evangelistic identity of the Estonian Baptists, but also the newly-available help from fellow Christians. If these Christians from other places were not sensitive to the local context this insensitivity posed problems.

One of the first massive evangelistic events took place in the Linnahall (City Hall), a major concert facility in Tallinn, on 24 July 1988.[106] It was organised with substantial help from Russian-speaking Pentecostals, and led by Josif Bondarenko, the leader of an independent church in Riga. Bondarenko was able to mobilise many believers from the Baltics and Ukraine, who came to

---

[101] Minutes of the Presbyters' Council meeting, no. 141 (16.05.1988). JKPLis, EEKBLA.

[102] Dimitri Lipping, oral information (21.03.2003).

[103] See also chapter 8 for further discussion on evangelism.

[104] Jüri Puusaag, oral information (08.05.2003); Jüri Puusaag, private letter (16.08.2002).

[105] Report of the Commissioner of the CRA of the year 1989 (13.02.1990). AÜ1971-1990, UNVA.

[106] According to Arpad Arder, it was the city council of Tallinn that offered this prestigious concert and sports hall for this event. The hall still bore the name of V. I. Lenin. See Arpad Arder, *Kus on Arpadi kuningas?* [Where is Arpad's King?] (Tallinn: [Logos,] 1992), p. 126.

attend. Approximately 7,000 people, both Russian and Estonian-speaking, took part in the 4-hour service. Among the speakers was the ECB pastor, Arpad Arder, from Estonia, as well as a German-Russian evangelist, Viktor Hamm, from Germany. Hamm's preaching in fluent Russian 'touched both mind and heart'.[107]Approximately 200-300 persons responded to the altar call.[108] The event was certainly successful, though hastily organised. Definitely, despite its success, it showed that when the initiators of evangelistic events came from outside of Estonia, there was an urgent need for better cooperation with local churches and with the UECBE.

In fact the lack of coordination and the tendency to seek immediate statistical results while ignoring the need to contextualise the message and to lead the converts to a life of discipleship in the local church constituted, together, a general problem during these years. A popular Christian music band Sõnajalg (Fern) together with Allan Laur, then the pastor of the Estonian Pentecostal Church in Toronto, organised in December 1989 a concert tour, promising that local churches would offer Christian literature later. Many ECB churches were quickly in trouble, as people came to ask for literature that had not yet arrived at the churches. 'Not keeping promises will compromise the evangelical message,' was the conclusion of the ECB leadership.[109]

But a more serious test was still to come. This was the issue of proselytism, to use the term that has become widely used in the Eastern European mission context.[110] In the case of Estonia, probably the most acute tension emerged between the UECBE and new, active free church movements. In July-August 1990, an Estonian Christian Seminar (Eesti Kristlik Seminar) was organised in Tallinn and Saaremaa Island in the western part of Estonia. The initiative came from three pastors, Märt Vähi, Harry Leesment and Allan Laur, who were serving Estonian Pentecostal churches in Australia and Canada.[111] In the following year this short-term training project was repeated. By spring 1991 it was clear that the training project served church planting goals: there was a plan to plant new Pentecostal churches in different parts of Estonia. The leaders of this mission project admitted that it was a mistake not to have consulted the UECBE before.[112] There were members of ECB churches who were attracted by the lively worship style, emotional experiences and

---

[107] Arder, *Kus on Arpadi kuningas?*, p. 127.

[108] Minutes of the Presbyters' Council meeting, no. 143 (12.09.1988). JKPLis, EEKBLA.

[109] Minutes of the UECBCE board, no. 1 (08.01.1990). JKPLis, EEKBLA.

[110] See Miroslav Volf, 'Fishing in the Neighbor's Pond: Mission and Proselytism as Challenge to Theology and Church Life in Eastern Europe', *Religion in Eastern Europe*, vol. XVI, no. 1 (February 1996), pp. 34-47; John Witte and Michael Bourdeaux, eds., *Proselytism and Orthodoxy in Russia. The New War for Souls* (Maryknoll, New York: Orbis Books, 1999).

[111] Minutes of the UECBCE board, no. 7 (17.09.1990). JKP, EEKBLA.

[112] Minutes of the UECBCE board, no. 15 (13.05.1991). JKPLis, EEKBLA.

charismatic theology of this active form of Evangelicalism and joined the new Pentecostal body that introduced itself as the Estonian Christian Church (Est. 'Eesti Kristlik Kirik').[113] Later, it became registered officially as the Estonian Christian Pentecostal Church (Est. 'Eesti Kristlik Nelipühi Kirik').[114]

The UECBE, at least officially, had taken a cautiously friendly approach toward this movement, trying to avoid confrontation.[115] It was stated, though, that the working methods of this new movement were foreign to Baptist churches – probably referring to 'dancing' elements in worship. Critical remarks – at times far from justified – could not be avoided from both sides during this period, with one movement trying to establish its role and find its identity, and another long-established movement trying to defend its traditional position. Mark Elliott and Anita Deyneka have described two views present in Protestant mission efforts in the former Soviet Union areas: one emphasises the faithfulness of Soviet Evangelicals, whereas another criticises their cultural isolation, authoritarian leadership, and inability to absorb new converts. Those supporting the latter opinion tend to see the solution in planting new churches.[116] This was exactly the case in the Estonian Pentecostal expansion at the beginning of the 1990s.

There were other charismatic movements, too, that posed new challenges to Estonian Baptists. New independent charismatic churches emerged. The Word of Life charismatic movement gained momentum after 1988, being inspired by Ulf Ekman's example in Uppsala, Sweden. In the early phases of this movement, many members requested permission to emigrate,[117] believing that apocalyptic tribulations would come over Estonia. In addition, so called 'prosperity theology' in general, and (from America) Kenneth Hagin's and Kenneth Copeland's books in particular, played an important role in forming the spirituality of these groups. Some of these ideas, probably arriving via Finland, had already influenced the youth in Tallinn Oleviste Church in the mid-1980s.[118] As later developments showed, there were other ECB churches that absorbed some of the theological ideas and practices of the new charismatics and Pentecostals. The ECB union, that had been rather uniform since the 1960s, was moving towards growing diversity in worship style and spirituality. Even the Effataa-movement of the 1970s and early 1980s was not such a challenge to the UECBE identity, partly because the state limited its influence with outward measures. Now the UECBE faced the inevitable reality.

---

[113] Minutes of the UECBCE board, no. 20 (09.12.1991). JKPLis, EEKBLA.

[114] Ilmo Au and Ringo Ringvee, *Kirikud ja kogudused Eestis* [Churches and Congregations in Estonia] (Tallinn: Ilo, 2000), p. 54.

[115] Minutes of the UECBCE board, no. 7 (17.09.1990). JKPLis, EEKBLA.

[116] Mark Elliott and Anita Deyneka, 'Protestant Missionaries in the Former Soviet Union', in Witte and Bourdeaux, eds., *Proselytism and Orthodoxy in Russia*, p. 207.

[117] Ramet, 'Religious Policy', p. 46.

[118] Minutes of the Presbyters' Council meeting, no. 116 (11.11.1985). JKP, EEKBLA.

Its identity and role as the biggest free church in Estonia was questioned by free church movements of the same kin.

However, there were influences from abroad that were easier to accept and deal with since they represented more central evangelical thinking. In August 1990 the Operation Mobilisation mission ship Logos II was in Tallinn harbour for two and a half weeks. Lectures, evangelistic events, a Christian bookstore and free medical help drew thousands of people to the ship. In the same year, the Estonian branch of Youth with a Mission was officially registered. Also, Campus Crusade for Christ, which had secretly organised some training in Estonia as early as 1986,[119] became more active. In March 1988 Campus Crusade president Bill Bright preached in Tallinn and met with the Estonian ECB leadership.[120]

There was also a local initiative for cooperation in evangelism and mission. On 18-19 September 1991 an evangelism conference with more than 200 delegates from different churches took place. This ecumenical initiative, marking the first stage in the work of the Estonian Evangelical Alliance in this period, came to serve as a constant challenge to Estonian churches to cooperate in mission work.[121] Though several ECB pastors became active in the Estonian Evangelical Alliance, warning notes were also expressed: the Alliance would involve many of the best pastors and the union's work would become more fragmented.[122] Estonian Baptists were also active in the Estonian Council of Churches, founded in the Kuremäe convent 16 February 1989.[123] The motive for this type of cooperation for Baptists was probably mainly practical, not growing out of deep ecumenical convictions. Baptists had good relationships at the leadership level with other traditional churches in Estonia, but the growing activities of other churches of all kinds caused not only joy because of the spreading of God's Kingdom, but also fear that ECB churches could lose their distinctive features. While Estonian Baptists affirmed evangelism as one of their main characteristics, in a new situation of 'opening doors' the forms and goals of the evangelistic activity undertaken by Baptists and other evangelicals raised new questions.

---

[119] Minutes of the Presbyters' Council meeting, no. 126 (11.11.1986). JKP, EEKBLA.
[120] Minutes of the Presbyters' Council meeting, no. 139 (14.03.1988). JKPLis, EEKBLA.
[121] Ingmar Kurg, 'Kristlikud organisatsioonid ja oikumeeniline suhtlemine Eestis' [Christian Organisations and Ecumenical Interaction in Estonia], in *Evangeelne kuulutus ja antievangeelne maailm. Aastaraamat 2001* [Evangelical Message and Anti-Evangelical World. Yearbook 2001] (Tartu: Eesti Evangeelne Allianss, 2002), p. 40.
[122] Minutes of the UECBCE board, no. 14 (15.04.1991). JKPLis, EEKBLA.
[123] Vello Salo, *Riik ja kirikud 1940-1991* (Brampton, Ontario: Maarjamaa, 2000), p. 41.

SOCIAL WORK

Estonian Evangelical Christians-Baptists – like the wider community of evangelicals – viewed commitment to evangelism as one of their core features. Using David Bebbington's words about British evangelicals: 'Preaching the Gospel was the chief method of winning converts.'[124] It took some time – and inspiration from abroad – before Estonian Baptists began to see the need and the opportunities for social work. Senior Presbyter Ülo Meriloo stated on 14 October 1988, after arriving back from Moscow: 'In the field of spiritual work, *perestroika* has advanced much further in Moscow and in other parts of the Soviet Union than with us. They [Russian Baptists] work in orphanages, hospitals and even in prisons. ... Besides social care, the proclamation of the gospel takes place.'[125] This remark characterises well the new situation. During the Soviet years, Estonian ECB identity had grown more toward a theological, ethical and congregational self-understanding, but had become weaker in its social dimension. Practical help was offered, but mostly to fellow Christians. However, it was not only because of external factors that Estonian Baptists were relatively slow to discover the social ministries which could reach outside church walls. It was also a matter of their values and self-understanding. Even before the Second World War, Estonian Baptists were only modestly involved in social work; Estonian Methodists had made much more effective attempts in this field.[126]

However, by the end of 1989 there were some initiatives, though often short term, in the field of social work and prison ministry in particular. On the initiative of the Russian speaking Baptists of Tallinn, groups of believers began to visit Iru Elderly Peoples' Home, in the neighbourhood of the Estonian capital. They helped to feed, wash and take care of the elderly people who were living in this home. In November a group of ECB Christians, led by Arpad Arder, visited a prison in Harku.[127]

The economic situation in Estonia was deteriorating rapidly in the years 1990-1991. The Estonian ECB union, following the pattern of helping those who belonged to the wider ECB community, established a central fund for pastors in need. In 1991 there were 10 pastors who received monthly support of 2,000 roubles from this fund.[128] Estonian Baptist partners abroad, first and

---

[124] David Bebbington, *Evangelicalism in Modern Britain. A History from the 1730s to the 1980s* (Grand Rapids, Michigan: Baker Book House, 1992), p. 5.

[125] Minutes of the Presbyters' Council meeting, no. 144 (14.11.1988), JKPLis, EEKBLA.

[126] S.T. Kimbrough, ed., *Methodism in Russia and the Baltic States: History and Renewal* (Nashville, Tennessee: Abingdon Press, 1995), p. 131.

[127] Minutes of the Presbyters' Council meeting, no. 156 (04.12.1989). JKPLis, EEKBLA.

[128] A report at the UECBE annual conferene of 1991. Aastakonverentsid 1989-1991, EEKBLA.

foremost in Finland, Sweden and Germany, responded to the situation of economic crisis by sending truck-loads of second-hand clothes and furniture, as well as food. Many local churches found themselves suddenly in a position of being humanitarian aid agencies. In order to coordinate the influx of humanitarian aid, the Union Board as it was now called – formerly the Presbyters' Council – founded a new 'department', the 'social work sector', consisting in practice of one person, who soon realised that the work load was unsustainable.[129] A committee was organised to solve the situation. As a result, by September 1991 the charitable foundation Sõbra Käsi (A Friend's Hand) was registered with the state authorities.[130] In Russia, Christian charity organisations had begun to emerge earlier, and 'charity' or 'mercy' (Russian 'miloserdye') had already become a 'buzz-word' by 1988-1989.[131]

As a great deal of humanitarian aid during these years was channelled through the churches, it offered an opportunity to meet new people and establish contacts with different organisations, such as schools, orphanages, hospitals, as well as with families in need. In spite of this, social work was seen as secondary by most of the churches; the preaching of the gospel and leading people to conversion was the priority. Social work was understood largely as a means for 'saving souls'. Was it the continuing effect of Soviet external pressures which deprived churches of opportunities to work in wider society? Or was it a dichotomy in Baptist anthropology, the preferring of 'soul' to 'body', which prevented them developing a more holistic approach to Christian service? Probably both factors had their effect. When the direct gifts from abroad ceased, social work faded out of the picture in most of the local churches. However, Sõbra Käsi – primarily based on support from abroad – continued to work, gradually decreasing its involvement in food projects and increasing its interest in supporting street children and orphans.

Estonian Baptist attempts to become involved in social ministry were limited by their understanding of themselves as an evangelical group whose main mission was to lead people to spiritual conversion. The concept of 'winning souls' rather than 'redeeming bodies'[132] had continued to be a part of Estonian ECB self-perception all through the Soviet years. However, the outward situation, with its obvious needs, at the beginning of the 1990s 'forced' them to become more involved in social ministries, and the foundation Sõbra Käsi was one of the results of this changing social context.

---

[129] Minutes of the UECBCE board, no. 11 (14.01.1991). JKPLis, EEKBLA.
[130] Minutes of the UECBCE board, no. 17 (16.09.1991). JKPLis, EEKBLA.
[131] Michael Bourdeaux, 'The Quality of Mercy: A Once-only Opportunity', in Witte and Bourdeaux, eds., *Proselytism and Orthodoxy in Russia*, p. 189.
[132] For theological discussion about soul-body dualism, see Nancey Murphy, *Theology in a Postmodern Age* (Prague: IBTS, 2003), pp. 24-58.

ORGANISATIONAL CHANGES AND CHALLENGES

New opportunities for Christian work and changes in society made it clear to ECB leaders that there was a need to make some rearrangements in the union's organisational structures. Examples of church administration models used in the West now became better known in Estonia. In addition to this, the general atmosphere of national awakening inspired Estonian Baptists to take steps toward independent decision-making and moved them away from the AUCECB.

The conference of the UECBE which took place in Tallinn from 8-10 December 1989 was of special importance both from the organisational and identity points of view. A unanimous decision of the delegates brought about the formation of an independent union – The Union of Evangelical Christian-Baptist Churches of Estonia – which separated from the AUCECB. 'We must have the possibility to decide the questions regarding the work of our churches here in Estonia; this would give us broader opportunities for spiritual work and allow us to solve emerging questions more quickly,' was the message of Deputy Senior Presbyter Joosep Tammo.[133] In spite of some separatist ideas among Russian speaking Baptists in Estonia,[134] Russian ECB churches such as those of Narva, Tallinn, Valga and Sillamäe joined the new 'Estonian' union.[135] The union continued as a multinational fellowship and was not divided along the lines of nationality.

The newly formed Union Board, the counterpart of the former Presbyters' Council, was trusted to deal with questions that might arise with the AUCECB regarding 'the declaration of the sovereignty of the Union of ECB in Estonia'. It was emphasised that the relationship with the AUCECB would remain based on 'the principles of brotherly love and equality'.[136] In reality, very soon the Estonians' eyes turned to the West, and for the next decade they were more concerned to establish and re-establish contacts with their Western partners than to continue and deepen their cooperation with the East. Sister-church projects developed with Baptist and Free Churches in Finland, Sweden, and Germany, and later with Texas Baptists in the USA, but these seldom grew to the level of long-term partnership and cooperation. Too often Estonians were content with the role of thankfully but passively receiving help. Lars Leven, a pastor of the Swedish Mission Covenant Church, said in 1993 that sister church relationships might begin with practical aid, making self-help possible, but needed to move toward mutual fellowship and learning, including

---

[133] Minutes of the UECBE conference (09.12.1989). Aastakonverentsid 1989-1991, EEKBLA.

[134] Minutes of the Presbyters' Council meeting, no. 127 (15.12.1986). JKP, EEKBLA.

[135] List of the UECBCE founding members (09.12.1989). Aastakonverentsid 1989-1991, EEKBLA.

[136] Declaration of the UECBE (09.12.1989). Aastakonverentsid 1989-1991, EEKBLA.

theologically, from each other.[137] These more mature relationships did not develop in most cases.

The UECBE Statutes of 1989 emphasised that the local churches joined the union on a voluntary basis and 'maintained their independence'.[138] This principle was one that had been violated during the Soviet years. Now this value was stressed again. However, the darker side of the Baptist principle of 'independence' and 'autonomy' was that this at times also involved a tendency toward separatism and the 'collective egoism' of a local church.[139] Commitment to unity in a situation of many scattering forces proved to be important. Contrary to the experience in Russia and Ukraine, in Estonia the different historical churches that had been brought together to form the UECBE remained in the same union after the end of communism, with some rare exceptions.[140] Different free church identities which were merged forcefully in 1945, had amalgamated and now held together around common values: belief in God's transforming work in individuals and an emphasis on evangelism.

The union's wider links were with Baptists rather than with any other denominational stream. After Estonia became politically free, the UECBE was received into full membership of the European Baptist Federation (EBF) on 25 September 1991 in Varna, Bulgaria,[141] together with Georgian, Latvian and Lebanese Baptists as well as the Hungarian Baptists in Romania.[142] The UECBE membership in the Baptist World Alliance was also re-established in 1991.[143] Relationships with the 'Moscow brotherhood' needed further clarification. A document of 3 June 1991 stated that 'all prayer houses located in the territory of Estonia belong to the Union of ECB Churches in Estonia', and 'the Union of ECB in SSSR does not have any claim on the church buildings or property of ECB churches in Estonia'.[144] With this official agreement, Estonian ECB leaders avoided any – at least theoretically possible – confusion and conflict about property, an issue that has been one aspect of post-

---

[137] Lars Leven, 'Näide kasvavast kogudusest Rootsis' [An Example of a Growing Church in Sweden], *Teekäija* (September 1993), p. 5.

[138] Eesti Evangeelsete Kristlaste-Baptistide Koguduste Liidu Põhikiri [Statutes of the Union of Evangelical Christian-Baptist Churches of Estonia] (09.12.1989). EEKBLA.

[139] On autonomy and denominational commitment see Nigel G. Wright, *New Baptists, New Agenda* (Carlisle: Paternoster Press, 2002), pp. 46-63.

[140] For example, the former Pentecostal church 'Eelim' in Tallinn has separated from the union.

[141] Peter Barber and Karl Heinz Walter to the UECBCE (25.09.1991). Aastakonverentsid 1989-1991, EEKBLA.

[142] Crabb, comp. and ed., *Our Favourite Memories*, p. 55.

[143] A report at the UECBCE annual conferece of 1991. Aastakonverentsid 1989-1991, EEKBLA.

[144] Udostoverenije, no. 56 (03.06.1991), EEKBLA. The document was signed by the Chairman of the Union of ECB of SSR G. Komendant, and by Vice-Chairmans A. Firisjuk, N. Kolesnikov and A. Bychkov.

communist Orthodox Church life and has caused conflict in Estonia since the 1990s.

There were also patterns for more democratic leadership that needed clarification. While the highest structure of the union was the annual conference, the leader of the union – now called President – still had considerable authority in spiritual, administrative and financial matters. The General Secretary was defined as the President's deputy, taking over leadership in the latter's absence. The General Secretary's duty was also to coordinate the work of the departments and to keep up communication with the member churches.[145] Perhaps the powerful role of the President when compared to the General Secretary reflected the continuing influence of the Soviet period, when the Senior Presbyter was the key person who had a great deal of information and actual power concentrated in his hands. However, the UECBE Statutes of 1989 officially gave this guiding and controlling role to the board. The board had right to confirm agreements, to oversee the activities of the local churches and departments of the union, and, if necessary, to make a proposal to the annual conference for deposing the President or General Secretary.

All through these turbulent years, Ülo Meriloo (born 13 February 1926) was the leader of the UECBE. He was elected the Senior Presbyter at the conference on 23 February 1985,[146] with Mikhail Zhidkov, the deputy chairman of the AUCECB present. Meriloo came from a pietistic background that included a variety of spiritual influences. In 1945 both his parents joined the Pentecostal church that was soon to merge into the ECB structures. He himself joined the Tapa Baptist Church in 1944. Later, his life became more closely related to Tallinn Oleviste Church, where he was ordained as a pastor on 28 November 1971.[147] With personal experience of cooperation with different free church movements – Evangelical Christians, Baptists and Pentecostals, and even with Herrnhut Brethren – Meriloo was well prepared to lead the Tallinn Oleviste Church, and later the UECBE, which had brought together and continued to embrace diverse free church traditions and spiritualities. Meriloo had to lead the union through a time in which there were fresh questions about identity.

In the position of Senior Presbyter, Meriloo supported the idea of arranging the work of the union according to nine regions, one or two members of the Presbyters' Council being responsible for each region. Regional meetings of church leaders and preachers were not absolutely new to the union. However, in the later 1980s these became a well established part of the organisational pattern of the UECBE. Meriloo also suggested that previously

---

[145] Eesti Evangeelsete Kristlaste-Baptistide Koguduste Liidu Põhikiri (09.12.1989). EEKBLA.

[146] Minutes of the UECBE conference (23.02.1985). JKP, EEKBLA.

[147] Ülo Meriloo, *Ränduri päevik* [A Diary of a Pilgrim] (Tallinn, 2001), pp. 14, 26, 37, 82.

informal departments should be rearranged into eight 'sectors', or more formal departments, each covering a certain area of responsibility.[148] These were the first steps toward shaping the life of the union according to more formal patterns. Meriloo, having been educated as an engineer, invested considerable time and energy in church building projects. With his initiative and advice, building projects in Ridala (1988) and Kuressaare (1993) were undertaken, to mention only two. While Robert Võsu as a Senior Presbyter can be characterised as an educator and recruiter of new church leaders, Meriloo's special gift was as an organizer and builder.

Meriloo's period of serving as Senior Presbyter, and later as President of the union, was characterised by rapid changes; new challenges demanded that the union quickly respond and react. Meriloo, his leadership model shaped by the Soviet period, was cautious, avoiding taking hasty steps. This evoked some criticism from more active, often younger leaders. In 1987, while admitting that the Senior Presbyter had 'honestly and faithfully' stood for the union's interests, the Presbyters' Council members expressed the need for more open discussions.[149] Reading between the lines of the minutes, one can find a deeper expectation: the expectation of a more collective type of leadership. However, it was the Soviet reality which had made the Senior Presbyter keep a great deal of information and also his emotions to himself. The Soviet context not only shaped Baptist practice, it also influenced personalities, and their leadership style.

Statistically, the UECBE reached a low point at the end of the 1980s. During the Soviet years the membership numbers had been dropping drastically. Whereas in 1980 there were 6,822 members in the UECBE,[150] at the beginning of 1990 there were 5,793 members.[151] Only during 1990 was it possible to turn the decline into modest growth, so that on 31 December 1990 there were 5,938 members in Estonian ECB churches. At the beginning of 1991, there were 52 presbyters, now usually called pastors. In addition there were 23 deputy pastors. Of the total of 75 pastors, approximately one third, 24 pastors, were working full time for the churches.[152]

In spite of some statistical growth after 1990 and significant expansion of Baptist activities, there was still a need for a far-reaching vision for the Estonian ECB union. This need was expressed at the conference in 1989:

[148] The 'sectors' covered the following areas: ministers' issues, evangelism, youth work, music, literature, economic issues, recording and reproduction of materials, theological studies and training.
[149] Minutes of the Presbyters' Council meeting, no. 136 (12.12.1987). JKP, EEKBLA.
[150] The UECBE statistical report 1980. The UECBE statistical reports 1964-1990, EEKBLA.
[151] The UECBE statistical reports 1989, 1990. The UECBE statistical reports 1964-1990, EEKBLA.
[152] Circular letter, no. 1 (1991). Eesti EKB koguduste 1990. a. aruanne [Report of the Estonian ECB churches of 1990]. Aastakonverentsid 1989-1991, EEKBLA.

'Within a month the new leadership should present their conceptual view for our spiritual situation and programmatic guidelines for future actions.'[153] However, rapid changes in the secular and religious spheres, which required immediate response, left little time for strategic planning. Both the local churches and the union found themselves in a situation of dealing constantly with 'emergency issues'. In 1991 the President of the union had to admit that alongside many areas of development within Estonian Baptist life there were considerable inadequacies; among these were weak cooperation with friendly unions and the minimal influence of ECB congregations in society.[154] The conference of 1991 stated that there was a need to prepare and publish a document expressing the spiritual principles of the union.[155] This proved to be more difficult and longer project than was expected. Only in 1998, after a series of discussions, was a theological summary, expressing the basic beliefs of Estonian Evangelical Christians-Baptists in the changed context, published.[156] Forging a new Baptist identity for a dramatically changed context was a huge challenge.

CONCLUSION

Estonian Evangelical Christians-Baptists found themselves in the midst of unprecedented changes at the end of the 1980s. The years 1985-1991 were years of opening doors. External restrictions were gradually removed, and now it was the growing freedom and the new opportunities for Christian work that demanded a response. Evangelical Christians-Baptists responded with a large-scale investment of energy into different activities such as theological education, publishing efforts, literature distribution and children's ministries. All these activities were seen as opportunities for evangelism. Baptist involvement in social work was a project 'borrowed from abroad' rather than growing out of their inner convictions. In political life, their voice was only modestly heard. Political activity did not fit into their 'self-portrait' – due to their pietistic-individualistic concept of faith as well as due to the experience of external pressures of Soviet times. Baptists were also aware of their limitations: lack of human resources and uncertain vision. This was also in part the heritage of the Soviet years; though there was joy about new opportunities, there was also an inclination to look back to past ideas and hesitance to innovate.

Estonian Baptists also realised that new religious movements and

---

[153] Minutes of the UECBE conference (09.12.1989). Aastakonverentsid 1989-1991, EEKBLA.

[154] Minutes of the UECBCE conference (23.11.1991). Aastakonverentsid 1989-1991, EEKBLA.

[155] Ibid.

[156] *Piibli õpetus Eesti Evangeeliumi Kristlaste ja Baptistide Koguduste Liidu kogudustes* [Biblical Teaching in the UECBCE Churches] (Tallinn: Eesti EKB Liit, 1998).

enthusiastic charismatic churches had a potential to cause divisiveness. Influences from abroad posed a challenge to Baptists to re-interpret their self-understanding and identity. However, not much theological reflection of a systematic kind can be found during these years. An important step at the organisational level was taken in 1989 when an independent Estonian union was formed and the leadership structures were revised. Beginning in August 1991, official relationships were established with the European Baptist Federation and the Baptist World Alliance. However, the UECBE continued to hold together the historical free church traditions which were merged into the union in 1945, evidence that in the Soviet 'melting pot' a more integrated ECB self-understanding had emerged. This self-understanding centred around an experience of 'new birth' which qualified a person to be a member of a bible-believing community of believers and which involved a commitment to passing on the message of new birth and offering a new way of life to others. These major themes in Estonian ECB life – the local church, the Bible, mission and sanctification – will be considered in depth in the second part of this volume.

PART TWO

Internal Dynamics of Identity

CHAPTER 6

Ecclesiological Perspectives:
Unity Out of Diversity

The first part of this study has considered the impact of external pressures on Estonian Baptist identity. But internal factors were also crucial. Joosep Tammo, the president of the Union of Evangelical Christians-Baptists of Estonia from 1992 to 1998, stated in 1989 that for the Estonian ECB churches the central value had always been a personal relationship with God. He added that this important feature of the ECB self-understanding had two expressions among believers: some had emphasised their personal relationship with Jesus Christ, and others an experience of the Holy Spirit.[1] Taking into account the diverse historical background of the UECBE, this observation is not surprising. Nevertheless, Tammo accurately defined the common starting point for both a personal faith journey and for an understanding of who should belong to a church community. This starting point was a personal faith experience, understood in relational rather than intellectual terms. 'How is your relationship with God?' This was a question that was often voiced in sermons and conversations during the Soviet times. The presbyter Osvald Tärk emphasised: 'Our spiritual life has to begin with regeneration. There is no other way into the Kingdom of God.'[2] However, Tammo was also correct in noting that the different Estonian free church traditions which formed the union in 1945 did not agree in every aspect of their theology and practice. One area in which there were major differences was ecclesiology, and in this chapter attention will be paid to the ecclesiological developments within the UECBE from the perspective of the concepts of church membership, baptism and the Lord's Supper. During the Soviet years, the understanding of the church became more uniform in the UECBE churches, and the Baptist ecclesiological tradition came to prevail over the Evangelical Christian approach. In worship, Pentecostal and Revivalist Free Church elements gradually lost their energy, though there were some exceptions. The identity of the churches was being shaped not only by external factors but also by internal developments.

---

[1] Joosep Tammo, *Kesköö on päeva algus* [At Midnight the Day Begins] (Tallinn: Eesti EKB Liit, 1998), p. 31.
[2] O[svald] T[ärk], *Teeviit* [Guidepost], typewritten manuscript, (n. p., n. d.), p. 18. KUSA.

PERSONAL CONVERSION AND THE BELIEVERS' CHURCH

In 1945, Johannes Lipstok, then still the president of the Estonian Baptist Union, expressed the position of Estonian free churches in the evangelical tradition – Pentecostals, Evangelical Christians, Baptists and Revivalist Free Church believers – about who should be in church membership: 'A church should consist of persons, who voluntarily and personally have received the teaching of Christ, have undergone a religious experience and actually show with their life a serious endeavour to live according to Christ's teaching.'[3] In the same passage, Lipstok does not hesitate to say that during the New Testament times only those were considered Christians who had personally professed faith.[4]

The conversion experience, and the radical, sometimes dramatic, spiritual transformation of 'becoming a child of God', is spoken of as an essential ingredient of ECB identity in the writings of the representatives of all the Estonian free church traditions which are analysed in this study.[5] Aleksander Sildos, an outstanding figure in the Evangelical Christian tradition, described his conversion during a Moravian (Herrnhut movement) prayer meeting, after a sudden experience of his sinfulness, as 'making a covenant with the Lord' and giving his life to Him. 'From this day on a new and holy page was turned in my life,' he added.[6] Albert Tammo, a long time pastor in the Pärnu ECB church, described in his personal notes the deep feelings of guilt and desperation that he felt before his conversion, and the 'overflowing peace, joy and unutterable well-being' that he knew after his new birth.[7]

Emphasis on a personal faith experience, which shaped the traditional Estonian evangelical view of the church, had roots deeply planted in Estonian free church history. In the nineteenth century the Estonian Baptists stated: 'Through the proclamation of the Word of God a person must be regenerated from above and come to repentance. – Through faith [a person will] become a

---

[3] Johannes Lipstok to the Commissioner of the CARC (10.07.1945). Eesti Baptisti Usuühingu kirjavahetus 1945 (EBUKirj1945) [Estonian Baptist Union correspondence 1945], KUSA.

[4] Ibid.

[5] See Evald Kiil, *Issandast kutsutud viinamäe tööle* [Called by God for the Work in the Vineyard] (Tallinn, 1993), pp. 17-19; A. Seppur, *Jees. Krist. Evg. Priikoguduse tekkimine ja levinemine Läänemaa ärkamises* [The Beginning and Development of Jesus Christ's Evangelical Free Church in the Revival in Western Estonia] (Toronto, 1970), pp. 17-18; Johannes Laks, *Mälestusi eluteelt ja töömaalt* [Memoirs from Life and Work] (Toronto: Toronto Vabakoguduse Kirjastus, 1965), pp. 23-26.

[6] Aleksander Sildos, *Elulugu* [A Biography], typewritten manuscript (1967), pp. 24-25. TPL.

[7] This information is based on Marek Talts' course paper 'Albert Tammo elulugu' [A Biography of Albert Tammo] (Kõrgem Usuteaduslik Seminar, 2005). Talts used Albert Tammo's notes which are in Joosep Tammo's personal archive.

child of God, whose sins are forgiven... Only regenerated persons can receive Baptism and partake in the Lord's Supper.'[8] In these early stages of evangelical life, it seems, major questions dividing evangelicals, such as the debate over 'open' or 'closed' communion, were not as acute, though these matters later became an issue of hot discussions between Baptists and Evangelical Christians. Rather, a new ecclesiological paradigm, deriving its strength from the experience of spiritual transformation and challenging the Lutheran-Protestant paradigm of church,[9] united the young emerging Estonian free churches. This was the basis for their later cooperation, including when they were under Soviet pressure. The theological and ecclesiological identity of the UECBE, which underwent changes in the united union, had a common core: regenerate church membership. Though in some other Baptist traditions 'the insistence on regenerate church membership has been applied with less and less vigor in the twentieth century',[10] this was not the case in Estonia.

In the 1930s, one of the most outstanding leaders of the Estonian Baptists, Karl Kaups, emphasised that what was required to be a church member was 'personal conversion, personal inner renewal'. He also found these values in the Gospels and Acts, and called Baptist churches the 'first New Testament churches in Estonia'. [11] Actually this statement played down, probably not intentionally, the role of Revivalist Free churches, which were historically even older than Baptists within the Estonian scene, as well as paying little attention to other believers' church traditions which emerged shortly thereafter. Kaups' strong conviction about the Baptists' special role in Estonia, however, indicates that when compared to others, Estonian Baptists were more eager to define and emphasise their identity.[12] Sometimes other free churches, especially the Evangelical Christians, perceived this as intolerance or rigidity.[13]

Nevertheless, there was commonality. The religious conversion experience

---

[8] *Eesti Baptisti koguduste ajaloolik Album 25 Juubeli aasta mälestuseks* [In Commemoration of the 25th Anniversary: An Historical Album of Estonian Baptist Churches] (Tallinn: J. Felsbergi ja A. Tetermanni trükk, 1911), pp. 6-7.

[9] See Toivo Pilli, 'Eesti baptistide eklesioloogiast *Teekäija* vaatepeeglis: 1904-1940' [About Estonian Baptist Ecclesiology in the Mirror of *Teekäija*: 1904-1940], in Toivo Pilli, ed., *Teekond teisenevas ajas: peatükke Eesti vabakoguduste ajaloost* [A Journey in Changing Time: Chapters from the History of Estonian Free Churches] (Tartu: Kõrgem Usuteaduslik Seminar ja Sõnasepp, 2005), pp. 30-31.

[10] Wayne Stacy, ed., *A Baptist's Theology* (Macon, Georgia: Smyth and Helwys, 1999), p. 119.

[11] Karl Kaups, 'Eesti Baptismi ideelised põhialused' [The Principles of the Estonian Baptist Movement], in R. Kaups, ed., *50 aastat apostlite radadel* [50 Years in the Ways of the Apostles] (Keila: E.B.K. Liidu kirjastus, 1934), pp. 11-12.

[12] Ibid., pp. 10-15.

[13] Johannes Laks, *Kakskümmendviis aastat vabakoguduslist liikumist Eestis 1905-1930* [Twenty-Five Years of a Free Church Movement in Estonia 1905-1930] (Tallinn, 1930), pp. 8-9.

was - theologically speaking - 'common ground' for the four free churches that continued in one union after 1945. To employ James McClendon's words - which he uses to characterize small 'b' baptist type of churches – they considered that 'new birth, life delivered by the nurturing divine Spirit' was a necessary condition of membership.[14] In 1968 Robert Võsu preached that the church must be based on 'personal faith'; only believers can belong to the church.[15] Repentance, which through faith in the redemptive work of Jesus Christ leads to forgiveness and new birth, was a central theme in the ECB churches' proclamation of the gospel in the Soviet years.[16] In general, the conversion experience continued to be understood as a clearly defined moment in time; a conscious response to Christ's calling, which would lead to a living relationship with Christ - as Frank Mangs, an evangelist who was influential in the Nordic countries, explained.[17] Mangs' writings were known among Estonian ECB Christians through typewritten translations. Other writings, too, were influential. The former Evangelical Christian pastor, Oskar Olvik, was inspired by the American evangelists, D. L. Moody and R. A. Torrey, in his understanding of preaching the gospel which would lead sinners to a conversion experience.[18]

The other important aspect of this common Estonian ECB identity was the notion of voluntarism. People were not coerced to become church members. It was their own choice to become part of the committed local church membership. As Durnbaugh put it: 'The Believers' Church, therefore, is the covenanted and disciplined community of those walking in the way of Jesus Christ.'[19] Estonian Evangelical Christians-Baptists, in their search for a new identity in the framework of the UECBE, were significantly helped by their emphasis on voluntary commitment to the local church.

VOLUNTARY CHURCH, COMMITTED MEMBERS

In his book *Riigikirik ja wabakogudus* (State Church and Free Church) Karl Kaups enthusiastically defended the free church concept as something that was in opposition to the state church or the idea of a national church. Though the

---

[14] James Wm. McClendon, Jr., *Systematic Theology: Doctrine*, vol. 2 (Nashville: Abingdon Press, 1994), p. 343.

[15] *'Kalju' koguduse karjase Robert Võsu jutlusi ajavahemikul 1944.-1969* [Sermons of 'Kalju' Church Pastor, Robert Võsu, from 1944-1969], typewritten manuscript, p. 132. KUSA.

[16] See O[svald] T[ärk], *Teeviit.*

[17] Frank Mangs, *Issanda tee* [The Lord's Way], typewritten Estonian translation (1970s?), pp. 3-4. KUSA.

[18] Oskar Olvik, *Mälestused* [Memoirs], part 1 (Tallinn, 1966), p. 219. Oleviste ECB Church library, Tallinn.

[19] Donald F. Durnbaugh, *The Believers' Church* (Scottdale, Pennsylvania: Herald Press, 1985), p. 33.

book preferred the term 'free church', Kaups was actually talking about the 'believers' church'. In addition to the 'new birth' experience, for Kaups there was another important pillar for his understanding of church: free choice in the matters of religion and in joining the local church.[20] Kaups was not alone in this position. Estonian free churches, in their earlier stages, derived much spiritual energy and also crucial material for verbalising their identity from being a 'counter-church', a church denying the existing ecclesiological patterns. To use the terminology of 'given church' and 'gathered church',[21] the early Estonian free churches defined themselves as 'gathered' groups, separate from the 'given' Lutheran-Protestant body.

At the end of the nineteenth and beginning of the twentieth century, separation from the dominating Lutheran Church and joining 'the despised small [believers' church] congregation' could happen only on the basis of a voluntary decision. Church members in these small groups were accepted into fellowship by 'spiritual considerations'.[22] This experience had the potential to bring the different Estonian free churches more closely together, though this happened to some extent through developing a 'negative' identity, emphasising their difference from Lutheranism, and also from Orthodoxy. However, there were positive consequences of this 'gathered church' identity, which was often spelled out in opposition to the 'given church'. Voluntary membership, personal convictions, refusal to rely upon power structures, focus on visible fellowship, acceptance of grass-root initiatives – these were precisely the shared features that helped all the Estonian free churches to adjust to the new situation in the 1940s. When social and political support was suddenly taken away from all Estonian religious bodies, then the flexibility of the Estonian free churches, coupled with a certain non-conformist identity, proved to be an advantage. Estonian Lutheran and Orthodox churches were much more vulnerable when they lost the support of all the power structures.[23]

In addition, William Brackney has pointed out that voluntarism in ecclesiology 'raises human worth and posits a strong anthropology'.[24] One may

---

[20] Karl Kaups, *Riigikirik ja wabakogudus* [State Church and Free Church] (Keila: Külvaja trükk ja kirjastus, 1934), pp. 60-63.

[21] See George H. Williams, 'The Believers' Church and the Given Church', in Paul Basden and David S. Dockery, eds., *The People of God: Essays on the Believers' Church* (Nashville: Broadman, 1991), pp. 325-332.

[22] Karl Kaups, *Riigikirik ja wabakogudus*, pp. 61, 86.

[23] Jaanus Plaat alludes to this in his article, but having chosen a sociological approach he does not analyse the theological background to this problem. Jaanus Plaat, 'Eesti vabakoguduste vastupanu nõukogude religioonipoliitikale võrreldes luterliku ja õigeusu kirikuga (1944-1987)' [The Resistance of Estonian Free Churches to Soviet Religious Policies, in Comparison with Lutheran and Orthodox Churches (1944-1987)], in Toivo Pilli, ed., *Teekond teisenevas ajas*, pp. 128-159.

[24] William H. Brackney, 'Introduction', in William H. Brackney, ed., *The Believers Church: A Voluntary Church* (Kitchener, Ontario: Pandora Press, 1998), p. 1.

add that the involvement of the laity is also higher in voluntarily gathered churches. The Soviet context made religious belonging even more of a voluntary act and brought out more vividly an element of identity that all the ECB church traditions agreed with: being a believer means radical commitment. The social support that had previously existed and been enjoyed by church members disappeared due to atheistic ideology. Motivation to be a nominal member of any church diminished. This was an especially difficult experience for the Lutheran Church. Whereas in 1936 there were 847,600 members in the Estonian Evangelical Lutheran Church,[25] in 1969 the baptised membership was approximately 300,000.[26] As to members who donated (paid their annual church fee) to the Lutheran Church, the figures were the following: in 1937 there were 272,340, in 1966 there were 98,323 and in 1978 there were 65,425.[27] Though Evangelical Christians-Baptists also lost many members during the Soviet years, their statistics reflected to a much greater extent the real involvement of church members in church life. Voluntary membership was accompanied by a higher level of commitment to the local visible church. In 1990, Joosep Tammo emphasised the need to stand against formal baptisms and 'nominal Christianity'. He continued: 'The winds of liberalism have influenced the elders of the churches toward performing quick baptisms, not waiting for a deep experience and serious life of faith. Fellow Christians are frustrated by the baptisms of nominal Christians.'[28] Commitment was being re-emphasised.

Voluntarism found its expression also in the ECB literature that was circulated. A short survey *Baptistide arengust ja põhimõtetest* (About the Development and Principles of Baptists), reflecting the ECB teachings of the 1960s, summarized the position with these words: 'Only those are accepted into church membership who have experienced repentance and who express the wish [to become a church member] by themselves. After testing, if the person's moral life and religious understandings are in accordance to Christian norms, the person is accepted. For those who wish to leave, no hindrance is made.'[29] Osvald Tärk stated in 1982, in an article about 'the principles of our brotherhood': 'According to the teaching of Evangelical Christians-Baptists the

---

[25] Jaan Gnadenteich, *Kodumaa kirikulugu* [Church History of the Home Country] (Tallinn: Logos, 1995), p. 102.

[26] Vello Salo, *Riik ja kirikud 1940-1991* [The State and Churches 1940-1991] (Brampton, Ontario: Maarjamaa Publications, 2000), p. 33.

[27] Jaan Kiivit, 'Eesti Evangeelne Luterlik Kirik pärast Teist maailmasõda' [Estonian Evangelical Lutheran Church after the Second World War], in J. Gnadenteich, *Kodumaa kirikulugu*, p. 111.

[28] Minutes of the Annual Conference of the UECBE (17.11.1990). Aastakonverentsid 1989-1991 [Annual conferences 1989-1991], EEKBLA.

[29] [Robert Võsu,] *Baptistide arengust ja põhimõtetest* [About the Development and Principles of Baptists] [1966], p. 10. Merike Uudam's personal library.

visible church consists of believers regenerated through the Holy Spirit...'[30] These believers, he insisted, confess that Jesus Christ is their Saviour and Lord, their teaching and ways of life are based on the Word of God, they voluntarily submit themselves to the Lord's commands and order of the church, they search for sanctification under the guidance of the Holy Spirit and they fulfil the tasks given by the Lord.[31] While the danger in focusing on voluntarism too much is that it tends to over-emphasise human action over against the divine initiative, Estonian Baptists attempted to keep a theological balance: human 'steps of faith' – initial and ongoing commitment – were seen as responses to God's sovereign power.

Two comments are pertinent here. First, Tärk preferred not to talk about 'spiritual' or 'inner' experience. In part this was because he was aware of the role of 'experience' in theological liberalism, which he could not agree with. But probably he had also grown cautious of the tradition of 'experience' in Pentecostalism and its newer expressions in charismatic groups, especially because some new influences of this kind were reaching Estonia via Finland in the 1970s. Furthermore, public expressions of religious experience in local churches, especially those of a more emotional or charismatic mode, usually provoked pressure and intensified negative attention from the side of the state authorities. Second, as if to balance the stress that there sometimes was on 'experience', Tärk emphasised the role of order in the church. 'Not every group of believers is a church, in the same way as accidentally gathered atoms do not constitute a molecule.'[32] Tärk's emphasis seems to have moved toward formal rules instead of the order created by the dynamic fellowship and mutual interaction and discipline in local congregations. Partly this was the need of the times, as disorders in local churches endangered the churches' opportunities to work. Partly also this reflected Tärk's own convictions, theological preferences and orderly personality, all of which had an influence on his understanding of how a church should operate and worship.[33]

Tärk was advocating a classic 'free church' concept, which he expressed in the following manner: 'The New Testament does not teach that all who are born in a parish should be taken to baptism without their consent and that through this they belong to the church. A people's church idea is alien to the teaching of Christ.'[34] Robert Võsu[35] and Efraim Joel Dahl[36] expressed similar

---

[30] Osvald Tärk, 'Meie vendluse põhimõtted' [Principles of Our Brotherhood], *Logos*, no. 1 (1982), p. 18.

[31] Ibid.

[32] Ibid.

[33] Ruudi Leinus, comp. and ed., *Osvald Tärk. Uskuge Jumalasse* [Osvald Tärk. Believe in God] (Tallinn: Eesti EKB Liit, 1999), pp. 28-33, 48-49, 66-67.

[34] Tärk, 'Meie vendluse põhimõtted', *Logos*, no. 1 (1982), p. 19.

[35] [Robert Võsu,] *Baptistide arengust ja põhimõtetest*, p. 7.

views; according to their interpretation, the 'people's church' was the state church, in contrast with the believers' church. Tärk also referred to Louis Berkhof when talking about the relationship between the 'body of believers and Christ as its head'. However, Estonian Evangelical Christians-Baptists, including Tärk, would not have agreed with Berkhof, who wrote from a Presbyterian perspective, that the visible church 'always does contain some who are not yet regenerated – there may be chaff among the wheat…'[37] Tärk's awareness of Louis Berkhof's *opus magnum* is interesting, although he modified and rejected some of the positions of Berkhof, who has been seen as characterised by 'simple piety, a high theology and an unswerving devotion to the Reformed faith'.[38]

Becoming a believer without any coercion, joining the church on a voluntary basis and being aware of the commitment it brings – these values find their way again and again into Estonian Evangelical Christian-Baptist ecclesiological argumentation during the Soviet years. Gradually, criticism directed toward the Lutheran Church lost its sharpness, as all Christian churches found themselves 'in the same boat'. Yet it remained true that by contrast with other Christian traditions, new birth and voluntary church membership constituted distinctive common ground for Baptist, Pentecostal, Evangelical Christian as well as Revivalist Free churches in Estonia. They could build their relationships under Soviet pressure and in the united ECB union on this mutual understanding. However, there were significant disagreements, especially in the areas of the theology of baptism as well as over questions of open or closed membership and communion. Is the criterion for believers' church membership and for partaking in communion only regeneration or should baptism (by immersion) as a believer be added as a *sine qua non*? This discussion took place mainly between the Baptist and Evangelical Christian traditions, with Baptist theology gradually gaining a stronger position within the union.

---

[36] Efraim Joel Dahl, *Evangeeliumi kristlate-baptistide tõekspidamistest* [About the Principles of the Evangelical Christians-Baptists], typewritten manuscript (n. p., n. d.). TPL.

[37] Louis Berkhof, *Systematic Theology* (Grand Rapids, Michigan: Eerdmans, 1949), p. 564; Tärk, 'Meie vendluse põhimõtted', p. 18. See also Toivo Pilli, 'Eesti baptistid ja nende teoloogilise mõtte kajastumine ajakirjas *Teekäija* kuni 1940' [Estonian Baptists and their Theology as Reflected in *Teekäija* until 1940], ThM thesis (Tartu: Tartu University, 1996), p. 73.

[38] 'Berkhof, Louis', in Timothy Larsen, ed., *Biographical Dictionary of Evangelicals* (Leicester, England: Inter-Varsity Press, 2003), pp. 45-47.

BAPTISM OF BELIEVERS:
A PREREQUISITE FOR CHURCH MEMBERSHIP?

Estonian Evangelical Christians had a different view of the role of baptism to that of the Baptists. Even if the UECBE was formally united, the varieties that existed in the free church traditions that had been brought together by the state did not disappear so easily. Baptists clearly expressed the view that 'believers baptism' had to be one of the criteria for church membership.[39] For Evangelical Christians the basic criterion for membership, and consequently for participation in the Lord's Supper, was 'regeneration' or 'conversion'. Theological tensions revolving around these different emphases were 'on the table' already in 1945, during the negotiations regarding the unification of the four Estonian free churches.[40] For Evangelical Christians, leaving the issue of baptism by immersion open was an important aspect of their historical identity. In their history the Evangelical Christians had tried to avoid the issue of baptism becoming a dividing line between believers, and they were generally critical of Baptist strictness (as they saw it) in doctrinal matters. The Evangelical Christians emphasised the ethics of love and tolerance instead.[41] Pentecostals and Revivalist Free churches reflected less on such theological issues, but in practice they shared Baptist rather than Evangelical Christian views about this question of baptism.

In pre-war Estonia, Evangelical Christians had a Moravian influence in their historical background,[42] which made it easier for them to see at least some value in infant baptism, on condition that a religious conversion followed later in the person's life. They emphasised that both 'members who have been baptised as believers and those baptised as infants have equal rights in a church'.[43] Their statutes from 1926 confirmed that they administered 'baptism

---

[39] Excerpt from minutes, no. 5 (30.04.1945). Eesti Baptisti Usuühingu kirjavahetus 1945 (EBUKirj1945) [Estonian Baptist Union correspondence 1945], KUSA.

[40] Excerpt from minutes, no. 5 (30.04.1945). EBUKirj1945, KUSA.

[41] The division could not be avoided even among Evangelical Christians. Eduard Lilienthal, an early Evangelical Christian leader, began to emphasise that believers' baptism should not be allowed at all. This view was not supported by the younger generation of leaders, including K. L. Marley and J. Laks, who stood for the principle of freedom, tolerance and flexibility in these matters. In 1923 a split took place. The more tolerant branch, led by Marley, became an influential free church movement and grew significantly. For the split, see Laks, *Kakskümmendviis aastat vabakoguduslist liikumist Eestis*, pp. 40-51.

[42] Oskar Olvik, 'Ülevaade Evangeeliumi Kristlaste ajaloost' [Overview of the History of Evangelical Christians], in *Eesti Evangeeliumi Kristlaste juubel 50: 1905-1955* [The 50th Jubilee of Estonian Evangelical Christians: 1905-1955], typewritten manuscript (1955), pp. 43-46. KUSA.

[43] Laks, *Kakskümmendviis aastat vabakoguduslist liikumist Eestis*, p. 27.

with water' both to infants and adults.[44] In the Lord's Supper those 'newborn believers could take part whose way of life did not hinder them from participating'.[45] For Evangelical Christians, this was a matter of 'freedom of conscience'.[46] They held the view that it was the individual believer who had to take responsibility for these decisions, while the Estonian Baptists, on the contrary, had traditionally emphasised the place of congregational responsibility. Paradoxically, one may argue, the Evangelical Christians applied the Baptist principle of 'soul freedom' or 'individual competency'[47] to almost an extreme; by extending it from an individual choice in conversion to the individual's choice as to if and when believer's baptism should take place. In summary, the Estonian Evangelical Christian theological identity before the Second World War was characterised by the following key concepts: the church consists of regenerated persons; the issue of believers baptism is a matter of every person's own conscience; the Lord's Supper is open to all 'children of God', including those who have experienced regeneration but who are not yet church members; and there should be respect toward and cooperation with all 'children of God', without attempts to convert them to the views of Evangelical Christians.[48] The Estonian Evangelical Christian identity had its specific features when compared to other Estonian free churches[49] as well as when compared to Russian Evangelical Christians, though the latter also considered the question of baptism upon the profession of faith as 'secondary' with reference to the requirements for participation in communion.[50]

At the meeting about becoming a union in Moscow in August 1945, however, Johannes Laks, the Estonian Evangelical Christian leader, had to accept the principle of believer's baptism as a requirement for church membership and communion. He said: 'As the representative of the Evangelical Christian Free Church, I was compelled, in spite of myself, to make a respective change in our fundamental principle of the freedom of baptism. This was inevitable for reaching the agreement about the conditions of our future

---

[44] *Evangeeliumi Kristlaste Vabakoguduse Põhikiri* [The Statute of The Evangelical Christian Free Church] (Keila: Külvaja trükk, 1926), p. 4.
[45] Laks, *Kakskümmendviis aastat vabakoguduslist liikumist Eestis*, p. 27.
[46] Ibid.
[47] Walter B. Shurden, *The Baptist Identity. Four Fragile Freedoms* (Macon, Georgia: Smyth and Helwys, 1993), pp. 23, 26-30.
[48] Olvik, 'Ülevaade Evangeeliumi Kristlaste ajaloost', p. 49.
[49] Often their commitment to cooperation and to so called 'alliance work' as well as their high ethical standards and demands on Christian lifestyle have been emphasised. Haljand Uuemõis, 'Evangeeliumi kristlaste liikumisest' [About the Evangelical Christian Movement], *Teekäija* (June 1995), p. 5; Olvik, 'Ülevaade Evangeeliumi Kristlaste ajaloost', pp. 49, 51-52.
[50] Paul D. Steeves, 'The Russian Baptist Union, 1917-1935: Evangelical Awakening in Russia', PhD dissertation (University of Kansas, 1976), p. 72.

existence.'[51] One gets an impression that pressure was put on Laks by the Estonian rather than the Russian 'brothers'. Back in Estonia, Laks was in a difficult situation when he had to explain this concession. Writing from the place to which he had emigrated, the former Evangelical Christian leader Karl Leopold Marley criticised this theological compromise severely. According to him, it would have been better if Evangelical Christians had been liquidated in Estonia rather than joining the Baptists.[52] He was upset by the information that Estonian Evangelical Christians had to give up, at least officially, one of their key historic positions.

All this was not a theological priority for Russian Evangelical Christians and Baptists, who were struggling with other serious questions in the 1940s. The Statute of Unity (1944) which was accepted (in Moscow) during the unification of Russian Evangelical Christians and Baptists, and was theologically a rather shallow document, stated that in the ECB congregations only ordained leaders were entitled to perform baptism and communion, and that both baptism with laying-on of hands and baptism without laying-on of hands had equal force.[53] This was an echo of a tension created by the influence of British evangelicals on Russian Evangelical Christians and German Baptist influence on Russian Baptists, especially in Southern Russia.[54] The Estonian situation was different. However, as the statute of the AUCECB 'adopted Baptist views with only slight modifications',[55] so in a similar way Baptist ecclesiology in the Estonian scene began gradually to influence the Evangelical Christian positions. The fact that this did not happen without discussion, and even strong debate, can be clearly seen when the views of one of the Estonian Evangelical Christian key persons, Oskar Olvik, are analysed in the light of Baptist positions.

Oskar Olvik came from a Lutheran-Pietistic background and joined the Evangelical Christian movement in the 1930s. He was convinced that infant baptism had some value when the parents were believers.[56] It is obvious that he had been influenced by his studies at Tartu University, in the so called 'Lutheran' theological department. However, the issue of baptism was not only a theoretical issue but a very personal matter for Olvik. Oskar Olvik's own spiritual journey had led him to a conversion experience. He 'became a believer', but did not seek for believer's baptism. He stated: 'When I became a

---

[51] Johannes Laks, *Mälestusi eluteelt ja töömaalt* [Memoirs from Life and Work] (Toronto: Toronto Vabakoguduse Kirjastus, 1965), p. 82.

[52] Oskar Olvik, *Mälestused*, part 2, p. 362.

[53] Walter Sawatsky, *Soviet Evangelicals Since World War II* (Kitchener, Ontario: Herald Press, 1981), p. 476.

[54] Wilhelm Kahle, *Evangelische Christen in Russland und der Sovetunion* (Wuppertal und Kassel: Oncken Verlag, 1978), pp. 209-210.

[55] Sawatsky, *Soviet Evangelicals Since World War II*, p. 89.

[56] Olvik, *Mälestused*, part 1, pp. 215-216.

believer I acknowledged the covenant that my parents had made, which was included in the human aspect of baptism, and I planned to live according to it.'[57] During the first Soviet years, Olvik led the 'Karmel' Evangelical Christian Church in Tallinn. In 1950 he became one of the two Oleviste Church presbyters; the other presbyter was Osvald Tärk.[58]

The formation of the Oleviste ECB Church,[59] consisting of different free church traditions and including more than 500 former Baptist church members, over 700 former Evangelical Christians, approximately 450 former Pentecostals and approximately 150 former Revivalist Free Church members,[60] probably put Olvik under some pressure to yield to more baptistic theological positions, though people who shared Evangelical Christian views were well represented in Oleviste. In addition, Olvik was increasingly influenced by the burial and resurrection imagery of Romans 6, which he interpreted in terms of sanctification. As he said, he at last made up his mind to 'give the old [human] nature to death, – once again, and in a decisive way', to overcome his 'defiance' in relation to baptism (as he put it), and to affirm to Christ in a practical way that his 'old nature' was crucified together with Christ. Olvik was baptised by immersion in the Finnish Gulf not far from Tallinn in 1951 by the UECBE Senior Presbyter, Aleksander Sildos.[61] It should be pointed out that it was not a congregational act – Olvik and Sildos were the only participants in this event. For Olvik, baptism was predominantly an individual and personal step of faith, as well as a sign of choosing the way of sanctification and humility.

In the Baptist tradition there was a somewhat different emphasis. Baptism was seen primarily as a public witness to Jesus' death and resurrection, and a profession of faith. Anthony Cross has emphasised in relation to British Baptists: 'The understanding of baptism as a profession of faith has been the most widely and firmly held Baptist view of baptism...'[62] This was true also of Estonian Baptists. However, the Evangelical Christian tradition put more emphasis on the moral aspect of baptism, and identifying with the ethical way of Christ. Baptists, even when using the 'burial' and 'resurrection' image, viewed it more dogmatically. It was confirming the truth of redemption. The fact that baptism had taken place would support the believer in situations of temptation in the future, reminding him or her about a new spiritual reality – a new life.[63] For the Evangelical Christian tradition, baptism was primarily

[57] Olvik, *Mälestused,* part 2, p. 405.
[58] Laks, Mälestusi eluteelt ja töömaalt, p. 88.
[59] See chapter 2, 'Merger of local churches'.
[60] This estimation is based on the UECBE churches statistical report of 1949. EEKBLA.
[61] Olvik, *Mälestused,* part 2, pp. 406-407.
[62] Anthony R. Cross, *Baptism and the Baptists* (Carlisle: Paternoster Press, 2000), pp. 30-31.
[63] Tärk, 'Meie vendluse põhimõtted', *Logos*, no. 4 (1982), p. 6.

related to personal sanctification and spiritual maturity, whereas, for the Baptist tradition, baptism was understood in the light of spiritual principles and obedience to Christ's command and example.

For Olvik, baptism and 'becoming a believer' were two phenomena that had both to be included, in whatever order, in the process of spiritual beginnings. In this respect Olvik's logic has some resonance with recent views expressed by Paul Fiddes, who from within the British Baptist tradition has interpreted baptism as one step in the process of Christian initiation.[64] In his later years, Olvik strongly emphasised repentance and was inclined to focus on the baptism of John the Baptist as a model. He believed that baptism could be seen as preparation in the process of becoming a believer.[65] This view was criticised by another ECB preacher and writer, Efraim Joel Dahl, in 1967. Dahl said that Olvik's position might open the door for the baptism of persons who did not have personal faith.[66] Dahl stated that baptism could be understood as a preparation 'for final salvation' in an eschatological sense, not as preparation 'for subjective personal salvation.' Repentance and faith in Jesus Christ as the Son of God, he argued, have to precede the act of baptism. Baptism itself cannot be understood as an act of repentance.[67] However, Olvik and Dahl both seemed to agree that baptism is first and foremost a human activity. Both Estonian Baptist and Evangelical Christian theology paid little attention to the Holy Spirit's presence in baptism;[68] they focused on the human aspect, at the cost of downplaying the divine aspect of baptism.

Estonian Evangelical Christians, together with Baptists, Pentecostals and Revivalist Free churches, agreed with the wider evangelical tradition, that 'only through conversion does a person become a Christian.'[69] However, the conclusions based on this belief led Evangelical Christians to follow their own way. They believed that the decision regarding believer's baptism should depend wholly on the person's conscience. Referring back to New Testament times, Olvik stated: 'It was critical that a person had become a believer. If this goal had been achieved, then it was not important when, where or by whom the

---

[64] See Paul Fiddes, 'Baptism and the Process of Christian Initiation', *The Ecumenical Review*, no. 54 (2002), pp. 48-65.

[65] Olvik, *Mälestused,* part 2, pp. 529-530.

[66] Efraim Joel Dahl, 'Kas ristimine kannab ainult usuelu ettevalmistavat iseloomu?' [Does Baptism have a Preparatory Character Regarding the Christian Life?] (12.12.1967), p. 14. Artikleid [Articles]. Robert Võsu materjalid [Materials of Robert Võsu], EEKBLA.

[67] Dahl, 'Kas ristimine kannab ainult usuelu ettevalmistavat iseloomu?' (12.12.1967), pp. 14-15. Artikleid. Robert Võsu materjalid, EEKBLA.

[68] The same 'lacuna' in the theology of baptism occurred among British Baptists during the first decades of the twentieth century. Cross, *Baptism and the Baptists*, p. 108.

[69] David Bebbington, *Evangelicalism in Modern Britain. A History from the 1730s to the 1980s* (Grand Rapids, Michigan: Baker Book House, 1992), p. 10.

person was baptised.'[70] This seems a very open-minded approach. Yet Olvik was critical both of Lutherans, who baptised infants 'decades before they become believers', and also of Baptists who 'do not lead those who have responded to invitation [i.e. experienced conversion] to the water, but instead keep them for months or years on probation.'[71] Making baptismal services a public witness, as Pentecostals and Baptists used to do before the Second World War, was not a procedure that was supported by Olvik. He argued: 'It seems that adult baptism is marching toward formal fulfilment of a ritual, to where infant baptism had arrived a long time ago.'[72] It seems that Olvik, by referring to pre-war times in his criticism, did not take fully enough into consideration the atheistic realities of the Soviet period. The Soviet government restrictions, allowing the ceremony to take place only in remote locations and at a time of the day when only a few people could move around,[73] diminished the aspect of public testimony, making baptism in ECB churches rather more of a personal act of testimony in the presence of a small group of fellow believers.

Olvik's theological critique of the practice of baptism within the Estonian ECB movement was largely neglected during the Soviet times. For pastoral reasons, in order to avoid confrontation and confusion among church members, he was also himself careful not to share his views too widely. More traditional Baptist positions in baptismal theology were advocated by Olvik's colleague in the Oleviste Church, Osvald Tärk, perhaps one of the most outstanding Baptist theologians during the Soviet years not only in Estonia, but in the whole Soviet Union.[74] In a series of typewritten articles from the beginning of the 1980s, Osvald Tärk made an attempt to describe what he considered Estonian ECB theological identity.

Tärk's views in fact re-stated the Estonian Baptist traditional positions. He defined Christian baptism as follows: 'Baptism is a spiritual ordinance established by the Lord; by immersing a believer into the water before God and other people it signifies that the person baptised has already abandoned his unconverted life and through regeneration stepped into a living relationship with the death and resurrection of Jesus Christ.'[75] Tärk was confident that 'only believers can be baptised', and found support for this position also in Karl Barth's *Church Dogmatics*, which he had read with care.[76] The emphasis in Tärk on there being a certain finiteness about the conversion experience before

---

[70] Olvik, *Mälestused,* part 2, p. 530.

[71] Ibid., pp. 532-33.

[72] Ibid., p. 543.

[73] A secret circular of the Commissioner of the CARC (19.06.1949). ERA, f. R-1989, n. 2, s. 1, p. 75.

[74] See Istorija evangel'skih hristjan-baptistov v SSSR (Moskva: Izdanije VSEHB, 1989), p. 271; Sawatsky, Soviet Evangelicals Since World War II, p. 265.

[75] Osvald Tärk, *Vaimulikud talitused EKB kogudustes* [Spiritual Ordinances in the ECB Churches] (1959), p. 2. Robert Võsu materjalid, EEKBLA.

[76] Tärk, 'Meie vendluse põhimõtted', *Logos,* no. 4 (1982), pp. 6-7.

baptism, and his avoidance of interpreting conversion and baptism as aspects of an ongoing process, means that there was a clear contrast between his thinking and Olvik's more flexible theological views. According to Tärk, baptism expresses the reality that repentance and a change have already taken place in the baptized person's life.[77] Baptism is the 'pledge of a good conscience toward God' (1 Peter 3:21); it is a visible confirmation that a believer has turned away from the 'old life', is 'buried into the death of Christ' and is living a renewed life, as Tärk explained, referring to Romans 6:1-14. Tärk emphasised strongly that 'saving' power was not in baptism but was in the redemptive work and resurrection of Jesus Christ. Tärk firmly held to the belief that baptism is the 'outward sign' of regeneration and that it lacked any sacramental value.[78]

Tärk was aware that there were some British Baptist authors who, in Anthony Cross' words, 'wished to reinstate and emphasize the "sacramental" aspect of baptism'.[79] However, Tärk was suspicious of the mechanical interpretation of the word 'sacrament' and preferred 'ordinance'. He was critical of the views expressed in the book *Christian Baptism*, edited by a British Baptist, Alec Gilmore, and published in 1959, which, according to Tärk's understanding, placed regeneration and baptism too close to each other.[80] He was convinced that the reason for this theological trend was twofold: the influence of ecumenical dialogue and a 'weak experience of regeneration'.[81] 'A person, who is absolutely convinced in regeneration, that his sin has been forgiven, will not search a new forgiveness in baptism,' was his later comment.[82] Tärk also stated: 'Taking into account the historically developed meaning of the words "media gracia" and "sacrament", neither of these expresses the teaching of free churches.'[83] For the Estonian ECB churches, the sacramental view of baptism, as discussed among some British Baptists,[84] was and is practically non-existent.[85] As Tärk's interpretation of

---

[77] Tärk, 'Meie vendluse põhimõtted', *Logos,* no. 4 (1982), p. 5.

[78] Tärk, 'Meie vendluse põhimõtted', *Logos,* no. 4 (1982), pp. 3, 5-6.

[79] Cross, *Baptism and the Baptists*, p. 100.

[80] It was probably not only a certain openness to sacramental views of baptism in Gilmore's book, but also the analytical and discussion-oriented style which made Tärk cautious. For example, see the arguments by S.F. Winward about the relationship of Scripture and tradition, or some questions which were raised by Gilmore who analysed the role of 'Jewish antecendents' for Christian baptism. Alec Gilmore, ed., *Christian Baptism* (London: Lutterworth Press, 1959), pp. 26-31, 82-83. Tärk, often for pastoral reasons, tried to offer rational and 'clear' answers to theological questions.

[81] Osvald Tärk, '"Uus suund" ristimise õpetuses' ['A New Trend' in the Teaching of Baptism], *Logos,* no. 5 (1982), pp. 25-27.

[82] Tärk, '"Uus suund" ristimise õpetuses', p. 27.

[83] Tärk, 'Meie vendluse põhimõtted', *Logos,* no. 4 (1982), p. 3.

[84] See Anthony R. Cross, 'Dispelling the myth of English Baptist Sacramentalism', *The Baptist Quarterly*, vol. 38, no. 8 (2000), pp. 367-91; Stanley K. Fowler, *More Than A*

'ordinances' became a standard element in the identity of ECB churches in Estonia, baptism was increasingly interpreted as an act of obedience to Christ's command.[86]

In 1966, a short survey of Evangelical Christian and Baptist life and faith in Estonia was written, most probably by Robert Võsu. It expressed Baptist positions on baptism and church membership as if these were the only possible approaches: 'When a person is thoroughly tested that his/her repentance is true and authentic, then this person has to give a witness of his/her decision publicly and to confirm it with a special outward act, which is baptism.' ... 'Only after passing this public and voluntary act the person is regarded as a member of a Baptist church.'[87] In the second half of the 1970s and in the 1980s, the 'traditional' Baptist positions were confirmed in the writings which circulated in the UECBE churches and among ECB presbyters.[88] Within former Baptist circles there were some theologians, such as Tärk and Võsu, who taught and wrote within the UECBE over a longer period of time than did the key-leaders of the Evangelical Christians, such as Olvik and Laks.[89] In this way Baptist ecclesiological positions became more clearly and thoroughly articulated in the UECBE.

Symbol: The British Baptist Recovery of Baptismal Sacramentalism (Carlisle: Paternoster Press, 2002).

[85] Estonian Baptists' refusal of both sacramental language and a sacramental interpretation of baptism was influenced by their opposition to Lutheranism and the theological impact of German Baptist models. See Toivo Pilli, 'Eesti baptistide eklesioloogiast Teekäija vaatepeeglis: 1904-1940', in Toivo Pilli, ed., *Teekond teisenevas ajas*, pp. 33-37 .

[86] For example Tärk prepared a small manual for ECB presbyters which included basic theological interpretation and practical guidance on how to administer 'ordinances'. The manual was widely used by ECB presbyters. Osvald Tärk, *Vaimulikud talitused EKB kogudustes* (1959).

[87] [Robert Võsu,] *Baptistide arengust ja põhimõtetest*, p. 14.

[88] In autumn 1975, teaching a semi-illegal Bible course group in Tartu, Robert Võsu gave a lecture about Baptist ecclesiology, based on the book by the German Baptist, Hans Luckey, about Baptists. Lecture notes 1973-1978, notebook 2. Uudu Rips' personal archive. Extracts from Luckey were also published in *Logos*, no. 4 (1983), pp. 6-9. See also E. J. Dahl, *Evangeelse maailma radadel* [On the Paths of Evangelical World], typewritten manuscript (Tallinn, 1976), pp. 48-49, 168-170. KUSA. Osvald Tärk's 'Meie vendluse põhimõtted' [Principles of our Brotherhood], published in 1981-1982 in *Logos,* has already been mentioned. In 1984, Robert Võsu emphasised that the person of Christ defines the church – and 'the borderline for church [membership] is baptism'. Robert Võsu, *Jeesus Kristus – koguduse alus* [Jesus Christ – A Foundation for Church], *Logos*, no. 2 (1984), pp. 4-9.

[89] Robert Võsu died in 1994, Osvald Tärk in 1984, Oskar Olvik in 1977, Johannes Laks in 1969. In this way, the Baptist theologians had approximately a decade or even more to say the 'last word' in this ecclesiological discussion.

THE LORD'S SUPPER: OPEN OR CLOSED TABLE?

The tensions between Baptist and Evangelical Christian traditions emerged also – inevitably – in the area of the understanding of the Lord's Supper. As with baptism, there was common ground. Indeed, all Estonian free churches agreed that a believer was called to obedience which involved responding to Jesus' invitation to participate in these 'ordinances'.[90] However, in regard to questions such as who should participate at the Supper, the two traditions differed: Evangelical Christians supported the view of 'open' communion, open to all believers; Baptists (together with the majority of Pentecostals and Revivalist churches) tended to hold to the view of a 'closed' communion, open only to those baptized as believers. This emerged from their different views on the criteria for church membership.

Evangelical Christians searched for fellowship and union between all 'newborn' believers. Karl L. Marley, writing from abroad in 1965, stated critically: 'Baptist teaching establishes borders and walls among those who are saved and are children of God; it denies them attending the Lord's table and deprives them of the fellowship of the church. However, this is "the Lord's table", not "the congregation's table".'[91] Marley, who addressed his letter to Oskar Olvik, Johannes Laks and Aleksander Sildos, the three most influential former Evangelical Christian leaders within the UECBE, tried to re-emphasise the positions of Evangelical Christians, the positions which had begun to grow weaker in the interrelationships of the united union.

The Estonian Baptist tradition held strongly to the view of 'closed' communion. In this they differed significantly even from the Russian Evangelical Christians and Baptists. In 1950, when the Oleviste Church was formed in Tallinn, there was a debate between Osvald Tärk and Aleksander Karev about how to conduct the communion services in this united church. Karev suggested that both those who were full church members and also 'born again' believers who were not yet church members could participate in communion. This was how things were arranged in the Moscow ECB church, Karev stated. Tärk disagreed. An argument followed. 'A. Karev argued that in the Bible there is no such sequence or reason. O. Tärk thought that they, i.e. Baptists have such a principle, which he is not planning to give up.'[92] Tärk wrote later: 'The church must have a clear teaching; who are members of the congregation, who can participate in the Lord's Supper.'[93] Listening more carefully to the AUCECB practices in these matters might have made the merger of different free church traditions a smoother operation in Estonia. The

---

[90] Tärk, 'Meie vendluse põhimõtted', *Logos*, no. 4 (1982), p. 3.

[91] Olvik, *Mälestused,* part 2, p. 362.

[92] Ibid., p. 379.

[93] O[svald] [Tärk], *Püha õhtusöömaaeg. Viis kõnet pühast õhtusöömaajast* [The Lord's Supper. Five Sermons on the Lord's Supper] (1965), p. 25. Robert Võsu materjalid, EEKBLA.

state had brought the traditions together, but this did not mean that theological unity had been achieved.

Again, it was Olvik who was prepared to be engaged in this theological discussion and to question the Baptist stance. He stated in some study material that he prepared: 'The only prerequisite for participation in the Lord's table is a cleansed heart. Since Jesus gave the ordinance of the Supper before Pentecost, i.e. before the birth of the church, then belonging or not belonging to church is not a criteria for participating in the Lord's Table. Belonging to the church is a recommendable, not a decisive condition.'[94] A 'response' from the Baptist tradition was voiced by others, for example by Adolf Pohl, a teacher at Buckow Baptist Theological Seminary, in his translated article: only being baptised as a believer, he argued, gives a person the right to take part in the Lord's Supper.[95] Pohl expressed the same positions that Osvald Tärk had advocated through his period of ministry.

However, there were many areas where the different theological identities within the UECBE converged and there were many issues about which leaders agreed with each other. The Lord's Supper was understood as a meal of fellowship, a meal of remembrance, and there was a rejection of any sacramental interpretation of this event. In accord with wider Baptist tradition, this meal was also understood in terms of obedient discipleship, thanksgiving and proclamation.[96] Efraim J. Dahl stated it in this way: the Lord's Supper is a symbolic remembrance of personal forgiveness of sins which is received through an inner experience.[97] This harmonises well with the general tendencies in Anglo-American Baptist thought in the twentieth century: 'The elements are only symbols of the Lord's completed sacrifice.'[98] Olvik emphasised the strengthened fellowship with Christ and between believers that came as a result of taking part in this rite.[99] Tärk interpreted the Lord's Supper as a meal where the church remembers Christ's death for sins and proclaims that the growth of the new forgiven life, which has already been received from Christ, depends fully on Christ's sacrificial death.[100] Though vehemently denying any sacramental, or, more specifically, *ex opere operato* value in the Lord's Supper, Tärk agreed with the symbolic value of 'the breaking of bread', a common phrase in the UECBE churches to denote the eucharist: 'Symbols help to guess

---

[94] Oskar Olvik, *Esimene Korintose kiri* [The First Epistle to the Corinthians], typewritten manuscript (1960), p. 76. KUSA.
[95] Adolf Pohl, 'Meie arusaam ristimisest' [Our Understanding of Baptism], *Logos*, no. 2 (1985), pp. 7-9.
[96] Walter B. Shurden, ed., *Proclaiming the Baptist Vision: Baptism and the Lord's Supper* (Macon, Georgia: Smyth and Helwys, 1999), pp. 117-126.
[97] Dahl, *Evangeelse maailma radadel*, p. 46.
[98] Dale R. Stoffer, ed., *The Lord's Supper: Believers Church Perspectives* (Scottdale, Pennsylvania: Herald Press, 1997), p. 239.
[99] Olvik, *Esimene Korintose kiri*, pp. 75-78.
[100] Tärk, *Vaimulikud talitused EKB kogudustes*, p. 8.

this part of the truth that goes beyond the rationality of definition.'[101] In his sermons Tärk, like Olvik, emphasised that this meal reminds a believer of Christ's redemption. Also, this is a meal of fellowship, spiritually with Christ and visibly with fellow believers.[102]

These were positions with which Pentecostals, Revivalist Free churches as well as Baptists and Evangelical Christians could easily agree. Focus on Christ's sacrifice and passion instead of his victory and resurrection power was probably due in part to the influence of Moravian piety. Songs for the Lord's Supper were usually chosen from the hymnal section 'About the Suffering of Christ', a typical Moravian emphasis.[103] Also, an emphasis on spiritual preparation before the Supper and ethical responsibility emerging from the believer's participation in the Supper were common features in Estonian ECB churches. While in the wider Baptist world, social trends influenced Baptist practices in relation to the eucharist, for example the trend toward using individual glasses,[104] in Estonia one or two chalices were passed around, usually filled with wine.

It must be noted that in spite of representing two rather different theological approaches, in personal relationships Olvik and Tärk were committed to maintaining fellowship and respect. Olvik was open-hearted enough to suggest baptism by immersion to a prospective church member who asked for his advice. 'If God has made it clear to you, then you have to be obedient to Him.'[105] However, it took years before the controversy about the Lord's Supper was settled in the union and in the local ECB churches, especially in cases when the state authorities had forced different free churches to merge. In the Oleviste Church, for 28 years, from 1950 to 1978, there were two communion services: one for former Evangelical Christians and another for former Baptists.[106] Only with a new pastor, Ülo Meriloo, who was elected in 1978, and based on the decision of the church's general assembly, was the situation changed.[107] Two separate communion services were practised also in

[101] Tärk, "Meie vendluse põhimõtted," *Logos,* no. 4 (1982), p. 3.
[102] O[svald] [Tärk], *Püha õhtusöömaaeg. Viis kõnet pühast õhtusöömaajast* (1965), pp. 18-21. Robert Võsu materjalid, EEKBLA.
[103] This section about Christ's passion and death included 23 songs, while the section 'About the Resurrection' included only 6 songs. *Evangeelsed laulud* [Evangelical Hymns] (Tallinn, 1975), pp. 239-256.
[104] Stoffer, ed., *The Lord's Supper: Believers Church Perspectives*, p. 238.
[105] Arpad Arder, *Kus on Arpadi kuningas?* [Where is Arpad's King?] (Tallinn: [Logos,] 1992), p. 86.
[106] Ülo Meriloo, *Ränduri päevik* [A Diary of a Pilgrim] (Tallinn, 2001), p. 82.
[107] Tarmo Lige, 'Kogudus põlvkondade vahetusel' [Church on the Threshold of Generations], in *Oleviste 50. Oleviste koguduse juubelikogumik* [Oleviste 50. The Anniversary Collection of Oleviste Church] (Tallinn: Oleviste kogudus, 2000), p. 32.

Pärnu 'Immanuel' Church in the 1950s.[108] What has been said of Baptists in general, was dramatically true for many years in the UECBE: 'Unfortunately, the Lord's Supper has been ... symbolic of the disunity of Christ's followers more than of their unity.'[109]

The differences in ecclesiology were more painful and difficult to overcome than the ECB believers would have wished. The later descriptions of love and unity, which occur often in the UECBE 'official story' of what happened during Soviet times, seem to be an 'invented tradition',[110] rather than reflecting the complexities of the reality of life in the union. Oleviste Church deacons were expected to agree with the position that new members joining the church had to accept the practice of believer's baptism, and accept that there were two separate gatherings for the Lord's Supper in one church (one 'closed' and one 'open').[111] In the second half of the 1980s and in the 1990s, in the context of rapid social and religious changes, the principle of 'closed' communion began to lose its strength in the UECBE. In 1989, when discussing Meelis Etti's candidature for a pastor's job in Rakvere, the UECBE board mentioned critically that Etti had allowed a person who 'was not baptised as a believer' to take part of the Lord's Supper.[112] In the end, however, the board supported his candidature. There were clear 'cracks' emerging in the doctrinal wall of closed communion.[113]

However, by the end of the 1970s the Baptist tradition in Estonia had largely 'won' the argument with Evangelical Christians over believer's baptism and the Lord's Supper. The reasons for the vitality of Baptist theological

---

[108] Voldemar Kaasik, 'Tagasivaade Pärnu Immaanueli kogudusele' [Pärnu 'Immanuel' Church in Retrospect], *Logos*, no. 4 (1984), p. 13.

[109] Shurden, ed., *Proclaiming the Baptist Vision: Baptism and the Lord's Supper*, p. 124.

[110] M. Scarot, 'Counterfactuals and the Invention of Religious Traditions', in Jan W. van Henten and Anton Houtepen, eds., *Religious Identity and the Invention of Tradition* (Assen: Van Grocum, 2001), pp. 29-30. Being inspired by Eric Hobsbawm's and Karl Popper's views, Scarot develops further the discussion about 'invention of tradition', 'religious identity' and the role of 'counterfactuals'.

[111] 'Diakonite jaoks' [For the Deacons], typewritten guidelines (No date). Osvald Tärgi materjalid, EEKBLA. The document dates from 1958 or later. The first deacons in the history of the Oleviste ECB Church were ordained in 1958. Lige, 'Kogudus põlvkondade vahetusel', p. 31.

[112] Minutes of the UECBE board, no. 152 (12.06.1989), Juhatuse koosolekute protokollid koos lisadega (JKPLis) [Minutes of the Executive Board, with attachments] (11.01.1988-02.03.1992). EEKBLA.

[113] In 1998, Joosep Tammo does not emphasise closed communion in his booklet about ECB principles, but rather states, allowing a somewhat ecumenical interpretation, that 'the Lord's Supper is for all newborn believers a sign of communion with the Redeemer and Saviour and with all members of his body'. Joosep Tammo, *Piibli õpetus Eesti Evangeeliumi Kristlaste ja Baptistide Koguduste Liidu kogudustes* [Biblical Teaching in the Churches of the UECBE] (Tallinn: Eesti EKB Liit, 1998), p. 34.

emphases in the Soviet period were varied. The Baptists were the only free church in Estonia that had offered systematic theological education at the seminary level in the 1920s and 1930s. Baptist pastors like Osvald Tärk and Robert Võsu played important roles in forming the theological identity of the UECBE. Their ability to express thoughts in a written form, and their constant involvement in preaching, spread their theological positions widely in local churches. Olvik, who was also an able preacher and writer, often chose not to press his theological views on others, in order to keep peace and unity. Arpad Arder, who considered Olvik his father in faith, was even more of a relationship-oriented individual, an 'apostle of love' in the UECBE, working across denominational borders. Being a member in Oleviste, he also obtained an official statement from Herrnhut that he had been accepted into the membership of the Moravian church.[114] The Evangelical Christian tradition was more relationship orientated, while Baptists focused more on theological truths and principles, and their main emphases tended to prevail.

WORSHIP AND MINISTRY IN LOCAL CONGREGATIONS

There was another spiritual dynamic which more clearly brings into the discussion the Pentecostal and Revivalist Free Church traditions. These two free church bodies in Estonia had always valued spontaneous and emotional worship.[115] Baptists and Evangelical Christians had preferred well planned and 'balanced' worship styles. One of the early controversies between Estonian Baptist and Revivalist traditions took place precisely over this issue in the last decades of the nineteenth century. Adam Reinhold Schiewe, a German Baptist from St. Petersburg, who helped to organise some of the early Baptist churches in Estonia, stood for an orderly and 'sober' worship style and considered clapping of hands, prophesying, loud shouts of praise and other similar phenomena alien to Baptist worship.[116] This led to a conflict in Kärdla Baptist Church in Hiiumaa Island in 1886, and a split occurred. A group of believers who supported revivalist spontaneity left. Later they founded Palade Revivalist

---

[114] Ingmar Kurg, 'Üks mälestus Arpad Arderist' [One Reminiscence about Arpad Arder], *Teekäija* (November 1995), pp. 20-21.

[115] Jaanus Plaat, *Usuliikumised, kirikud ja vabakogudused Lääne- ja Hiiumaal: usuühenduste muutumisprotsessid 18. sajandi keskpaigast kuni 20. sajandi lõpuni* [Religious Movements, Churches and Free Churches in West-Estonia and Hiiumaa Island: Transformational Processes of Religious Entities from the mid-18th Century to the End of the 20th Century] (Tartu: Eesti Rahva Muuseum, 2001), pp. 77, 172; Evald Kiil, *Meenutusi nelipühi ärkamisest Eestis* [Memories of the Pentecostal Revival in Estonia] (Tallinn: Logos, 1997), p. 25; A. Seppur, *Jees. Krist. Evg. Priikoguduse tekkimine ja levinemine Läänemaa ärkamises*, pp. 15, 20-21.

[116] Pilli, 'Eesti baptistid ja nende teoloogilise mõtte kajastumine ajakirjas *Teekäija*', p. 13.

Free Church, which after the Second World War joined the ECB union.[117]

Another aspect of differences in worship had been in the use of music. The Revivalist Free churches, especially in their early stages, preferred simple worship with joyful congregational singing *a capella*,[118] and in some cases they considered Baptist choirs to be 'sheer secularity' and Baptist church order to be immersed in 'the German spirit'.[119] However, some changes took place in Revivalist Free churches during the Soviet times. In the former Revivalist Free church in Loona the local church leadership had opposed the idea of having a choir, but the Senior Presbyter stated in 1956 that there were signs that their position was changing.[120] The rich music tradition of Baptists and Evangelical Christians had its impact on Revivalist Free church worship, and in 1980s some former Revivalist churches in Saaremaa Island used harmoniums to accompany congregational singing.[121]

However, many of the former Revivalist churches continued to hold to their traditional repertoire of worship songs, even after 1975 when the UECBE was allowed to publish a new hymnal. The songs which the Revivalist Free churches usually valued most, came from *Laulud Talle Kiituseks* (Songs for the Glory of the Lamb), which was a combination of spiritual songs and secular folk melodies,[122] dating back to the nineteenth century. These songs were first characterised by local people as 'dance tunes, but with holy words'.[123] Anne Allpere has characterised the worship which was inspired by the so called West Coast revival of the 1870s and 1880s in Estonia in this way: 'The prayer meetings swung with merry and dotted song-rhythms.'[124] It was often through their distinctive practice of communal singing that the former Revivalist Free churches and also the Pentecostals[125] attempted to maintain their more enthusiastic spirituality during the Soviet times.[126]

---

[117] Richard Kaups, *Hea Sõnum ja Eesti Baptisti Kogudused* [A Good Message and Estonian Baptist Churches] (Santa Barbara, California, 1974), pp. 81-82; Plaat, *Usuliikumised, kirikud ja vabakogudused Lääne- ja Hiiumaal*, p. 111.

[118] Seppur, *Jees. Krist. Evg. Priikoguduse tekkimine ja levinemine Läänemaa ärkamises*, p. 15

[119] Kaups, *Hea Sõnum ja Eesti Baptisti Kogudused*, p. 83.

[120] Inspection report, no. 7 (06.07.1956). Revideerimisaktid 1956-1957 [Inspection reports 1956-1957], EEKBLA.

[121] Margus Mäemets, private letter (12.04.2005). Toivo Pilli's personal archive.

[122] Plaat, *Usuliikumised, kirikud ja vabakogudused Lääne- ja Hiiumaal*, p. 83.

[123] M. Busch, *Ridala ärkamise ajalugu* [A History of the Revival in Ridala] (Keila: K.-Ü. 'Külvaja' trükk, 1928), p. 12.

[124] Anne Allpere, *Estonian Cantometric Attempt II: The Sacred and the Profane – Can It Be Heard?* (Tallinn: Academy of Sciences of the Estonian SSR, 1989), pp. 10-11.

[125] The traditional Pentecostal hymnal *Võidulaulud* [Songs of Victory] (1928) also continued to be used in the UECBE churches, mostly during weekly gatherings and prayer meetings.

[126] Even in 2001 there were some ECB churches where *Laulud Talle Kiituseks* (printed in 1921) or the Pentecostal hymnal *Võidulaulud* (the 1935 edition) were used in parallel

Nevertheless, there is no doubt that during the Soviet years worship in the ECB churches lost much of the diversity that had characterised the free churches. In part, this was due to the monitoring of the state authorities who were suspicious of 'pentecostal' elements in worship.[127] Another factor was the influence of the Baptist and Evangelical Christian traditions which stood for structured and pre-planned worship. Knowing that 'disorderly worship' might cause difficulties from the state authorities, the ECB leaders emphasised the need to keep order in worship. Everything, both in conducting 'ordinances' and in leading worship, should be done 'solemnly and without confusion'.[128] In the united church of Oleviste it was agreed that there must be order in the worship service, and speaking in tongues, for example, should not be allowed unless an 'interpreter' would be translating the message.[129] During sermons and prayers there must be silence, and prophets should not perform on their own account.[130] The elements of Revivalist Free Church and Pentecostal worship were discouraged, or adjusted to a more 'sane' way of worship. However, in the 1970s and 1980s, a new and more lively worship style, which had reached some of the Estonian ECB churches, caused debates, and almost divisions, in the union. Yet this more lively worship style, which included music that appealed to young people, and enthusiastic preaching as well as some charismatic phenomena, inspired several churches, especially in Tallinn, but also in Hiiumaa and Saaremaa Islands, the traditional regions of Revivalist Free churches.[131] A rather experiential and emotional worship, though restricted by Soviet pressures, found its way back into the UECBE. New charismatic worship elements supported the former Pentecostal and Revivalist worship tradition.

The role of music in general, and congregational singing in particular, cannot be underestimated in the Estonian context. Meego Remmel has pointed out that 'the holy narrative in Christian music was kept alive and developed

---

with more recent hymnals. Ene Paldre, 'Ühislaulu areng ja tähendus EKB Liidu kogudustes' [Development and Meaning of Communal Singing in the UECBE Churches], BTh thesis (Tartu: Tartu University, 2001), p. 47. Ain Riistan has pointed out that visiting Hiiumaa Island with a youth choir in the 1990s, some Revivalist Free Church members, warm and emotional in their style of worship, commented: 'Your songs are too "academic"! We are simple people here and we like simple "evangelical" songs which touch our hearts.' Ain Riistan, 'The Union of Estonian Evangelical Christian and Baptist Churches: Diversity in Unity or Issues Concerning Spirituality and Identity', a paper in a Church History course (Prague: IBTS, 1997), p. 2. TPL.

[127] The chairman of the CARC, I. Polianski, to the Commissioner, J. Kivi (21.09.1945). ERA, f. R-1989, n. 2, s. 2, pp. 36-39.

[128] Tärk, *Vaimulikud talitused EKB kogudustes*, p. 2.

[129] 'Diakonite jaoks' [For the Deacons], typewritten guidelines (No date). Osvald Tärgi materjalid, EEKBLA.

[130] Olvik, *Mälestused*, part 2, p. 367.

[131] Margus Mäemets, private letter (12.04.2005).

throughout the years of totalitarian occupation'.[132] It can be argued that there was more than one narrative of congregational singing, music and worship in the UECBE during Soviet years. Being aware of the danger of oversimplification, I would put it in this way: in the Pentecostal and Revivalist approach, singing served as a language for experiential faith; in Baptist and Evangelical Christian traditions, in general, singing and music offered a commentary on the preaching and the biblical texts. These different spiritual approaches became intertwined and modified during the Soviet years, but the distinct traditions did not die out altogether. It should also be mentioned that music offered a natural link between the ECB religious identity and the national identity of Estonians. Yet, not all music styles in the ECB churches survived the test of time. For example, mandolin choirs in the ECB churches were 'dying out' by the 1980s. But other choirs flourished throughout the communist period. In 1950, in Tallinn 'Kalju' ECB Church, a church which maintained a traditional Baptist spirituality, thirty per cent of the church members were involved in choir activities.[133] In 1991 there were 81 choirs with 1547 singers in the UECBE. The total membership of the union was 6087.[134]

There is one more aspect which should be discussed. In Estonia, from the 1950s, a gradual shift took place in understanding how an ECB church, of whatever spiritual strand, should look and operate. It is well known that the Soviet government restricted the life of the congregations to the church buildings. Hans Brandenburg stated: 'At a pinch, the Orthodox Church with its liturgy could be satisfied with this. But for the Evangelical Christians and Baptists, it meant a significant limitation.'[135] Brandenburg is right, but the whole issue has another aspect attached to it. The atheistic government also confiscated several church buildings, merging local churches which had significantly different spiritual atmospheres. Tallinn Oleviste Church was formed by an unprecedented merger of eight local churches in 1950,[136] though since 1948 the Tallinn Revivalist Free Church had shared a building with the

---

[132] Meego Remmel, *The Role of Christian Ethics in Postmarxist and Postmodern Estonia* (Bonn: Verlag für Kultur und Wissenschaft, 2002), p. 61.
[133] A survey of Tallinn 'Kalju' Church activities in 1950. Kirjavahetus ja dokumendid 1950-1974: Kalju kogudus [Correspondence and documents 1950-1974: Kalju Church], EEKBLA.
[134] Robert Võsu, 'Eesti EKB Liidu tegevusest 1991. a.' [About the Activities of the UECBE in 1991], *Teekäija*, no. 10 (1992), pp. 16-17.
[135] Hans Brandenburg, *The Meek and the Mighty: The Emergence of the Evangelical Movement in Russia* (New York: Oxford University Press, 1977), p. 189.
[136] For closures and mergers of the Estonian ECB churches, see Toivo Pilli and Tõnis Valk, 'Ühest ateistliku töö meetodist: evangeeliumi kristlaste-baptistide palvemajade sulgemine Eestis 1945-1965' [A Method of Atheistic Work: Closures of Evangelical Christian-Baptist Prayer Houses in Estonia, 1945-1965], in Toivo Pilli, ed., *Teekond teisenevas ajas*, pp. 89-127 .

Evangelical Christians 'Karmel' Church.[137] Oleviste, a 'mammoth-size church' (at least for the Estonian setting), began to shape the ECB understanding of church and spiritual leadership. Certainly, cooperation needed to be learned, though Olvik admitted that it was difficult in 1948-1950, as some believers (from the Pentecostal tradition) 'liked to pray so loud that it sounded far outside the building'.[138] Tärk also seemed to have had difficulties with the Pentecostal wing.[139] But there was more to it. The example of Oleviste gradually changed the church model that had been common to Baptists, as well as Pentecostals and Revivalist Free churches. This was a model of a relatively small congregation, often located in the countryside or in small towns, where people knew each other well and where close fellowship could develop between 'brothers and sisters'. The new model for Estonian Evangelical Christian-Baptist churches was one that was more 'urbanised' and 'structured'.

Oleviste Church created a new paradigm, first forced upon the ECB union, but soon accepted. This approximately 1900-member church required more hierarchical leadership structures. A fellowship or 'brotherhood' model, visualised by meeting in simple prayer houses rather than in classical church buildings, became gradually marginalised in much ECB thinking. Oleviste Church, located in an old cathedral and symbolising an urban type of congregational life, became the 'mother church' of the union. Smaller ECB churches, instead of looking toward Haapsalu or the West-Coast of Estonia, where the nineteenth century religious revivals took place, began to look toward Tallinn and Oleviste. In addition, Oleviste Church was influential through its ministries. During the period 1950-2000 Oleviste sent into pastoral ministry approximately 40 persons.[140] The Oleviste music ministry, as well as the evangelism patterns in the 1970s inspired other ECB churches all over Estonia.[141] All four strands of free church life that made up the ECB found that their traditional identity was changed and they engaged in a process in which a new identity was forged.

CONCLUSION

In 1945, the Estonian Evangelical Christians, Baptists, Pentecostals and Revivalist Free churches sensed that there was a danger that they might lose

---

[137] The UECBE statistical report 1948. Evangeeliumi Kristlaste-Baptistide koguduste statistilised aruanded 1945-1963 [The UECBE statistical reports 1945-1963], EEKBLA.
[138] Olvik, *Mälestused,* part 2, pp. 336, 340.
[139] Ibid., p. 389.
[140] Ü. Meriloo, 'Karjaste läkitamine' [Sending out the Pastors], in *Oleviste 50,* pp. 39-40.
[141] For example, a youth choir in Hiiumaa Island established in 1968-1969, copied the example of Oleviste youth choir. Viljo Liik, *Meenutusi möödunust* [Memories from the Past] (Kärdla: Kärdla Baptistikogudus, 2005), p. 21.

some essential elements of their identity in the union imposed on them by the state. The smaller traditions felt the pressure, whether well founded or not, to adjust to the Baptist way of being a free church.[142] There were undoubtedly uniting elements. All four churches which were joined together had a common understanding that the new birth is a basis for church membership. All four traditions had the historical experience of being a 'gathered church' – or 'gathering church', to use a more dynamic term now being employed.[143] But there were significant differences which did not disappear overnight.

Tensions emerged, especially between the Baptist and the Evangelical Christian traditions, more specifically in the field of ecclesiology, in the understanding of baptism and the Lord's Supper. In the August 1945 meeting in Moscow, between Estonian representatives and the AUCECB leadership, the following understanding was reached: 'Toward those who had still remained on the basis of infant baptism the attitude must be respectful and one should try to convince them that they should let themselves be baptized in faith...'[144] Though a certain flexibility was shown, the course that was taken was one of uniformity. Those representing Baptist views in the UECBE took seriously the task of convincing those of other viewpoints. The traditional Estonian Baptist understanding that believer's baptism must be a prerequisite for church membership as well as the practice of 'closed' communion became the predominant teaching and practice in the union by the 1970s. The Baptist case was, it seems, better argued. In 1974, Karl L. Marley argued that Evangelical Christians lost much of their identity because when joining the union 'the small countryside churches had not developed to their full maturity...'[145]

One may only guess what might have happened if in this ecclesiological debate more attention had been paid to searching actively for a common theology and a 'core identity', instead of defining the borders of different traditions. Was there a chance of developing a unique 'small "b" baptist' identity,[146] informed by wider evangelical experience, instead of supporting the large 'B' baptist positions? In the field of Revivalist and Pentecostal worship styles, 'where everyone has a contribution to make to the service',[147] the spontaneous and joyful-emotional elements were gradually marginalised. In the UECBE, worship became increasingly centred on the pulpit and the choir

---

[142] J. Kivi to the chairman of the CARC, I. Polianski (15.07.1945). ERA, f. R-1989, n. 2, s. 2, pp. 18-20.
[143] The term 'gathering church' was introduced in Keith Jones, *A Believing Church* (Didcot: The Baptist Union of Great Britain, 1998), pp. 38-39.
[144] Laks, *Mälestusi eluteelt ja töömaalt*, p. 82.
[145] K.L. Marley to Robert Võsu (07.04.1974). Robert Võsu materjalid, EEKBLA.
[146] For a short description of a small 'b' baptist vision, see James Wm. McClendon, Jr., *Systematic Theology: Ethics*, vol. 1 (Nashville: Abingdon Press, 1986), p. 35.
[147] Alan Anderson, *An Introduction to Pentecostalism: Global Charismatic Christianity* (Cambridge: Cambridge University Press, 2004), p. 9.

podium. The church members were not encouraged to participate actively in worship, except in times of free prayer, and the principle of 'order' was emphasised. Some churches, however, maintained for a longer time their 'awakening spontaneity, deep conviction of sins and ensuing joy',[148] which resonated with the new charismatic worship style of the 1970s. Even if Pentecostals and Revivalist Free churches did not have trained theologians to express their identity in a more explicit way, their grassroots identity, lived out in congregational practices, helped to an extent to maintain the fellowship model of church in the UECBE.

Stronger traditions have a tendency to 'swallow up' smaller ones. Karl Leopold Marley, in 1980, strongly criticised the UECBE: human power, he argued, was used to strengthen activities in the spiritual field; the pastor's role was overestimated and the priesthood of all believers was downplayed; spontaneity and earnestness had become lost; teaching and 'seminars' were overemphasised; and 'the spirit of the world' had penetrated into the churches. Though Marley's words have to be taken *cum granum salis*, he is certainly right in suggesting that different historical movements have a complementary nature and that instead of one movement dominating, it would have been constructive if there had been a more consistent desire to learn from the 'truths of different movements and to fill in the gaps'.[149] Evangelical Christians were convinced that 'dogmatics divides' but that prayer and worshipping together unites.[150] In the name of unity Evangelical Christians were more willing to make compromises over doctrinal issues, but even they had difficulties accepting some Baptist or Pentecostal or Revivalist elements.

Increasingly the UECBE leaders presented the union of 1945 through the prism of Baptist identity. Robert Võsu took it for granted in 1968 that the ECB union should be understood as a Baptist union. He was also aware that the ECB believers were often referred to by outsiders simply as 'Baptists'. 'A name does not spoil a man, if a man does not spoil the name … if we should consider it necessary to give up this name, … then it would be because we do not deserve this name. … Let the Lord be merciful that we could deserve the name of Baptists.'[151] Oskar Olvik, by contrast, believed and argued that the UECBE should be a movement 'where every previous point of view would be respected' and thus that it should not be 'a Baptist Union, which has principally remained the same, with only some letters changed in the name'.[152] In reality, however, at least in the field of ecclesiology, the traditional Baptist approach and traditional Baptist identity became dominant. The tendency to uniformity

---

[148] Alland Parman, Merike Uudam and Norie Roeder, *Kui kristlik on Eestimaa?* [How Christian is Estonia?] (Tallinn: Estonian Evangelisation Alliance, 1997), p. 23.

[149] K.L. Marley to Robert Võsu (03.01.1980). Robert Võsu materjalid, EEKBLA.

[150] Olvik, *Mälestused*, part 2, pp. 331-335.

[151] *'Kalju' koguduse karjase Robert Võsu jutlusi ajavahemikul 1944.-1969*, p. 135.

[152] Olvik, *Mälestused*, part 2, pp. 360-361.

reflected other spheres of life in Soviet society, and as the first part of this study has shown that brought a pressure to bear on the churches, but within the UECBE there was a further set of spiritual dynamics at work deriving from the need for different free church traditions to find spiritual unity and forge a new ecclesial identity.

CHAPTER 7

Word and Spirit: A Creative Tension

It has usually been emphasised by Estonian Baptist authors that from the very beginning Estonian Baptists were Bible-based or 'Word-orientated' in their understanding of the Christian life. One early leader, August Johannson, was convinced that it was the Baptist influence in the wider religious scene in Estonia at the end of the nineteenth and the beginning of the twentieth century that contributed to 'a clearer understanding of the Bible, study of the Word of God and a [better] preaching style'.[1] High regard for scripture was typical of all Estonian free church traditions. During the Soviet era the Estonian Evangelical Christian-Baptist leaders often highlighted the authority of the Bible.[2] Their views harmonized with those of Arthur Mitskevich, one of the AUCECB's key figures, who stated at the Tenth Baptist World Congress: 'Our believers [in the Soviet Union] stand on the foundation of full confidence in the Bible, biblical discipline and a deep devotional and moral life.'[3] However, there was another element, also present in the Estonian Baptist identity from the beginning – the awareness of and focus on the work of the Holy Spirit. In the Estonian Baptist publication *Teekäija* (Pilgrim), the work of the Holy Spirit was discussed extensively in the first half of the twentieth century. Revivalist and holiness teachers from America and Britain, such as D.L. Moody, F.B. Meyer, Jessie Penn-Lewis and R.A. Torrey, through their translated articles, reminded Estonian Baptists about the need for the 'filling' or 'baptism' of the Spirit for a 'victorious' Christian life.[4] Karl Kaups, who in 1934 called Estonian Baptists 'a

---

[1] August Johannson, 'Juubeli aasta Eesti Baptisti Ühenduses' [An Anniversary Year in the Estonian Baptist Union], *Teekäija*, no. 3 (1909), p. 18.

[2] See Osvald Tärk, *Piibli teoloogia* [Biblical Theology], typewritten manuscript (1958), p. 2. KUSA.; Robert Võsu, *EKB koguduste ajalugu* [A History of ECB Churches], typewritten manuscript (1959), p. 2. KUSA.

[3] Tenth Baptist World Congress. Official Report (Nashville, Tennessee: BWA and Broadman Press, 1961), p. 187.

[4] Toivo Pilli, 'Eesti baptistid ja nende teoloogilise mõtte kajastumine ajakirjas *Teekäija* kuni 1940' [Estonian Baptists and their Theology as Reflected in *Teekäija* until 1940], ThM thesis (Tartu: Tartu University, 1996), pp. 47-55.

movement of Biblical truths',[5] also stated that 'we must not deny the gifts of the Spirit'.[6] Estonian Pentecostal and Revivalist Free churches emphasised this aspect even more. The dynamics of Spirit-orientedness and Word-orientedness in the process of shaping Estonian ECB identity continued under Soviet pressure. In the 1940s and 1950s the 'Word approach' was widely encouraged in the Estonian ECB churches, while in the 1970s and 1980s a resurgence of a 'Spirit approach' can be detected.

A SEARCH FOR STABILITY IN THE WORD

In the post-war situation, the Evangelical Christian-Baptist believers in Estonia needed to find new stability. Atheistic pressures from outside and the pains of adjustments inside the multifaceted UECBE required a stabilizing factor. In 1962, Robert Võsu, in his sermon 'Note the Times', summarized this post-war experience: 'There are times when it is popular to be a devout person. But before the second coming of Christ the situation is contrary to this. Heaven above the believers is dense with clouds.'[7] He suggested that the believers needed to learn to see 'buds of faith in the chaos', and to believe that these dark 'clouds will become the throne of the Son of Man'.[8] Where did the believers in the UECBE find strength for their faith, an unswerving centre in their diversity and an anchor in turmoil? This centre was found in the written and preached Word. Estonian ECB believers were assured that their beliefs and lifestyle should be based on the Word of God.[9] They were convinced that spiritual stability was achieved on this basis. In the immediate context of change, the theological heritage of Word-centredness was reconfirmed. It should also be remembered that the Spirit-emphasis in the Estonian ECB union was marginalised during the decades after the war, as the Soviet government felt uneasy about the spontaneity of Pentecostal-type devotional practices. The government officials were suspicious that, under Pentecostalist influences, former Baptists and Evangelical Christians might start 'praying in the Spirit' and 'speaking in tongues'.[10] However, there were inner factors which moulded

---

[5] Karl Kaups, 'Eesti Baptismi ideelised põhialused' [The Principles of the Estonian Baptist Movement], in R. Kaups, ed., *50 aastat apostlite radadel* [50 Years in the Ways of the Apostles] (Keila: E.B.K. Liidu kirjastus, 1934), p. 10.

[6] Karl Kaups, 'Katsuge vaimud läbi' [Test the Spirits], *Teekäija*, no. 23 (1924), pp. 334-335.

[7] *'Kalju' koguduse karjase Robert Võsu jutlusi ajavahemikul 1944-1969* [Sermons of 'Kalju' Church Pastor, Robert Võsu, from 1944 to 1969], typewritten manuscript, p. 97. KUSA.

[8] Ibid.

[9] Osvald Tärk, 'Meie vendluse põhimõtted' [Principles of Our Brotherhood], *Logos*, no. 1 (1982), p. 18.

[10] The chairman of the CARC, I. Polianski, to the Commissioner, J. Kivi (21.09.1945). ERA, f. R-1989, n. 2, s. 2, p. 37.

the theological identity of Estonian Evangelical Christians-Baptists regarding the issues of Word and Spirit.

The leadership of the UECBE highlighted a Word-orientated understanding of faith, as they were well aware that issues of pneumatology had caused diverse views among Estonian free churches before the Second World War, a situation which, for example, had adversely influenced Baptist and Pentecostal relationships.[11] Probably there was some awareness among Estonian ECB leaders of difficulties which marked Baptist and Pentecostal relations in Scandinavia.

During the Soviet era, in matters of pneumatology, Estonian Baptist and Revivalist Free church traditions were closer to each other than were Baptist and Pentecostal traditions. There was a need to adjust and learn from each other. Again, it was hoped that scripture would serve as the point of unity. The young Estonian preachers were taught that while interpretations regarding the work of the Spirit may differ, 'our teaching is the New Testament, and there is no deviation from this'.[12] Paraphrasing Gordon Fee and Douglas Stuart, one may say that Estonian ECB believers were convinced that 'the plain meaning' of a scripture text 'often lies on the surface'.[13] In a somewhat naïve but sincere way they believed that obedience to this 'plain meaning' is of prime importance, and they paid much less attention to the process of interpreting the text. Osvald Tärk said in his later years that during his lifetime he had seen two world wars and eight changes of political order – ranging from tsarism to socialism – but the Word of God remained the point of support, even 'though the earth give way and the mountains fall into the heart of the sea' (Psalm 46: 2).[14] What Tärk verbalised as an important personal lesson, was subconsciously followed as a principle by the ECB union in the post-war confusions and in the process of different free church traditions adjusting to each other after the merger in 1945. Trust in the scriptural text was expected to provide a necessary centre for ECB identity. Paradoxically, emphasis on the Bible made Estonian Baptists cautious about any written confession of faith, as 'confessions of faith may separate, but living faith unites'. 'We may, indeed, be united on the basis of a written confession of faith, and my suggestion would be that this confession be the New Testament,' said Osvald Tärk.[15]

There was another aspect of the same issue of stability: relations between 'doctrine' and 'experience'. These two words appear often in Soviet era ECB

---

[11]The Estonian Baptist herald *Teekäija* published criticism of Pentecostalism. Also Karl Kaups, though positive about the work of the Holy Spirit and Spirit Baptism, was critical of some emotional phenomena in Pentecostalism.

[12] Lecture notes 1973-1978, notebook 3. Uudu Rips' personal archive.

[13] Gordon D. Fee and Douglas Stuart, *How to Read the Bible for All Its Worth* (Grand Rapids, Michigan, Zondervan, 1993), p. 13.

[14] Tärk, 'Meie vendluse põhimõtted', *Logos*, no. 1 (1981), p. 8.

[15] Osvald Tärk, *Efesose kiri* [The Epistle to the Ephesians], typewritten manuscript (1957), p. 84. KUSA.

literature in Estonia. 'Doctrine', for Estonian believers, was an attempt to
explain and apply the teaching of the Bible. 'Experience' referred to more
subjective elements of faith, the experienced – not only rationally argued –
signs of God's presence. In 1977 it was stated in a semi-illegal ministerial
training session that teaching about the 'new birth' was the same in all ECB
churches, but 'experience of the new birth' was different for every person.[16]
Doctrine, therefore, had a unifying role. Robert Võsu complained in the 1970s,
however, that 'both piety and doctrine are pushed into the background', and
that 'experience' had come to the forefront. These comments were made
against the background of a new interest in the charismatic phenomena, which
had by then reached Estonia. Võsu concluded that the early church, which
Estonian Baptists often saw as their model,[17] 'continued in teaching, not in
emotions or experiences'. Being himself a systematic thinker, he argued that in
a 'healthy charismatic movement' teaching should be a priority. According to
him, a 'healthy doctrine' is Christocentric, draws its criteria and balance from
the Bible, is in accordance with 'common sense' and is free from extreme
positions, has a healing effect on the church, develops the fruit of the Spirit, and
has teachers who are not arrogant.[18]

Ants Rebane, who became known as a systematic preacher and teacher in
ECB circles in the 1980s, said that 'in Christianity teaching is always a
priority'; experience and ethics will follow. 'This sequence cannot be
reversed.'[19] Again, the unifying role of 'teaching' was emphasised. However,
this position was challenged by the new awareness of the work of the Holy
Spirit and the consequent need to reflect on it theologically. In 1978, Manfred
Otto's translated article, 'A Tension Area of the Charismatic Movement',
reminded Estonian believers that charismatic unity was a unity in common
experience, not in common doctrine. The author agreed that the unity of the
church is endangered when one group presents its experience in absolute terms.
However, help is found 'not in emphasising right teaching'. Rather, 'where
experiences are related to the Spirit and the Word' the right perspective can be
found.[20] This approach, aiming at taking the Spirit's role seriously, became
increasingly widespread in the UECBE, though the leadership promoted the
Word-emphasis.

[16] Lecture notes 1973-1978, notebook 3. Uudu Rips' personal archive.
[17] Riho Saard has pointed this out also. See his 'Eesti varase baptismi
eneserefleksioonist' [About the Self-Reflection of Early Estonian Baptists], in Toivo
Pilli, ed., *Teekond teisenevas ajas: peatükke Eesti vabakoguduste ajaloost* [A Journey in
Changing Time: Some Chapters from History of Estonian Free Churches] (Tartu:
Kõrgem Usuteaduslik Seminar ja Sõnasepp OÜ, 2005), pp. 18-20.
[18] Lecture notes 1973-1978, notebook 2. Uudu Rips' personal archive.
[19] Ants Rebane, 'Kristuse koguduse ühtsus' [The Unity of Christ's Church], *Logos*, no. 1
(1985), p. 10.
[20] Manfred Otto, 'Harismaatilise liikumise pingeväli' [An Area of Tension in the
Charismatic Movement], *Lectio V* (1978), p. 11.

The tension between 'teaching' and 'experience' can be detected also at the level of church members. In 1981, Osvald Tärk remarked critically that ECB believers were seldom able to explain their beliefs 'with the help of the Word of God'. He said that the basis for the church members' faith was often 'personal experiences', sometimes stimulated and strengthened by 'dreams and literature about revelations'. Tärk lamented that 'dogmatic education in our churches has grown very weak'.[21] There were even ideas that the local churches should have some kind of 'confirmation teaching', similar to the practice of the Lutheran Church.[22] Solid doctrinal teaching was supposed to balance unstable, often individualistic experiences, a need which has from time to time been expressed in the wider evangelical world.[23] However, in Estonia, there were also other voices. Oskar Olvik, a former Evangelical Christian, argued that movements that had become 'petrified', in the sense of no longer being open to change, 'highlighted dogmatics even when faith and love were not up to the standard any more.'[24] One of Olvik's main concerns, in the line of Evangelical Christian tradition, was a shallow ethical application of Christian beliefs; he did not underestimate theological reflection, as some charismatically-orientated circles in Estonia tended to do in the 1970s and 1980s. If Estonian Baptists had more thoroughly analysed the whole issue of 'experience', instead of simply contrasting it to 'teaching', they would probably be better equipped to meet the challenges of the present era when the experiential is again highlighted, both in culture and in Christian worship.[25]

There was another element, perhaps more dynamic than doctrinal, which offered a 'meeting point' for the different traditions within the Estonian ECB union. This was - as Robert Võsu pointed out - 'Christocentrism';[26] a piety and understanding of faith which focussed on the person of Jesus Christ. Despite different emphases related to theological understandings of scriptural teaching and spiritual experience, all four free churches in Estonia traditionally agreed that 'fellowship with Christ is crucial'.[27] The Holy Spirit transforms believers into Christ-likeness.[28] Believers in Estonian ECB churches would find no difficulty identifying with Larry Christenson's view that renewal requires submission to the Lordship of Christ and that the gifts of the Spirit increase the

---

[21] Osvald Tärk, 'Meie vendluse põhimõtted', *Logos*, no. 1 (1981), p. 8.

[22] Lecture notes 1973-1978, notebook 2. Uudu Rips' personal archive.

[23] See, for example, Gerald Bray, *Biblical Interpretation: Past and Present* (Downers Grove, Illinois: InterVarsity Press, 1996), p. 562.

[24] Oskar Olvik, *Mälestused* [Memoirs], part 2 (Tallinn, 1966), p. 388.

[25] For example, see Leonard Sweet, *Postmodern Pilgrims* (Nashville, Tennessee: Broadman and Holman Publishers, 2000), pp. 27-52; and Bob Rognlien, *Experiential Worship* (Navpress, 2005).

[26] Lecture notes 1973-1978, notebook 2. Uudu Rips' personal archive.

[27] Olvik, *Mälestused*, part 2, p. 592.

[28] Ibid., pp. 592-597.

awareness of the presence of Christ among his people.[29] Later, in the 1980s, the semi-illegal ECB typewritten publication *Logos* emphasised the need to focus on the words of Christ and on Christ as the Word.[30] In biblical interpretation, too, the Christocentric approach was widespread. Explaining the Ethiopian official's story (Acts 8:26-40), Oskar Olvik was convinced that Isaiah 53, which the Ethiopian read, 'very directly speaks of Christ's redemptive work'.[31] Many Old Testament scholars would probably debate this issue. However, Christocentrism in Estonian ECB theological identity functioned as a stabilizing factor, aiming to keep the centrifugal and centripetal forces in balance. Both the Word and Spirit approaches had the potential to find common ground in focusing on Christ.

UNDERSTANDING AND APPLYING THE WORD

Though academic study of the Bible was not a priority for Estonian Evangelical Christians-Baptists, they were aware of formal methods of biblical interpretation. Robert Võsu was convinced that 'recent archaeological excavations' proved 'the honesty' of the biblical authors.[32] Efraim Joel Dahl, referring to Stanley Jones' views, stated that biblical criticism was a child of the Enlightenment, but 'instead of preparing Christ for burial, … it liberated Him from burial linen…'.[33] Osvald Tärk evaluated the historical-critical method of biblical interpretation in his typewritten textbook *Uue Testamendi sissejuhatus* (Introduction to the New Testament). Though Tärk did not deny the role of the historical-critical method for understanding the scriptures, he was critical of the method's 'liberal' connotations, and rather emphasised personal faith, ethical lifestyle and a focus on Jesus, more than the rational conclusions which could be derived from the Bible.[34] He did have sympathy with common sense philosophy, 'the view that common sense rightly recognizes some ideas as true and needing no defence'.[35] Nevertheless, any method of biblical interpretation was weighed on the scales of local Baptist identity and used with a sense of pastoral responsibility.

The priority for Estonian Baptists was a simple openness to the biblical

[29] Larry Christenson, 'Palu, et Kristus valitseks' [Pray that Christ would Rule], *Lectio V* (1978), pp. 17-20.
[30] *Logos*, no. 1 (1981), no. 1 (1982), introduction, without pagination.
[31] Olvik, *Mälestused*, part 2, p. 525.
[32] Lecture notes 1973-1978, notebook 1. Uudu Rips' personal archive.
[33] Efraim Joel Dahl, *Evangeelse maailma radadel* [On the Paths of the Evangelical World], typewritten manuscript (Tallinn, 1976), p. 116. KUSA.
[34] Ruudi Leinus, comp. and ed., *Osvald Tärk. Uskuge Jumalasse* [Osvald Tärk. Believe in God] (Tallinn: Eesti EKB Liit, 1999), p. 30.
[35] William W. Klein et al., *Introduction to Biblical Interpretation* (Nashville: Thomas Nelson Publishers, 1993), p. 55.

text as a guide for Christian living, often with attention to the 'literal meaning' of the text. They had a high view of biblical authority, in line with pre-war spiritual leaders, such as Johannes Laks and Karl Kaups.[36] In general, it was an 'ordinary theology',[37] not a scholarly theology, that constituted the framework for the ECB way of understanding the Bible. Paradoxically, although they sometimes failed to see benefits in the historical-critical method, some Estonian Baptist theologians and presbyters still used some of its tools.[38] According to Heikki Räisänen, the historical-critical method, aiming 'to reach objective facts and conclusions', could be hierarchical and authoritative, and create passivity among church members in the process of interpreting biblical texts.[39] In part, this was true in Estonia, though in the UECBE interpreting scriptures was never the privilege of only a small group of pastors-theologians. Freedom of interpretation by individual believers, which is 'fundamental to Baptist thought',[40] continued to influence UECBE identity. Ideally, Estonian Baptists wanted to leave space for an individual believer to think, and not to be enslaved by theological systems.[41] The believer could engage directly with the Bible.

Estonian Baptists in Soviet years emphasised that scripture is the inspired Word of God. How the 'inspiration' should be understood was not interpreted unanimously. For example, early Baptists, such as Karl Kaups, in their fight for the 'normative authority' of the Bible, were convinced that 'inspired persons could not write non-inspired words'[42] and tended to see biblical text and the Word of God almost as identical.[43] Billy Graham, in his book *Püha Vaim* (The Holy Spirit), which was translated into Estonian in the 1980s, soon after its original publication, expressed views which point toward verbal inspiration.[44] However, not all Estonians agreed. Dahl argued that 'verbal inspiration' places

---

[36] Johannes Laks, *Kakskümmendviis aastat vabakoguduslist liikumist Eestis 1905-1930* [Twenty-Five Years of a Free Church Movement in Estonia 1905-1930] (Tallinn, 1930), p. 27. Karl Kaups, 'Pilke tulevikku' [Visions for the Future], in R. Kaups, ed., *50 aastat apostlite radadel*, p. 206.

[37] This term has been used by Jeff Astley, *Ordinary Theology: Looking, Listening and Learning in Theology* (Ashgate, 2002), p. 56.

[38] Especially the students who, as an exception, had an opportunity to study in Germany in the early 1980s.

[39] Heikki Räisänen et al., *Reading the Bible in the Global Village* (Atlanta: Society of Biblical Literature, 2000), p. 10.

[40] Walter B. Shurden, *The Baptist Identity. Four Fragile Freedoms* (Macon, Georgia: Smyth and Helwys, 1993), pp. 18-20.

[41] Tärk, 'Meie vendluse põhimõtted', *Logos*, no. 1 (1981), p. 10.

[42] Karl Kaups, 'Protestantism' [Protestantism], *Teekäija*, no. 21 (1931), p. 252.

[43] Pilli, 'Eesti baptistid ja nende teoloogilise mõtte kajastumine ajakirjas *Teekäija*', p. 38.

[44] Billy Graham, *Püha Vaim: Jumala väe virgutav jõud inimese elus* [The Holy Spirit: Activating God's Power in Your Life], typewritten Estonian translation (n. p., n. d.), pp. 54-58. KUSA.

'spiritual understanding solely on the basis of an [intellectual] principle. ... But this principle is not yet a convictional revelation or faith.'[45] 'Inspiration' is divine, but 'verbal inspiration' is a purely human idea, Dahl declared. 'If I have to be constantly afraid of my intellect and the results of its explorations, then my faith and commitment to God are not one hundred per cent sincere.'[46] As Senior Presbyter, Robert Võsu argued that the Bible was written in order to meet the needs of its own time, but contained eternal truths which go beyond the borders of past times.[47] This kind of 'middle way' was also supported in the 1980s by Ingmar Kurg, a representative of a younger generation of Estonian Baptists influenced by classical Protestant thinking, who saw the Bible and the Word of God linked together but not absolutely identical. Kurg criticised the theory of verbal inspiration, saying that it made the biblical text 'flat' and failed to distinguish between its periphery and high points. If the text is understood in this way it would be possible to prove anything, if only suitable Bible verses could be found, Kurg argued. However, he was equally critical of those who denied any inspiration, seeing in the Bible only a 'book of history' with no normative authority.[48] Estonian ECB believers affirmed the authority of the biblical text, though wider views also shaped their arguments.

Estonian Baptists were convinced that every reader needed God's Spirit in order to grasp the meaning of Scripture. [49] The Spirit not only inspired the scriptural writers, but also inspired and inspires the readers of Scripture. Võsu argued that if God does not open the reader's eyes and heart to understand scripture, then this is not the Word of God for the reader. The Spirit gives guidance according to the reader's situations and needs.[50] However, while affirming the need for supernatural help in understanding the Bible, and rejecting the tendencies in biblical studies which undermined the miraculous elements in the Bible, the Word-orientated wing of Estonian Baptists saw coherence in the Bible.[51] Though somewhat critical of the nineteenth-century 'scientific' approach that '[reason] is the best tool with which to study the Bible'[52], the Word-emphasis in the UECBE often relied on rational arguments and presented biblical truths in a logical and systematic way. This caused a reaction. In the 1970s, there were several presbyters and church members who began to seek direct, inner guidance from the Spirit, along the lines of a Finnish charismatic leader, Niilo Yli-Vainio, who believed that 'baptism with the

---

[45] Dahl, *Evangeelse maailma radadel*, p. 117.

[46] Ibid., p. 118.

[47] Robert Võsu, 'Püha Vaimu olemus' [The Nature of the Holy Spirit], *Logos*, no. 5 (1982), p. 17.

[48] Ingmar Kurg, 'Jõuludeks: Jumala Sõna lihakssaamine' [For Christmas: The Incarnation of God's Word], *Logos*, no. 6 (1983), pp. 12-13.

[49] Osvald Tärk, 'Meie vendluse põhimõtted', *Logos*, no. 1 (1982), 18.

[50] Robert Võsu, *Evangeelne eetika* [Evangelical Ethics] (Tallinn: Logos, 1996), p. 56.

[51] Lecture notes 1973-1978, notebook 1. Uudu Rips' personal archive.

[52] Klein et al, *Introduction to Biblical Interpretation*, p. 52.

Spirit' teaches how to use scripture in the context of 'false teachings and false spirits'.[53] The Spirit's guidance, though using the Word, was understood in these circles as a mystical-miraculous act of God, which marginalises or even excludes human intellect. The advocates of the Spirit-approach seldom realised that to be left with competing subjective 'Spirit' interpretations of the text can be as dangerous as a view that puts too much trust in human reason in the process of understanding the Bible.

These two approaches in the UECBE identity, often in tension with each other, became clearer in the 1980s. In some extreme cases, the 'inner guidance' of the Spirit tended to underestimate the scriptural written word altogether. This was why Osvald Tärk said: 'It is not enough that we have an inner sign. We need also an outward sign through the Word. If somebody thinks that a new being does not need it, then he has placed himself outside the New Testament.'[54] The Word should be 'absorbed in our way of thinking and in our feelings'; the believer should be immersed in the Word.[55]

Though there was a clear tendency toward taking biblical passages at their 'face value', without consciously engaging in interpretative processes, this does not mean that interpretation was altogether lacking – both in individual Bible reading and in Bible study efforts in local churches. Sometimes individual reading missed the wider context of biblical texts. Efraim J. Dahl even argued that Bible verses which are torn out of context, though lacking a general-dogmatic meaning, may still have a literally understood meaning for the reader's individual needs. 'Sometimes inspiration can be drawn also from one sentence,' he argued. It is impossible every time a believer is in a critical moment in his or her life and needs guidance, for that believer to analyse a Bible verse theologically and with scholarly tools. Rather, a sincere openness to the message of God is needed. Tärk, taking a different approach, suggested finding a point of support in 'the general teaching' of the New Testament, not in separate verses; i.e. scripture in itself – Old and New Testaments – contains major principles for the exegesis of any particular text.[56] It was important to be aware of the biblical context, because 'false teachers play with truths as if they play with dice'.[57] However, in their personal Bible reading, individual believers practised seeking for direct guidance in one or two Bible verses, a method with many blessings and with even more dangers. In many cases, however, they took the traditional teaching of the church and its inherited piety to be the major

---

[53] Niilo Yli-Vainio, *Väe saladus* [Mystery of the Power], Estonian translation, typewritten manuscript (n. p, n. d.), p. 60.

[54] Tärk, *Efesose kiri*, p. 100.

[55] Osvald Tärk, 'Märkmeid O. Tärgi jutlustest 1981-1982.a.' [Notes from the Sermons of O. Tärk from the years 1981-1982], 1982 peetud jutlused [Sermons delivered in 1982], typewritten manuscript, pp. 54-55. KUSA.

[56] Tärk, 'Meie vendluse põhimõtted', *Logos*, no. 1 (1981), p. 10.

[57] Tärk, *Efesose kiri*, p. 96.

keys to interpreting scripture, even if they did not state this explicitly.

The scriptures were understood as a basis for Christian ethical life and devotion. In accordance with the wider evangelical understanding, Estonian Baptists saw the need for personal Bible reading, in order to deepen their relationship with Christ and to become more mature in their spirituality and discipleship. What D.W. Bebbington said about early evangelicals in Britain, can easily be applied to Estonian Baptists during the Soviet era: their 'overriding aim' was 'to bring home the message of the Bible and to encourage its devotional use'.[58] The Bible is not a collection of formal rules, argued Võsu. 'The Word is a door to the world of God's light, God's kingdom of love. Some remain exploring the door, but never step inside through it.'[59] For Estonian Baptists, to 'step inside' meant to apply the biblical message to their lives. Both Old and New Testaments were important for this aim, though Osvald Tärk emphasised that the Old Testament should be interpreted in the light of the New.[60] Tärk gave practical advice: read with a sense of sympathizing with the biblical story, read with a prayerful mind, and read every day. 'Read until the Holy Spirit brings you into a personal fellowship with Christ.'[61] The worship service and fellowship helped to maintain the 'influence of the Word'. 'We need only to cease attending the worship services and [neglect] personal reading of the Bible and our spiritual life will disappear,' was Tärk's warning.[62] God's message can reach a believer also in spiritual songs or preaching, or by some other means, which convey truths from the Bible.[63] Also classic Christian books, such as Thomas à Kempis' *The Imitation of Christ* and John Bunyan's *The Pilgrim's Progress*, were helpful because 'this literature had taken its thoughts from the Bible'.[64]

There was an interrelation of communal and individual elements in understanding the Bible. Some authoritative presbyters, such as Tärk, Võsu and Olvik emerged as outstanding 'saintly interpreters ... whose wisdom, insights, and lives shed particular light on the gospel', to use the language of E. Davis and R. Hays.[65] However, the local congregations continued to function as

---

[58] David W. Bebbington, *Evangelicalism in Modern Britain. A History from the 1730s to the 1980s* (Grand Rapids, Michigan: Baker Book House, 1992), p. 14.

[59] Võsu, *Evangeelne eetika*, p. 56.

[60] Tärk, 'Meie vendluse põhimõtted', *Logos*, no. 1 (1981), pp. 8-9.

[61] Tärk, 'Märkmeid O. Tärgi jutlustest 1981-1982.a.', 1982 peetud jutlused, pp. 56-59.

[62] Ibid., p. 56.

[63] Efraim Joel Dahl, *Usutervistamine Piiblis, algkristluses ja tänapäeval* [Healing through Faith: In the Bible, Early Christianity and Today], typewritten manuscript (n. p., n. d., 1980?), p. 42. KUSA.

[64] Tärk, 'Märkmeid O. Tärgi jutlustest 1981-1982.a.', 1982 peetud jutlused, p. 55.

[65] Ellen F. Davis and Richard Hays, eds., *The Art of Reading Scripture* (Grand Rapids, Michigan: Eerdmans, 2003), pp. 147-148.

'hermeneutic communities', similar to Radical Reformation patterns.[66] Estonian ECB understanding of the biblical message was never seen only in individual terms. The communal element – through lay preaching and discussion groups – was always present. This was emphasised by E.J. Dahl who believed that 'the ideal church was a Berea church, where the believers "examined the Scriptures every day" (Acts 17:11).'[67] Dahl was convinced that Bible study and prayer groups, led by experienced and well-prepared people, who 'use a concordance and a Bible lexicon', could 'broaden spiritual understanding and create a spiritual micro-climate'.[68] It should also be pointed out that the Evangelical Christian tradition had in its earlier history extensively used discussion groups for biblical interpretation. Oskar Olvik had a polemical, sometimes even provocative style when leading a Bible study. 'Some accidental visitor may have got a first impression that here a group of free-thinkers has gathered,' Olvik recalled in his memoirs.[69] The goal, however, was to reach a common and Christocentric understanding of the passage. The quest for uniformity in understanding the biblical texts was counterbalanced by the theological ideal that every believer has a right to interpret the Bible with the guidance of the Holy Spirit. This brought a 'danger of losing the focus', as Tärk said, but 'our differences in interpreting the Bible show that we need each other'; only together can we offer at least some picture of Christ's perfection.[70] Ideally, Tärk saw the value of diversity within the UECBE, both in biblical interpretation and views about the Holy Spirit. 'Our motto should be: diversity within the limits of the Word'.[71] Not only individual reading of the Bible, but also listening to and learning from each other shaped Estonian Baptist identity.

Estonian Baptists in the Soviet era had a high regard for scripture, which was seen as offering God-given guidance for Christian faith and life. This guidance was sought both in personal devotion and also in the process of 'communal hermeneutics'. Those among the ECB believers who inclined toward Word-orientedness, though never denying the role of the Holy Spirit in understanding the Bible, often started from an assumption that there is a rational coherence in the Bible and it is possible to base knowledge of scripture upon universal 'all-encompassing, self-evident, and self-legitimating foundations'.[72] A more Spirit-orientated wing in the UECBE, especially in the 1970s and 1980s, claimed that more emphasis should be placed on direct

[66] See the chapter 'Congregational Hermeneutics' in Stuart Murray, *Biblical Interpretation in the Anabaptist Tradition* (Kitchener, Ontario: Pandora Press, 2000), pp. 157-185.
[67] Dahl, *Usutervistamine Piiblis, algkristluses ja tänapäeval*, pp. 124-125.
[68] Ibid., pp. 125-126.
[69] Olvik, *Mälestused*, part 1, p. 251.
[70] Tärk, 'Meie vendluse põhimõtted', *Logos*, no. 1 (1981), pp. 9-10.
[71] Tärk, *Efesose kiri*, p. 52.
[72] Davis and Hays, eds., *The Art of Reading Scripture*, p. 110.

supernatural guidance of the Spirit and on Spirit-baptism if a believer wanted to have a right apprehension and application of the Bible. These differing approaches were reflected also in preaching within the UECBE.

PREACHING THE WORD, TRUSTING THE SPIRIT

Preaching was a central element for the identity of the ECB churches. Osvald Tärk stated in 1976 that 'God himself has chosen the pulpit as a means by which to lead people to Jesus Christ'.[73] Pentecostal as well as Baptist tradition had always valued 'the gift of power and proclamation' in a preacher.[74] The preaching styles in the UECBE, however, varied considerably. While Baptists and Evangelical Christians traditionally gave more space to intellectual and systematic reflection in preaching, Revivalist Free Church and Pentecostal preaching was less structured and relied more on the spontaneous impulse from the Spirit. In the 1950s, in the Oleviste church, former Pentecostal preachers, such as Voldemar Nurk and others, tried to continue preaching with an enthusiastic fervour. But the audience, in this united ECB church, was now different. Neither did the large medieval cathedral support emotional services. Olvik commented: 'This probably often brought sadness among the rows of Pentecostals and Revivalist Free church believers.'[75] In the countryside the Revivalist Free church preaching maintained its specific features much longer, and some outstanding evangelists, such as Johannes Jääger[76] and Paldor Teekel,[77] emerged from Pentecostal and Revivalist traditions, with convincing sermons, vivid biblical imagery and down-to-earth language. However, the model for Estonian ECB preaching became increasingly shaped by the systematic, logical and ethically orientated preaching of Tärk, Võsu and Olvik. Arpad Arder, from an Evangelical Christian background, with his narrative style and message of God's love and care, was a preacher with a distinctive approach. Also Edgar Rajandi had a very individual style: his sermons could be 'compared to a love letter – at the beginning one does not know where it ends'.[78] There were also some women preachers who were well known in the union, such as Ilse Katvel and Emilie Bertelson. Different sermon styles continued to live in parallel with each other in the united union, influencing each other.

---

[73] Osvald Tärk, 'Jutlustaja kantslil' [A Preacher in the Pulpit], a presentation at the presbyters' conference, 29.05.1976, typewritten manuscript, p. 1. TPL.

[74] Evald Kiil, *Issandast kutsutud viinamäe tööle* [Called by God for the Work in the Vineyard] (Tallinn, 1993), p. 42.

[75] Olvik, *Mälestused*, part 2, p. 466.

[76] Johannes Jääger, *Tema kutsus mind* [He Called Me], typewritten manuscript (1984), pp. 21, 31-35, 55. TPL.

[77] 'Eesti Vabariigi priiusk on kõige parem usk' [Revivalist Free Faith in the Estonian Republic is the Best Faith], interview with Astrid Teekel, *Teekäija* (March 1994), p. 4.

[78] Olvik, *Mälestused*, part 2, p. 350.

Preaching was and remained in the centre. The 'preached word', based on the 'written word', was expected to take the hearers to Christ, the 'revealed word', to use Karl Barth's threefold view of 'the Word', of which Estonians were aware.[79] Adolf Pohl, a German Baptist theologian, emphasised in a translated article that there was no experience of Christ outside the biblical Word.[80] Ingmar Kurg expressed a 'golden rule' which Estonian Baptists shared with classical Lutheranism and with Pietists such as Estonian Moravians: '...every sermon should be directed toward Christ'.[81] Preaching should proclaim the crucified Christ and God's Kingdom, which finds its manifestation in the fulfilment of God's will in all creation, as Olvik argued.[82] The latter part of Olvik's statement sounds rather exceptional in the Estonian Baptist context, where usually personal salvation and personal yielding to God's plans were emphasised. In traditional Baptist understanding, the Holy Spirit enlivened the Word and helped a believer to approach Christ. However, Baptist sermons were sometimes sliding toward being lectures, offering little opportunity for experiencing the message. This was balanced with preaching which attempted to take the immediate presence of the Spirit into account. Both approaches, though in different combinations, appealed to the audience's intellect, will and emotions, giving much less nourishment to their imagination.

A good sermon, for many ECB (Baptist) presbyters and lay preachers, inevitably involved quoting a variety of biblical passages. A description of a Baptist worship service, though referring to pre-war times and coming from a person critical of 'sectarians', is probably also true of many countryside ECB churches in the Soviet era: the prayer meeting usually began with corporate singing, then the believers knelt for prayer, and after another song there was the sermon, which included reading from the Bible and the preacher's comments, which did not show much rhetorical skill. 'The main emphasis, then, was put on quotations from Scripture which were known by heart.'[83] The use of numerous biblical quotations was typical also of 'more experienced' preachers. Aleksander Sildos, for example, during his lifetime, read the Bible through

---

[79] Ingmar Kurg, 'Jõuludeks: Jumala Sõna lihakssaamine', p. 10. Karl Barth's theological focus on the sovereignty of God appealed to several ECB presbyters-theologians in the 1980s in Estonia, such as O. Tärk, J. Tammo and others.

[80] Adolf Pohl, 'Piibel ja sinu tänane Kristuse kogemus' [The Bible and Your Present Experience of Christ], *Logos*, no. 2 (1982), p. 2.

[81] Ingmar Kurg, 'Homileetilisi märkmeid' [Homiletical Notes], *Logos*, no. 1 (1986), p. 27.

[82] Oskar Olvik, *Homileetika* [Homiletics], typewritten manuscript (1957), pp. 33-34. KUSA.

[83] Jaanus Plaat, *Saaremaa kirikud, usuliikumised ja prohvetid 18.-20. sajandil* [Churches, Religious Movements and Prophets in Saaremaa Island in the 18th-20th Centuries] (Tartu: Eesti Rahva Muuseum, 2003), pp. 145-146.

more than 160 times[84] and knew long passages by heart. However, the church members were often less diligent Bible readers. In 1976 Tärk complained that 'people know the Bible very little' and even added that 'the believers read the Bible little at home'. He suggested reading longer passages at worship services.[85] Typically, it was hoped that when increasing the 'quantity' of Bible reading, 'quality' would follow automatically.

Word and Spirit dynamics also influenced attitudes toward training preachers. In the pre-war period Estonian Pentecostals organised short-term evangelism and preaching courses, with visits from some leading Pentecostal teachers from abroad (Eino Manninen from Finland, Donald Gee from Britain, Carl Forsberg from Sweden).[86] Baptists attempted to give even more thorough education to future preachers. However, preaching in Estonian free churches, including in the Baptist tradition, was never only a matter of formal homiletical skills; they had always acknowledged the 'charismatic gift' of preaching.[87] Much attention was paid to an inner calling, a conviction about being commissioned to preach, which was often understood in a Spurgeonic way, though with more emphasis on the empowerment of the Spirit.[88] In the 1920s, Baptist theological seminary students were encouraged to seek the help of the Holy Spirit, because 'homiletics should be secondary'.[89] Training for younger preachers, especially during Soviet years, happened through the use of the apprenticeship model, in which more experienced preachers mentored and advised younger preachers.[90]

The Pentecostal tradition, which re-emerged in the UECBE in the 1970s, emphasised the need for a special experience for being a fruitful preacher - a Spirit-baptism or anointing of the Spirit. A Finnish charismatic preacher, Niilo Yli-Vainio, who was known in Estonia, expressed this view: a 'common man', a man 'from behind the plough', can as a result of baptism with the Spirit 'proclaim the Word of God as a teacher'.[91] Though traditional Baptist and

---

[84] Johannes Vink, comp., *Aleksander Sildose surm* [Death of Aleksander Sildos], typewritten manuscript ([Vancouver], 1977), p. 12. TPL.

[85] Tärk, 'Jutlustaja kantslil', p. 3.

[86] Kiil, *Issandast kutsutud viinamäe tööle*, p. 31.

[87] Tärk, 'Jutlustaja kantslil', p. 1.

[88] See for example, C.H. Spurgeon, *Lectures to My Students: A Selection from Addresses Delivered to the Students of the Pastors' College, Metropolitan Tabernacle,* vol. 1 (London: Passmore and Alabaster, 1876), pp. 19-32. Spurgeon emphasised the need for future preachers to reach a conviction and feel a desire to preach; however, he also stressed the need to evaluate one's abilities and gifts, and to listen for guidance from others as to one's qualification for the vocation of preacher.

[89] Minutes, no. 23 (n. d. [1923?, 1924?]). Eesti Baptisti Usuteaduse Seminari protokolliraamat 1920-1940 [Baptist Theological Seminary minute book 1920-1940], KUSA.

[90] Olvik, *Mälestused*, part 1, p. 304.

[91] Yli-Vainio, *Väe saladus*, p. 59.

Pentecostal preaching differed in methods and style, they both tended to see the preacher as a 'teacher', and consequently saw the audience as 'students'. As to formal education, the most reluctant to recognize the value of homiletical training were probably the believers who had a Revivalist Free Church background, though in 1982 Robert Võsu argued that 'in the united union' Revivalist churches 'have received well the sermons [delivered] by preachers with seminary education'.[92]

The Evangelical Christian tradition in Estonia also enriched the understanding of preaching in the ECB union. Oskar Olvik, a former Evangelical Christian, wrote a textbook of homiletics for future presbyters. Though following rather classical patterns of guidelines for sermon preparation and delivery, obviously using the approach to homiletics he had himself studied years ago at Tartu University, Olvik, nevertheless, put much emphasis on the personality of a preacher, which he considered especially important in times when 'the pulpit was no longer the centre of cultural life and the preacher's authority was not self-evident'.[93] The speaker's ethics and personal qualities must be seen as part of the message. Both modern communication theory and evangelical theology can affirm this, though on different grounds.

The criteria for preachers were summarised by Robert Võsu. A preacher should know the Bible as a whole, be orientated toward the teachings of Christ and the apostles, submit to fellow Christians, respect the church and its discipline and leaders, and keep his or her life and faith 'healthy' and 'pure'.[94] Evangelistic sermons were of primary importance. These were expected to be 'simple and clear, as if the audience does not know anything [about the Christian faith] beforehand'.[95] The biblical text itself, preached simply and not mixed 'with human opinions', as Ermo Jürma emphasised in 1974, would benefit the people. [96] This belief was deeply rooted among Estonian Baptists during the Soviet era. Mid-week worship services often included an expository type of preaching, 'sermons of sanctification' as the Estonian saying goes. It should, however, be noted that in the 1970s, models for Estonian ECB preachers included not only C.H. Spurgeon and Billy Graham, but also Pentecostal figures such as Oral Roberts and Yonggi Cho. Openness to new influences re-modelled the Estonian Baptist identity. Inspired by interest in the supernatural work of the Spirit, a more enthusiastic, narrative, and often testimony-like preaching emerged in charismatically-oriented circles in the UECBE. This preaching was intended to lead the audience to the experience of the Holy Spirit's presence and to manifestations of the Spirit. Yet, in all ECB

---

[92] Robert Võsu, 'Sada aastat priikoguduse algusest' [One Hundred Years from the Beginning of the Revivalist Free Church], *Logos*, no. 4 (1982), p. 2.
[93] Olvik, *Homileetika*, pp. 7-8, 14-15.
[94] Lecture notes 1973-1978, notebook 2. Uudu Rips' personal archive.
[95] Lecture notes 1973-1978, notebook 1. Uudu Rips' personal archive.
[96] Lecture notes 1973-1978, notebook 1. Uudu Rips' personal archive.

churches, the task of preaching was predominant. Today, Estonian Baptists would see pastoral responsibilities more broadly, as including counselling and other ministries. Also, in thinking about spiritual growth non-verbal elements, such as community experience or visual art as an expression of faith, are slowly being valued. In Soviet years, even the role of the Holy Spirit was often understood in verbal terms; the Spirit announced God's will, talked to Christians in prayer, and enabled a believer to give witness about the Lord.

HOLY SPIRIT – POWER FOR SPIRITUAL LIFE

In more traditional Baptist churches the main focus was on the person of Christ rather than the person of the Spirit. However, it was unanimously believed that the Holy Spirit, the third person of the Trinity, brought a transformed life through faith.[97] Popular translated and typewritten literature, circulating in ECB churches, emphasised this aspect.[98] Osvald Tärk, the leading ECB theologian, said: 'A spiritual life without the Holy Spirit is an oxymoron.'[99] He added: '...who will receive the word of Christ through proclamation, he will also receive His Spirit, because his words are spirit and life'.[100] The Spirit was understood to offer power for a Christian to follow Christ in discipleship.[101] In a critical moment on his own spiritual journey (in 1946) Tärk had been deeply encouraged by reading James H. McConckey's *Three-Fold Secret of the Holy Spirit*, which emphasised committing one's life fully to God.[102] From an Evangelical Christian background, Oskar Olvik argued that the Holy Spirit was a 'heavenly worker' who liberated a believer from 'everything which was old' and purified the believer's abilities for the service of God.[103] These insights, broadly in accordance with the 'the first wave of Pentecostalism' of the early 1900s,[104] were fairly unanimously supported by Estonian Evangelical Christians-Baptists. The Holy Spirit was God working for the salvation, renewal and sanctification of human beings. The presence and work of the Spirit, however, required committed discipleship and trust on the believer's part. The Holy Spirit's role was seen predominantly in individualistic terms; Estonian Baptists seldom discussed the Spirit's work in the world or even in the wider church. Jürgen Moltmann has argued that '[t]he creation of community is

---

[97] See also Graham, *Püha Vaim*, pp. 13, 24.

[98] Frank Mangs, *Issanda tee* [The Lord's Way], typewritten Estonian translation (1970s?), pp. 19-21. KUSA.

[99] Tärk, *Efesose kiri*, p. 138.

[100] Ibid., p. 26.

[101] Olvik, *Mälestused*, part 2, pp. 592-597.

[102] Ruudi Leinus, comp. and ed., *Osvald Tärk. Uskuge Jumalasse*, p. 18.

[103] Olvik, *Mälestused*, part 2, p. 589; See also Tärk, *Efesose kiri*, p. 139.

[104] Kevin Springer, *Kolmas aalto* [Riding the Third Wave] (Hämeenlinna: Päivä OY, 1990), pp. 27-28.

evidently the goal of God's life-giving Spirit in the world of nature and human beings.'[105] This approach remained foreign for Estonian ECB believers; their pneumatological vision was rather narrow.

Different views became evident when interpretations of Spirit-baptism came to be discussed. Attempts to position 'baptism' and 'filling' of the Spirit (or with the Spirit) on the scale of a Christian's life caused sharp debates. A more 'conservative' approach, in line with Billy Graham's views, saw Spirit-baptism as something happening simultaneously with the conversion experience.[106] This experience, according to this understanding, happened once at conversion, and was not a subsequent event. Osvald Tärk, however, stated that a believer needed the filling of the Spirit, which was a repeated experience.[107] Robert Võsu believed that the filling and the baptism of the Spirit were one and the same thing. He explained this experience using the language of psychology. Filling, for him, had something to do with releasing the hidden resources in the human subconsciousness, though the 'consciousness has to remain in control'.[108] However, it would be wrong to assume that for Võsu the 'filling of the Spirit' was only an experience limited to the human 'soul' – rather, he saw it as God working in and with human realities.

Olvik was less concerned about the terminology of 'baptism' and 'filling'. He taught: 'To receive the Holy Spirit, a person has to repent and believe. To receive a greater amount of the power of the Holy Spirit, one has to give oneself unconditionally to Christ and to believe. I cannot give any other rule.'[109] The Spirit magnified Christ, and the presence of the Spirit had ethical consequences for a believer's life, moulding it in accordance with the will of God and the image of Christ.[110] According to Olvik, believers should give more space in their lives to the Spirit. This could happen step by step or abruptly - the latter being what some believers call baptism in the Spirit. Olvik was convinced, however, that this division between Spirit-baptism and Spirit-filling could not be found in the Bible. It is not important, he argued, what a phenomenon is called, but rather the new life that the Holy Spirit brings.[111]

In his memoirs Olvik described his own spiritual journey and personal yearning to receive more blessings in the Spirit. Inspired by Stanley Jones' writings he gave himself fully to Christ and believed that the gift of the Holy Spirit belonged personally to him. 'Suddenly a great peace, deep silence, filled my soul. I felt that now I am allowed to testify that I am the temple of the Holy

---

[105] Jürgen Moltmann, *The Spirit of Life: A Universal Affirmation* (London: SCM Press, 1992), p. 219.

[106] Graham, *Püha Vaim*, pp. 88, 153.

[107] Tärk, *Efesose kiri*, p. 138.

[108] Lecture notes 1973-1978, notebook 3. Uudu Rips' personal archive.

[109] Oskar Olvik, *Mälestused*, part 2, p. 600.

[110] Ibid., p. 601.

[111] Ibid., pp. 591-592.

Spirit; I am allowed to say that the fullness of the Holy Spirit has also stepped into my life.'[112] There were no outward manifestations, but a deep experience of fellowship with Christ. A Christocentric and 'controlled-by-the-Bible' approach in this area was widespread among Estonian Baptists in the Soviet era. A German Baptist, Adolf Pohl, in a translated article in 1982, said bluntly: 'Who leaves the Biblical Christ aside, in order to experience Christ only and directly in the Spirit, is grasping only air, intensifies his imagination and becomes receptive to mental illnesses.'[113] Pohl's views did not fully correspond with Estonian Baptist theological identity. Estonians did traditionally affirm an element of mysticism in their search for unity with Christ.

However, Baptist identity in the field of pneumatology was open to new influences and shifts in emphasis. The role and work of the Holy Spirit, as one who gives supernatural experiences and direct guidance in a believer's life, came to be re-emphasised in the UECBE. Though Estonian free churches, including Baptists, in the 1920s and 1930s, were interested in pneumatology,[114] it was in the 1970s that the influences from Finnish Pentecostal and Charismatic circles on Estonian ECB identity increased. For example, Niilo Yli-Vainio's book *Väe saladus* (Mystery of the Power) became available in Estonian as a typewritten text and was privately circulated in local churches. Yli-Vainio, a Finnish charismatic evangelist who was involved in prayer healing, emphasised that the baptism of the Spirit is promised to every believer, because believers need strength in 'the great contest of the last days against the powers of darkness'.[115] The eschatological elements in Estonian Baptist pneumatology came to be emphasised. It was in the 'last days' that the pouring out of the Spirit would take place. Yli-Vainio taught that Spirit-baptism enabled a Christian to fulfil his or her calling. Separate from the event of Spirit-baptism was the filling of the Spirit, which was a repeated experience.[116] The work of the Spirit was to bring vigour and enthusiasm into a Christian's life.[117] There was a stress on the 'victorious Christian life'. Criticism of rational elements in the Christian life were part of this change in Baptist thinking: 'Right teaching can still be without vitality.'[118] Estonian Baptist understanding of the Holy Spirit increasingly embraced a more immediate and emotionally loaded experience.

---

[112] Ibid., pp. 444-445.

[113] Pohl, 'Piibel ja sinu tänane Kristuse kogemus', p. 2.

[114] For Estonian Baptist views in the inter-war period about the role of the Holy Spirit, see Pilli, 'Eesti baptistid ja nende teoloogilise mõtte kajastumine ajakirjas *Teekäija*', pp. 47-55.

[115] Yli-Vainio, *Väe saladus*, p. 23.

[116] Ibid., pp. 28, 44.

[117] Christenson, 'Palu, et Kristus valitseks', p. 22; see also Veli-Matti Kärkkäinen, *Pneumatology: The Holy Spirit in Ecumenical, International and Contextual Perspective* (Grand Rapids, Michigan: Baker Academic, 2002), p. 91.

[118] Yli-Vainio, *Väe saladus*, p. 24.

In general, Estonian Baptists tended to see the Holy Spirit, or specifically the blessing of the Spirit in the lives of believers, as an 'instrument' for empowered practical ministry, sanctification and evangelism. This was in accordance with tendencies in wider Pentecostal piety.[119] Though theological reflection about the 'baptism' and 'filling' of the Holy Spirit certainly took place, both at the grass roots level in local churches and also among church leaders, Estonians could generally sympathise with the practical advice of Frank Mangs: 'Do not care about chapters [in books] and debates about humanly-established teachings. Let those who do not need anything, debate and fight. But you humbly fall on your knees and pray that the Lord Jesus, because of his great mercy, would deal with your life and would fill you with the Holy Spirit.'[120] This was good practical advice. But it also reflected certain drawbacks: Estonian Baptists tended to see the Holy Spirit as an agent in leading a person to salvation and deeper devotional life; the broader theological panorama which envisions the Spirit in the framework of the Trinity and sees the Spirit's work in all creation was seldom explored beyond general doctrinal statements. However, there was an area where a more careful and detailed theological discussion happened – the area of various manifestations of the Spirit.

MANIFESTATIONS OF THE SPIRIT

The manifestations of the Spirit - praying for the sick, speaking in tongues and prophesying - were not excluded from the Estonian Baptist understanding of the Christian life, but there was a certain modesty about these manifestations. They were seen as belonging to the private rather than the public sphere of Christian life. Osvald Tärk, in his book *Markuse evangeeliumi seletus* (Explaining the Gospel of Mark), written in the 1970s, affirmed that 'we are allowed today to pray for healing', but he also emphasised that if we cannot heal, we at least should help and visit the sick.[121] Some ECB believers, such as those participating in the Effataa movement in Tallinn in the 1970s, nevertheless began to expect the manifestations of the Spirit to take place publicly. Inspired by Finnish Free Church leader, Tapio Nousiainen, and his interpretation of the 'full gospel', which included 'authority over sickness and over powers of darkness', Rein Uuemõis, a preacher in the Oleviste Church, and his co-workers, began a healing and prayer ministry, which usually took place after general evangelistic worship services.[122] The UECBE leadership, as

---

[119] Kärkkäinen, *Pneumatology*, p. 92.

[120] Mangs, *Issanda tee*, p. 36.

[121] Osvald Tärk, *Markuse evangeeliumi seletus* [Explaining the Gospel of Mark] (Tallinn: Logos, 1993), pp. 63-64.

[122] Rein Uuemõis, *Jumala teenistuses* [In the Service of God] (Tallinn: Oleviste kogudus, 2001), pp. 37-38.

well as local pastors and church members, facing these new emphases shaping the union's identity, were forced to re-interpret their approach to the manifestations of the Spirit.

One issue which needed analysis was speaking in tongues. Robert Võsu, holding rather traditional Baptist views, was cautious about manifestations of the Spirit, though he did not deny them. In 1976 he said, critically evaluating recent developments, that speaking in tongues had been made a primary issue among many believers, though it should be a secondary matter. According to Võsu, in the 'new Pentecostalism', as he called the Charismatic movement, the 'new birth experience' had lost its centrality; the movement was dependent on feelings and weak in doctrine.[123] The identity of the UECBE was under pressure because of the debates about the Spirit's manifestations. However, Estonian Baptists and the Senior Presbyter Robert Võsu emphasised that the Bible did not prohibit 'speaking in tongues'; this experience had an 'enlivening influence in the believer's life'. The danger was that the person who had this gift was inclined toward spiritual pride. Gifts receive their value from love, which builds up the church. 'To reconcile the speaking-in-tongues-movement with the church is very difficult.'[124] However, where this succeeds, it gives 'positive results'. Võsu suggested that speaking in tongues belonged to private spirituality; in public worship services it might have a negative effect on the church's mission, as it might give a 'bad impression' to 'outsiders' who did not understand it.[125]

Oskar Olvik believed that speaking in tongues was a special gift for some but not for all believers.[126] Estonian Baptists and Evangelical Christians traditionally held to the views of R.A. Torrey who claimed that the evidence of the Spirit-baptism was not glossolalia, but rather 'power for Christian service'.[127] Also recent Pentecostal theology itself has admitted that 'whether glossolalia can be regarded as normative will always remain an open question'.[128] However, some Pentecostal and charismatic literature, translated into Estonian in the 1970s, emphasised that 'the result of the baptism with the Spirit is always speaking in tongues'.[129] This view was held also by early Estonian Pentecostals, but had not been a part of Baptist identity. Efraim J. Dahl, who highly appreciated the sincere trust in God which he found in the Pentecostal movement, was nevertheless critical of an exaggerated view of

---

[123] Lecture notes 1973-1978, notebook 3. Uudu Rips' personal archive.

[124] Ibid.

[125] Ibid.

[126] Oskar Olvik, *Esimene Korintose kiri* [The First Epistle to the Corinthians], typewritten manuscript (1960), p. 81. KUSA.

[127] Kenneth J. Archer, *A Pentecostal Hermeneutic for the Twenty-First Century: Spirit, Scripture and Community* (London, New York: T&T Clark, 2004), p. 80.

[128] Simon Chan, *Pentecostal Theology and the Christian Spiritual Tradition* (Sheffield: Sheffield Academic Press, 2000), p. 42.

[129] Yli-Vainio, *Väe saladus*, p. 50.

speaking in tongues. His evaluation of the practice of speaking in tongues was that it was a product of 'emotional discrepancy' which was characteristic of 'highly rationalistic and materialistic times' – this discrepancy forced people to seek emotional experiences in religion.[130] Dahl, however, was not fully correct in ascribing glossolalia to over-concern with emotions; for early Pentecostal tradition it was a matter of being faithful to 'a straight-forward reading of Acts', naive as this biblicism may be.[131]

Views about speaking in tongues certainly varied among Estonian Baptists. There were attempts to emphasise the unifying elements in the UECBE identity and in particular in relation to pneumatology. In 1977 Võsu declared that Baptists and Pentecostals in Estonia differed only over the question of speaking in tongues.[132] It is not clear if he was referring to recent developments within UECBE identity, especially within the framework of the Effataa movement, or if he was referring back to the pre-war period. However, the union leaders, who felt responsible for the theological identity of the churches, tried to address the issues that were causing tensions, especially as the issue of tongues moved from the private to the public arena.

The same movement – from the private sphere to the public sphere – took place also in the field of praying for healing. Oskar Olvik used to pray for the sick, and reported some miraculous answers to his prayers in his memoirs. However, these were pastoral cases rather than something belonging to public worship or 'prayer ministry'. With the Effataa movement and the new external theological influences, praying for healing became more visible. Some ECB preachers moved, though cautiously, toward a position that all sicknesses should be healed. The healing depended on trust in God – as Tommy Lee Osborn taught: 'When we are walking by faith, we delight to cast aside the senses and enjoy the Father's already-provided blessings.'[133] This deviated from more traditional Baptist positions: 'According to the word of God, healing is God's gift and a special grace, not a religious self-certainty or something which we have a right to demand.'[134] God manifests his power in human suffering and sickness in different ways: God can heal but he can also teach some valuable lessons to people, using illness as a means. In weakness the power of God will be revealed.[135] Thus, the problem was not with praying for healing, which is part of Christian tradition, but rather claims made about how those prayers were answered. In the 1970s, Osvald Tärk, the leading theologian of the Estonian Baptists, made an attempt to interpret the biblical evidence on

---

[130] Dahl, *Evangeelse maailma radadel*, pp. 153-154.

[131] Chan, *Pentecostal Theology and the Christian Spiritual Tradition*, pp. 41-42.

[132] Lecture notes 1973-1978, notebook 3. Uudu Rips' personal archive.

[133] Quote in William K. Kay and Anne E. Dyer, eds., *Pentecostal and Charismatic Studies: A Reader* (London: SCM Press, 2004), p. 73.

[134] Dahl, *Usutervistamine Piiblis, algkristluses ja tänapäeval*, p. 33.

[135] Olvik, *Mälestused*, part 2, pp. 462, 564-577.

the topic of faith and healing and to offer an approach which avoided extremes. He expressed his convictions in a treatise *Usk ja haigused* (Faith and Illnesses). God is omnipotent, he argued, but this does not mean that every illness will be healed in this world. God may have higher goals than physical healing; it would be too one-sided to say that all illness is the result of sin or caused by demonic forces.[136]

Tärk was clearly reacting against some new emphases, coming to Estonia through literature and personal contacts with charismatically-orientated Christians and those from abroad involved in healing ministries. For example, Oral Roberts' book *If You Need Healing, Do These Things*, originally published in 1965, was available in Estonian as a typewritten text. Roberts clearly emphasised that God's will is to heal all people; sickness is an oppression that comes from Satan.[137] T.L. Osborn expressed similar views.[138] These new theological emphases prompted different interpretations of some biblical passages, for example regarding the 'thorn' in the apostle Paul's flesh (2 Corinthians 12: 7-9). Roberts was sure that this was a demonic power which brought physical problems to Paul.[139] Later, in 1994, Udo Veevo, one of the key persons in the prayer and healing ministry in Oleviste in the 1970s, argued that Paul's weakness was not an illness.[140] Theological presuppositions shaped biblical interpretation. Also, both the 'charismatic' and 'conservative' wing of Estonian Baptists tended to argue from the position of God and his nature, trying to find 'eternal truths' about suffering, instead of identifying with the suffering person.

A theology of healing and views about the manifestations of the Holy Spirit were closely linked to an understanding of faith. The Korean Pentecostal leader, Yonggi Cho, in sermons he delivered in 1975 in Stockholm, which were later translated into Estonian, emphasised the need to pray with confidence and to pray concretely.[141] He taught that much depends on a person's mindset. 'If you bear in your mind a picture of yourself as a sick person, then you have to live your life as a sick person.'[142] Oral Roberts, in turn, suggested using some

---

[136] Osvald Tärk, *Usk ja haigused* [Faith and Illnesses], typewritten manuscript (n. p., n. d.). KUSA. See also Osvald Tärk, *Armastuse käsu all* [Under the Law of Love] (Tallinn: Eesti EKB Liit, 2004), pp. 82-87.

[137] Oral Roberts, *Kui tahad saada terveks, siis talita järgmiselt* [If You Need Healing, Do these Things], typewritten Estonian translation (n. p., n. d.), pp. 7, 41. KUSA.

[138] Tommy Lee Osborn's booklet *Three Keys to the Book of Acts* (Est. Kolm võtit) (1968) circulated in the UECBE churches as a typewritten manuscript.

[139] Roberts, *Kui tahad saada terveks, siis talita järgmiselt*, p. 29.

[140] Udo Veevo, 'Veel Pauluse vaiast' [More about Paul's Thorn], *Teekäija* (January 1994), p. 16. For a more flexible interpretation see Tarmo Toom, 'Ikka veel Pauluse vaiast' [Even More about Paul's Thorn], *Teekäija* (March 1994), p. 16.

[141] Yonggi Cho, *Loov usk* [Creative Faith], typewritten Estonian translation (n. p., n. d.), pp. 34-46. TPL.

[142] Cho, *Loov usk*, p. 19.

physical means 'to release one's faith', such as putting a 'prayer cloth' on sick parts of the body.[143] To some extent, this was practised in Estonia. Efraim J. Dahl, as an Estonian, expressed theologically a more 'centrist' evangelical view: 'Real faith is there where the Lord is allowed to be initiator and leader, and where people have learned to act hand in hand with him...'[144] Ideas from abroad were sometimes taken over with little critical evaluation, but there were attempts to filter these ideas through the local tradition. Charismatic phenomena were certainly not excluded from Estonian Baptist identity. For example, Dahl was positive about campaigns by the American evangelist, Kathryn Kuhlmann, which he considered as well planned but not artificial. He believed that Kuhlmann's campaigns had a supportive 'microclimate' which helped people to trust God in 'child-like faith'.[145]

There is little doubt that those in the UECBE who were emphasising supernatural manifestations of the Holy Spirit, were sincerely seeking for the signs of God's power. Others, however, interpreted the signs of God's power more broadly rather than in terms of specifically charismatic phenomena. They found support from more moderate evangelists such as Billy Graham, who believed that physical suffering can be used for the glory of God, and that real faith is in total surrender to God's will, whatever that may be.[146] The leaders of the union, such as Tärk, Võsu and Olvik made efforts to balance the teachings related to healing and suffering: God's kingdom is 'already here' but 'not yet' here in its fullness.[147] This complete healing, for example, was not to be expected 'now'. However, the tendency to demonise sickness, and to advocate the view that if full recovery did not arrive it was either hindrance from Satan, weak faith or some secret sin in the sick person, became more widespread among Estonian Baptists.

The Presbyters' Council of the UECBE, in dealing with these issues - praying for healing, the laying on of hands, as well as people falling down during the prayer - sought to give theological and practical guidance. Their hope was that serious division in the UECBE churches would be avoided. The UECBE leadership emphasised the need to keep unity in the churches, and to be orientated toward reconciliation if conflicts over the 'new movement' emerged. The theological thinking and ultimately the identity of Estonian Baptists was being reshaped by these new challenges. A centrist or moderate position emerged, which was neither fully Pentecostal/charismatic, nor anti-charismatic. The union leadership, in a circular document which has no date,

---

[143] Roberts, *Kui tahad saada terveks, siis talita järgmiselt*, pp. 13-17.

[144] Dahl, *Usutervistamine Piiblis, algkristluses ja tänapäeval*, p. 35.

[145] Ibid., pp. 21, 23, 31, 66.

[146] Graham, *Püha Vaim*, pp. 265, 269.

[147] 'Kingdom of God', in Sinclair B. Ferguson and David F. Wright, eds., *New Dictionary of Theology* (Leicester, England, and Downers Grove, Illinois: Inter-Varsity Press, 1988), pp. 367-369.

but was probably prepared in the mid-1970s,[148] took such a moderate position, not condemning the manifestations, but calling for a balanced evaluation and for a prayer ministry which gives honour and glory to God and avoids human exaggerations, spiritual pride and disorderly activities during worship or prayer services. Praying for healing with laying on of hands should be considered as one method among others. It was believed that the moderate position could be found in the Bible, that laying on of hands was practiced cautiously and selectively in the New Testament and the Early Church.[149]

In a way, the tensions and new emphases in the field of Baptist identity in Estonia can be seen as an attempt to find a balance between the 'gifts of the Spirit' and the 'fruit of the Spirit'. While in the wider world, the 'Spirit-movement', as Estonians said, was often a reaction toward a Christianity which was defined predominantly by a rational mindset,[150] the picture in Estonia was more colourful. Estonian Baptists, even in their pre-war history, had not excluded the baptism, filling and gifts of the Spirit from their understanding of the Christian life. They affirmed, and practised, supernatural gifts, though there was a tendency to see fruit of the Spirit and an ethical lifestyle as the primary signs of the presence and fullness of the Spirit.[151] Võsu commented: 'Fruits can not be replaced by anything else. Some have tried to replace these with the gifts of the Spirit... Gifts are given by God for serving the church. The value of gifts depends on how much they serve the church.'[152] The changes in Estonian Baptist identity, in the field of understanding the role of the Spirit, meant that supernatural gifts moved toward the more public sphere in Christian life and worship. At the same time Estonian Baptists became more aware that different gifts needed to be integrated into the whole life of the churches.[153] Emphasis on the work of the Spirit became related to the power to evangelise, and demonstrate God's presence, and not only to the strength to live a life of sanctification and discipleship.

CONCLUSION

An important aspect of Estonian Baptist identity which underwent reshaping

[148] Koguduste presbüteritele ja nõukogudele [To the presbyters of churches and to the church boards]. O. Tärgi materjalid [Materials of Osvald Tärk], EEKBLA [The Archive of the Union of Evangelical Christian and Baptist Churches of Estonia]. See also Rein Uuemõis, *Jumala teenistuses*, pp. 37-38.
[149] Dahl, *Usutervistamine Piiblis, algkristluses ja tänapäeval*, p. 19.
[150] Otto, 'Harismaatilise liikumise pingeväli', pp. 6-9.
[151] See thorough discussion about the fruit of the Spirit in Võsu, *Evangeelne eetika*, pp. 121-134.
[152] Võsu, *Evangeelne eetika*, p. 133.
[153] Siegfried Grossmann, 'Harismaatiline integratsioon koguduses' [Charismatic Integration in the Church], *Lectio V* (1978), pp. 13-15.

during the Soviet era was related to an understanding of the role of the Word and the Spirit. Immediately after the Second World War, when the UECBE was formed, there was a tendency to seek unity on the basis of scriptural texts. This is a common practice in wider Baptist life,[154] though interpretations of what 'Biblical foundations' means may vary, and today some Baptist theologians would suggest abandoning 'foundationalist' language.[155] However, the language of 'foundations' or a 'biblical basis' was widespread among Soviet Baptists, including Estonians, and Robert Võsu, an outstanding Estonian Baptist leader, stated: 'To be a Baptist means to teach and live on the basis of the Bible.'[156] While there was space for different interpretations of the biblical text, both individually and in church communities, Estonian Baptists were predominantly seeking for spiritual guidance and for the deepening of their devotional life through reading the Bible. The Bible was often taken at 'face value'. Though Estonian Baptists highlighted biblical authority, and believed that the Bible had inner coherence, they focused on Christ and the ethical value of the Bible, rather than trying to build rational constructs of interpretation. They also emphasised the need for the assistance of the Holy Spirit for understanding the message of the Bible. Preaching remained at the centre of worship, and verbal elements in Estonian Baptist spirituality and identity were affirmed all through the Soviet years.

New influences, moulding the Estonian Baptist understanding of the Word and Spirit, reached Estonia through Pentecostal and charismatic literature as well as through personal contacts, especially in the 1970s and early 1980s. Prayer and healing ministries, especially in the Effataa movement, expressed this new emphasis within the UECBE identity. This new emphasis focused on the baptism and filling of the Spirit, as well as on manifestations of the Spirit such as speaking in tongues and healing. Though these elements had been part of Estonian Baptist identity, they had always been restricted rather to the private sphere of spiritual life. Now, with a new desire to receive power for evangelism and the Christian life, the manifestations of the Spirit became a part of public worship and prayer ministry. Though Ingmar Kurg stated critically that Estonians have often 'gluttonously swallowed teachings in foreign languages, instead of taking the Bible as truth for our nation and proclaiming this',[157] one cannot deny that the new Spirit-oriented trend in ECB life brought vigour and revived commitment to Baptist churches. There certainly were attempts to critically evaluate theological impulses coming from abroad or

---

[154] L. Russ Busch and Tom J. Nettles, *Baptists and the Bible* (Nashville, Tennessee: Broadman and Holman, 1999), p. 4.
[155] See Stanley Grenz and John Franke, *Beyond Foundationalism: Shaping Theology in a Postmodern Context* (Louisville, Kentucky: Westminster John Knox Press, 2001), pp. 28-92.
[156] *'Kalju' koguduse karjase Robert Võsu jutlusi ajavahemikul 1944-1969*, p. 135.
[157] Kurg, 'Jõuludeks: Jumala Sõna lihakssaamine', p. 12.

emerging in the midst of the Estonian Baptist community. Baptist leadership, affirming the Spirit-orientated aspects of the UECBE identity, made efforts to avoid extremes in theology and practice. They called for a balanced view of the scriptures and the Spirit in Christian life, order in worship services, and the fruit of the Spirit as the final criteria for evaluating the experiences of the Holy Spirit.

The dynamics of understanding the work of the Spirit had a distinctive development in Estonia; different, for example, from the Baptist theological positions in Russia or Ukraine, where the official AUCECB tended to reject totally any charismatic phenomena. Estonian Baptists, being informed in their earlier years by holiness and early Pentecostal views on the Holy Spirit, continued to maintain openness toward this area also during the Soviet years, though the pneumatological discussion in these years tended to be limited. The thinking that did take place was prompted by new charismatic influences in devotional and church life, and by the immediate need to avoid extremes and to evaluate manifestations of the Spirit, rather than being inspired by broader reflections on the Trinity or on the Spirit working in the wider church and in creation.

CHAPTER 8

A Common Goal: Evangelism and Mission

Both before and after the Second World War, mission – or, rather, evangelism – was a common goal for all Estonian free churches, despite their variations in theological preferences. The belief that every believer is called to bear witness in the world created deeper mutual understanding between different traditions in the ECB union, and helped to shape ECB identity in Estonia. As to terminology, this chapter follows Graham Tomlin's simple explanation that 'the actions that demonstrate or recall God's rule over the world are "mission", and the words that explain those actions are "evangelism".'[1] Though it is not possible to draw a clear line between these two, mission – in general – is a more holistic concept, including Christian service and lifestyle, while evangelism tends to be predominantly verbal. As a rule, Estonian Baptists tended to see these terms as almost synonymous, or on some occasions they saw 'mission' as 'foreign mission' and 'evangelism' as the task of sharing the gospel in one's local surroundings.[2] Whatever the nuances of definition, Estonian Baptists – in the past and today – would gladly assent to the statement by Claude L. Howe: 'The mission impulse should propel the total Baptist experience, for missions is the purpose of the church that functions as the body of Christ.'[3]

In the 1960s the UECBE Senior Presbyter Aleksander Sildos stated that 'the decline in the moral life of the society' was the result of the fact that the atheistic government had diminished the influence of religion. 'We want to pray for the full-scale opportunities for evangelism, because the gospel is the only force which is able to guide sinners to the right path.'[4] Evangelism was

---

[1] Graham Tomlin, *The Provocative Church* (London: SPCK, 2002), p. 64.

[2] See Richard Kaups, 'Evangelisatsioon' [Evangelisation], in R. Kaups, ed., *50 aastat apostlite radadel* [50 Years in the Ways of the Apostles] (Keila: E.B.K. Liidu kirjastus, 1934), pp. 22-26, Karl Kaups, 'Eesti baptistide osa paganamisjonis' [The Role of Estonian Baptists in Mission Work Among the Heathen], in R. Kaups, ed., *50 aastat apostlite radadel*, pp. 165-171.

[3] Claude L. Howe, 'The Mission Impulse Propels the Baptist Experience', in Charles W. Deweese, ed., *Defining Baptist Convictions. Guidelines for the Twenty-First Century* (Franklin, Tennessee: Providence House Publishers, 1996), p. 156.

[4] The UECBE Senior Presbyter's Report of 1964. EKB vanempresbüteri aruanded (VpAruanded) [The UECBE Senior Presbyter's reports], EEKBLA.

such an important part of Soviet Baptist identity that it broke through, despite
atheistic restrictions and penalties.[5] The local authorities complained in 1981
that the presbyter of Kuressaare ECB church, Hermann Mäemets, turned even a
reception after a funeral service into an evangelistic and prayer event.[6] At the
same time, an exemplary lifestyle and faithfulness in everyday responsibilities
were also emphasised as forms of Christian witness. The charismatic winds of
the 1970s also brought along the Pentecostal evangelistic ideas of the 'full
gospel', which proclaimed freedom both from sin and sickness.[7]

Estonian Baptists tried to reflect theologically upon the role of evangelism.
The Senior Presbyter Robert Võsu systematically evaluated the possibilities for
the UECBE churches to fulfil their calling to proclaim the gospel. While
Estonian free churches traditionally related evangelism to 'preaching
campaigns' and 'revival weeks', Võsu introduced local churches to the idea of
personal evangelism. Attempts to reflect upon the impact of the gospel in wider
society were made by some theologians, but Estonian Baptists, in general,
maintained a somewhat narrower paradigm of mission: individualistic, rather
pragmatic, propagating 'Christian knowledge' even if mixed with emotional
experiences, having its roots in revivalism, and orientated to church growth
rather than transformation in the wider cultural environment. While the modern
paradigm of mission also included optimism about social change, in the
Estonian context this aspect was much less emphasised.[8] However, there was
an interpretative process taking place. Estonian ECB believers – coming from
different historical traditons – were seeking a more adequate understanding of
evangelism and mission. This chapter focuses on some facets of this process as
these relate to their identity.

AN EVANGELISTIC VISION INHERITED FROM THE PAST

Estonian Baptist identity had been shaped by a commitment to evangelism from
the early stages of the Baptist story. The later years of the nineteenth century
were for Estonian Baptists a period of spontaneous revivalist enthusiasm,

---

[5] Sometimes presbyters were fined if they preached in neighbouring churches or at
'revival weeks' in churches other than their own without permission from local
authorities, though the officials were not always consistent in pursuing these cases.

[6] Õiend usuühingute tegevuse kohta Kingissepa rajoonis 1980. aastal [A Report about
activities of religious societies in Kingissepa region in 1980] (08.01.1981). Aruanded ja
ülevaated kirikute tegevuse kohta ENSV-s 1971-1990 [Reports and surveys about the
activities of churches in the ESSR 1971-1990], UNVA.

[7] For a short explanation of the 'full gospel', see Veli-Matti Kärkkäinen, *Pneumatology:
The Holy Spirit in Ecumenical, International and Contextual Perspective* (Grand
Rapids, Michigan: Baker Academic, 2002), p. 93.

[8] For 'modern missionary motives and motifs', see David J. Bosch, *Transforming
Mission: Paradigm Shifts in Theology of Missions* (Maryknoll, New York: Orbis Books,
1997), pp. 262-345, especially pp. 315-345.

inspired by Nordic pietism and German Baptist missionary endeavours.[9] 'Brothers ... motivated by their love for the Lord and the inner need for winning souls, went from village to village, from town to town, and held warm revival meetings.'[10] These lay preachers proclaimed the need for personal conversion, baptism by immersion, and the principle of the believers' church. In 1891, a six-week Baptist mission training course took place in Haapsalu, a town in western Estonia: the students prayed 'for revivals', studied the Bible and held evangelistic meetings in the evenings. By the end of the course, 'seventy persons had been saved and the majority of them joined the local church'.[11] Persuasive preaching and dramatic repentance were important elements of Estonian Baptist theological identity through the twentieth century.

This enthusiastic approach to evangelism was shared by other Estonian free churches. The pre-war Evangelical Christians were keen to lead 'sinners' to a conversion experience. They were more alert to social problems in the society than Baptists or Pentecostals, and worked closely with the organisation *'Sinine Rist'* (Blue Cross), which aimed to help alcoholics. Johannes Laks, later a key leader in the UECBE, described one of the Evangelical Christian revival events, which took place in the facilities of *'Sinine Rist'*. The contrast between the people sitting on the seats in the worship hall, with their obvious social problems, and those preaching and singing on the podium, was striking and was vividly preserved in his memory.[12]

Though Evangelical Christians as well as Baptists in the 1920s and 1930s ran small orphanages and made cautious efforts to reach out with practical ministries, their main focus was on verbal proclamation and on the 'new birth' experience of repentant 'sinners'. 'Social ministry' in Estonia, as was the case in many other parts of Europe among evangelicals, remained mostly on the level of alleviating the consequences, not dealing with the roots of social problems.[13] Nevertheless, there was a sincere – though somewhat short-sighted – conviction that effective evangelism would help the converts to step into a better social reality. Gospel 'seed' would bear good 'fruit' – Estonian Baptists shared this modern view of causality with the wider evangelical world.[14] The church's primary task was to preach the gospel in a convincing and intelligible

---

[9] Toivo Pilli, 'Eesti baptistid ja nende teoloogilise mõtte kajastumine ajakirjas *Teekäija* kuni 1940' [Estonian Baptists and their Theology as Reflected in *Teekäija* until 1940], ThM thesis (Tartu: Tartu University, 1996), pp. 12-14.

[10] Kaups, 'Evangelisatsioon', p. 22.

[11] Martin Schmidt, 'Eesti Baptisti jutlustajate usuteadusliku hariduse ajaloost' [About the History of Estonian Baptist Preachers' Theological Education], in R. Kaups, ed., *50 aastat apostlite radadel*, p. 175.

[12] Johannes Laks, *Mälestusi eluteelt ja töömaalt* [Memoirs from Life and Work] (Toronto: Toronto Vabakoguduse Kirjastus, 1965), pp. 23-24.

[13] Claude Welch, *Protestant Thought in the Nineteenth Century 1870-1914*, vol. 2 (New Haven and London: Yale University Press, 1985), p. 239.

[14] Bosch, *Transforming Mission*, p. 342.

way.[15] From an individual believer's perspective the main calling of a Christian was to evangelise others, to 'win souls'.[16]

Foreign mission was an area where practical service and verbal teaching more naturally intermingled; 'mission' in the minds of Estonian believers often remained detached from local realities and limited to some far-away countries where there were pressing 'needs' of all kinds. Evangelical Christians, in the pre-war period, invested more into foreign mission, when compared to other Estonian free churches. Individuals such as Ester Sirotkin, Melita Marley and Aleksandra Liblik worked as missionaries in Egypt. The latter, Aleksandra Liblik, was the founder of the so called 'village mission' approach in Egypt;[17] and in many ways she was an 'Estonian Mother Theresa' in North Africa. Also, in the first decades of the twentieth century, Henrik Tuttar (Hinrek Tutar), a former Estonian Lutheran missionary in German West Africa (Ovamboland), and later a Baptist preacher back at home, helped the Estonian Baptist tradition to understand more fully the theological motivation for foreign mission.[18] This type of missionary work, however, was not possible for Baptists in the Soviet era, and foreign mission faded away from the picture of Estonian ECB identity for almost fifty years.[19]

Estonian Revivalist Free church believers as well as Pentestostals were, traditionally, fully involved in evangelistic work. At the beginning of the twentieth century, Revivalist Free preachers expanded their activities to Southern Estonia and even beyond the Lake Peipsi,[20] which was then under Tsarist Russia. Their theological focus was on deep repentance and experiencing God's grace, which was expected to result in overwhelming praise

---

[15] Toivo Pilli, 'Eesti baptistide eklesioloogiast *Teekäija* vaatepeeglis: 1904-1940' [About Estonian Baptists' Ecclesiology in the Mirror of *Teekäija*: 1904-1940], in Toivo Pilli, ed., *Teekond teisenevas ajas: peatükke Eesti vabakoguduste ajaloost* [A Journey in Changing Time: Chapters from the History of Estonian Free Churches] (Tartu: Kõrgem Usuteaduslik Seminar ja Sõnasepp OÜ, 2005), pp. 43-44.

[16] See, for example, Daniel H. Matson, 'Hingedevõitmine' [Winning Souls], *Teekäija*, no. 21/22 (1930), pp. 265-266.

[17] Karin Hiiemaa, *Südame kutsel: Eesti misjonärid Aafrikas* [On the Call of the Heart: Estonian Missionaries in Africa] (Tallinn: Olion, 2000), pp. 61-72.

[18] For example, see his articles in *Teekäija* in 1909.

[19] The so called 'foreign mission' was revived among Estonian Baptists after the renewed political and religious freedom of the 1990s. In 2006 there were two married couples and four single missionaries from Estonia working in different parts of the world, including Turkey, Bosnia and China. *Aastaraamat 2006: Eesti Evangeeliumi Kristlaste ja Baptistide Koguduste Liit* [Yearbook 2006: The Union of Evangelical Christian and Baptist Churches in Estonia] (Tallinn, 2006), pp. 11-12.

[20] Peeter Võsu autobiograafia [Peeter Võsu's Autobiography], manuscript (1951), electronical version, pp. 11-36. Toivo Pilli's personal archive.

and joy.[21] Pentecostals, in the 1920s, organised 'revivals' in different locations in the Estonian countryside. Also Pentecostal missionaries from Sweden were active in these outreach efforts.[22] Behind this activism was a deep conviction that a believer is called to be 'an instrument of evangelism in the world'.[23] Karla Poewe has said, referring to wider Pentecostal identity: 'Expansion is essential to the Pentecostal movement. The goals of evangelistic campaigns illustrate that ultimately the message is meant for the whole of humanity.'[24] Estonian Pentecostals had perhaps more modest goals, but they were inspired by the same spirituality, and they took this – sometimes expressed in fervent forms of witnessing – into the Soviet context. A 'pentecostalist' approach to evangelism continued to influence the Estonian Baptist identity in the UECBE, though rational arguments for 'Christian truths' were not lacking – indeed were prominent – in evangelistic thinking.

All Estonian free church traditions, working together in the Soviet context, recognized the basic task of evangelism which was, for them, motivated by the 'Great Commission' (Mt 28:18-20).[25] In 1975, Robert Võsu, the Senior Presbyter of the UECBE, emphasised that the task of Christians was to bring the gospel to 'as broad [a range of the] masses of the people as possible'.[26] Võsu's approach to evangelism was closer to the evangelical Lausanne Covenant of 1974, which emphasised the proclamation of the gospel,[27] than to the World Council of Churches approach, as articulated for example in 1975 in the Nairobi assembly, which emphasised that the gospel always includes

---

[21] A. Seppur, *Jees. Krist. Evg. Priikoguduse tekkimine ja levinemine Läänemaa ärkamises* [The Beginning and Development of Jesus Christ's Evangelical Free Church in the Revival in Western Estonia] (Toronto, 1970), 16-17; M. Busch, *Ridala ärkamise ajalugu* [A History of the Revival in Ridala] (Keila: K.-Ü. 'Külvaja' trükk, 1928), pp. 18-21.

[22] Evald Kiil, *Meenutusi nelipühi ärkamisest Eestis* [Memories of the Pentecostal Revival in Estonia] (Tallinn: Logos, 1997), pp. 20-68.

[23] L.G. McClung, 'Evangelism', in Stanley M. Burgess and Gary B. McGee, eds., *Dictionary of Pentecostal and Charismatic Movements* (Grand Rapids, Michigan: Zondervan, 1988), p. 284.

[24] Karla Poewe, ed., *Charismatic Christianity as a Global Culture* (Columbia, South Carolina: University of South Carolina Press, 1994), p. 35.

[25] For example, see a reference to it in a Baptist publication. Kaups, 'Evangelisatsioon', p. 22.

[26] [Robert Võsu], '1975 – evangelismi aasta' [1975 – The Year of Evangelism], typewritten sermon. Lecture notes 1973-1978, notebook 2. Uudu Rips' personal archive.

[27] Võsu was well informed about the theology and the practice of evangelism in the wider world. The Lausanne Covenant was translated into Estonian in 1980. 'Lausanne'i leping: Kuulgu maailm tema häält!' [Lausanne Covenant: Let the Earth Hear His Voice], typewritten Estonian translation, in *Evangelismikogumik I* [A Collection of Articles on Evangelism I] (1980). TPL.

'struggle for justice and human dignity'.[28] This desire for effective evangelism was an important element in Estonian ECB practice, a kind of 'uniting glue', which consolidated the Estonian ECB identity around one of its central theological ideas: to witness and to win the 'lost' to Christ. Linked with this was revival theology.

REVIVALIST THEOLOGY

Revivalist theology formed the background to the Estonian Baptist undersanding of evangelism, even if no systematic attempts were made to define the word 'revival'.[29] In the wider evangelical scene the term has denoted the 'spiritual revification of individual Christians', or 'renewal of the church through the sovereign act of the Spirit of God', or 'religious movements of enthusiasm'.[30] To a certain extent, all these views were present and were intermingled in Estonia. However, the most important aspect of 'revival' for Estonian believers was that it was a special God-given time for preaching the gospel, a time when the hearts of people were 'softened' by the Holy Spirit and receptive to the Word, and when conversions happened without much human effort.

There were some historical examples in the minds of Estonians that helped them to define when and how revivals should happen. The pre-war Estonian Baptist magazine *Teekäija* (Pilgrim) made references to the evangelistic views of C.H. Spurgeon, C.G. Finney, D.L. Moody and R.A. Torrey, as well as to the Welsh Revival of the beginning of the twentieth century.[31] There were different elements that were distilled out of these examples: a focus on key preachers, the need for preparing for revivals with prayer, and an emphasis on the role of the Holy Spirit. In 1965 some presbyters suggested that the last three months of the year should be a prayer time for revivals, though ECB leaders were aware that sometimes prayer can be a pretext for a low level of evangelistic activity among church members.[32]

The American nineteenth-century evangelist Charles G. Finney's views about revivals were especially influential in Estonian Baptist churches. An

---

[28] Emilio Castro, 'Evangelism', in Nicholas Lossky et al., *Dictionary of the Ecumenical Movement* (Geneva and Grand Rapids: WCC Publications and Eerdmans, 1991), p. 396.

[29] The English words 'revival' and 'awakening' are in Estonian expressed by one word *'ärkamine'*, which has the connotation of somebody waking up from dreams or even from the verge of death. For this semantic reason, I use 'revival' and 'awakening' as synonyms.

[30] Andrew Walker and Kristin Aune, eds., *On Revival: A Critical Examination* (Carlisle: Paternoster, 2003), p. xxi.

[31] Pilli, 'Eesti baptistid ja nende teoloogilise mõtte kajastumine ajakirjas *Teekäija*', pp. 59-60, 62-64, 81.

[32] The UECBE Senior Presbyter's report of 1965. VpAruanded, EEKBLA.

Estonian translation of his *Lectures on Revivals on Religion* circulated as a typewritten manuscript in local churches in the Soviet years.[33] Finney emphasised the need for a renewed love and compassion toward 'sinners', the commitment of believers to the cause of Christ, and the repentance of Christians themselves. All these were needed if revivals were to be expected.[34] He also had a high view of prayer. In his autobiography he said that he had regarded all that he had been able to accomplish as an answer to prayer. Finney continued: 'The spirit of prayer came upon me as a sovereign grace...'.[35] This approach resonated in Estonian Baptists' hearts. Finney's ideas about the cooperation of human effort and God's work in revivals also spread among Estonians. In 1986, Imant Ridaliste, presbyter of the Tartu 'Kolgata' church, wrote referring to Finney: 'If the believers do the preparatory work with faith and commitment, then revival will come.'[36]

Estonians tended to emphasise, in accordance with a rather stereotypical evangelical understanding, that a 'revival' must involve, first and foremost, 'a powerful re-intensification of God's comprehensive saving work in and through his people', as Max Turner has put it.[37] During the Soviet years in Estonia, 'revival' became a key word which expressed the hope that God would intervene and would turn the numerical decline of ECB churches into a new growth and that the 'spiritual lukewarm situation' would be transformed into a new 'fire' and into 'first love'. Even the Commissioner of the CRA in 1969 was aware that the believers regretted the lack of revivals.[38]

There was another dimension of evangelical thinking which saw revival as a special ministry of the Holy Spirit leading a believer to a deeper spiritual life. According to this approach, 'revival' was evangelism directed toward the evangelised. Osvald Tärk emphasised that not only non-believers but also 'half-believers' need awakening. They do not, he suggested, apply the Bible in its fullness and they rely on human opinions instead of receiving the 'renewal of life'.[39] The place of spiritual maturity and growth is here seen as being in the church community. 'Those who want to escape the status of a half-believer should give full attention and full faith to the gospel, but also full commitment

---

[33] Charles Finney, *Kõned ärkamiste üle* [Lectures on Revivals of Religion], typewritten Estonian translation (n. p., n. d.). KUSA.

[34] Ibid., no pagination.

[35] Charles G. Finney, *The Autobiography*, condensed and edited by Helen Wessel (Minneapolis, Minnesota: Bethany House Publishers, 1977), p. 177.

[36] Imant Ridaliste, 'Ärkamise ettevalmistamine' [Preparing for Revival], *Logos*, no. 2 (1986), p. 4.

[37] Max Turner, 'Revival in the New Testament', in Walker and Aune, eds., *On Revival: A Critical Examination*, pp. 4-5.

[38] The Commissioner of the CRA report of 1969. ERA, f. R-1989, n. 2, s. 43, p. 80.

[39] Osvald Tärk, 'Ärkamine Samaarias' [Revival in Samaria], sermon, in [O. Tärk], *Märkmeid O. Tärgi jutlustest 1965. a.* [Notes from O. Tärk's sermons in 1965], typewritten sermon collection (1966?), pp. 246-250. KUSA.

to the church of Christ.'[40] The church, just like the ten virgins with lamps in the Gospel story, is waiting for Christ, but still needs a 'shout of awakening'. This voice prepares the way for the Lord, and usually a new blessing follows. The believers' task is to focus on Christ and to renew their activism and to be constantly prepared to meet Christ.[41]

Oskar Olvik, from the former Evangelical Christian background, agreed with Tärk in his stand against 'lukewarm Christianity': '[O]ur spiritual life requires enlivening and we need seriously to fight lest carelessness and a lukewarm [mentality] will conquer us.' This lukewarm Christianity was characterised by poor faith, lack of love, and spiritual lethargy; and it lacked an inner passion to serve the Lord. Lukewarm Christianity becomes theoretical and mediocre, warned Olvik.[42] In 1950, Robert Võsu stated the goals for the spiritual work in Tallinn 'Kalju' church: a wider spiritual awakening, especially awakening among men; a more intense prayer-life; and the implementation of different spiritual gifts in the church.[43] These became matters of spiritual identity within the ECB.

A new emphasis on the work of the Holy Spirit, especially in the 1970s and 1980s, brought the word 'revival' again into the minds and on to the lips of Estonian Baptists. Now it was understood as a renewal of the Spirit. The 'Effataa revival' embodied the theological expectations of a number of Estonian ECB believers for a committed and victorious Christian life. It saw evangelism as witnessing under the guidance of the Spirit. Referring to the early stages of the Effataa movement in Tallinn Oleviste church, Haljand Uuemõis stated: 'There emerged a serious need to search for God, to pray to Him, to find what is the priority. Believers searched for … a goal in their Christian life. It was a true prayer revival, which was brought forth by the Spirit of God.'[44] There was hope that the state of intense spiritual experience could be maintained; that believers could continue to live on the 'mountain of transfiguration'. The believers with renewed enthusiasm sometimes forgot that it was not possible to live permanently in 'rainbow days', as John Ortberg has described the experience when God feels close and it is easy to witness to Christ.[45]

---

[40] Tärk, 'Ärkamine Samaarias', p. 252.

[41] Osvald Tärk, 'Näoga Jeesuse poole' [Turning Your Face to Jesus], sermon, in [O. Tärk], *Märkmeid O. Tärgi jutlustest 1965. a.*, pp. 344-351. KUSA.

[42] Oskar Olvik, *Neli kõnet* [Four Sermons], typewritten manuscript (1964), pp. 36-39. EEKBLA.

[43] Tallinna Kalju EKB koguduse 1950. a. tegevuse ülevaade [A survey of Tallinn 'Kalju' ECB Church activities in 1950]. Kirjavahetus ja dokumendid 1950-1974: Kalju kogudus [Correspondence and documents 1950-1970: 'Kalju' Church], EEKBLA.

[44] Haljand Uuemõis, 'Effataa-ärkamine' [Effataa Revival], in *Oleviste 50. Oleviste koguduse juubelikogumik* [Oleviste 50. The Anniversary Collection of Oleviste Church] (Tallinn: Oleviste kogudus, 2000), p. 22.

[45] John Ortberg, *God Is Closer Than You Think* (Grand Rapids, Michigan: Zondervan, 2005), pp. 33-35.

These theological views, deriving new energy from an emphasis on the work of the Spirit, spread to other ECB churches in Estonia. For example, in Kuressaare the youth experienced a special time of 'upper room experience' (a reference to Jesus and the disciples in the upper room) in 1984, spending much time in prayer, often until the early morning hours. The participants described the spiritual framework of this local 'revival' as follows: a spirit of repentance and an experience of God's love, openness to prophecy and speaking in tongues, a sense of fellowship and a readiness 'to do whatever is needed for others', and new enthusiasm in reading the Bible. One participant said: 'I felt a touch of the Holy Spirit. I felt how much God loved me. It was as if I had been saved once again.'[46] Both in Tallinn and Kuressaare, and in some other places, the Effataa revival intensified local grassroots efforts in evangelism, often on the level of prayer groups or youth fellowships. Besides praying for the sick, an invitation to come forward 'to give one's life to God' was an essential aspect of the Effataa-style worship services.[47] As to methods, Korean-style 'cell group evangelism' also came to be known to Estonian ECB believers, though some leaders warned that such 'group work' could cause splits and separation within churches.[48]

In addition, Billy Graham's theological preferences shaped Estonian Baptist evangelistic identity. For Estonians, Graham was an evangelist *par exellence*. In his book *The Holy Spirit* he emphasised that 'revival' brings new vision to Christians regarding sin, repentance and salvation; a new sense of responsibility for evangelizing the world; and dependence on the work of the Holy Spirit, - though Graham saw the work of the Spirit in a less charismatic way than, for example, the leaders of Effataa revival.[49] Graham saw revival as a situation where Christians find new motivation for committed witness. The hindrance to revival, according to Graham, was sin in the lives of believers and an unrepentant attitude which means that one does not give one's life fully over to God.[50] Graham's Bible-focused theology and his evangelistic model inspired Estonians for at least three decades, from the 1960s to 1990s, and, in part, this influence continues today. In 1991 forty-five Estonian Baptists took part in

---

[46] Margus Mäemets, 'Kuressaare koguduse noortetöö 1970 kuni 2005 – ajalooline vaatenurk' [Youth Work in Kuressaare Church from 1970 to 2005: A Historical Perspective], diploma thesis (Tartu: Kõrgem Usuteaduslik Seminar, 2006), p. 34, see also pp. 33-40.

[47] Allan Kroll, 'Effataa ärkamine' [Effataa Revival], diploma thesis (Tallinn: EMKTS, 2006), pp. 13-17.

[48] H. Veermets, *Albomi juurde. Haapsalu koguduse 100 aastapäev* (1984)) [To the Album. The 100th Anniversary of the Haapsalu Church (1984)], pp. 3-4. EEKBLA.

[49] Billy Graham, *Püha Vaim: Jumala väe virgutav jõud inimese elus* [The Holy Spirit: Activating God's Power in Your Life], typewritten Estonian translation (n. p., n. d.), pp. 358-364. KUSA.

[50] Ibid., pp. 365-368.

Graham's major evangelism training in Moscow.[51]

Estonia belongs geographically to a region where spiritual awakenings were part of the pietistic forms of Lutheranism.[52] Indirectly, this has had an impact on Estonian Baptists. More directly, Estonian Baptist revivalist theology has been shaped by the Anglo-American 'soul winning' type of evangelicalism, with some significant Pentecostal and charismatic influences. While during the Soviet years there was a need – forced both by external pressures and an internal theological search – to reinterpret the evangelistic task of the church and find new methods, the revivalist vision continued to be a crucial part of Estonian Baptist identity. At the centre of this vision was a conviction that spiritual conversion – the new birth – is basic, the *sine qua non* starting point, for a person's Christian life.

THE 'NEW BIRTH' AS A CENTRAL THEOLOGICAL CONCEPT

For Estonian ECB believers, mission and evangelism had a clear aim: to lead people to Christ, to the experience of conversion and new birth. Through 'making a decision' for Christ in faith, which 'is the most important part of conversion', … 'a person crosses the borderline between the world and God's kingdom.'[53] Osvald Tärk was assured that it was important for a person to take his or her stand, in other words to make a decision, when faced with the message of the gospel.[54] The invitation to make a personal decision for Christ reflected American revivalist methods and language – used by D.L. Moody, Billy Graham and others.[55]

In the Estonian ECB context, sin was understood as a rebellion against God, God's redemption as a message of amnesty, and repentance as a process of a human being turning from an enemy of God to his friend.[56] This was standard evangelical thinking. Similar logic is expressed in a theological document of the ECB from the 1990s, which in a way summarizes earlier theological positions: 'The only way to be saved from perishing is conversion, repentance and new birth through Jesus Christ.'[57] Peeter Roosimaa, who received his theological education at Buckow Baptist Theological Seminary in

---

[51] Ülo Meriloo to N.A. Kolesnikov (14.06.1991). Folder 'Üleliiduline keskus' [All-Union Centre], EEKBLA.

[52] Björn Ryman et al., *Nordic Folk Churches: A Contemporary History* (Grand Rapids, Michigan, and Cambridge, UK: Eerdmans, 2005), pp. 140-143.

[53] Robert Võsu, *Isiklik evangelism* [Personal Evangelism], typewritten manuscript (Tallinn, 1971), p. 95. Robert Võsu materjalid [Materials of Robert Võsu], EEKBLA.

[54] Tärk, 'Ärkamine Samaarias', p. 251.

[55] John M. Terry, *Evangelism: A Concise History* (Nashville, Tennessee: Broadman and Holman, 1994), pp. 154, 170.

[56] Võsu, *Isiklik evangelism*, pp. 91-101.

[57] *Piibli õpetus Eesti Evangeeliumi Kristlaste ja Baptistide Koguduste Liidu kogudustes* [Biblical Teaching in the UECBCE Churches] (Tallinn: Eesti EKB Liit, 1998), p. 16.

the German Democratic Republic, has emphasised that the 'new birth' – according to him a process during which a non-Christian becomes a Christian – has both 'juridical' aspects and 'existential' aspects.[58] Roosimaa's approach has attempted to reconcile the typical Lutheran-Protestant understanding of 'objective' justification by faith and the free church understanding of a 'subjective' experience of spiritual inner renewal. Roosimaa has also tried to draw a theologically justified line between 'conversion' and 'new birth' – the first being the act of a human being (turning away from sin, *metanoia*) and the second being the sovereign act of God.[59] However, Estonian Baptists have often seen these two terms as synonymous, the central characteristic of the phenomenon being 'self-transformation within a religious context', to use the language of religious psychology.[60]

Traditionally Estonian Baptists viewed the 'new birth' as a sudden event, even if it had been preceded by a period of prayer, seeking and repentance. In this sense the ECB believers supported the 'classic model of conversion' which suggests 'an instantaneous change', a view widespread among evangelicals.[61] However, when the general atmosphere in Estonian society was hostile to Christianity and there were no significant revivals - there were some local awakenings (the role of which has sometimes been overestimated in the UECBE)[62] - many new converts came from church members' families, and their evangelical faith grew gradually. This has been the general tendency in history: when fresh awakenings arc lacking, then instead of sudden conversions taking place members are increasingly 'recruited through socialization processes within the movement'.[63]

For Estonian Baptists this posed a theological dilemma. Many churches continued to expect dramatic experiences at the beginning of a person's Christian journey. Presbyter Paldor Teekel, from a Revivalist background, expressed doubts that people who became Christians 'quietly' could become 'serious believers'.[64] Many other presbyters, however, admitted that the 'new birth' could take place over a longer period of time. This 'new birth theology' had its effect on the understanding of evangelism: it was either aiming at a personal and sometimes emotional 'turning around' event or it was seen as a

---

[58] Peeter Roosimaa, *Pöördumine ja uussünd* [Conversion and New Birth] (Tartu: EKB Liidu Kõrgem Usuteaduslik Seminar, 2003), p. 24.

[59] Ibid., pp. 67-70.

[60] Bernard Spilka et al., *The Psychology of Religion: An Empirical Approach* (New York, London: The Guilford Press, 2003), p. 345.

[61] Tomlin, *The Provocative Church*, p. 89.

[62] Jüri-Valdur Kibuspuu, '50 aastat tagasi toimus Hiiumaal suur ärkamine' [50 Years Ago a Large Revival Took Place in Hiiumaa Island], *Teekäija*, no. 9 (2006), p. 22.

[63] Ryman et al., *Nordic Folk Churches*, p. 141.

[64] Minutes of the Executive Board meeting, no. 115 (14.10.1985). Juhatuse koosolekute protokollid (JKP) [Minutes of the Executive Board] (30.01.1981-12.12.1987), EEKBLA.

process of growth toward God in the supportive atmosphere of a Christian community.[65] Some theologians have stated that the focus on new birth – regeneration – is related to crisis evangelism, while the focus on gradual transformation is related to process evangelism.[66] Estonian Jüri Puusaag stated boldly that conversion is a process that lasts throughout a human person's whole lifetime, and that the only right context for this is local church.[67] Not everyone in the UECBE rushed to agree with him.

Evangelism, however, could only *help* a person to establish a personal relationship with God. The final responsibility lay on the potential convert. Estonian ECB believers were convinced that every person can and must approach God without any mediator. 'Father meets with every child in immediate fellowship and every child can directly turn to the heavenly Father in prayer.'[68] American Baptist sources tend to call this quality 'soul freedom'. This is linked in American literature to voluntarism. 'All authentic missions and evangelism are predicated upon the possibility, the opportunity, and the responsibility of a voluntary response.'[69] Though Estonian Baptists have never argued for 'voluntarism' as strongly as their American counterparts, the principle has been essential for them, often 'accepted silently'. In 1965, the Senior Pesbyter said that an emphasis on personal commitment is an advantage for free churches, because people detach themselves from formal Christianity.[70]

Oskar Olvik described a typical conversion in a former Evangelical Christian church in 1945-1950. 'Those who came to faith did not come under the influence of emotions or feelings, but with deep repentance, change of mind and with a wish seriously to improve their life with the help of God.'[71] I would argue that this gives too rational a picture of the conversion theology of the UECBE. Subjective feelings – joy, peace, being filled with emotions of love and liberation – also continued to be important in conversion. This more emotional 'tradition' derived from wider revivalist models, as well as from the Estonian Revivalist Free Church and from Pentecostal theology and practice.[72]

---

[65] See also Spilka et al., *The Psychology of Religion*, pp. 348-354. The authors suggest that sudden conversions tend to be more emotional, and gradual conversions more cognitive.

[66] Tomlin, *The Provocative Church*, p. 94.

[67] Jüri Puusaag, 'Kogudusekeskne evangelism' [Church-Centered Evangelism], *Logos*, no. 3 (1988), pp. 10-11.

[68] Robert Võsu, 'Baptistide ajaloolised põhimõtted' [Historical Principles of Baptists] (Oleviste, 05.02.1956), pp. 3-4. Robert Võsu materjalid, EEKBLA.

[69] Grady C. Cothen and James M. Dunn, *Soul Freedom: Baptist Battle Cry* (Macon, Georgia: Smyth and Helwys, 2000), p. 21.

[70] The UECBE Senior Presbyter's report of 1965. VpAruanded, EEKBLA.

[71] Oskar Olvik, *Mälestused* [Memoirs], part 2, typewritten manuscript (Tallinn, 1966), p. 312. Oleviste ECB Church library, Tallinn.

[72] See Seppur, *Jees. Krist. Evg. Priikoguduse tekkimine ja levinemine*, pp. 11, 51; Evald Kiil, *Issandast kutsutud viinamäe tööle* [Called by God for Work in the Vineyard]

But whatever the emphasis – rational or emotional or a combination of both – the new birth remained a central concept. However, this does not mean that the theology and practice of evangelism were static; conversion required interpretation and was put to the test by changing social and religious realities. Much discussion revolved around the issues of evangelistic strategies.

PERSONAL OR CAMPAIGN EVANGELISM?

The Estonian ECB vision for evangelistic revivals was traditionally 'meeting-driven', although an individual Christians' responsibility in witnessing to Christ was also emphasised. Through the Soviet years, 'personal evangelism' was even more systematically explored and taught by some church leaders. Sociologically, campaign evangelism is most effective in settings where people are – at least superficially – aware of the Christian message.[73] Atheism, which eroded the knowledge of Christianity in Estonian minds, also undermined the social conditions for 'old time revivals' – when numerous conversions happened in a short period of time. This was aggravated by secularisation in the wider European scene. It was 'more difficult to argue from a common basis of Christian knowledge.'[74] Also urbanisation played a role.[75] In 1965, it was clear that the most rapid decline in ECB membership had taken place in churches in the countryside, in areas that had been the former seedbeds of 'revival meetings'.[76] Estonian Baptists' response to these developments was a renewed emphasis on personal witness.

Nevertheless, 'campaign evangelism', often in the form of 'revival weeks' in local churches, was not abandoned. In particular, believers with a Revivalist Free background cherished a hope that God would miraculously intervene and numerous conversions would follow. During special 'evangelistic meetings' much energy was devoted to an invitation time, when people were expected to come forward or to raise their hand as a sign of a wish to 'receive Christ'. Johannes Jääger, a fiery evangelist, used every opportunity to invite people to

---

(Tallinn, 1993), pp. 17-19. Several stories reflecting emotional aspects of conversion can be found in Aare Tamm, comp., *Teel allikale* [On the Way to a Fountain], vols. 1-2 (Tallinn: Logos, 2002).

[73] Meic Pearse, 'Revivals as Historically Situated Events: Lessons for the Future', in Walker and Aune, eds., *On Revival: A Critical Examination*, pp. 162-163.

[74] Ryman et al., *Nordic Folk Churches*, p. 142.

[75] Plaat, Jaanus, 'Eesti vabakoguduste vastupanu nõukogude religioonipoliitikale võrreldes luterliku ja õigeusu kirikuga (1944-1987)' [The Resistance of Estonian Free Churches to Soviet Religious Policies, in Comparison with Lutheran and Orthodox Church (1944-1987)], in Toivo Pilli, ed., *Teekond teisenevas ajas*, pp. 152-155.

[76] The UECBE Senior Presbyter's report of 1965. VpAruanded, EEKBLA. In 1979 the Senior Presbyter Võsu clearly stated that the evangelistic frontier was in the cities. The UECBE Senior Presbyter's report of 1979. VpAruanded, EEKBLA.

repentance.[77] This type of evangelistic theology relied less on rational
arguments and more on religious experience; it used biblical imagery and had a
high, even prophetic view of an evangelist-preacher. Jääger, who never used
written sermon notes, stated: 'God will remind me what to say, he never forgets
anything!'[78] This locally modified 'campaign evangelism' found its models
both in Estonian free church history and also in the wider world - for example
from Billy Graham's ministry. Graham's approach was not spontaneous, but
his campaigns belonged to the evangelical tradition of preacher-centred
revivals.[79]

   Revival weeks were expected to happen in a 'warm' atmosphere. One
writer described Baptist evangelism in Saaremaa island: 'Every speech was
followed by communal singing. It was characteristic that ... "more powerful
brothers in the Lord" were among the last [preachers]. Also more joyful and
rythmic songs came at the end. ... The content of sermons was more or less the
same for every [preacher]: a person has been born with original sin and would
go into the fires of hell. It is possible to be saved from this by means of prayer
and by "being born from above".'[80] Though the quote referred to the pre-war
period, it could also fairly accurately describe an evangelistic meeting in a
countryside Baptist church in the Soviet period. Gradually, the style of 'revival
preaching' began to change, especially in urban churches, where the language
expanded beyond hell-and-heaven-images to include consideration of moral
decline in society, the loss of meaning in life and personal spiritual struggles,
which came to be used as arguments for seeking forgiveness and new life in
Christ. The gospel is the saving power of God: it awakens consciousness, leads
to an experience of grace, and reshapes a person's will, emotions and
thinking.[81]

   However, there was some questioning of the effectiveness of 'revival
meetings' – and more cautiously, of the practical theology behind these events.
It was argued that sometimes 'mass-revivals can even be dangerous';[82] an

---

[77] Johannes Jääger, *Tema kutsus mind* [He Called Me], typewritten manuscript (1984),
pp. 28-73, 102-107, 120-123. TPL.

[78] 'Johannes Jääger in memoriam', *Logos*, no. 3 (1986), pp. 59-60.

[79] See, for example, William Martin, *A Prophet with Honor: The Billy Graham Story*
(New York: William Morrow and Company, 1991), pp. 32-52.

[80] Jaanus Plaat, *Saaremaa kirikud, usuliikumised ja prohvetid 18.-20. sajandil*
[Churches, Religious Movements and Prophets in Saaremaa Island in the 18th-20th
Centuries] (Tartu: Eesti Rahva Muuseum, 2003), p. 146.

[81] See a systematic presentation by Osvald Tärk, 'Evangeelium on Jumala vägi' [Gospel
is the Power of God], in *Eesti EKB koguduste presbüterite konverents Tallinnas, 15.-18.
veebruaril 1968. a.* [The Estonian ECB Presbyters Conference in Tallinn, 15-18
February 1968], typewritten manuscript [1968], pp. 154-155. Ülo Meriloo's personal
library.

[82] The UECBE Senior Presbyter's report of 1979. EKB vanempresbüteri aruanded
(VpAruanded) [The UECBE Senior Presbyter's reports], EEKBLA.

increase in nominal Christianity and 'fallings away from faith' could accompany mass-conversions.[83] Võsu's theological reflections led him to emphasise again the value of personal relationships in evangelism. His conclusions found expression in a small book *Isiklik evangelism* (Personal Evangelism), which first appeared as a typewritten text in 1971. This book marked a significant change in Estonian Baptist thinking on the topic. For many, it was a theological guideline for the years to come.[84]

In the typical evangelical manner of the 1960s and 1970s, Võsu found the theological mandate for evangelism in the Great Commission and in other texts of the New Testament which refer to Jesus sending his disciples (Mk 16: 15, Mt 28: 19, John 20: 21, Acts 1: 8).[85] There were practical advantages to personal evangelism, such as its simplicity, its independence from the need to access financial resources and its flexibility. Nevertheless, the main argument was biblical: personal evangelism was the model set by Jesus and the apostles, though 'sometimes they proclaimed also to crowds'. Võsu concluded: 'No doubt, the method he [Jesus] gave us is the best.'[86] This encouragement to follow the 'method of Jesus' aimed to help people to experience spiritual transformation and confidence in being 'a child of God'. In 1981 it was taught in the 'underground' UECBE correspondence Bible courses: 'It is necessary to know Christ and to present him to the world in a way that their understanding will change.'[87]

Personal evangelism appealed to the sense of responsibility of every believer. The 1965 Senior Presbyter's report said, in a standard Baptist manner: '[W]e need to grow a spirit of evangelism in our believers, so that every believer will be a committed missionary.'[88] In revival meetings local church members often became passive observers, while guest speakers took the main responsibility. For Võsu, evangelism required total personal commitment and spiritual maturity of every Christian: 'If we want the work of Kingdom to develop, we need people who commit themselves fully to this work.'[89] In 1965 the Senior Presbyter, Aleksander Sildos, stated: 'We need God's grace but also our own endeavours, to bring along a new awakening … we can increase revitalisation locally.'[90] In 1972 he commented: 'We may sing in a choir, go to

---

[83] The UECBE Senior Presbyter's report of 1967. VpAruanded, EEKBLA.

[84] In 1988 Kalju Raid, a veteran presbyter in the UECBE, expressed his appreciation for the book. Minutes of the Executive Board meeting, no. 141 (16.05.1988). Juhatuse koosolekute protokollid koos lisadega (JKPLis) [Minutes of the Executive Board, with attachments] (11.01.1988-02.03.1992), EEKBLA.

[85] Võsu, *Isiklik evangelism*, pp. 1-3.

[86] Ibid., p. 5.

[87] Lecture notes 1973-1978, notebook 3. Uudu Rips' personal archive.

[88] The UECBE Senior Presbyter's report of 1965. VpAruanded, EEKBLA.

[89] Robert Võsu, 'Tagasi Jeesuse juurde' [Back to Jesus], handwritten notes (n. d.), no pagination. Robert Võsu materjalid, EEKBLA.

[90] The UECBE Senior Presbyter's report of 1965. VpAruanded, EEKBLA.

church and even preach, and still not have compassion for souls'.[91] In addition to commitment and a compassionate heart, there was a need to trust the renewing power of the Spirit, and to pray with confidence.[92] To the extent that these spiritual-theological elements were 'tested' in actual witnessing situations; the Baptist view that faith finds its expression in personal discipleship and witness was strengthened in the UECBE.

However, neither Võsu nor other ECB leaders said that personal evangelism had to replace the wider mission of the church, but rather that it had to cooperate with other ministries in a believer's community: prayer groups, evangelistic meetings, revival weeks and Bible study circles.[93] Jüri Puusaag, presbyter of Tallinn 'Kalju' ECB Church, took a step further in trying to put into practice the idea of evangelism as a 'calling' for all church members. Võsu's book was mainly a manual for individual evangelistic efforts. Puusaag made more conscious attempts to interpret personal evangelism and the wider mission of the church as going hand in hand. It was the witness of the whole church and the transforming effect of a Christian community – expressed, however, through its members – that came to be re-emphasised in Tallinn 'Kalju' Chuch, one of the leading local churches in the UECBE.

Puusaag added a new dimension to the ECB's evangelistic theology. He systematically encouraged church members to build personal relationships 'outside the church walls'. 'We are missionaries for educated atheists', he explained, 'we need to learn the language, in order to converse with today's educated world'.[94] Some translated articles in the semi-illegal publication *Logos* also paid attention to the cultural context in which the gospel was shared.[95] This fresh view of evangelism saw the local church community as the centre for proclaiming the gospel.[96] Puusaag encouraged church members to build long-term relationships with people from 'the world'. It was believed that the Christian message must convey a clearer picture of a gracious God, not 'scare away people' with sermons about punishment. First of all, the church must be attractive and bring people into its fellowship; only then catechetical work could and must follow.[97] Puusaag's model was based on a renewed

---

[91] Aleksander Sildos, 'Läkitus ülesannetele' [Sending Out for a Mission], typewritten sermon (1972). Robert Võsu materjalid, EEKBLA.
[92] Võsu, *Isiklik evangelism*, pp. 12-13.
[93] Ibid., pp. 137-146.
[94] Lecture notes 1973-1978, notebook 3. Uudu Rips' personal archive.
[95] Günther Wieske, 'Euroopa kristlased piibli ja kultuuri pingeväljas' [European Christians in the Tension Area of the Bible and Culture], *Logos*, no. 3-4 (1987), pp. 42-48; Francis Schaeffer, 'Uus religioosne laine' [A New Religious Wave], *Logos*, no. 4 (1982), pp. 28-32, no. 5 (1982), pp. 19-24.
[96] Jüri Puusaag, 'Kogudusekeskne evangelism' [Church-Centered Evangelism], *Logos*, no. 3 (1988), p. 10.
[97] Jüri Puusaag, 'Inimeste püüdja või inimeste hirmutaja?' [Fishing for Men or Scaring Men?], *Logos*, no. 2 (1986), pp. 9-10.

theological understanding of the priesthood of all believers. Tallinn 'Kalju' Church wanted to be known for its hospitality toward non-members.[98] In a sort of Finneyan way, Puusaag believed in cooperation between God and man in proclaiming the gospel, but he abandoned the 'campaign' approach.[99]

However, the 'campaign' and 'personal' methods were creatively combined in the Effataa movement, which believed that with a new blessing of the Holy Spirit the work of evangelism would be renewed. The Effataa 'revival' believed that effective evangelism must have a renewed pneumatological centre. Early Pentecostalism saw Spirit baptism as a door to sanctification, but for later Pentecostalism 'the second blessing' gave 'power for witness'.[100] Also, some Pentecostal theologicans have interpreted speaking in tongues from a missionary perspective, as a sign of the power and even the language for preaching the gospel.[101] In the Effataa movement in Estonia there was not much theoretical-theological analysis, but their practice demonstrated their deep conviction that the baptism or filling of the Holy Spirit was essential for a renewed commitment to evangelism.

Effataa supporters believed that God miraculously intervened in human life not only for healing but also for manifesting his power in personal salvation. Those ECB groups which were influenced by Effataa ideals found new motivation for sharing the gospel. Before evangelistic meetings sometimes one thousand invitations were distributed in Tallinn – despite the fact that this was viewed as an illegal activity by the authorities.[102] In the 1980s, the youth of Kuressaare church travelled in neighbouring churches, gave their testimonies, and helped with music programmes during 'revival weeks' in local churches.[103] Also, it was Effataa evangelism that tried to reach the 'marginalised in the society' – youth from problematic families, and people with alcohol and drug problems. During the Soviet years there was a tendency in the UECBE to suggest that the 'best soil' for evangelism was 'children of believers'.[104] This view was broadened now. Effataa youth were also engaged in 'personal' evangelism on every possible occasion and in every possible place – on public

---

[98] Jüri Puusaag, 'Sajandivanune Tallinna 'Kalju' kogudus' [A Century-Old Tallinn 'Kalju' Church], *Logos*, no. 3 (1984), pp. 5-8.

[99] See also Jüri Puusaag, 'Evangeelse töö mured ja rõõmud' [Joys and Sorrows of Evangelistic Work], *Logos*, no. 3 (1985), pp. 10-15.

[100] Kärkkäinen, *Pneumatology: The Holy Spirit in Ecumenical, International and Contextual Perspective*, p. 96.

[101] Simon Chan, *Pentecostal Theology and the Christian Spiritual Tradition* (Sheffield: Sheffield Academic Press, 2000), pp. 42-46.

[102] Lecture notes 1973-1978, notebook 3. Uudu Rips' personal archive.

[103] Mäemets, 'Kuressaare koguduse noortetöö', pp. 26, 44.

[104] Robert Võsu, 'Külvakem rohkesti!' [Sow Abundantly!], *Logos*, no. 1 (1983), p. 2; Aleksander Sildos, 'Tee valmistajad' [Those Who Pave the Way], typewritten sermon, no pagination. Robert Võsu materjalid, EEKBLA.

transportation, in cafeterias, on streets and in parks.[105]

Osvald Tärk, 'the grand old man of Estonian Baptists', also talked about the 'power of the gospel' – though from a different angle than the Effataa group. Tärk's approach was an attempt to go behind 'methods': the power of the gospel is not in singing or sermons, it is in the power of the Spirit; and the Spirit is not 'it' but 'Him'. This power becomes visible through Christ's body, the church.[106] Even if the majority of evangelistic discussions remained on the level of 'strategies', Tärk's theological arguments were helpful in giving biblical and theological perspectives.

Both campaign evangelism and personal evangelism had their place in the evangelistic self-understanding of Estonian Baptists. Nevertheless, during the Soviet years, when the level of 'religious literacy' in the society diminished, campaign evangelism – in Estonia often in the form of 'revival weeks' – lost its social basis. The Effataa 'revival', with its evangelistic and healing ministry, was socially supported, rather like a youth protest against a stagnant Communism, and it led a significant number of young people to seek religious experiences. Some ECB church leaders pointed out that there was a need for the whole church to be motivated for evangelism, and charismatic influences through Effataa activities in Tallinn added a pneumatological dimension. However, all these approaches tended to see evangelism as verbal. Were Estonian Baptists unaware of the 'incarnational' aspects of evangelism? ECB semi-illegal literature testifies that there were, indeed, attempts to see evangelism in a more service-orientated way, though that was less conspicuous than verbal proclamation. Whether in personal or campaign evangelism the ECB churches expressed their missional identity largely in sharing the 'words of life'.

LIFESTYLE EVANGELISM AND SERVANT SPIRIT

Honesty, exemplary work, and loving relationships were, for Soviet ECB believers generally, not just a matter of personal sanctification, but also a means of witnessing to the life-changing power of the gospel.[107] This was also true in Estonia. Personal faith and God's grace were to be expressed in everyday life by a person's changed character and good deeds. Võsu stated in

---

[105] A little tract *Neli vaimuliku elu tõsiasja* [Four Spiritual Laws] was widely used in witnessing. Also some typewritten texts were helpful, such as Rosalind Rinker, *Te võite veendunult tunnistada* [You Can Witness with Confidence], typewritten Estonian translation (n. p., n. d.). KUSA. The original was published in 1962 by Zondervan.

[106] Osvald Tärk, 'Evangeelium on Jumala vägi' [The Gospel is the Power of God], in *Eesti EKB koguduste presbüterite konverents Tallinnas, 15.-18. veebruaril 1968. a.*, pp. 152-154.

[107] Steve Durasoff, *The Russian Protestants, Evangelicals in the Soviet Union: 1944-1964* (Rutherford: Farleigh Dickinson University Press, 1969), pp. 217-219.

1982 that 'separation between the church and the world is so large that people do not understand spiritual language anymore', and – according to him – a lifestyle type of witness opened up new avenues for evangelism.[108] However, in practice Estonian Baptist evangelism remained overwhelmingly verbal – partly because of revivalist influences and partly because of their Word-centered theology. Wider activities in the society were also hindered by Communist regime.

As a theologian, Võsu pursued his argument further. He explained that evangelism in homes and the workplace was the method of Jesus. The activity of Jesus was not limited to synagogues; he moved daily among people and often visited homes. He preached along the shores of lakes, a 'common workplace'. Jesus did not draw a line between everyday life and spiritual life. 'In our days a dividing line between Sunday piety and everyday life becomes more and more visible,' Võsu stated, while arguing for a more holistic view of Christian witness. The walls of prayer houses should not separate Christians from real life and church members should not become 'prayer-house-believers', lest their witness in the world be hindered.[109] Võsu had a positive attitude also toward the Oxford Group movement, with its commitment to explaining and living out the gospel in contemporary ways, a movement which was known in Estonia through literature published in the 1930s.[110]

Aleksander Sildos paid much attention in his sermons to a believer's lifestyle and moral character. 'Children of God' pave the way for non-Christians, Sildos explained. Believers who are full of self-righteousness, or who do not have confidence in their salvation, or who are under burdens of worry cannot show the way to others. 'Proclamation is important, but even more important is a holy life, which is in harmony with proclamation. There are people, who cannot and do not know how to speak, but with their holy life they have prepared the way for many others. … Quiet patience, peacefully standing against all injustice and roughness, has a greater influence than a weak sermon.'[111] Also Ants Rebane, who received his theological education in the 1980s, saw witness in practical life as 'central in the Sermon on the Mount and as a core topic in the epistles'.[112]

---

[108] Robert Võsu, 'Kristlase kohustused' [Responsibilities of a Christian], *Logos*, no. 1 (1982), pp. 1-2.

[109] Robert Võsu, 'Tagasi Jeesuse juurde', handwritten notes, no pagination. Robert Võsu materjalid, EEKBLA.

[110] For example, see *Oxford-rühmade liikumisest* [About the Oxford-Group Movement] (Tartu: Eesti Kristlik Üliõpilasühing, 1934); cf. I.M. Randall, '"Arresting People for Christ": Baptists and the Oxford Group in the 1930s', *The Baptist Quarterly*, vol. 38, no. 1 (1999), pp. 3-18.

[111] Aleksander Sildos, 'Tee valmistajad', typewritten sermon, no pagination. Robert Võsu materjalid, EEKBLA.

[112] Ants Rebane, 'Piibellik pühitsus' [Biblical Sanctification], *Logos*, no. 2 (1982), pp. 11-12.

Indeed, often the lifestyle of church members caused a 'cognitive dissonance'[113] in their co-workers and neighbours. The real life experience of unbelievers who came to know believers was often so different from the atheistic picture, which described believers as unintelligent or irresponsible. This needed explanation, and sometimes raised interest in Christian beliefs. However, Baptists tended to see exemplary lifestyle as a means for verbal witness – 'paving the way', to paraphrase Sildos. The aim was to lead a person to the 'sinner's prayer'. Estonian Baptists seldom thought that a life of justice and honesty had value in itself as a form of witness, expanding the borders of God's kingdom in the world. Rather, effective witness only took place, it was believed, when the end result of the activity was that people accepted the truth about salvation through Jesus and experienced conversion.

Having said this, it is important to note that Estonian ECB leaders did reflect upon Christian influence on society, even if this did not become a guiding vision for local churches. The 'social gospel' was thought of as something that might lead someone astray from the main goal – preaching the Word. In this sense, Estonian Baptists were in accord with much of the wider evangelical world.[114] This is why it is somewhat surprising to find that Robert Võsu, prophetically for the UECBE, talked about 'the Christianity of servanthood' and about the social dimension of the gospel.[115] Jesus, Võsu argued, met the needs of people and chose Isaiah 61:1-3, with its stress on the good news as it is worked out for the benefit of the poor, as the *leitmotif* for his ministry. 'Our churches have become preaching churches. Social activity is limited and marginalised and mainly involves only taking care of the sick.'[116] Though Võsu did not give to 'servanthood' an independent value, his theology was much more balanced than in the ECB churches in general. Proclamation and servanthood, as he saw it, should be inseparable from each other. The world outside the church evaluates faith according to how it is practised. Võsu also referred to Matthew 25:35-36 – the call to feed the hungry, clothe the naked, etc. Christians must not leave these areas of ministry and service to politicians and economists. Faith that does not take seriously this mission will be 'put aside'. The stark warning of Võsu was that this judgement was already taking place.[117]

Estonian Baptists were aware, however, of some models which reminded them that the gospel had other dimensions than just preaching. For example, in

---

[113] See R.L. Timpe, 'Cognitive Dissonance', in D. Benner, ed., *Baker Encyclopaedia of Psychology* (Grand Rapids, Michigan: Baker Book House, 1985), p. 188.
[114] John Wolffe, ed., *Evangelical Faith and Public Zeal: Evangelicals and Society in Britain 1780-1980* (London: SPCK, 1995), p. 177.
[115] Robert Võsu, 'Tagasi Jeesuse juurde', handwritten notes, no pagination. Robert Võsu materjalid, EEKBLA.
[116] Ibid.
[117] Ibid.

a typewritten manuscript, probably dating from the end of the 1960s, a selection of Martin Luther King Jr.'s sermons and speeches were made available for Estonian Baptist believers. This collection inclued King's summary of his own development toward social and political activism. King was confident that the gospel should embrace the whole person – not only spiritual needs, but also bodily well-being. He also admitted in this collection that he was influenced by the ideas of Walter Rauschenbusch.[118] Walter Rauschenbusch was known to Estonian Baptists only as a name in textbooks, and via some short translated articles from the pre-war period,[119] but there was no deeper or more direct impact of or connection with this Baptist 'father of the social gospel' in Estonia. However, contacts through the written word, like this, must have broadened the Estonian Baptist understanding of evangelism and mission. In 1986, influenced by the concept of 'Diakonie' among German Baptists, Ermo Jürma said: 'God can be present in every humanitarian deed, even if He is not specifically mentioned.' … 'Serving other people is also evangelism.'[120]

Regarding the impact of the gospel in the society, Estonian Baptists did not think so much in terms of social justice, but rather in terms of moral purity. The task of believers was to raise the moral level of the whole society – but the change began with personal transformation. Christians were to be 'salt and light' for society – in a moral sense.[121] It was Võsu who taught that it was God's will that the gospel message should penetrate into the whole society.[122] He emphasised in 1946 that God uses 'a small remnant' in order to 'build up the people' of the whole country.[123] In his 1964 report the Senior Presbyter, Sildos, expressed a wish that evangelism would raise up the moral level of the

---

[118] Martin Luther King, *Kõned ja jutlused* [Speeches and Sermons], typewritten Estonian translation (n. p., n. d.), p. 178. KUSA.

[119] Toivo Pilli, 'Eesti baptistide eklesioloogiast *Teekäija* vaatepeeglis: 1904-1940' [About Estonian Baptists' Ecclesiology in the Mirror of *Teekäija*: 1904-1940], in Toivo Pilli, ed., *Teekond teisenevas ajas*, pp. 45-46. In neighbouring Latvia, for example, a number of Baptist pastors were influenced by the ideas of the social gospel, even leaning toward socialist ideas. See Valdis Teraudkalns, 'Socialist Ideas among Latvian Baptists in the First Half of the Twentieth Century', in Toivo Pilli and Sharyl Corrado, eds., *Eastern European Baptist History: New Perspectives* (Prague: IBTS, 2007), pp. 102-118.

[120] Ermo Jürma, 'Diakooniast' [About Diaconie-work], *Logos*, no. 1 (1986), pp. 28-30.

[121] For Robert Võsu, Matt 5: 13-16 and Mk 4: 3-9 were key texts for interpreting the task of Christians in the world. See, Lecture notes 1973-1978, notebook 2. Uudu Rips' personal archive.

[122] *'Kalju' koguduse karjase Robert Võsu jutlusi ajavahemikul 1944-1969* [Sermons of 'Kalju' Church Pastor, Robert Võsu, from 1944 to 1969], typewritten manuscript, p. 123. KUSA.

[123] Ibid., pp. 11-13.

society.[124] Osvald Tärk preached that the gospel also brings judgement which, in turn, will give guidance to people about how to find God's grace and mercy. 'The lifestyle of believers has to admonish the immorality of the world in the name of the light of the gospel.'[125]

However, Baptists were rather modest in fighting publicly with the 'structural sins' of the communist regime. The traditional evangelical revivalist approach remained predominant. Another factor was that the development in Estonia was different, for example, from the story of Scandinavian pietism and Baptist evangelicalism, movements with which the Estonian free church movements used to have much in common in their earlier stages. In Scandinavia 'the new church activities including social and diaconal work created a spirituality that differed from the old pietistic spirituality that concentrated solely on "the one thing needful", the preaching of the gospel to save souls.'[126] In Estonia the Baptists continued to seek the "one thing needful" – and from there they believed some positive changes could take place in the society. Political activism was almost excluded – even at the end of the 1980s, when the collapse of Communism was at hand.

Graham Tomlin has suggested: 'The priority for the Church is neither evangelism nor social action; it is to live under the lordship of Christ. In other words, the central thing is not a human task, but a divine action.'[127] This was one of the main theological problems for Estonian Baptists. They saw evangelism as a human activity and as expressed in certain tasks, including life-style evangelism and servanthood – no doubt, to be fulfilled with the help of God – but they were lacking a clear theological vision of God in mission, the *missio Dei*.

EVANGELISM OF THE CHURCH OR MISSION OF GOD?

The lack of a far-reaching missiological perspective was probably one internal reason – reinforced of course by external pressures – that produced a comparatively narrow practice of evangelism in the UECBE. There was little reflection on God who is on a mission in this world. The focus was on evangelism as a human task and responsibility. The effectiveness of evangelism was measured by human activities and the numbers of converted persons. Sometimes Estonian believers complained that they had done too little. As a response to the feelings of inadequacy in evangelism, Estonian Baptists continuously sought for new methods. In 1963 Robert Võsu, perhaps the most prolific Estonian writer on the topic of evangelism, said: 'What can we do that

---

[124] The UECBE Senior Presbyter's report of 1964. VpAruanded, EEKBLA.

[125] Osvald Tärk, *Efesose kiri* [The Epistle to the Ephesians], typewritten manuscript (1957), p. 129. KUSA.

[126] Ryman et al., *Nordic Folk Churches*, p. 144.

[127] Tomlin, *The Provocative Church*, p. 67.

the sinners would come? Old methods have grown ineffective.'[128] A decade later he reminded his fellow presbyters again: new situations require change both in thinking and in methods.[129] Sometimes self-criticism was rather severe. In 1976 the Senior Presbyter said that the UECBE churches had not been able to adjust their evangelism to new situations.[130] The report probably did not do justice to the efforts of local churches: the 1970s saw an increase in evangelism activities in the UECBE. However, the subjective feeling, as the report reflected, was that not enough had been done.

In the 1980s the evangelism 'department' of the UECBE prepared a report which pointed out the main problems in evangelism.[131] The report was discussed at the Presbyters' Council meeting in May 1988,[132] and presented at the presbyters' conference in October 1988.[133] The report criticized local churches for sticking to the *status quo* in evangelism. It described the reasons for this: too little attention to the 'holy life'; negligence of the fact that 'works proclaim more loudly than words'; discrepancies in love for and patience with people; too little real faith; 'the atmosphere of death' in churches; a loss of vision for biblical evangelism. The document said that evangelism in the UECBE had become the privilege and responsibility of some, not the vision of the whole church.[134] The authors gave some guidelines for improvement: believers were called to live a life of transformative influence in the world; they should intensify prayer; and churches should develop an atmosphere of confidence in evangelism. Most of the suggestions were methodological: send out more workers; plant new mission stations; evangelize in urban settings; organise better training; pay attention to literature and audiovisual aids in evangelism; and plan ahead carefully.[135]

The document summarized many topics which had already emerged in ECB practice and in ECB written texts during Soviet years. I would argue that

---

[128] *'Kalju' koguduse karjase Robert Võsu jutlusi ajavahemikul 1944.-1969*, pp. 102-103.

[129] The UECBE Senior Presbyter's report of 1970-1972. VpAruanded, EEKBLA.

[130] The UECBE Senior Presbyter's report of 1975 at the presbyters' conference (29.05.1976). VpAruanded, EEKBLA.

[131] This was a work-group rather than an official or formal department of the union. In Estonian it was called *'evangelismi sektor'* (evangelism unit). See the document, 'Evangeelsest tööst Maarjamaal' [About Evangelism Work in the Land of Mary] (1988), EEKBLA. The title refers to the name of Estonia from Medieval times, when this land was dedicated to the Virgin Mary. Certainly, this does not mean that Estonian Baptists had any leanings toward Mariology.

[132] Minutes of the Executive Board meeting, no. 141 (16.05.1988). Juhatuse koosolekute protokollid koos lisadega (JKPLis) [Minutes of the Executive Board, with attachments] (11.01.1988-02.03.1992), EEKBLA.

[133] The presbyters' days took place 14-16 October 1988. See *Logos*, no. 3 (1988), pp. 2-4.

[134] 'Evangeelsest tööst Maarjamaal', pp. 18-21, 31.

[135] 'Evangeelsest tööst Maarjamaal', pp. 32-44.

it demonstrated some basic characteristics of the UECBE evangelistic identity. First, it was motivated by a conviction that evangelism – interpreted as proclamation of the Word – is the number one task given to Christians.[136] Second, it placed emphasis on human responsibility rather than on God's ongoing work in the world.[137] Third, in typical evangelical fashion, if evangelistic results fell short of expectations this was attributed to a lack of holiness on the part of believers.[138] Fourth, in response to changes in society it suggested methodological improvements. There was no analysis of the more basic missiological paradigm.[139] The theological shift toward 'recognition that mission is God's mission',[140] and not only a task of the church or of individual believers, did not have much influence on Estonian Baptist thinking. This is slightly surprising, especially when one recognizes that Karl Barth – who introduced this view – inspired some Estonian Baptist theologians, such as Osvald Tärk[141] and Joosep Tammo[142].

While the 1981 ECB document was comparatively sharp in its tone, the 1968 paper by Osvald Tärk at the presbyters' conference, though theologically thorough, was much more pastoral. After noting the problems in evangelism, it said: 'I am not going to offer a self-made new medicine which would remedy

---

[136] Robert Võsu begins his book *Isiklik evangelism* with this argument. Võsu, *Isiklik evangelism*, pp. 1-4. It is surprising that Osvald Tärk in his important identity document, does not bring out 'mission' or 'evangelism' as separate facets of ECB identity. It may be because of the external atheistic pressures that Tärk does not specifically point out this aspect, though there is no doubt that he was well aware of the importance of witnessing for ECB self-understanding. See Osvald Tärk, 'Meie vendluse põhimõtted' [Principles of our Brotherhood], *Logos*, no. 1 (1981), no. 1-4 (1982), no 1-2 (1983).

[137] For example, the Senior Presbyter emphasized the responsibility of the believers' churches to 'make Christ known' in the society. The UECBE Senior Presbyter's Report of 1965. VpAruanded, EEKBLA.

[138] Thus Osvald Tärk warned in 1982 that sin is the main hindrance to mission – then the church does not move out into the world but the world moves into the church. Osvald Tärk, 'Tööraskuste õigest kasutamisest' [How to Use Difficulties in Ministry for Good], *Logos*, no. 6 (1982), p. 15.

[139] See also the writings of Efraim Joel Dahl. According to him, Estonian Baptists tended to import evangelism models from abroad without 'deeper reflection' or stood against some evangelistic practices because these were too 'unusual'. 'This causes rigid clinging to primitive methods in mission work,' he concluded. Efraim Joel Dahl, *Usutervistamine Piiblis, algkristluses ja tänapäeval* [Healing through Faith: In the Bible, Early Christianity and Today], typewritten manuscript (1980?), pp. 121-122. KUSA.

[140] Bosch, *Transforming Mission*, p. 393.

[141] Ruudi Leinus, comp. and ed., *Osvald Tärk. Uskuge Jumalasse* [Osvald Tärk. Believe in God] (Tallinn: Eesti EKB Liit, 1999), p. 31.

[142] Joosep Tammo, e-mail message (09.10.2006). Toivo Pilli's personal archive. Tammo's graduation thesis at Buckow Theological Seminary, German Democratic Republic, was on Karl Barth's views of anthropology.

all problems. I do not dare to offer the medicines that have been imported during last years or mixed locally. We do not know yet the consequences of these.' Instead, he based his suggestions on the message of the apostle Paul in the epistle to the Romans: repentance should include not only personal sins but also the collective sins of believers; believers should be involved not in a superficial prayer life but in a prayer battle; believers should maintain high moral standards and seek the life of sanctification, and they should be faithful.[143]

It is not possible to know what might have been the consequences of the Estonian Baptists pursuing a missionary strategy informed by the wider concern of *Missio Dei*. Their story, as it actually unfolded, was driven by very different theological presuppositions. If Estonian Baptists had distanced themselves from the position that saw the goal of preaching the gospel only as saving sinners from eternal punishment, and if they had moved toward a more trinitarian position which interprets mission as participating in the sending of God,[144] the consequences would probably have been paradigmatic. It could have increased their openness to be involved in social and political life and would have encouraged them to think more thouroughly not only about how to share the gospel, but also what the gospel is. It could have prepared them to see that 'the *locus* of God's salvation is not the church, but the world',[145] and to recognize that evangelism is clearly different from church membership recruitment. In short – it could have helped them to move from a conviction that the church is called to do evangelism, toward a position that the church is called to be a missional church. There was a chance for the UECBE to participate more in the society in the 1980s and 1990s, when atheistic restrictions were removed. In fact the sharing of the gospel continued to be interpreted predominantly as a proclamation.[146] In other words – it was difficult to find a new identity. Estonian evangelistic identity had centred on a

---

[143] Osvald Tärk, 'Evangeelium on Jumala vägi' [Gospel is the Power of God], in *Eesti EKB koguduste presbüterite konverents Tallinnas, 15.-18. veebruaril 1968. a.*, pp. 158-164.

[144] Bosch, *Transforming Mission*, pp. 389-390.

[145] David L. Watson, 'The Mystery of Evangelism: Mission in an Age of Cosmic Discovery', in Howard A. Snyder, ed., *Global Good News: Mission in a New Context* (Nashville: Abingdon Press, 2001), p. 37.

[146] Joosep Tammo, 'Nüüdisaegse evangeelse töö põhimõtted ja võimalused' [Principles and Opportunities for Present Day Evangelism], *Logos*, no. 3 (1988), pp. 5-9. See also other articles on evangelism in *Logos* in the 1980s. Joosep Tammo, 'Kristlus ja maailmareligioonid' [Christianity and World Religions], *Logos*, no. 1 (1986), pp. 38-43; 'Kogudused ja vendlus koondumise ja läkituse pingeväljas' [Local Churches and the Brotherhood in the Tension Area of Being Gathered and Being Sent], *Logos*, no. 3 (1986), pp. 8-12; Michael Green, 'Algkristliku evangelisatsiooni meetod ja taktika' [The Method and Tactics of Evangelism in the Early Church], *Logos*, no. 3-4 (1987), pp. 8-17.

commitment to 'save souls', and the challenge was to embrace a new view of mission as participation in God's work of transforming the world.

CONCLUSION

Despite some varieties in the style of evangelism, for all four free church traditions which were united in the Union of Evangelical Christians-Baptists in Estonia preaching the gospel was a leading idea. The theological dynamics meant that there was a clear answer to the question of whether there was a need to preach the gospel. The answer – through the Soviet years and across the ECB churches – was a unanimous 'yes'. The result of sharing the good news was expected to be a personal conversion experience, often called 'new birth' in typical baptistic language. However, the canvas of Estonian Baptist theological identity in the Soviet era appears to have involved more varieties and colours when the following question was asked: 'What should be the method of preaching the gospel?' Or we might ask another question: 'How was 'the good news' understood by Estonian Baptist theologians and church members?'

Though Estonian Baptists saw the value of lifestyle in witnessing, their main focus was still on verbal proclamation. Romans 10:14-15 was one of the key verses which helped them to understand evangelism: 'And how can they believe in the one of whom they have not heard? And how can they hear without someone preaching to them?' Revivalist Free Church and Pentecostal traditions were more enthusiastic in their proclamation when compared to their Baptist and Evangelical Christian counterparts. However, they all derived much from Anglo-American revivalist spirituality. Effective evangelism was often 'meeting driven', decision-orientated and concentrated on a 'charismatic' preacher-figure. In the situation of atheistic restrictions, as well as in part because of their inherited theology, Estonian Baptists generally did not understand evangelism and mission as an activity of the church to expand the realm of God's kingdom in human society and bring 'salvation' from 'social sins': injustice, dishonesty, or political manipulation. An ethical lifestyle was emphasised, but it was believed that the transformation must always start from an individual Christian: in this context the Baptist leaders talked about the responsibility of believers to 'raise up the moral level of society'. Nevertheless, personal inner renewal was the starting point.

As to evangelism methods – while evangelistic meetings and 'revival weeks' continued, more and more attention was paid to personal evangelism. This was advocated mostly by Robert Võsu, Senior Presbyter in the 1970s and 1980s. Jüri Puusaag emphasised the need to motivate the whole church to reach out, be culturally relevant and build friendly relationships outside the church walls. The Effataa movement, a Charismatic-Pentecostal strand in the UECBE, was convinced that a renewed pneumatological focus was a key to effective Christian witness. Robert Võsu was probably the most outstanding Estonian Baptist theologian who spoke about the social dimension of the gospel in his writings and sermons. However, his ideas, especially those refering to the social aspects of the gospel, were not always fully understood or practised by the local churches.

The Estonian Baptist concept of evangelism was predominantly ecclesiologically grounded. The strength of this position was that to reach out to the world was seen as a primary responsibility and calling of the church. It was also a key part of Estonian Baptist identity that the church was God's agent in the salvation process. The weakness was that much of this was seen in individualistic terms – the believers were challenged to seek to save people (individuals) who were 'perishing in their sins' and 'lost to God'. Crucially, evangelism and mission were understood as part of the *missiones ecclesiae* – the activities and ministry of the church – rather than as a participation in the *Missio Dei* – God's renewing and saving work in individuals, human society and the whole world.

CHAPTER 9

Bearing Fruit: Challenges in Ethics

Estonian Baptists were convinced that individual spiritual regeneration, which took place as a result of hearing the good news, the gospel – had to be followed by signs of a transformed life.[1] The evangelical understanding of discipleship and – indirectly – of pietist spirituality were both constitutive elements for Estonian Evangelical Christian-Baptist patterns of faith and ethics. A famous faith development theorist John Westerhoff has stated that conversion is a 'radical turning' from 'faith given' to 'faith owned'. He comments: 'Conversion is radical because it implies ownership and the corresponding transformation of our lives.'[2] This transformation was largely seen by Estonian ECB believers in terms of moral behaviour and a Christ-like mentality. Robert Võsu stated in his comprehensive treatise on evangelical ethics: 'In regeneration it is first and foremost a person's moral nature that will be transformed.'[3] Ethical living was believed to be 'the main goal of the church's activity'.[4]

The AUCECB leadership in Moscow stated in 1946: 'The purity of the Church and high standards in the Christian life of its members are most important to us.'[5] This stance was sometimes to be interpreted in Russia as a downplaying of the role of evangelism. Estonian Baptist leaders in this period, when compared to the Moscow leadership, appear to have kept a better balance between evangelism and sanctification. Both were important facets of the Estonian ECB identity, and were seen as two sides of one and the same coin. Ülo Meriloo, later the Senior Presbyter of the UECBE, expressed this balance: he argued that 'sanctification should be the highest endeavour of every church member', but at the same time believers should not wait until the world comes

---

[1] [Robert Võsu,] *Baptistide arengust ja põhimõtetest* [About the Development and Principles of Baptists] typewritten manuscript [1966], p. 14. Merike Uudam's personal library.

[2] John Westerhoff, *Will Our Children Have Faith?* (New York: The Seabury Press, 1976), p. 39.

[3] Robert Võsu, *Evangeelne eetika* [Evangelical Ethics] (Tallinn: Logos, 1996), p. 76.

[4] [Robert Võsu,] *Baptistide arengust ja põhimõtetest*, p. 12.

[5] A letter from Soviet Baptists to American Baptists, sent to Louie Newton in 1946. Quoted in Serge Bolshakoff, *Russian Nonconformity* (Westminster Press: Philadelphia, 1950), p. 126. The letter was signed by five members of the Presidium of the AUCECB.

to them, but they should go out into the midst of people.[6]

In this context there are some simple, but very telling 'definitions' of sanctification in Estonian Baptist writings. Oskar Olvik, a former Evangelical Christian leader, said: 'Sanctification is ... the Christian character of the members of God's church, i. e. separation from the masses of people who have sinful natures and, instead, devoting oneself as committed persons to the service of God.'[7] Another author suggested: 'The life of sanctification is a process of covering the gap that exists between a person's human life and the life of Christ.'[8] A focus on moral character and seeing Christ as a model – these aspects were all-important for the Estonian Evangelical Christian-Baptist understanding of living a fruitful Christian life and thus for the identity of the Baptist community. In addition, in an environment of persecution, ethical issues such as how to maintain unity and trust between 'brothers and sisters' were also crucial.

A SANCTIFIED LIFE – FROM THE INSIDE OUT

Estonian Baptists, like Baptists elsewhere, were concerned with sanctification and discipleship. Many of them read, in translation, a collection of speeches by Martin Luther King, Jr., the famous American Baptist and civil rights leader, in which he stated that while the world had progressed regarding material wealth, it was a moral 'falling behind' that was posing the main dilemma for modern man.[9] The discrepancy between technical progress and moral development was also noted by Estonian authors.[10] But Estonian believers, while agreeing that ethical issues were of the highest importance, interpreted this challenge in a slightly different way than Martin Luther King, Jr.: for them the ethical life was seen first and foremost in terms of personal sanctification. The transformation of one's 'heart', and good fruits exhibited in a person's character – these were key words and phrases for Estonian Baptists. Also 'giving one's "flesh" to death' and 'being crucified with Christ' was the language of pre-war Estonian Pentecostals, as well as other free churches, when they explained sanctification. This use of individualistic language continued in Soviet times in the ECB

---

[6] H. Veermets, *Albomi juurde. Haapsalu koguduse 100 aastapäev* [To the Album. The 100th Anniversary of the Haapsalu Church], typewritten manuscript (1984), pp. 5-10. EEKBLA.

[7] Oskar Olvik, *Esimene Korintose kiri* [The First Epistle to the Corinthians], typewritten manuscript (1960), p. 9. KUSA.

[8] Valdur Rosenvald, *Pühitsuselu* [The Life of Sanctification] ([Tallinn]: Vaimulik kirjavara, 1999), p. 5. The manuscript was written in the 1950s.

[9] Martin Luther King, *Kõned ja jutlused* [Speeches and Sermons], typewritten manuscript (n. p., n. d.), pp. 4, 111. KUSA.

[10] For example, Robert Võsu, *Mäejutlus* [The Sermon on the Mount], typewritten manuscript (Tallinn, 1957), pp. 109-110. EEKBLA.

churches. Sanctification as a calling for the whole faith community, not simply its individual members, was much less present in ECB theological thinking.

In the ECB churches during the Soviet years, personal moral characteristics and ethical behavioural patterns were taught from the pulpits, endorsed by typewritten texts and reinforced through 'brotherly and sisterly admonition'. Honesty, moral purity and abstinence from alcohol were often mentioned as signs of a believer's 'sanctified life'.[11] The change in a person that produced an ethical life was seen by Estonian Baptists as fundamentally an inner religious transformation and indeed a miraculous renewal; this change was primarily neither an act of a person's human will nor a gradual maturing of one's personality.[12] Christian faith and ethics were seen as inseparable. Oskar Olvik commented: 'If faith has disappeared in the heart then moral values and the whole happiness of a person is in danger.'[13] A new desire to follow God's will begins in the heart of a human being, he argued, and out of that 'an improvement ... of outward life begins, until the full reign of God ultimately arrives.'[14]

Thus a core 'sin', according to Estonian Baptist theologians, was to defy God and his will. Osvald Tärk, in one of his sermons, stated that the beginning of the ethical life was a surrender to God's grace, a giving up of one's personal pride. 'Human nature, spoiled by sin, is proud, and does not want to receive grace.'[15] Pride was also portrayed as a root cause of sin and vice in a book by Andrew Murray, a South African Reformed minister and a propagator of Keswick holiness ideas.[16] Murray's book *Humility* was known in ECB churches through a typewritten Estonian translation.[17] Võsu believed that an inner attitude of pride paves the way for envy and for every other evil.[18] In this sense,

---

[11] 'Suhtlemine maailmaga Kristuse meelsuses' [Christ-Centred Relations with the World], typewritten paper (n. p., n. d.), p. 5. Osvald Tärgi materjalid [Materials of Osvald Tärk], EEKBLA.

[12] Võsu, *Evangeelne eetika*, pp. 33-78.

[13] Oskar Olvik, 'Usulise ja kõlbelise elu probleeme meie kogudustes' [Problems of Religious and Moral Living in our Churches], in *Eesti EKB koguduste presbüterite konverents Tallinnas, 15.-18. veebruaril 1968. a.* [The Estonian ECB Presbyters Conference in Tallinn, 15-18 February 1968], typewritten manuscript [1968], p. 111. Ülo Meriloo's personal library.

[14] Oskar Olvik, *Homileetika* [Homiletics], typewritten manuscript (1957), p. 34. KUSA.

[15] Ruudi Leinus, comp. and ed., *Osvald Tärk. Uskuge Jumalasse* [Osvald Tärk. Believe in God] (Tallinn: Eesti EKB Liit, 1999), pp. 74-75.

[16] For the Keswick movement history, see Charles Price and Ian Randall, *Transforming Keswick* (Carlisle: OM Publishing, 2000).

[17] Andrew Murray, *Alandus* [Humility], typewritten Estonian translation (n. p., n. d.), pp. 7-8. KUSA. Robert Võsu refers to Andrew Murray. Robert Võsu, 'Tasadus ja alandus Pauluse käsitluses' [Meekness and Humility in the Understanding of Paul], *Logos*, no. 1-2 (1987), pp. 28-32.

[18] Võsu, *Evangeelne eetika*, p. 188.

Estonian Baptists were in accord not only with expressions of 'younger' evangelical spirituality such as Keswick but also with the centuries-old tradition of theological thinking which saw pride ('the inordinate desire to excel over others and God') 'as the essence and root of sin'.[19]

So according to Estonian ECB believers, the ethical life, a life bearing 'good fruit' as it was often put, had to start from a person's inner experience. The role of the local church community or perhaps formation through Christian family traditions, or more broadly the influence of social conditions, were not totally neglected in practice; but in theological discussions these communal – in certain respects, external – aspects of ethics were usually presented as secondary or were missed altogether. Certainly the starting point was the individual. In this respect, all Estonian free church traditions, from their earliest stages, shared a common ethical emphasis. Võsu stated in one of his writings: 'Goodness in this world is spread by the influence of a renewed personality on its surroundings.'[20] A person has to begin the task of 'improving the world' with the act of 'improving himself';[21] though – and Estonian evangelicals always emphasised this – the ultimate initiative in such a process always comes from God.[22] As an American theologian, Frank J. Matera, has said: 'The moral life of believers is a response to God's work of salvation.'[23]

The belief that 'a life bearing good fruit' grows from the inside out was expressed also in the conviction that not only a person's deeds but also their thoughts and their motivations must be surrendered to God's will. Christian ethics not only had to do with behaviour and human relationships, but also the invisible 'roots' of people's deeds and words. Thus Oskar Olvik emphasised the need to sanctify the realm of thoughts. If Christ has been allowed to sanctify our thinking, Olvik argued, then the thoughts are good thoughts and Christ will use these to show his presence. 'Christ would like to think through our thoughts ... so that these would serve God and God's greatness. If Christ is in us, then human thoughts are pure, these are selfless thoughts.'[24] A sanctified Christian is thinking not only about what will be of benefit to him or her, but what will bring glory to Christ.[25] In his treatise on the Sermon on the Mount, Robert Võsu said that '[f]ruit is life that flows out from the nature of a person'; it is made

[19] D.L. Okholm, 'Pride', in David J. Atkinson and David H. Field, eds., *New Dictionary of Christian Ethics and Pastoral Theology* (Downers Grove, Illlinois, and Leicester, England: InterVarsity Press, 1995), p. 685.
[20] Robert Võsu, *Isiklik evangelism* [Personal Evangelism], typewritten manuscript (Tallinn, 1971), p. 88. EEKBLA.
[21] Lecture notes 1973-1978, notebook 2. Uudu Rips' personal archive.
[22] Võsu, *Evangeelne eetika*, pp. 65-66.
[23] Frank J. Matera, *New Testament Ethics: The Legacies of Jesus and Paul* (Louisville, Kentucky: Westminster John Knox Press, 1996), p. 248.
[24] Oskar Olvik, *Neli kõnet* [Four Sermons], typewritten manuscript (1964), p. 27. EEKBLA.
[25] Olvik, *Neli kõnet*, p. 28.

possible through the power of the Holy Spirit and is characterised by peace, love, and other features (Gal 5:22).[26]

An important feature of Estonian Baptist identity in this area during the Soviet years, as seen in the quotation from Võsu, was the pneumatological connotations of sanctification. James H. McConkey's book *Three-Fold Secret of the Holy Spirit*, was known to Estonian readers. McConkey, however, warned against constant observation of one's internal life and spiritual condition; rather he supported the attitude of trust that God would give the fullness of the Spirit so that the believer could undertake a committed life of service, and he argued that a believer does not need to 'dig out the seed, to check if it has grown already'.[27] Also Oskar Olvik believed that the Holy Spirit would give power for Christian living and bring forth peace, joy, love, patience and other fruits of the Spirit.[28] Presbyter Ants Rebane stated: 'The Holy Spirit carries out sanctification in us, which manifests itself as the fruit of the Spirit. If the Holy Spirit lives in a believer, the fruits of the Spirit become evident. But if the Holy Spirit cannot lead us, then the old "self" rules, and the "works of the flesh" appear.'[29] ECB believers were unanimous in believing that the Holy Spirit was the 'agent' of God in sanctification, but the Spirit's role was interpreted in different ways. More Pentecostal or Revivalist groups emphasised 'filling of the Spirit' as a special experience along with other supernatural elements in sanctification. The more traditional Baptist wing focused on a faithful life of discipleship and obedience to the example and words of Jesus – also with the help of the Spirit. The former often spoke about 'gifts of the Spirit' while the latter referred to 'the fruits of the Spirit'. It can be noted that while Estonian Baptists placed emphasis on character formation they largely neglected 'gifts of understanding and knowledge' in the context of ethical reasoning – which, by contrast, was an important topic in Roman Catholic moral theology.[30]

The emphasis on the inner life meant that for some in the UECBE sanctification was defined in terms of deeper spirituality: being closer to God. Efraim Joel Dahl, a Baptist writer, believed that 'the whole content of Christian life is coming closer to God – the beginning [of this life] is awakening and the

---

[26] Võsu, *Mäejutlus*, p. 110.

[27] James H. McConkey, *Püha Vaimu kolmekordne saladus* [The Three-Fold Secret of the Holy Spirit], typewritten Estonian translation (n. p., n. d.), p. 52. KUSA.

[28] Oskar Olvik, *Mälestused* [Memoirs], part 2 (Tallinn, 1966), pp. 592-597. Oleviste ECB Church library, Tallinn.

[29] Ants Rebane, 'Kristuse ihu ja Kristuse vaim II' [The Body of Christ and the Spirit of Christ II], *Logos*, no. 1 (1986), p. 17.

[30] See Romanus Cessario, *The Virtues or the Examined Life* (London and New York: Continuum, 2002), pp. 19-30.

continuation [of it] is sanctification.'[31] However, he was critical of what he saw as an element of 'emotional superficiality and non-practical understanding of sanctification' among Estonian Baptists.[32] Indeed, Dahl was concerned that some ECB believers, especially those who had a background in the 'enthusiastic Christianity' of Pentecostalism or Revivalist Free churches, tended to identify sanctification with extraordinary emotional experiences. Such a view was present, but the general attitude in the UECBE was that the sanctified life, which was bound up with a person's individual relationship with God, had to become visible 'in practical life' – at the workplace, at home, and in the church. Discipleship – understood in an ethical sense – was an inseparable part of the Estonian Baptist identity during the Soviet years. This life of discipleship was lived out in the context of atheistic pressures and in an environment that was hostile to Christianity. This feature has to be analysed.

ETHICAL LIFE IN THE MIDST OF PERSECUTION

Estonian Baptists, like Soviet Baptists as a whole, had to seek to interpret persecution and to understand their identity in the light of the experience of being persecuted. This was not just a theoretical task, but a challenge which had its consequences for practical life and human relationships. In many cases, persecution was understood by believers as something that called out from them a deeper commitment to Christ. The experience of persecution was the experience of a 'refining fire'. It included standing firm against constant external opposition. One of the major motivations for being faithful in persecution was that Christ had also been misunderstood and criticised. Suffering for Christ was a means by which Christian character was, it was believed, to be formed.[33] Osvald Tärk said that an inappropriate response to persecution was a weakness that characterised many believers: 'They are not able to remain peaceful, when somebody speaks against them'.[34] The hostile environment in which they lived certainly underlined the view – one that Estonian Baptists shared with many in the wider evangelical tradition – that 'the process of Christian development is a battle'. [35]

---

[31] Efraim Joel Dahl, *Evangeelse maailma radadel. Pühitsus Piiblis ja ajaloos.* [On the Paths of the Evangelical World: Sanctification in the Bible and in History], typewritten manuscript (Tallinn, 1976), p. 1. KUSA.
[32] Efraim Joel Dahl, *Usutervistamine Piiblis, algkristluses ja tänapäeval* [Healing through Faith in the Bible, Early Christianity and Today], typewritten manuscript (1980?), p. 121. KUSA.
[33] Osvald Tärk, 'Märkmeid O. Tärgi jutlustest 1981-1982.a.' [Notes from the sermons of Osvald Tärk from the years 1981-1982], 1982. peetud jutlused [sermons delivered in 1982], typewritten sermon collection (n. p., n. d.), pp. 27-29. KUSA.
[34] Tärk, 'Märkmeid O. Tärgi jutlustest 1981-1982.a.', 1982. peetud jutlused, p. 32.
[35] Efraim Joel Dahl, *Evangeelse maailma radadel*, p. 8.

Texts translated into Estonian and statements by Estonian leaders all supported the view that the experience of suffering was ethical in its nature. Frank Mangs, a Scandinavian free church evangelist, argued in a typewritten translated text that persecution was part and parcel of the Christian life because winter fights against spring. The high calling of the Christian, he continued, is to be identified with Christ, and 'in this way to bring the great mystery and power of redemption into the lives of other people'.[36] Robert Võsu believed that persecution of the followers of the Lord would increase. 'They have to give an account of their faith, they will be purified, tested, until whatever remains is really from the Lord.'[37] Tärk stated: 'If somebody suffers because of the church, this always serves the glory of God, even if this is not understood by his contemporaries.'[38] The challenge of persecutory suffering involved a challenge to remain faithful to God and also to explain one's views to others. But at a deeper level it was an ethical test and a way toward a deeper spirituality. Suffering was a necessary tool for those who strove to develop Christ-like virtues.[39] Joosep Tammo said in 1988: 'In the centre of our faith is a suffering person'.[40] At the presbyters' conference in 1981 which took place under the title 'Become holy in all your ways of life' it was stated that sanctification required full commitment from a Christian and that sufferings were the part of Christian life 'because of Christ'.[41]

In this situation, some Estonian Baptist authors found inspiration in sixteenth-century Anabaptist history. For Anabaptists, suffering was 'readiness to yield one's life for Christ's sake'; it was also a means of identification with Christ.[42] Some ECB presbyters were convinced that for the Anabaptists the hostile environment intensified their commitment to an ethical life, their main focus being on sanctification: 'on bearing one's cross, on a morally purified life and on separation from the world'. Persecution moulds a Christian so that the 'sanctified life will be brought to the fore and will take shape'.[43] Estonian Baptists considered the Anabaptists to be a good model, one which helped them to find their own identity in oppressive situations. They found spiritual

---

[36] Frank Mangs, *Issanda tee* [The Lord's Way], Estonian translation, typewritten manuscript (1970s?), p. 76. KUSA.

[37] *'Kalju' koguduse karjase Robert Võsu jutlusi ajavahemikul 1944.-1969* [Sermons of 'Kalju' Church Pastor, Robert Võsu, from 1944 to 1969], typewritten manuscript, p. 97. KUSA.

[38] Osvald Tärk, *Efesose kiri* [The Epistle to the Ephesians], typewritten manuscript (1957), p. 63. KUSA.

[39] Võsu, *Mäejutlus*, p. 16

[40] Joosep Tammo, 'Meil on suur ülempreester Jeesus' [We Have a Great High Priest - Jesus], *Logos*, no. 1 (1988), p. 4.

[41] 'Informatsioon' [Information], *Logos*, no. 1 (1982), pp. 20-21.

[42] C. Arnold Snyder, *Following in the Footsteps of Christ: The Anabaptist Tradition* (London: Darton, Longman and Todd, 2004), pp. 164, 166-168.

[43] Ants Rebane, 'Piibellik pühitsus' [Biblical Sanctification], *Logos*, no. 1 (1982), p. 10.

encouragement in the Anabaptists whom they considered historically their 'soul-mates'.[44]

Some Estonian presbyters occasionally idealised suffering. For example, presbyter Eerik Rahkema said that an innocent person who was suffering was a blessing for many and indicated that such a person was on the way toward godly perfection.[45] However, in general, Estonian Baptists avoided the temptation to idealise persecution, in contrast with many of the ECB underground believers in Russia. Estonians usually did not defy the oppressive laws or the atheistic structures – their response was spiritual and ethical: 'giving one's life fully over to God' was an expression often used by Estonian Baptists in the Soviet years. 'Life with no compromises, in the service of truth and love, has always undermined the dominion of falseness and greed...'.[46] In their relations with atheistic society, Estonian ECB believers tried to give to Caesar what is Caesar's but also to God what is God's (Matthew 22:21). In everything a believer was to have as the ultimate goal of his or her actions, *telos*, bringing glory to God.[47] For example, if the Communist government required 'voluntary' work (the socialist working Saturdays, *subbotniks*), a Christian was supposed to work with sincere commitment. So if a Christian was required to take on 'so-called tasks for the benefit of society' then the believer should 'take it as a task to bring glory to God, do it from your heart'.[48] There were, however, more difficult ethical dilemmas than whether or not to participate in these tasks.

One of these serious challenges was how to maintain an atmosphere of trust and unity in a believers' community. Persecution, as well as differences in the religious practices of the formerly independent free churches, caused inner tensions in the ECB union. On the one hand, the government attempted to play some groups of believers against others. Thus the state generally opposed Pentecostal practices. At the same time, from the perspective of the inner life of the churches, 'the otherness' of those speaking in tongues, or alternatively those preferring supposedly 'dry' Bible study, caused tensions. The forceful merger of Estonian free churches after the Second World War posed an ethical question: How to learn to respect and love other traditions? Oskar Olvik remembers that between himself, as a former Evangelical Christian who had come from a Lutheran background, and Johannes Lipstok, a Baptist, there was

---

[44] Robert Võsu, 'Baptistide ajaloolised põhimõtted' [Historical Principles of Baptists] (Oleviste, 05.02.1956), pp. 1-3. Robert Võsu materjalid [Materials of Robert Võsu], EEKBLA.

[45] Eerik Rahkema, 'Süütult kannatades' [Suffering Innocently], *Logos*, no. 3-4 (1987), pp. 18-22.

[46] 'Suhtlemine maailmaga Kristuse meelsuses', pp. 5-6. Osvald Tärgi materjalid, EEKBLA.

[47] Võsu, *Evangeelne eetika*, pp. 290-293.

[48] 'Suhtlemine maailmaga Kristuse meelsuses', p. 3. Osvald Tärgi materjalid, EEKBLA.

a certain 'coldness' in the early stages of their cooperation. Also, there were accusations levelled against Osvald Tärk from the Pentecostal 'wing' in the Oleviste church.[49] Maintaining an atmosphere of trust, honesty and integrity was one of the primary ethical tasks for church members in the UECBE in the Soviet years. This was also one of the important challenges facing Russian Baptists.[50]

The issue of trust and integrity was directly or indirectly present in relationships between fellow presbyters, as well as church members. The Senior Presbyter, Robert Võsu, emphasised in 1976 that the Estonian Senior Presbyter and the Presbyters' Council had to submit themselves voluntarily to the test of trust. This was why in 1976 re-elections of leaders in the UECBE took place, even if the official statutes 'did not say anything about the length of service of the members of the Presbyters' Council'.[51] There was also the important issue of how to maintain trust in situations of external pressure. Johannes Togi, an authoritative member of the Presbyters' Council, emphasised in 1979 that the Presbyters' Council must consist of persons who were 'transparent' in their views and attitudes, who did not pretend to agree in meetings but then, afterwards, talked quite differently and did something else behind the backs of their colleagues.[52] Ambiguity in words was seen as a dangerous temptation.[53]

Undoubtedly a factor here was the activity of the KGB. For example Olvik spoke of a concrete ethical dilemma he faced in 1953: how to 'keep a pure heart' when interrogated by the secret police. The Soviet officers did not regard the argument that one should keep a 'confessional secret' as a valid ethical argument. A member of Olvik's church was accused of destroying some documents in an archive and Olvik, who was interrogated in relation to this case, had to choose between two 'evils' – to lie to the KGB or to betray what the church member had entrusted to him. Remaining silent was a sign of disobedience in the eyes of the authorities. Olvik later – when the person had already told the full story to the officer – apologized to the officer for his reluctance to tell him what he knew. 'Whether the officer understood the problem of my pure heart – I cannot know', was Olvik's comment.[54] Robert Võsu was also aware of similarly complicated situations in which it was

---

[49] Oskar Olvik, *Mälestused*, part 2, pp. 359-361, 388-389.

[50] For further discussion, see Toivo Pilli, 'Christians as Citizens of a Persecuting State: A Theological and Ethical Reflection from a Historical Perspective', *Journal of European Baptist Studies*, no. 1 (September 2006), p. 18.

[51] The UECBE Senior Presbyter's report of 1975 of the Presbyters' Conference (29.05.1976). EKB vanempresbüteri aruanded [The UECBE Senior Presbyter's reports], EEKBLA.

[52] Minutes of election committee, no. 2 (09.10.1979). Kalju Raidi kirjavahetus ja märkmed [Correspondence and notes of Kalju Raid], KUSA.

[53] Võsu, *Evangeelne eetika*, pp. 189-191.

[54] Olvik, *Mälestused*, part 2, p. 436.

necessary to choose between 'truth and love'. He believed that the value of a human being was to be placed above the value of abstract principles. 'If there is no way to avoid it, then a Christian should choose love. The mistake is then smaller and [more easily] forgivable.'[55]

There were also moments when suspicion crept into the brotherly relations of the ECB leadership. In 1979, Robert Võsu, the Senior Presbyter, obtained 80% support (60 out of 74 votes of the presbyters), and was re-elected as the leader of the UECBE. Six voted against and eight abstained. According to normal democratic standards this would have been seen as a very successful election, but Võsu was hurt by the result. He expected something approaching unanimous support. He commented: 'This election showed that there are splits in our brotherhood. ... Without grounds, dark shadows are cast on fellow brothers.' Probably in the last sentence Võsu was referring to accusations of co-operation with the KGB either on the part of himself or of one of the candidates he suggested for the post of assistant senior presbyter. Obviously these accusations were never publicly expressed, but they were passed on in personal conversations between presbyters. Võsu's response confirmed his commitment to unity and cooperation: 'For my part, I am not going to divide brothers into supporters or opponents, I want to trust and love everyone.'[56] Clearly   the context of persecution posed serious challenges to Estonian Baptists. It was not easy to maintain an atmosphere of mutual trust and integrity within the churches in an environment that was so hostile towards believers and was designed to weaken the churches. However, ECB believers were convinced that difficulties and pressures were tools in God's hands for their purification and for character formation.

CHRIST-LIKE DISCIPLESHIP

Identification with Christ and becoming more Christ-like were seen as important goals for the Christian life. These goals, however, had to do with more than following a path that involved persecution and opposition. It meant also radiating the character of Christ – his love, meekness and transforming power. Oskar Olvik said: 'A human being can manifest the life of Christ, in all its glory and power. This is what Jesus expects ... from those who love him ... that the life of Christ would be visible through the life of a human being. This is the highest ideal of a human being that he would spiritually be similar to Christ. ... [W]e want to stand as high in our spiritual life as Jesus once stood, we want to have the power that would protect us from evil and enable us somehow to make visible the divine life, to show light to others. This is possible when

---

[55] Võsu, *Mäejutlus*, p. 59.

[56] 'Vanempresbüteri usalduse hääletus' [Confidential vote of Senior Presbyter], notes [1979]. EKB vanempresbüteri aruanded, EEKBLA.

Christ lives in us.'[57] He added: 'If Christ is in us then ... we have enough strength to suffer, to stay quiet ... then we have strength to live a sanctified life ... then it is Christ who will bear fruit in us...'.[58] Estonian Baptists saw Christ as the one who embodied the highest ethical ideal, though their vision of Christ was certainly not limited to ethics.

The ethical demands of Jesus were considered to be so high that it might not even be possible to meet the standard at the time of a believer's death and entry into the eternal state. Võsu made this unusual statement: 'This ideal is so great that our present life is not [long] enough to reach it perfectly, this [process] continues even after physical death.'[59] This was going beyond the traditional Protestant teaching of theologians such as John Calvin who taught that God's transformation would be completed in the Christian at the last day.[60] Discipleship for Estonian Baptists was demanding. It was more than just knowing the basics of evangelical Christianity or a set of Bible verses. It was a continuous refinement of one's character, including distancing oneself from things 'that seem to be evil'. This sometimes meant believers distancing themselves from cultural events which in Soviet reality were intertwined with Communist ideology or which glorified a lifestyle that believers considered non-biblical. Discipleship was ultimately a journey towards a closer unity with Christ.

Sometimes this 'unity with Christ' was understood in rather mystical ways and also in ways that seemed dualistic. An important aspect of Estonian Baptist understanding was that holiness was 'giving up one's self'. This process – usually seen as painful and difficult – would make more 'space' for Christ in a person's life. This person, having given over that space, would not restrict the rule of Christ.[61] Believers were called to a constant giving up of their 'old being' in order to promote a 'new being'. 'Give up one's self – to serve others', was the Baptist advice.[62] Paul's terminology of 'flesh' and 'spirit' was often used to describe the situation (Romans chapter 8). Within this there was a tendency toward a rather dualistic approach to ethics, as well as a tendency to rigid moralism. This view was also nurtured by a negative view of anthropology – the 'self' was seen as fallen and ready to defy God's will, instead of containing God-given positive potential. Such ethical dualism reached Estonian Baptists through evangelical literature that was translated and reproduced on typewriters. Watchman Nee, a Chinese Christian leader widely admired in the evangelical world, said that it was necessary for each believer to

---

[57] Olvik, *Neli kõnet*, pp. 24-25.

[58] Ibid., p. 33.

[59] [Võsu], *Baptistide arengust ja põhimõtetest*, p. 14.

[60] P.J.H. Adam, 'Jesus', in David J. Atkinson and David H. Field, eds., *New Dictionary of Christian Ethics and Pastoral Theology*, p. 509.

[61] Olvik, *Neli kõnet*, p. 26.

[62] Lecture notes 1973-1978, notebook 2. Uudu Rips' personal archive.

give himself or herself over to Christ, to put the old creation to death.[63]
Following Christ was characterised as denying oneself, as Frank Mangs
emphasised, referring to the teaching of the Sermon on the Mount. The mass of
the people, he added, did not favour taking this way, but it is the way of Jesus.[64]

The views of Estonian believers themselves often correlated with
translated texts. Being a disciple meant nothing less than taking up the cross
and following Christ, as was emphasised by one Estonian author.[65] The 'mind
of Christ' in a believer was often explained in terms of 'giving up the rule of
self', or more dramatically as being 'on the cross with Christ', as well as using
the more standard terminology of following 'Christ's example'.[66] This meant
disciples showing humility, 'turning the other cheek', being patient in suffering,
and expressing love and care to others.

Devotion and spirituality were seen as inseparably linked with the ethical
life. For example, prayer was not only an element of worship; it was believed
that prayer would help a person to 'walk in Christ', to find the will of God and
to live an ethically 'right' life. The ECB semi-illegal publication *Logos* taught
in 1982 that 'our thoughts, emotions, wishes, words and deeds must harmonize
with God's will'.[67] In prayer believers were looking for the 'voice' of God or a
'leading' or 'inner confidence' from God.[68] Oskar Olvik stated: 'If we have in
our life or work deviated from God's will, then in prayer God's Spirit will
remind us that we need to settle this. ... This is a great benefit of prayer: not
only that we receive answers to our prayers, but that the Spirit of God works in
us. Everyone who prays will come out of the prayer room more cleansed than
entering the prayer room.'[69] Reading and applying the Bible were also
important. Osvald Tärk asked in 1982: 'Brother is your division between good
and bad, permissible and deniable, where the Bible draws it?'[70] Estonians
would have agreed with today's authors, such as Glen H. Stassen and David P.
Gushee, who said: 'Scripture is the central source of authority for Christian
ethics and ... Jesus is the key to interpreting Scripture.'[71] One's devotional life

[63] Watchman Nee, *Loomulik usuelu* [The Normal Christian Life] (Rakvere, 1993), pp.
48-49, 52-53. A typewritten translation of this book circulated in Estonian ECB
churches in the Soviet years.
[64] Mangs, *Issanda tee*, p. 46.
[65] Ants Rebane, 'Üks ristimine' [One Baptism], *Logos*, no. 1-2 (1987), p. 36.
[66] Lecture notes 1973-1978, notebook 1. Uudu Rips' personal archive.
[67] Robert Võsu, 'Kristlase kohustused' [Responsibilities of a Christian], *Logos*, no. 1
(1982), p. 2.
[68] Olvik, *Mälestused*, part 1, pp. 228-229.
[69] Oskar Olvik, *Palve: kaheksa kõnet palvest* [Eight Sermons on Prayer], typewritten
manuscript (Tallinn, 1965), pp. 68-69. EEKBLA.
[70] Osvald Tärk, 'Tööraskuste õigest kasutamisest' [How to Use Difficulties in Ministry
for Good], *Logos*, no. 6 (1982), p. 15.
[71] Glen H. Stassen and David P. Gushee, *Kingdom Ethics: Following Jesus in
Contemporary Context* (Downers Grove, Illinois: InterVarsity Press, 2003), p. 98.

was the basis for an ethical lifestyle. Obedience to Christ was an ethical and spiritual characteristic. It was essential to be obedient to Christ's commands. 'Never do what the Lord forbids, and never leave undone what he commands', was the advice of Osvald Tärk.[72] The life of following Christ was believed to be so demanding that it required supernatural power: the help of the Holy Spirit, prayer, faith, and becoming absorbed with the Word.[73]

This position, that devotion and the ethical life belong together, was strongly supported by Osvald Tärk, whose pastoral and theological influence on Estonian Baptist identity was remarkable. In a sermon given in 1952, Tärk emphasised that prayer can change situations and offer moments of transfiguration and transformation. On the mountain of prayer, a believer needs to pray for great things. In prayer we 'are raised from our context of small issues into the atmosphere of God's great thoughts'.[74] This change, a renewed spiritual awareness, was believed to lead a believer closer to Christ, into the life of fruitfulness in the Spirit. A sincere relationship with God was expected to protect a person from temptations and from the influences of evil.[75] Estonians, however, never supported perfectionism – either in Wesleyan or Finneyan lines.[76] Robert Võsu was careful not to use the triumphalist language of 'perfect sanctification' or 'life in the Spirit'. Instead, he rather spoke about modesty and humble persistence on the way of sanctification, directed to the shaping of a Christ-like character.[77]

Christ, as the model for disciples, was seen as humble, mild, loving and compassionate. He was also believed to have been a master of controlling his negative emotions. Andrew Murray, who was influential in Estonian Baptist circles, condemned inadequacies of love, indifference towards other people, sharp expressions that hurt others and quick judgements - all of which were expressions of agitation. Instead, a humble person, 'in whom Jesus lives', does not feel envy or jealousy; he can praise God when others are preferred over him. The sanctified life is a sincere and authentic life.[78] An important feature of a Christian character was considered to be 'humility'. Aleksander Sildos, Senior Presbyter in the 1960s, argued: 'Where satan has sowed pride and pompousness into the [human] heart, then most of these cases have ended in the

---

[72] Tärk, 'Märkmeid O. Tärgi jutlustest 1981-1982.a.', 1981. peetud jutlused, p. 61.

[73] Võsu, *Evangeelne eetika*, pp. 91-104.

[74] Osvald Tärk, 'Palve usuelu uuendamise vahendina' [Prayer as a Means for the Renewal of Faith-Life], typewritten sermon (07.01.1952), no pagination. Robert Võsu materjalid [Materials of Robert Võsu], EEKBLA.

[75] Olvik, *Palve: kaheksa kõnet*, p. 18.

[76] For further discussion on perfectionism, see Keith J. Hardman, *Charles Grandison Finney 1792-1875: Revivalist and Reformer* (Grand Rapids, Michigan: Baker Book House, 1990), pp. 325-349.

[77] Võsu, *Mäejutlus*, pp. 15, 116.

[78] Murray, *Alandus*, pp. 15, 36, 44.

flesh and tragically [brought] shame ... for God and fellow believers.' [79] Unfortunately, Sildos stated, many believers do not know the holy life. 'They become irritated about everything, become angry and block the way to God.'[80] Sildos pointed to hindrances in the spiritual life such as pride, aggressiveness, covetousness, envy, jealousy, taking offence quickly, and other emotional, personality and behavioural characteristics.[81] Instead, forgiveness was expected to characterise a believer.

Robert Võsu devoted a sermon to the subject of forgiveness, in which he developed a rather interesting idea. He suggested that there was no teaching in the Bible about asking forgiveness from other people, though the Bible did not prohibit this. Forgiveness, he argued, should be requested from God. Sometimes, he believed, asking forgiveness from other people could cause 'fleshly thinking' – probably Võsu had in mind 'a feeling of superiority' in the person who was forgiving someone else. However, Võsu insisted that the Word repeatedly reminded believers to offer forgiveness: to forgive other people's debts to them, which might be debts because there had been offensive behaviour, debts incurred within the family or debts in terms of failures in carrying out church responsibilities.[82] The forgiveness offered was offered in the name of Christ and a forgiving spirit signified that the believer was Christ-like. Aleksander Sildos said: the person who does not forgive, 'will spoil his heart and cannot be a blessing to others'.[83] Võsu's argument seems to be rather exceptional; ECB churches in general taught that members needed to ask forgiveness both from God and from other people.

At times, discipleship was viewed as 'taking life seriously' – even to the extent of excluding playfulness and humour and other 'lighter' aspects – as if *homo ludens* cannot be a sanctified follower of Christ.[84] Oskar Olvik stated that for his own ministry a 'deep spiritual attitude and mindset' were important. 'All joking and small talk was left far away. Instead of this came spiritual happiness, helpfulness, friendly and trustworthy mutual understanding.'[85] Even if Olvik's

---

[79] Aleksander Sildos, 'Tee valmistajad' [Those who Prepare the Way], typewritten sermon (1972), no pagination. Robert Võsu materjalid, EEKBLA.

[80] Ibid.

[81] Aleksander Sildos, 'Komistuskivid usuteel' [Stumbling Blocks on the Way of Faith], typewritten sermon (1972), no pagination. Robert Võsu materjalid, EEKBLA.

[82] *'Kalju' koguduse karjase Robert Võsu jutlusi ajavahemikul 1944.-1969*, p. 46.

[83] Aleksander Sildos, 'Tee parandamine' [Repairing the Way], typewritten sermon (1972), no pagination. Robert Võsu materjalid, EEKBLA.

[84] For an attempt to interpret the element of creativity, aesthetics and play in culture, see Johan Huizinga, *Mängiv inimene* [Man as Player], Estonian translation (Tallinn: Varrak, 2003).

[85] Olvik, *Mälestused*, part 2, p. 304.

view was narrow, it emphasised the ethics of character and integrity.[86]

Typically in Estonian free churches, especially in the Baptist and Evangelical Christian tradition, sermons gave much attention to ethical issues. Baptist preaching at the end of the 1960s spoke of moral decline in Soviet society; preachers mentioned the devastating consequences of alcoholism and divorce, as well as the 'sinful life' of young people.[87] In 1978, presbyter Herman Mäemets emphasised at a meeting with local soviet authorities that the believers' churches had resources for the healthy moral education of youth.[88] The government was aware of the ethical ideals of Baptists: the Commissioner reported to the Council for Religious Affairs that Baptist preaching in Estonia included moral topics. Presbyters taught about joy, persistance, faithfulness and humility.[89] As the majority of ECB writings focus on individual sanctification, it is slightly surprising to find at least some awareness of ethics and society. Robert Võsu emphasised a wider social dimension: 'A Christian must always think socially, from the perspective of the whole city or the whole country. We must always see ourselves as members of this country.'[90] Võsu's vision for Christian ethics, expressed in his major work *Evangeelne eetika* (Evangelical Ethics) was exceptionally broad – he analysed the ethical role of a Christian in society and touched upon economic life, human relations with the created world, war and peace.[91] These theological reflections did not, however, express the ethical thinking of all local churches.

Nevertheless, Estonian ECB believers saw discipleship and ethics as closely related to each other. The goal of a believer's life – lived out in a hostile society - was to behave and serve like Christ. In this pursuit Estonian Baptists found encouragement from the wider evangelical world – as well as using writers such as Andrew Murray and Watchman Nee some authors mention Karl Barth and Dietrich Bonhoeffer as sources of inspiration for understanding Christian ethics.[92] In general, Estonian Baptists focused on finding and applying God's will, developing Christ-likeness, and being a blessing for others. To be like Christ was their ethical task. This was not primarily a mystical unity with the Lord but rather a practical way of being a Christian.

---

[86] For wider discussion, see Joe E. Tull and James E. Carter, *Ministerial Ethics: Moral Formation for Church Leaders* (Grand Rapids, Michigan: Baker Academic, 2004), pp. 47-63.

[87] The Commissioner of the CRA report of 1969. ERA, f. R-1989, n. 2, s. 43, p. 82.

[88] Minutes of the meeting with church executive board representatives and pastors in the Kingissepa region (03.03.1978), Kirjavahetus usukeskustega vabariigis 1977-1990 [Correspondence with religious centres in the Republic 1977-1990], UNVA.

[89] The Commissioner of the CRA report of 1971. Aruanded ja ülevaated kirikute tegevuse kohta ENSV-s 1971-1990 (AÜ1971-1990) [Reports and surveys about the activities of churches in the ESSR 1971-1990], UNVA.

[90] Võsu, *Mäejutlus*, p. 36, see also p. 37.

[91] Võsu, *Evangeelne eetika*, pp. 199-256.

[92] Rebane, 'Piibellik pühitsus', *Logos*, no. 1 (1982), pp. 11-15.

Võsu considered that 'following Christ does not mean an attempt to copy him in every situation, but to own his mentality'.[93] In some cases Estonian Baptists believed that to be a disciple meant living as separately as possible from the wider culture or sticking to rigid moralism. However, Estonian Baptists also knew that to live an ethical Christian life a relationship with God was needed rather than just a 'moral map'. To follow Christ meant having an on-going personal relationship, which was nourished by prayer and the practice of the faith.[94] Though this was often understood in individualistic terms it also had an ecclesial dimension.

<h2 style="text-align:center">CHURCH DISCIPLINE AND CHRISTIAN ETHICS</h2>

This chapter has argued that Estonian Baptists viewed sanctification as the personal ethical development of a Christian. This statement, however, needs some further clarification. The Christian life itself always has a communal aspect to it. Church fellowship – symbolized in participation at Holy Communion – was considered by Estonian ECB believers as giving strength for the life of discipleship. Osvald Tärk said that during thirty years he had been absent from the communion table only three times – for health reasons.[95] By such actions leaders offered important examples. While sanctification was understood in terms of individual Christian development and maturity, the context for this was communal. The local church played an important role in setting ethical norms and monitoring the conduct of believers – even if its role was neither analysed theologically nor set out in written form. Stanley Hauerwas has said: 'As Christians we believe we not only need a community, but a community of a particular kind to live well morally. We need people who are capable of being faithful to a way of life, even when that way of life may be in conflict with what passes as "morality" in the larger society.'[96] For Estonian Baptists, this 'particular kind of community' not only exhorted its members; it also disciplined them in order to maintain a certain way of life.

Estonian free churches had always practiced church discipline: there was admonition of church members, and also in some cases exclusion from the Lord's Table or even excommunication from the church. Before the Second World War, Evangelical Christian Free churches had 'watch-care teams' that took responsibility for overseeing the church members' spiritual life. Church meetings had a variety of purposes; among those was the aim of educating and guiding the church members. The items considered included: how a believer

---

[93] Võsu, *Evangeelne eetika*, p. 105.

[94] Tärk, 'Märkmeid O. Tärgi jutlustest 1981-1982.a.', 1982. peetud jutlused, pp. 2-4.

[95] Tärk, 'Märkmeid O. Tärgi jutlustest 1981-1982.a.', 1981. peetud jutlused, pp. 72, 83.

[96] Stanley Hauerwas, 'On Keeping Theological Ethics Theological', in Stanley Hauerwas and Alasdair MacIntyre, eds., *Revisions: Changing Perspectives in Moral Philosophy* (Notre Dame: University of Notre Dame Press, 1983), p. 35.

should behave, how to raise children or how to pray.[97] Ethical and lifestyle issues were often clarified when a baptismal candidate's case was discussed. However, during the Soviet years, the main issues which could lead to disciplining a church member were related to sexuality and marriage. This was a distortion as over against a more comprehensive concern with issues that needed pastoral care or might have provoked a need for discipline.

Sexuality was understood as an important spiritual and moral area of human life. Dating was seen as a serious step. Oskar Olvik, who continued to represent Evangelical Christian ideals in the UECBE, said that 'courting' should be condemned; even a closer 'friendship' between a girl and a boy – walking together, spending time together – was seen as a negative or perhaps a potentially 'dangerous' thing. The pastoral advice was to get engaged or finish the friendship.[98] Some young people in ECB churches were probably not given an opportunity to get to know each other sufficiently before marriage. But the most serious matter discussed by presbyters as well as church members was divorce and remarriage. It seems that Estonian Baptists in the Soviet years moved towards stricter positions regarding remarriage: they accepted divorce in some cases, but practically excluded the possibility of remarriage as long as the other 'party' was alive. They believed, together with many other evangelicals, that the marital bond could be dissolved only by death.[99]

Osvald Tärk, who took a strict position, was regarded as something of an authority in this area, and his views were sometimes taken in even narrower directions by those who followed him. Jüri Jürgenson, then the pastor of Tartu 'Salem' Church, said in 1987 that the demands of Jesus in the realm of marriage were very strict. He was concerned that people had been trying to weaken the norms for family life, and he condemned this trend. In his view 'we are faced with a choice, whether we want to walk a narrow road or the wide road'. Jürgenson's rather extreme warning was that if divorced persons re-married then clear norms would be blurred and as a next step a door would be open also for homosexuality and the use of drugs among believers. The issue of remarriage, for him, was a crucial one, dividing grain from chaff.[100] Even if Jürgenson's biblical interpretation or theological-ethical conclusions may be questioned, Jürgenson clearly demonstrates how important – and how emotionally loaded – was the topic of the ethics of marriage in Estonian ECB churches.

---

[97] Olvik, *Mälestused*, part 1, p. 257.

[98] Olvik, *Mälestused*, part 2, p. 305.

[99] For further argumentation for this position, see William A. Heth, 'Divorce, but No Remarriage', in H. Wayne House, ed., *Divorce and Remarriage: Four Christian Views* (Downers Grove, Illinois: InterVarsity Press, 1990), pp. 73-129.

[100] Minutes of the Presbyters' Council meeting, no. 131 (13.04.1987). Juhatuse koosolekute protokollid [Minutes of the Executive Board] (30.01.1981-12.12.1987), EEKBLA.

At times pastoral arguments somewhat softened doctrinal positions. This was particular true in connection with the confusion caused by the Second World War. For example, the case of Johannes Kappel in Tallinn 'Kalju' church can serve as a 'case study' for throwing light on some of these dilemmas.[101] Kappel was divorced by a decision of the Estonian Supreme Court in 1954, because his wife left Estonia in 1944, and he had been separated from her for ten years. Political realities made re-uniting impossible. Kappel planned to marry Liidia Kõrge, whose story was similar. The presbyter of Tallinn 'Kalju' church, Robert Võsu, after prayer and consultation with other 'brothers', refused to marry the couple. They were married in Tallinn 'Kaarli' Lutheran church, and the service was conducted by a Lutheran pastor. According to the report, the position of the local Baptist church was not too rigid at the beginning. Võsu stated that 'there are some rights left to the church to bind and loose'. He added: 'Also the Senior Presbyter br[other] Lipstok has a standpoint, that only the church can do something about it - and according to inner clarity to give mercy. Exceptional situations and the person's behaviour can be taken into account.'[102] So, at least theoretically, there was a possibility that remarriage of a divorced person could be accepted under certain exceptional conditions. And the conditions for Kappel and Kõrge were exceptional indeed.

However, Kappel was reluctant to let his case to be discussed in the church community, and made the decision to re-marry without having a proper consultation with the church. The report considered that Kappel had left the church's fellowship. One gets the impression that the church and its leaders were not sure how to resolve the whole issue. Perhaps it was not only Kappel's defiant behaviour – as the church interpreted it – but also hesitance on the part of the church and its leaders (as they thought about the decision they had to make) which aggravated the situation. Võsu commented: 'On the one hand, I felt compassion towards the brother's burden, but on the other, there is the Word of God, the spiritual attitude of the brother and other [issues].'[103] Ultimately Kappel was excommunicated. But did this happen because the marriage took place without local church approval, or because the marriage was against the Estonian Baptist interpretation of the text in Matthew 19:9 about marriage and divorce? This is not clear from the report. It seems likely that the interpretation of Matthew 19:9 allowed exceptions, depending on the person's attitude and willingness to yield to the community's discernment. The pastoral aspects of this ethical dilemma were at least seriously considered.

---

[101] See 'Seletus kogudusele venna Joh. Kappeli kohta, Kalju palvelas, 22. aug. 1954. a.' [A Report about Brother Joh. Kappel, in 'Kalju' church, 22 August 1954]. Kirjavahetus ja dokumendid 1950-1974: Kalju kogudus [Correspondence and documents 1950-1974: 'Kalju' Church], EEKBLA.
[102] Ibid.
[103] Ibid.

While Baptists used biblical interpretation and communal discernment to seek to solve these dilemmas, they seldom thought that there might be cases when remarriage could be considered as part of a concern for 'the wholeness and well-being of all persons affected by the marital dissolution', as Stanley Grenz has argued.[104] This approach would have required more careful consideration of contextual elements in ethical decisions. This was what Estonian Baptists were hesitant about. They cherished a hope that biblical guidelines 'determine in advance what circumstances entail a proper divorce and the right to remarriage'.[105] Probably influenced by Osvald Tärk's position, Tallinn Oleviste church asked candidates for the diaconate if they agreed that divorced persons could not marry while their former spouse was alive (if a person was divorced and remarried before becoming a believer, he or she could be a church member, but these persons could not serve as presbyters or deacons).[106] The presbyters' conference in 1987 warned that churches should not allow the divorced to re-marry.[107] There was a clear shift by this time from a pastoral emphasis towards a doctrinal emphasis.[108]

There were other occasions when exclusion from the Lord's Supper or excommunication was used by Estonian Baptists in order to secure certain ethical norms. For example, the use of alcohol was considered a serious sin. Presbyter Albert Sergo had used alcohol when celebrating his fiftieth birthday and, according to Olvik's memoirs, 'got drunk'. He was 'put aside' from the ministry for six months. However, for Olvik the more serious ethical problem was that Sergo neither understood his mistake nor repented.[109] According to Meego Remmel, in spite of the fact that 'abstinence was seen as a Christian virtue' in ECB churches, 'Estonian churches never refused using wine at the Lord's Supper or home-made small beer at a rural lunch'.[110] There was space for flexibility, especially in the earlier stages of the UECBE's life. In the case of Sergo, the issue of an unrepentant mind was seen as more problematic than the issue of excessive use of alcohol. Osvald Tärk stated in a somewhat warning tone: 'We need prayer and repentance, because among the believers there are many transgressions which have become allowed. It is astonishing to

---

[104] Stanley Grenz, *Sexual Ethics: A Biblical Perspective* (Carlisle: Paternoster Press, 1998), p.138; see also pp. 134-145.

[105] Ibid., p. 137.

[106] 'Diakonite jaoks' [For Deacons], typewritten guidelines (n. d.). Osvald Tärgi materjalid [Materials of Osvald Tärk], EEKBLA.

[107] 'Presbüterite konverents 24.-26.04.1987 Tallinnas' [Presbyters Conference in Tallinn, 24-26 April, 1987], *Logos*, no. 1-2 (1987), p. 4.

[108] For Tärk's positions on marital ethics, see also Osvald Tärk, 'Abieluküsimusi: 1. Kor., 7. pt.' [Marriage Issues: 1. Cor., ch. 7), parts 1-3 (13.03.1981, 08.04.1981, 14.05.1981), audiotape. KUSA.

[109] Olvik, *Mälestused*, part 2, p. 471.

[110] Meego Remmel, *The Role of Christian Ethics in Postmarxist and Postmodern Estonia* (Bonn: Verlag für Kultur und Wissenschaft, 2002), p. 61.

hear how believers have begun to allow and excuse their mistakes.'[111] However, repentance could also be seen in a more positive light: as evidence of an ability to listen to scriptural guidance, as showing respect towards the brothers and sisters, and as an attitude which could open the way for growth in maturity and closeness to God.

Another important aspect of ethics was related to witness. An ethical lifestyle should be a witness for outsiders: this was the Estonian Baptist conviction. If an offence or hindrance to the 'outsiders' had occurred, or in other words if the sin was 'public', the church tended to take more serious disciplinary measures.[112] No doubt this had the possible danger that 'public' sins were condemned but 'secret' sins – misuse of power in human relationships or gossiping, for example – were taken as being less serious offences. Olvik said that believers who had fallen back into alcoholism or lies had caused much damage to the Kingdom of God, because 'the world does not separate them from true believers, saying that this is what they all are'.[113] The witness of the church was an important element in decisions related to ethics in Baptist church communities in Soviet Estonia. Evangelistic identity was expressed also in the area of ethics.

For some people the church discipline carried out in the UECBE was too demanding. The Senior Presbyter's report of 1970-1972 stated that some members had left for other denominations not because of doctrinal differences but because 'we have too strict demands' for a believer's life and ethics.[114] In 1970-1972 there were 72 persons who left for other denominations – for a variety of different reasons, however – and 207 who were erased from church membership lists.[115] Võsu considered church discipline as being an important aspect of Baptist identity: 'The Church's discipline … is one of those bases on which our brotherhood stands. The church has here a spiritual authority, which requires spiritual discernment.'[116] On another occasion the Senior Presbyter said that one reason to be happy was that no presbyter had been 'disqualified' from his position for reasons of an impure life.[117]

The exercise of church discipline – especially in matters of behaviour – in the UECBE is an example which shows the communal element that was in operation in maintaining ethical norms in the ECB tradition in Estonia. Nevertheless, in many cases, the community was a tool for achieving 'better'

---

[111] Osvald Tärk, 'Jumalast antud meeleparanduse aeg' [A God-given Time for Repentance], *Logos*, no. 1-2 (1987), p. 7. The sermon was originally preached in the 1950s.

[112] 'Suhtlemine maailmaga Kristuse meelsuses', p. 3.

[113] Olvik, 'Usulise ja kõlbelise elu probleeme meie kogudustes', p. 112.

[114] Senior Presbyter's report of 1970-1972. EKB vanempresbüteri aruanded, EEKBLA.

[115] Ibid.

[116] Robert Võsu, 'Baptistide ajaloolised põhimõtted' (Oleviste, 05.02.1956), p. 8. Robert Võsu materjalid, EEKBLA.

[117] Senior Presbyter's report of 1967. EKB vanempresbüteri aruanded, EEKBLA.

results in the area of personal sanctification; it was a measure against which individual ethical achievements or non-achievements were measured. In Estonian ECB churches the priority was individual behaviour and much less thought was given to ethical meaning related to how the community functioned together, how it solved its problems, or how it made decisions. It is also notable that transgressions in some aspects of ethical behaviour – especially those aspects related to marriage and sexuality – were more likely to result in disciplinary measures by the church community. 'Public' mistakes were condemned more promptly. This is not to say that elements of motivation and the inner life were neglected. As we have seen, this was far from being the case. To an extent Estonian Baptist ethical thinking in Soviet years can be described as a combination of 'virtue ethics' and 'rule ethics'.

VIRTUE ETHICS AND RULE ETHICS

The UECBE understanding of the ethical task involved both an emphasis on Christian norms and on spiritual maturity. Mari Vahermägi has demonstrated that 'rule ethics' and 'virtue ethics' were both represented in the Soviet times in the UECBE.[118] Jean Porter writes: 'The virtues are generally regarded as praiseworthy traits of character … or valuable traits of intellect.'[119] On rules, Richard Miller has this to say: '[R]ules refer to normative regulations of individual or corporate behaviour.'[120] In the UECBE, written Bible studies, sermon collections, as well as theological treatises, show the presence of these two conceptual approaches. They are different, but they do not completely contradict each other.

Two images may help to explain these two approaches. One considers a believer to be like a child who is not aware of dangers, and who has a tendency to break good rules that parents have set. He or she needs discipline, and clear normative statements. Oskar Olvik often, though not always, represented this approach, which tended to place dogmatic truth into the centre, and which sometimes slid into legalism. Also Osvald Tärk often emphasised 'norms',

---

[118] Mari Vahermägi, 'Vooruslikkusest pühitsuselus Osvald Tärgi ja Robert Võsu kirjapärandi valgel' [About Virtues in Sanctification in the Light of the Literary Heritage of Osvald Tärk and Robert Võsu], in Toivo Pilli, ed., *Teekond teisenevas ajas: peatükke Eesti vabakoguduste ajaloost* [A Journey in Changing Time: Chapters from the History of Estonian Free Churches] (Tartu: Kõrgem Usuteaduslik Seminar ja Sõnasepp OÜ, 2005), pp. 160-180.

[119] Jean Porter, 'Virtue', in Gilbert Meilaender and William Werpehowski, eds., *The Oxford Handbook of Theological Ethics* (New York: Oxford University Press, 2005), p. 206.

[120] Richard B. Miller, 'Rules', in Meilaender and Werpehowski, eds., *The Oxford Handbook of Theological Ethics*, p. 220.

'responsibility' and 'obedience' in ethics.[121] The other picture, perhaps better expressing Robert Võsu's approach, sees the human person in slightly more optimistic colours. This view strongly believes that the inner renewal and work of the Spirit transforms a person so thoroughly that gradually new 'fruit' will become visible. This approach puts more emphasis on the spiritual and ethical development of the person, and tends to solve ethical dilemmas from human and contextual rather than from dogmatic perspectives. Võsu, who tried to give a systematic survey of evangelical ethics, stated: 'Life is very complicated and it is impossible to give guidelines for every single situation.'[122]

In reality, in some cases the UECBE churches, despite Võsu's caution, tended to develop a rather rigid moralism. Especially some former Evangelical Christian leaders, such as Oskar Olvik, were apt to prescribe moral norms in a rather detailed way. For example, in 1968, Olvik complained that 'the world is bringing its ways of life and mentalities into the church' and 'believers do not have unified views about many moral problems'.[123] Before the Second World War, Karl L. Marley tended to define a Christian lifestyle by a particular dress code or by a special hair style.[124] Legalism was the negative aspect of a sincere commitment to be a witness by living a moral Christian life. It was a 'shortcut' to this goal, to be achieved by defining external (sub)cultural 'signs' that had to be observed. Osvald Tärk, though with a less legalistic tone, complained that 'present day worldly customs and ways have their impact on Christians'.[125]

Olvik argued that the church community should exercise clearer control over the moral life of its members. But if control was attempted then rules and 'clear borders' had to be defined in detail. This was what Olvik tried to do on several occasions during the Soviet years. He saw serious danger if a believer married a non-Christian partner, he warned against promiscuous sexual relationships, he criticized church members for stealing potatoes from kolkhoz fields, he was worried that in the hairstyles being adopted by women in the church there was 'something of a worldly mentality', and he was concerned that for men and women to swim at the same beach posed a serious moral danger.[126] No doubt Olvik as a presbyter was right to consider ethical questions at the grassroots level, but he often prescribed 'acceptable' behaviour rather than giving tools for ethical discernment. Also Osvald Tärk tended in his

---

[121] See Tärk, 'Märkmeid O. Tärgi jutlustest 1981-1982.a.', 1981. peetud jutlused, pp. 9-10.

[122] Võsu, *Evangeelne eetika*, pp. 168-169.

[123] Olvik, 'Usulise ja kõlbelise elu probleeme meie kogudustes', p. 123.

[124] Toivo Pilli, 'Albert Ruutsoo vabakoguduslikust vaimulaadist' [Albert Ruutsoo on Free Church Spirituality], manuscript of an unpublished article based on an interview with Ruutsoo from the early 1990s, pp. 3-4. TPL.

[125] Tärk, 'Tööraskuste õigest kasutamisest', p. 14.

[126] Olvik, 'Usulise ja kõlbelise elu probleeme meie kogudustes', pp. 123-134. See also Oskar Olvik, 'Koguduse siseseid ja –väliseid distsipliini küsimusi' [Internal and Exernal Issues of Church Discipline] (11-13.05.1973), audiotape. KUSA.

writings as well as in counselling situations to offer clear-cut answers, though his theological depth helped him to avoid some petty legalisms. However, Estonian Evangelical Christians-Baptists could not completely avoid the age-old temptation: 'the temptation of self-justification and the corresponding danger of works-righteousness'.[127]

However, the UECBE ideal for the Christian life was different. For example, Ants Rebane criticized the understanding of sanctification in terms of rigid guidelines, positive thinking or extraordinary spiritual experiences.[128] The latter expression probably referred to charismatic influences in the 1970s, which tended to emphasise miraculous guidance in ethical decisions, instead of discernment in the light of the Word. Võsu stressed that Christian ethics were not 'a codex of morality' – notice the subtle reference to Communist use of language! – where good and bad characteristics and behaviours are listed. Rather, an evangelical approach to ethics throws light on the religious and moral situation of a person: the reasons for ethical and spiritual decline and the ways to reverse this tendency. It also shows God at work in transformation, so that the formerly 'wild and bad tree' is enabled to 'bear good fruit'.[129] Võsu explained that a believer's true fruit is a life that is lived for the benefit of others and which in a natural way grows out of fellowship with Christ.[130] Again, the image of 'bearing fruit' – an organic and natural process – was central. Using a quotation from recent literature in this area: 'To character and its virtues must be added conduct and its values: the perspectives, obligations and aspirations...'[131]

Sometimes 'separation from the world' as an ethical task – both virtue and rule – was emphasised, though Osvald Tärk pointed out that although the church is different from the world it is not taken totally out of the world.[132] It is its mission and vision that marks the church. It cannot identify itself with a culture that neglects God, but it can offer help. It is good for a person who is sinking, it was noted, if a helper is on the shore.[133] Also, Estonian Baptists believed that contrasts grow over time: good becomes better and bad becomes worse.[134] Kalju Raid, using the language of 'defining limits', said in 1960 that 'every church member should define the limits and determine where the

---

[127] Miller, 'Rules', in Meilaender and Werpehowski, eds., *The Oxford Handbook of Theological Ethics*, p. 225.

[128] Ants Rebane, 'Piibellik pühitsus', *Logos*, no. 5 (1982), pp. 3-4; see also Robert Võsu, 'Püha Vaim ja valevaimud' [The Holy Spirit and Wrong Spirits], *Logos*, no. 5 (1985), pp. 14-16.

[129] Võsu, *Evangeelne eetika*, pp. 10-11.

[130] *'Kalju' koguduse karjase Robert Võsu jutlusi ajavahemikul 1944.-1969*, p. 35.

[131] Tull and Carter, *Ministerial Ethics*, p. 52.

[132] Tärk, 'Märkmeid O. Tärgi jutlustest 1981-1982.a.', 1981. peetud jutlused, pp. 25-26.

[133] *'Kalju' koguduse karjase Robert Võsu jutlusi ajavahemikul 1944.-1969*, p. 69.

[134] Ibid., p. 96.

church's space gives way to that of the world'.[135] This was very often interpreted also as avoiding a lapse into 'nominal Christianity'. However, Estonian believers were also warned that there was a danger in losing contact with the world; what Günther Wieske, a German Baptist, called 'emigration into sanctification' or propagating one's own church-centred lifestyle as the only right option.[136] Osvald Tärk argued in a balanced way: 'Wasn't it that Jesus himself lived in the world of sinners, but he remained pure. He ate with sinners and touched lepers. His purity was so great that it infected others, but the sins of other people could not influence him. There are believers whose purity protects them. Holiness, simplicity and integrity create a zone of protection around them, in front of which people with mean plans and immoral talk have to stop. Neither rules nor prohibition nor teachings protect these people, but a miraculous divine influence.'[137]

It was because of higher ideals, because of their ultimate goal, which was the glory of God, that Christians gave up some things. Võsu argued that Christians might detach themselves from many pleasures or hobbies not because these were prohibited, but because believers considered time too valuable a treasure to spend aimlessly. He continued: 'From this aspect they evaluate all cultural issues: literature, theatre, movies, parties, concerts, etc. Nothing is forbidden of these, but everyone has to ... choose what helps him in the moral fight towards perfection and put aside everything that does not help to achieve this goal or might even be a hindrance.'[138] It was Robert Võsu, when compared to other UECBE leaders, whose focus in matters of ethics was most clearly on Christian virtues instead on dogmatic positions.

According to UECBE leaders, the central virtue for a Christian community was love. The statement that 'God is love' expresses God's moral nature. Love is the consummation of a moral personality, the *summa* of all virtues.[139] Robert Võsu spoke about love in many of his writings.[140] Võsu taught that the relationship of a human being with God is moral; this means it is based on will and deeds over against wishes and emotions. Love is also expressed in human relationships – in 'brotherly love' as Võsu said. This takes the form of

---

[135] Kalju Raid, notes (24.07.1960). Kalju Raidi kirjavahetus ja märkmed [Correspondence and notes of Kalju Raid], KUSA.

[136] Günther Wieske, 'Euroopa kristlased piibli ja kultuuri pingeväljas' [European Christianity in the Tension Area of the Bible and Culture], *Logos*, no. 3-4 (1987), pp. 43-44.

[137] Osvald Tärk, 'Kuidas vabaneda nimekristlusest?' [How to Get Rid of Nominal Christianity], typewritten sermon (06.01.1962), p. 22. Palvenädal Olevistes, 1-8 January 1962, Robert Võsu materjalid, EEKBLA.

[138] [Võsu,] *Baptistide arengust ja põhimõtetest*, pp.15-16.

[139] Robert Võsu, 'Armastuse tähendus apostel Johannese kirjades' [The Meaning of Love in the Epistles of the Apostle John], *Logos*, no. 3 (1986), p. 27.

[140] See also Robert Võsu, *Armastusest* [About Love], typewritten manuscript (1965). KUSA.

fellowship and self-sacrifice, giving up time, interests and means for the benefit of others.[141] Love respects others even if it has its own views.[142] The deeper the self-sacrifice, the deeper the love.[143] Võsu emphasised that holiness and sanctification can be repulsive if they are not accompanied by love, which is what attracts people to God and to church. Deeper than the purity of external behaviour is purity of heart.[144] Purity itself was not the ultimate aim for Võsu. 'How often we are satisfied with our own purity, but do not inspire a yearning for purity in others. Our purity has to be so authentic that it attracts other people.'[145] Seeking for justice is not enough: a Christian has to seek love and compassion which surpass justice.[146]

Love was not just an abstract theological-ethical topic for Estonian Baptists in the Soviet years. It was a challenge, a task that needed to be fulfilled. Responding to atheistic pressure with dignity and love required more than just knowing about 'right behaviour'. Human relationships were like litmus paper, indicating the value and depth of Christian ethics. Also in comparatively small local church communities personal relationships could not stay only on the level of formal politeness or business-like activism. Relationships had ethical connotations. Osvald Tärk complained of 'unsettled relationships'.[147] He also warned that gossiping, 'speaking badly about others', must be given up and that quarreling about different theological views must stop.[148] In the 1970s the depth of relationships in the ECB churches were also tested by the new charismatic influences and lively music styles.[149] In addition, more democratic patterns of church government meant that not only leaders, but the church members as a whole, were responsible for the life and conduct of the community.[150] 'We take to ourselves a freedom to think in certain ways. This freedom we must grant also to others. ... Perhaps we are closer to the truth than others ... but if we despise those who think differently, then we have gone astray.'[151] The virtue of love was central to a believers' church.

As noted, Estonain Baptists emphasised a wide variety of virtues, such as

---

[141] Võsu, 'Armastuse tähendus apostel Johannese kirjades', pp. 31-32.

[142] 'Presbüterite konverents 24.-26.04.1987 Tallinnas', p. 4.

[143] Võsu, *Mäejutlus*, p. 9

[144] *'Kalju' koguduse karjase Robert Võsu jutlusi ajavahemikul 1944.-1969*, pp. 103-104.

[145] Ibid., p. 104.

[146] *'Kalju' koguduse karjase Robert Võsu jutlusi ajavahemikul 1944.-1969*, p. 105; Võsu, *Mäejutlus*, p. 21.

[147] Tärk, 'Jumalast antud meeleparanduse aeg', p. 7.

[148] Ibid.

[149] [R. Võsu,] 'Kodumaa vaimulik olukord' [The Spiritual Situation in our Homeland] (1979). EKB vanempresbüteri aruanded, EEKBLA.

[150] Robert Võsu, 'Baptismist' [About the Baptist Movement], *Logos*, no. 4 (1986), p. 20.

[151] [R. Võsu], 'Kodumaa vaimulik olukord' (1979). EKB vanempresbüteri aruanded, EEKBLA.

faithfulness, meekness, honesty, self-discipline and joy.[152] One other important aspect of ethics should be mentioned in the context of 'virtue ethics'. This was a spirit of servanthood, which was considered as a central characteristic of a believer and a key for the ethical life. Robert Võsu criticised many believers who, he claimed, went to worship in order to receive encouragement, or to seek peace in their hearts or perhaps new strength, but who did not go to worship with the desire to be transformed so that they might be more helpful, more ready to serve and more willing to give themselves in a self-sacrificial way. Referring to Harry E. Fosdick, a very prominent American Baptist of the early twentieth century and one who held broad theological views, Võsu said he was convinced that 'a great day for Christianity will dawn' when servanthood would become a part of a believer's everyday responsibilities.[153] To overcome egotistic striving and find an altruistic way was truly to follow the model of Jesus, Võsu taught.[154] Võsu referred to Hans Küng, the outstanding Roman Catholic theologian, who in *Christ Sein* said that love is service, and service is a way to real greatness.[155]

Finally Estonian Baptists – or, at least, their leading theologians – placed the quest for ethical virtues in the wider perspective of the Kingdom of God. In Estonian Baptist thinking 'the Kingdom' referred broadly to God's reality which goes beyond human efforts. Sometimes the Kingdom was seen as a realm to which a person belongs inwardly – 'with his inner spiritual attitude'.[156] But the Kingdom was also in the midst of the people; it was where people fulfilled the will of God. [157] Perhaps Oskar Olvik was the most consistent – probably because of his Protestant theological education from Tartu University – in relating ethical principles and the Kingdom. He believed that preparation for God's Kingdom takes place in every denomination, thus emphasising the ecumenical dimension, and that applying the ethical laws of the Kingdom would improve social life in the nation and deepen relationships between believers, including those belonging to different traditions.[158] However, on the whole Estonian Baptists tended to see God's Kingdom as a spiritual or eschatological reality, though at times they came surprisingly close to some present-day evangelical ethicists, who believe that 'Jesus offered not hard sayings or high ideals, but concrete ways to practice God's will ... in other words, he taught his followers how to participate in God's reign'.[159]

---

[152] Vahermägi, 'Vooruslikkusest pühitsuselus', in T. Pilli, ed., *Teekond teisenevas ajas*, pp. 168-175.

[153] Võsu, *Mäejutlus*, p. 110.

[154] Ibid., p. 9.

[155] Võsu, 'Armastuse tähendus apostel Johannese kirjades', p. 34.

[156] Võsu, *Mäejutlus*, p. 6.

[157] *'Kalju' koguduse karjase Robert Võsu jutlusi ajavahemikul 1944.-1969*, p. 123.

[158] Olvik, *Homileetika*, p. 34.

[159] Stassen and Gushee, *Kingdom Ethics*, p. 31.

CONCLUSION

Estonian ECB believers, living in a hostile atheistic environment and seeking ways to encourage mutual respect and cooperation in a united Evangelical Christian-Baptist union, faced several ethical challenges. They struggled to maintain trust and integrity. At the same time, they strongly believed that the ethical life, the way of sanctification, and spiritual development were inseparable. Osvald Tärk, referring to the new birth, said: 'The requirement of Christian ethics is: first a new person, then new ethics.'[160] The sanctified life was believed to grow from the inside out. It was believed to be a life of humility, yielding to God and 'giving one's old self to death'. One of the high goals for believers was to grow into a closer relationship with Christ, to become more Christ-like. Sometimes this was portrayed in somewhat mystical language, though mostly Christ-likeness was interpreted in terms of character formation and as having the mind of Christ. 'Taking up the cross' and 'following Christ's example', searching for God's will and being ready to apply this will in life's decisions and human relationships – all this was bound up in the sanctified life.

The ethical life was also lived out in the context of persecution. Meego Remmel has pointed out that during the Soviet years the primary resource for thinking about ethical matters in the UECBE was within the ECB tradition itself.[161] This is true, though the Estonian ECB tradition included elements and influences from wider Protestant thinking as well as from a number of evangelical authors. It is slightly surprising to realise that authors such as Andrew Murray or Watchman Nee, who were not Baptists, were influential in shaping the Estonian Evangelical Christian-Baptist understanding of sanctification. Also Robert Võsu, who wrote significantly on the topic of ethics, admitted that he was indebted to the Estonian Lutheran theologian, Elmar Salumaa.[162] Võsu's book *Mäejutlus* (The Sermon on the Mount) gives evidence that he was also influenced by Stanley Jones' *The Christ of the Mount*. But specifically in their striving to understand the meaning of persecution, Estonian Baptists found encouragement in the example of the sixteenth-century Anabaptists. Estonian believers taught that the suffering they endured, like the suffering endured by the Anabaptists, could bring glory to God, if a person was committed to fulfilling the will of God and keeping a 'pure heart'. This was a test of authentic discipleship for ECB church members. Christ invited his followers to become identified with him. Here was their ultimate focus and identity.

Estonian Baptists were comparatively individualistic in their understanding of sanctification – it was mostly personal sanctification that was

---

[160] Tärk, *Efesose kiri*, p. 108.

[161] Remmel, *The Role of Christian Ethics in Postmarxist and Postmodern Estonia*, p. 59.

[162] Võsu, *Evangeelne eetika*, p. 7.

talked about. Võsu gave advice about family and church issues but he did not
see 'the Christian family as a vocation of the kingdom' nor did he have a vision
of the kind of 'ecclesial formation' espoused (for example) by the Orthodox
Church.[163] However, the church community helped – even if this help was not
always verbalised – to shape the ECB believers' ethical identity. One way in
which this happened was through church discipline – an inherent feature of
Estonian free churches. Church discipline, which could mean exclusion from
the Lord's Supper or even excommunication, was often practised in relation to
marital/sexual ethics. For Estonian Baptists a major issue was whether a
divorced person was allowed to remarry. During the Soviet years the ECB
position in this matter became more dogmatic and rigid. However, there were –
especially in the 1950s, but also later – clear signs that congregational
discernment was believed to be a valid tool in solving these situations. Robert
Võsu was convinced that local congregations could 'bind and loose'.[164] In an
atheistic and hostile context, Baptists were especially sensitive in cases of
'public sins', which portrayed the whole believers' community in a bad light. In
such cases church discipline was more likely to be applied than in less open
cases of moral misbehaviour.

Both virtue ethics and rule ethics were taught and practised by Estonian
Baptists during the Soviet years. Meego Remmel has argued that Robert Võsu
paid considerable attention to virtue ethics.[165] However, Võsu himself was not
always consistent in his views and in the context of the rather individually-
orientated ethical background of the ECB Võsu was often a 'voice in the
wilderness', especially when trying to offer a more global and socially-inclined
perspective on ethics. But the image of 'bearing fruit' as a symbol of the
process of sanctification became widespread in the UECBE – largely due to the
writings and sermons of Võsu himself. Võsu emphasised that any individual
virtue needed to be combined with other 'fruits of the Spirit' in order that its
true and full meaning would come to the fore. Otherwise, for example, a
humble person could be envious or untrustworthy.[166]

The Estonian understanding of Christian ethics focused mainly on a
character that had certain features – such as trustfulness, joy, self-sacrifice and
kindness in human relationships. The most comprehensive virtue, occurring
most often in Estonian Baptist literature, was 'love'. This was the 'basic' virtue.
The way of love was the way of Christ. While Estonian Baptists did not always
avoid the temptation of falling into legalism in their efforts to live an ethical
life, at the same time the outstanding Baptist ethicists, such as Võsu, and also

---

[163] Vigen Guroian, *Ethics After Christendom: Toward an Ecclesial Christian Ethic*
(Grand Rapids, Michigan: Eerdmans, 1994), p. 154; see also the whole of chapter 6, pp.
133-154.

[164] Võsu, *Evangeelne eetika*, p. 169.

[165] Remmel, *The Role of Christian Ethics in Postmarxist and Postmodern Estonia*, p. 60.

[166] Võsu, 'Tasadus ja alandus Pauluse käsitluses', p. 31.

Tärk, clearly made an effort to move beyond the 'must and must-not' way of understanding ethics. Though the complex dynamics of individual human responsibility, biblical norms and pastoral considerations could be explained differently by a variety of authors writing in varying situations, one theme was clear: the transformed 'heart', transformed into the likeness of Christ, was to produce 'good fruit' in the church and in the world. This was an inseparable part of Estonian Baptist identity during the Soviet years.

CHAPTER 10

Conclusion

In this volume, I have explored developments in the identity of the Evangelical Christians-Baptists (known usually as Baptists) in Estonia during the years of communist atheistic pressure, from 1945 until 1991. The reactions of the believers to external restrictions, changing organisational patterns and religious practices, and the dynamics of theological interpretations in the Union of Evangelical Christians-Baptists in Estonia (UECBE), have all been studied. The picture that has emerged in this book is more complex than the one usually presented during the Soviet years in Estonia. In those years the leaders of the UECBE – a multifaceted ecclesial body consisting of former Baptists, Evangelical Christians, Pentecostals and Revivalist Free Church believers – often emphasised unity and common features in their identity rather than disparate elements. Robert Võsu, the UECBE Senior Presbyter from 1970 to 1985, often pointed out the unifying features.[1] These four streams of free church life in Estonia certainly shared many beliefs and practices – such as commitment to evangelism, an emphasis on the centrality of the experience of the new birth, or an understanding of sanctification as a journey toward Christ-likeness. Nevertheless, this study has demonstrated that distinctives in the different traditions, as undercurrents in the confluence that created a new stream of Estonian baptistic life, continued to exist. The strands of free church life became intertwined and affected each other. The shaping of Estonian Baptist identity within the communist context was a dynamic and long-term process, which was influenced by external and internal forces and which incorporated elements from the free church traditions which were merged into one union.

ESTONIAN BAPTIST IDENTITY: EXTERNAL INFLUENCES

Soviet reality, which was hostile toward believers, was a major factor which from 1945 until 1991 moulded Estonian Baptist behaviour and faith. Chapters 2 to 5 of this study have examined this process. The Soviet government allowed

---

[1] For example, see 'Baptismi ajalugu' [History of Baptists], typewritten collection of articles [1984], pp. 59-60. EEKBLA. Võsu emphasised unifying factors also in his numerous oral presentations and reports.

religious practices only in the private sphere of life or inside the church walls.[2] Even there, worship was far from being free: the state prohibited unregistered worship meetings in private homes, interfered with the selection of church leaders and carefully kept an eye on sermon topics and the content of Baptist preaching.[3] In wider society, the churches and believers were marginalised and their life was continuously monitored. The UECBE leadership style and denominational structures, under the directions that came from the Soviet authorities and especially from the Council for Religious Affairs, became more centralised – at times even hierarchical – when compared to traditional Estonian free church patterns in the pre-war period. This was a severe distortion of Baptist ecclesiological identity. Cultural-political factors played a more formative role in shaping a religious identity than believers themselves realised. Also, in Soviet Estonia several church activities became impossible, such as public mission and social ministries. Estonian Baptists, who shared the main distinctives found in the wider evangelical world,[4] often expressed themselves through their activism, and the restriction of their mission was a serious blow to their identity. Nevertheless, this study has also shown that Baptists in Estonia were not passive objects under the 'hammer' of Soviet religious persecution. Baptist identity found ways through the wall of atheistic restrictions, though it could not always be fully expressed and though the identity itself was inevitably changed in this process. This study adds weight to the case that there is no uniform Baptist identity.[5]

There were different ways in which Estonian Baptists reacted to the external pressures. In some cases they were forced to give up elements of their

---

[2] See Philip Walters, 'A Survey of Soviet religious policy', in Sabrina P. Ramet, ed., *Religious Policy in the Soviet Union* (Cambridge and New York: Cambridge University Press, 1993), p. 13; Jaanus Plaat, *Usuliikumised, kirikud ja vabakogudused Lääne- ja Hiiumaal: usuühenduste muutumisprotsessid 18. sajandi keskpaigast kuni 20. sajandi lõpuni* [Religious Movements, Churches and Free Churches in West-Estonia and Hiiumaa Island: Transformational Processes of Religious Entities from the mid-18th Century to the End of the 20th Century] (Tartu: Eesti Rahva Muuseum, 2001), pp. 186-190.

[3] The reports from local Soviet government offices, now preserved in the archives in the Ministry of Internal Affairs of the Estonian Republic, in Tallinn, give a good overview of Baptist preaching themes and how the Soviet officials interpreted the sermon messages.

[4] For the basic distinctives of evangelicalism, see David W. Bebbington, *Evangelicalism in Modern Britain. A History from the 1730s to the 1980s* (Grand Rapids, Michigan: Baker Book House, 1992), pp. 2-18; Kenneth J. Collins, *The Evangelical Moment: The Promise of an American Religion* (Grand Rapids, Michigan: Baker Academic, 2005), pp. 41-60.

[5] For more see Ian Randall, Toivo Pilli and Anthony R. Cross, eds., *Baptist Identities: International Studies from the Seventeenth to the Twentieth Centuries* (Milton Keynes: Paternoster, 2006).

identity. In other cases they waited until they could revive some of the patterns of their faith tradition. Thus, after twenty years of waiting they were able to revive collective leadership: the Presbyters' Council and all-Estonian ECB conferences were able to begin functioning again in the 1960s. In 1975 (to take another example) permission was finally given to publish an ECB hymnal, after decades in which the Soviet authorities evaded the issue or postponed making a decision. The hymnal was an important tool for congregational singing, which was essential for the expression of ECB identity in worship. Singing created a sense of belonging together.[6]

In some cases, Baptists made efforts to get round external restrictions. Youth and children's work – though semi-illegal and in Soviet years never officially permitted – was cautiously revived in the 1970s, often under the guise of birthday parties or family evenings. New and bolder methods of evangelism emerged, together with a wave of charismatic renewal, which centred in Tallinn Oleviste ECB church. Needless to say, many activities that strengthened identity were severely handicapped, such as literature production and theological education. However, it is surprising how much energy Estonian Baptists put into publishing semi-illegal typewritten publications and how persistent they were in organising informal study groups, especially in the 1970s and 1980s. There was considerably more creativity exhibited by evangelical believers in Estonia in maintaining their faith practices and values than some Western authors have suggested when analysing church life in the Soviet Union.[7] Not every generalisation which was relevant for Soviet Baptists was applicable to Baptists in particular republics such as Estonia.

Nonetheless, Soviet atheistic persecution of churches hindered Estonian Baptists from expressing their full identity. It also suppressed some of the latent potential present within the free church traditions. For example, before the Second World War some Estonian Baptists had made attempts to be involved in the political sphere of life. The Baptist leader Karl Kaups was a member of the Estonian Parliament from 1938-1940.[8] After 1945, this dimension, expressing socio-political responsibility in Estonian Baptist life, was ruthlessly cut off, and, as has been argued here, was never fully recovered – even when new freedoms arrived at the beginning of the 1990s. Estonian Baptists were slow to find inner motivation for political activity. Soviet shadows, and a

---

[6] Steven James Pierson, 'We Sang Ourselves Free: Developmental Uses of Music Among Estonian Christians From Repression to Independence', PhD dissertation (Deerfield, Illinois: Trinity International University, 1998), pp. 85-87.

[7] See, for example, Walter Kolarz, *Religion in the Soviet Union* (London and New York: Macmillan and St. Martin's Press, 1961), especially pp. 283-321; Michael Bourdeaux, *Religious Ferment in Russia. Protestant Opposition to Soviet Religious Policy* (London and New York: Macmillan and St. Martin's Press, 1968).

[8] Karl Kaups, 'Mineviku teedel' [On the Ways of the Past], in *Põllu Vagudel* [On the Furrows of the Fields], no. 31 (1966), pp. 92-103.

pietistic and individual-orientated theology, created an impression that believers could do little in society.[9] Similar processes also occurred in the area of social ministry. In Soviet years social help could not be formally organised by believers, though mutual support within the church community was an inseparable part of ECB identity. At the end of the 1980s, when the churches could expand their activities outside the church walls, social care and humanitarian aid projects were often initiated by Estonian Baptists' foreign partners rather than growing out of initiatives by Estonians themselves. There were some notable exceptions: a small prison ministry as well as a social foundation, Sõbra Käsi (A Friend's Hand), survived the test of time.[10] However, the effects of the external pressures continued significantly longer than the pressurizing factors themselves.

Chapters 2-5 of this research offer a periodisation of Estonian Baptist history from 1945 until 1991. The first period, 1945-1959, was characterised by several adjustments on the part of the UECBE to the new political situation. Estonian ECB believers had to learn how to survive in a hostile context, and had to find a method of communication with the governmental authorities, especially with the Commissioner of the CARC.[11] Moreover, ways of relating to the AUCECB, an ecclesial structure for the evangelicals in the whole of the Soviet Union, had to be established.[12] Estonians tried to maintain respectful and friendly relations, but with Nordic stubbornness were never fully obedient to all the orders they received – either those from the local Commissioner of the CARC or those from the AUCECB headquarters in Moscow. This kind of passive resistance helped to maintain local Estonian Baptist identity, even if changes in practice and theology were inevitable. The sources used in this study clearly show that Estonian evangelical believers were more concerned about losing their religious-denominational identity than they were about losing their national identity through being merged into the All-Soviet and Russian-speaking structures.

---

[9] At the end of the 1990s this attitude gradually began to change. In 1998 the Eesti Kristlik Rahvapartei (Estonian Christian People's Party), from 2006 Eesti Kristlikud Demokraadid (Estonian Christian Democrats), was established, and Baptists were involved in the activities of this political party.

[10] For further discussion, see chapter "'Mul oli nälg ja te andsite mulle süüa'": vabakogudused ja sotsiaalne vastutus' ['"I Was Hungry and You Fed Me": Free Churches and Social Responsibility'], in Toivo Pilli, *Usu värvid ja varjundid: Eesti vabakoguduste ajaloost ja identiteedist* [Shades and Colours of Faith: About Estonian Free Church History and Identity] (Tallinn: Allika, 2007), pp. 125-155.

[11] See also Otto Luchterhandt, 'The Council for Religious Affairs', in Ramet, ed., *Religious Policy in the Soviet Union*, pp. 57-58.

[12] For the early stages of the AUCECB see Walter Sawatsky, *Soviet Evangelicals Since World War II* (Kitchener, Ontario: Herald Press, 1981), pp. 78-104.

The second period, 1959-1972, consigned Estonian Baptists to an era of lethargy. Khrushchev's atheistic campaign, which affected Estonian ECB believers from approximately 1959 to 1964, imprisoned local churches and the ECB union alike within a 'still life' canvas. In the early 1960s, even the local Estonian Senior Presbyter's post was liquidated. It was only re-established after Khrushchev was removed from his position as the leader of the Soviet Union. However, it was not the severe atheistic campaign itself, but rather the Estonian Baptist response to it that has been the main focus of interest in this volume. By the mid-1960s, Estonian Baptists to an extent accepted their position as 'second-class citizens'. They kept a low profile and concentrated on 'keeping the positions'. Nevertheless, the 'still life' was 'still a life'. Though the general mentality of Estonian Baptists was rather passive in these years, there were signs of some developments in church life: conferences and church anniversaries were used as opportunities for strengthening believers' fellowship – a traditional aspect of Estonian Baptist identity. Some Estonian authors, such as Jaanus Plaat, have argued from statistical data that constant decline characterised Estonian churches.[13] This research has sought to go beyond statistics since the state of a religious movement cannot be determined only through sociological and statistical approaches, although these are important.

In the third period, from 1972 to 1985, Estonian Baptist life recovered from its general paralysis and a new evangelistic thrust was evident. Undoubtedly charismatic spirituality from and via Finland, strengthening the historic Pentecostal and Revivalist undercurrents in UECBE identity, played a role. A charismatically-orientated youth movement that emerged in Tallinn became known as the Effataa revival. Its message and spirituality spread in Estonia and beyond – in the wider Soviet Union. This is a phenomenon that has not yet been adequately analysed.[14] Evangelistic youth worship services and youth camps were organised in a number of ECB churches in Estonia. While in Soviet society the period has been described as one of political 'stagnation', Baptist churches, in contrast, developed an active music ministry and strengthened their evangelistic efforts, even if statistically they continued to register decline. Though reliable data is lacking, it is probable that the 1970s and early 1980s were the highest point in Estonian Baptist activism in

---

[13] Jaanus Plaat, 'Eesti vabakoguduste vastupanu nõukogude religioonipoliitikale võrreldes luterliku ja õigeusu kirikuga (1944-1987)' [The Resistance of Estonian Free Churches to Soviet Religious Policies, in Comparison with Lutheran and Orthodox Churches (1944-1987)], in Toivo Pilli, ed., *Teekond teisenevas ajas: peatükke Eesti baptismi ajaloost* [A Journey in Changing Time: Chapters from the History of Estonian Free Churches] (Tartu: Kõrgem Usuteaduslik Seminar ja Sõnasepp OÜ, 2005), pp. 128-159.

[14] The 'standard' ECB history, published in Moscow in 1989, is silent about this phenomenon. See *Istorija evangel'skih hristjan-baptistov v SSSR* [History of Evangelical Christians-Baptists in the USSR] (Moskva: Izdanije VSEHB, 1989), pp. 343-345, 347-348.

'publishing' *samizdat* typewritten literature.[15] In addition, informal theological study groups helped to resist the worst results of atheistic pressure and to maintain some vital elements of Baptist theological identity. Though church life was far from normal – atheistic propaganda continued and contacts abroad were hindered – the 'otherness' of the Baptist faith was attractive to many from a younger generation who were disappointed by empty communist rhetoric. While Estonian Baptists did not attempt public opposition to Soviet policies, as the Russian Reform Baptists did, silent disagreement with the atheistic system existed – through lifestyle, upholding of values and, sometimes, through giving help to 'underground' believers.

The fourth period, from 1985 until 1991, takes in the emerging emphasis on *perestroika*, a relative liberalisation in the interpretation and implementation of restrictive religious legislation, and other changes that took place in the period of Gorbachev's leadership of the USSR.[16] Estonian Baptists used the new freedoms to revive some aspects of their traditional identity. For example, at last permission was given to re-establish a theological seminary. The traditional Baptist focus on the written word found its expression once more in increasing publishing activity, now officially permitted. Though excitement about public opportunities for organised Christian witness meant that lifestyle witness and personal evangelism tended to move to the background, at least for a while, the new context offered opportunities for a long-cherished commitment to evangelism to be expressed more fully in Baptist life. Mass evangelism, involving some large-scale events at the beginning of the 1990s, was a part of the picture. However, decades of external pressure unquestionably had their effect. The Baptist voice in wider society – regarding such issues as social ethics, politics or national identity – remained muted and cautious.

THE INTERNAL DYNAMICS OF IDENTITY

Chapters 6-9 of this book deal with the complex influences of different theological trends within the UECBE. The constitutive role of these internal forces has been analysed in these chapters under four main subtopics: views on the new birth and ecclesiology, the dynamics of Word and Spirit, the concept and practice of evangelism and mission, and the topic of ethical reasoning and the understanding of sanctification. In some areas all four free church traditions which continued within the merged ECB union held common views. For example, evangelism was predominantly understood as verbal proclamation, which should 'lead a person to Christ', to a spiritual conversion. Also in their emphasis on an ethical life, sometimes interpreted in a rather narrow, even

---

[15] Riho Saard has pursued research on *samizdat* literature, but the results have not been published so far.

[16] Sabrina P. Ramet, 'Religious Policy in the era of Gorbachev', in Ramet, ed., *Religious Policy in the Soviet Union*, pp. 31-52.

legalistic way, the general perspective of the four traditions was similar. Nevertheless, certain distinctive emphases can be identified. There were substantial differences of thinking within the union in the fields of ecclesiology and pneumatology. In their understanding of sanctification those within the Evangelical Christian tradition tended to define the 'borders' of the Christian life and of what was acceptable in very clearly defined detail. Certainly, Evangelical Christian views of sanctification left their mark on UECBE spirituality and identity.

Theological nuances emerged also in the writings of individual theologians, such as Robert Võsu, Osvald Tärk and Oskar Olvik. Their influence, through their personal contacts and writings which were translated into Russian, reached beyond Estonia.[17] Alexei Bychkov, a long-time General Secretary of the AUCECB, commented that Tärk was loved and highly respected in the ECB churches in the Soviet Union, in Russia, Ukraine, and other places.[18] Robert Võsu, a systematic writer, sometimes brought into theological discussions themes and approaches which sounded innovative for Estonian Baptists. In his book *Evangeelne eetika* (Evangelical Ethics) Võsu challenged his readers to reflect upon an ethical approach to the created world, to work-relations and to the economy. In a context in which ethics and sanctification were understood mostly in individual terms, 'as growing in Christian maturity and increasing in personal holiness',[19] this was unusual. Indeed, sometimes Võsu's views did not express the general theological understanding of the churches, but were rather a challenge to 'grassroots theology'. However, in the majority of his writings Võsu's approach was pastoral and was aimed at the edification of his readers. His *Isiklik evangelism* (Personal Evangelism) was a practical handbook which was designed to help believers in their witness.

Osvald Tärk was a theologian who was well aware of his responsibility as a spiritual leader. His views were always well balanced and his authoritative voice offered guidance for many people in the UECBE. For Estonian Baptist theological identity, Tärk's exegetical works as well as his series of articles 'Meie vendluse põhimõtted' (Principles of Our Brotherhood) were crucially important. Influenced by Reformed theology as well as by Anglo-American

---

[17] For example, exegetical works on the Books of Ephesians, Romans and on the Gospel of Mark, by Osvald Tärk, were translated into Russian. Also explanation on the Sermon on the Mount as well as other works by Robert Võsu were also translated into Russian. In 2005 a two volume set of translated works by Tärk was printed in Moscow. O.A. Tärk [Tjark], *Izbrannye trudy* [Selected Works], vols. 1-2 (Moskva: Izdanie Sojuza EHB Rossii, 2005).

[18] Ruudi Leinus, comp. and ed., *Osvald Tärk. Uskuge Jumalasse* [Osvald Tärk. Believe in God] (Tallinn: Eesti EKB Liit, 1999), p. 59.

[19] Roger E. Olson, *The Westminster Handbook to Evangelical Theology* (Louisville and London: Westminster John Knox Press, 2004), p. 263.

revivalism,[20] Tärk has sometimes been viewed in popular opinion in the churches as if he were the only theologian who shaped Estonian Baptist self-understanding.[21] This was not the case. In the light of what is set out in this study, both Robert Võsu and Oskar Olvik should not be forgotten.

Oskar Olvik – who had studied theology in the Protestant theological faculty of Tartu University – was a respected pastor and a theologian whose positions often contained pietistic overtones. Together with his colleagues, he contributed considerably to ECB theological identity in Estonia. In some areas, such as in interpreting the meaning of God's Kingdom and partly even in his understanding of baptism, his views reflected the Protestant thinking of the first half of the twentieth century. The Schleiermacherian tradition (with its initial influences in the nineteenth century) also had an impact on Olvik, who emphasised the 'centrality of Jesus Christ' and the 'living witness of the religious life', to use pertinent quotes from a book on the kind of Protestant thought that influenced Olvik.[22]

To highlight the role of these three theologians is not to imply that these were the only voices. There were pastors and theologians such as Aleksander Sildos, Efraim Joel Dahl, Jüri Puusaag amongst others who contributed to theological discussions, though they were less systematic in their writings and argumentations. As to written theology, writers from Evangelical Christian and Baptist traditions in Estonia were particularly productive, probably because a number of their leaders were trained in theology before the Soviet era.[23] Pentecostal and Revivalist Free traditions had their theological nuances, but as a rule these remained in the form of sermons – in oral rather than in written form.

Whilst Estonian Evangelical Christian and Baptist identities, brought together in the UECBE, were similar in many respects, they differed significantly in the field of ecclesiology. Estonian Baptist convictions about closed membership and closed communion, rooted in the pre-war period, were unpalatable to Evangelical Christians. Evangelical Christians, historically coming from the background of Lutheran pietism, saw no problem in accepting into church membership persons who were baptised as infants but who had experienced spiritual renewal later in life. Together with the wider evangelical

---

[20] Leinus, comp. and ed., *Osvald Tärk. Uskuge Jumalasse*, pp. 29, 33.

[21] There are a number of books by Tärk that were published after 1990, as well as several memoirs by relatives, colleagues and church members. The number of printed pages by and about Võsu and Olvik, published during the last 15-20 years, is considerably smaller.

[22] John Dillenberger and Claude Welch, *Protestant Christianity: Interpreted Through its Development* (New York and Toronto: Macmillan Publishing Company, 1988), pp. 192-193.

[23] Toivo Pilli, 'Finding a Balance between Church and Academia: Baptist Theological Education in Estonia', *Religion in Eastern Europe*, vol. XXVI, no. 3 (August 2006), pp. 21-29.

world, Estonian Evangelical Christians emphasised conversion or the new birth
as the crucial sign of a believer. Baptists, as they saw it, added 'another door' to
church membership, and consequently to communion – baptism by immersion
on profession of faith by the baptismal candidate. Evangelical Christians, in
contrast to the 'German' Baptist tradition deriving from Oncken, were in favour
of open membership and open communion. On these issues Pentecostals and
Revivalist Free churches tended to side with the Baptists. Gradually, the
traditional Baptist elements of ecclesiology came to prevail in the UECBE.
Some changes also took place in worship. The more enthusiastic worship style
of Pentecostals and Revivalist Free churches moderated over the years, though
new charismatic worship within the UECBE in the 1970s revived some
traditional Pentecostal elements. Estonian Baptist identity was not fixed; it
developed over the years of the Soviet period, in mutual interaction with the
evangelical faith-patterns within the UECBE.

Another field where the dynamics of theological identity found expression
was the understanding of the roles of the Bible and the Spirit. Estonian Baptists
had their roots not only in the German Baptist movement but also in Anglo-
American revivalism which was pneumatologically more open. While biblical
preaching and sincere trust in the Bible were inseparable parts of all the
Estonian free church traditions, there were notable variations depending on
whether the emphasis was put on the written Word or on the work of the Spirit.
Immediately after the Second World War, in times of confusion and turmoil,
the newly formed UECBE found stability in focusing on the written Word.
There was a common belief which united different 'wings' in the UECBE.
Shared with a wider conservative Protestantism, there was confidence that the
Bible offered solid foundations for faith and conduct.[24] But Pentecostal and
Revivalist Free traditions, which appreciated the emotional and experiential
side of the work of the Spirit, found it difficult to understand the more cerebral
approach that tended to characterise traditional Baptist and Evangelical
Christian theological thinking. The charismatic tendencies of the 1970s and
1980s played their role in this dynamic of Word and Spirit. Estonian Baptists
had never denied the importance of the Spirit, but some charismatic tendencies
posed new questions. The Effataa movement, advocating as it did the direct
guidance of the Spirit and miraculous powers, challenged the identity of the
UECBE. Manifestations of the Spirit invaded public worship; in earlier times
they were restricted to private spirituality. Generally, Estonian Baptists lacked
wider theological perspectives on issues related to Word and Spirit. Their focus
on the authority of the Bible tended to take the form of literal interpretation,
with a sincere aim of putting the words of the Bible into practice. Gifts of the
Spirit were discussed, but – for example – the role of the Spirit in relation to the

---

[24] For the 'foundationalist' character of theological understanding, see Stanley Grenz
and John Francke, *Beyond Foundationalism: Shaping Theology in Postmodern Context*
(Louisville, Kentucky: Westminster John Knox Press, 2001), pp. 28-37.

other persons of the Trinity did not receive much attention. Nevertheless, a pneumatologically-orientated spirituality was a strand in the UECBE, and was re-confirmed in the 1970s.

During the Soviet years, Estonian Baptists unanimously agreed about the evangelistic calling of the church; that, as Roger Olson has described the convictions of evangelical believers, proclamation of the gospel 'in order to facilitate conversions' to faith in Christ is vitally important.[25] This linked Estonian Baptists (even when they were politically cut off) to the wider evangelical world, which – inspired by Pietism and the spirituality of awakenings – stressed the experience of saving faith and the spread of the gospel message.[26] However, this study has shown that the evangelistic methods used by Estonian Baptists were many-fold. In general, Baptist evangelism, deriving from a revivalist evangelistic tradition, was 'meeting-driven'. Revival weeks as a method, however, quickly lost their social basis. In an atheistic society people soon lacked the 'religious language' and knowledge of Christian basics for such a methodology to be successful. Reacting to this situation, personal evangelism was promoted by Robert Võsu. Tallinn 'Kalju' Church focused on fellowship as a context for gradual growth towards personal religious convictions, a method which is characterised now as beginning with 'belonging'.[27] The Effataa movement highlighted the power of the Spirit in evangelism. There was also a stress on rationally trustworthy biblical arguments. Much of the emphasis was individual. Personal redemption from sin was taught, but practically no reflection occurred on how the gospel could transform the structures of society. Yet the focus on evangelistic commitment was, despite variations and some lack of depth, an important factor which helped to unify and tie together different historical undercurrents in the union.

The fourth important internal area was concerned with ethics; in Estonian Baptist terminology 'sanctification'. Baptists in Estonia were convinced that signs of a transformed life, 'good fruits', had to accompany a believer's spiritual journey in the world. Believers were to be 'salt' and 'light' (Matthew 5:13-16). The dynamic in this field was not so much between different historical free church traditions but rather between different theological emphases which could appear in all four traditions. For example, there were attempts to find deeper unity with Christ, an approach which had mystical features. Some believers used the language of 'life through the death of the old self' to describe the process of sanctification. There was an emphasis on the

---

[25] Olson, *The Westminster Handbook to Evangelical Theology*, p. 175.

[26] For a wider background, see W.R. Ward, *The Protestant Evangelical Awakening* (Cambridge: Cambridge University Press, 1992); Mark Noll, *The Rise of Evangelicalism: The Age of Edwards, Whitefield and the Wesleys* (Leicester: Inter-Varsity Press, 2004).

[27] For a helpful discussion on 'believing' and 'belonging' (and 'behaving') see Stuart Murray, *Church after Christendom* (Milton Keynes: Paternoster Press, 2004), pp. 10-38.

help of the Holy Spirit in sanctification. In general, there was a tendency to establish clear normative rules. Some theologians, nevertheless, emphasised character formation, thus representing virtue ethics rather than rule ethics.[28] A combination of different approaches and different 'languages of sanctification' characterised the ethical search of Estonian Baptists in the Soviet years. Nevertheless, a specific feature of the period studied was the response to the context of persecution. Maintaining trust and relationships of integrity in the believers' community became an important ethical challenge. The Estonian Baptist concept of sanctification, no doubt deriving inspiration from the earlier free church traditions in Estonia, tended to be concerned with individual spiritual and ethical development. The role of ethics in the communal life of the church – decision-making processes or leadership styles, for example – was less important for Estonian Baptists. But the community was present in Estonian Baptist ethical identity: it shaped individual ethics especially through the exercise of church discipline. At the heart of the sanctified life, in Estonian Baptist thinking, was the desire for deeper Christ-likeness.

THE WIDER CONTEXT

Throughout this volume references have been made to theological influences which shaped, or at least coloured, Estonian Baptist self-understanding during the Soviet years. These influences came mostly via literature, but sometimes also through personal contacts. Estonian Baptists in the Soviet years found inspiration from a variety of sources. Although this study could not cover the full scale of this literature and the contacts made, one conclusion can safely be drawn – the sources utilised were far from being exclusively Baptist. Thus the identity was not narrowly denominational. This conclusion has implications for research into Baptist life in other regions in Eastern Europe. The Estonian Baptist movement was a 'mixed bag', not only because of the merger which took place after the Second World War, but also because of a certain openness to theological ideas reaching Estonia from beyond its political and theological borders. I have sought to place Estonian Baptist movement within a broader picture, correcting an earlier imbalance in the historiography.[29]

---

[28] Mari Vahermägi, 'Vooruslikkusest pühitsuselus Osvald Tärgi ja Robert Võsu kirjapärandi valgel' [About Virtues in Sanctification in the Light of the Literary Heritage of Osvald Tärk and Robert Võsu], in Pilli, ed., *Teekond teisenevas ajas*, pp. 160-180.

[29] During Soviet years, Robert Võsu, himself a church historian and Baptist leader, often presented Estonian Baptist history as a part of the Soviet ECB story. However, for political reasons, it was almost impossible to explore more deeply the relations (including differences) of Slavic and Estonian Baptists. Rather, Võsu placed the two stories side by side, and gave information about the Slavic ECB movement for the edification of Estonian believers. This helped Estonians to understand the Soviet ECB

One area from which Estonian Baptist believers found spiritual inspiration was wider evangelicalism, especially Anglo-American revivalism, which 'personalised' and 'emotionalised' religion, as Richard Kyle has argued.[30] Thus this volume contributes to the wider study of evangelicalism, study which has so far focused more on the English-speaking world.[31] Charles G. Finney and Reuben A. Torrey were well-known names among Estonian free church believers in the first half of the twentieth century and their ideas continued to be referred to in Soviet times. As D.L. Moody's 'brand of Evangelicalism ... spread over the globe',[32] it is not surprising to find signs of its influence also in Estonia. Also Andrew Murray's teaching on 'abiding in Christ' inspired Estonian believers – specifically in their search for a deeper devotional life. Stanley Jones' interpretation of the Sermon on the Mount was highly valued among Estonian Baptists.

As Scandinavia is Estonia's neighbour, it is only to be expected that ideas and literature from this area reached Estonian believers. For example, a free church evangelist and writer Frank Mangs gave simple, 'easy to read' guidance for Christian life and witness. Finnish Pentecostal Niilo-Yli Vainio became a popular name in the 1970s in the ECB churches in Estonia. This period also saw the 'invasion into Estonia' of some other authors, either related to church growth or the charismatic movement or both: for example Yonggi Cho, a successful Korean Pentecostal pastor, and Larry Christenson, an American charismatic preacher and writer from Lutheran background. This is not to say that more traditional Baptist perspectives were absent. Contacts with German Baptists were revived at the end of the 1970s, when some Estonians began to study in the Buckow Baptist Theological Seminary. Also, Baptist figures such as Johann G. Oncken, Charles H. Spurgeon and Billy Graham were in many ways 'icons' of Estonian Baptist identity. However, any attempt to impose a 'pure' Baptist model on Estonian Baptist identity would be unfruitful.

There was also another wider theological context from which Estonian Baptists drew ideas. Some Estonian Baptist authors were encouraged by the

---

context where they now belonged, but rarely invited them to analyse their own identity in the light of the Slavic background. See [Robert Võsu,] *Baptistide arengust ja põhimõtetest* [About the Development and Principles of Baptists], typewritten manuscript [1966]. Merike Uudam's personal library.

[30] Richard Kyle, *Evangelicalism: An Americanized Christianity* (New Brunswick and London: Transactions Publishers, 2006), p. 34.

[31] Mark Noll, *American Evangelical Christianity: An Introduction* (Oxford: Blackwell Publishers, 2001); David W. Bebbington, *The Dominance of Evangelicalism: The Age of Spurgeon and Moody* (Leicester: Inter-Varsity Press, 2005); Richard Carwardine, *Transatlantic Revivalism: Popular Evangelicalism in Britain and America, 1790-1865* (Milton Keynes: Paternoster, 2006).

[32] David W. Bebbington, 'Moody as a Transatlantic Evangelical', in Timothy George, ed., *Mr. Moody and the Evangelical Tradition* (London and New York: T. & T. Clark International, 2004), p. 92.

Reformed theologian Karl Barth, especially his emphasis on the sovereignty of God, on God as subject. Robert Võsu admitted his theological debt to the Estonian Lutheran theologian, Elmar Salumaa. Some Lutheran-Moravian spirituality also continued to live on in Evangelical Christian circles, though this requires further research to clarify the details of this source of influence. Also, though to a lesser extent, some recent Roman Catholic authors offered stimulus in theological reflection, in spite of the fact that access to theological literature was difficult. Hans Küng, for example, was a name known in Estonia, though the influence of his ideas was limited to a comparatively small group of Baptist pastors and students of theology. Contacts with the ideas of Protestant and Catholic authors, sometimes critically explored, sometimes welcomed wholeheartedly, widened Estonian Baptist theological horizons and 'forced' them to reflect upon Baptist theological core elements.[33] Interest in theological education – an inherent part of Estonian Baptist identity – helped Estonian Baptist theologians and pastors to be open to different ideas, and to absorb and select theological input according to local Baptist values. Baptist theological reflection sometimes remained narrow, reconfirming traditional emphases rather than exploring new venues, but the effort to explore more widely cannot be denied. The parts of this book dealing with Estonian Baptist theological identity can offer perspectives for research into theological thought in Estonia.[34]

The UECBE was a part of the AUCECB, the All-Russian Baptist structure. This offered another context for the Estonian union. However, Russian ECB influence on Estonians was more in the field of organisational and leadership structures and much less in the field of theological identity. Russian evangelical influence was certainly significant in Russian-speaking churches in Estonia, which used elements of Slavic Baptist worship style and had much easier access to Christian literature in the Russian language, scarce as it was during Soviet times. As to Estonians, there is no doubt that their vision was broadened by the fact that the small Estonian union became a part of a larger ecclesial body. This added confidence to Estonians, but cultural

---

[33] Contacts with Orthodox theology were practically lacking, as far as written sources show. This route of theological discussion has recently been opened among British evangelicals as well as at the Baptist International Theological Seminary in Prague. See Ian Randall, ed., *Baptists and the Orthodox Church: On the Way to Understanding* (Prague: International Baptist Theological Seminary, 2003); *Evangelicalism and the Orthodox Church: A Report by the Evangelical Alliance Commission on Unity and Truth among Evangelicals* (London: ACUTE, 2001). In Estonia, during the Soviet years, Baptists made no effort to invite anyone representing Orthodox theology and practice to be conversation partners.

[34] Some significant steps in exploring theological thought in Estonia, although focusing mostly in the Protestant area, have recently been taken. See Riho Altnurme, ed., *Eesti teoloogilise mõtlemise ajaloost: sissejuhatavaid märkusi ja apokrüüfe* [History of Theological Thought in Estonia: Introductiory Remarks and Apocrypha] (Tartu: Tartu Ülikooli Kirjastus, 2006).

differences also led them to pursue their own pathways. For example, whereas there were those within the Estonian Baptist tradition who adopted a Pentecostal-Charismatic outlook, Russian-Slavic Baptists within the AUCECB were suspicious of charismatic expressions of faith. Estonians were often more active in finding ways to maintain or revive some ministries which were part of their identity: children's and youth work was revived much sooner than in the official ECB churches in Russia. There were certainly common values shared by Estonian and Slavic Baptists related to general evangelical identity. Also Estonians appreciated the Slavic 'close to the Bible' preaching style. However, I would argue that it is important in studying Soviet evangelical life to recognise that there were specific regional variations in identity.

CONCLUSION

The Estonian Baptists during the Soviet years developed their own unique identity. This had similarities with both Western and Slavic Baptists, but it cannot be identified fully with either of these. The historical context, the nature of the atheistic pressures, specific theological preferences, the mutual influences of the evangelical traditions within the UECBE – all of these factors contributed to a development which resulted in the 'Estonian way of being a Baptist'. The Soviet period was a melting pot in which the religious identity of Estonian Baptists was shaped and re-shaped. The 'ingredients' of a new identity were offered by the four free church traditions which were merged into one union in 1945-1947. A complex set of elements – both external and internal – contributed to the process of identity formation. What was the result? A new combination of characteristics emerged; yet these were rooted in the evangelical tradition and expressed a certain sense of consistency, which allowed the Estonian ECB union to continue without splitting apart after political freedom arrived. The Estonian Baptist experience during the Soviet years demonstrates that the shaping of Baptist identity is a dynamic process in which features of the cultural and political context, as well as the theological heritage and the search for an authentic spiritual life, all play their different parts. In the Estonian case, what emerged was a Baptist identity which was a mosaic, something multicoloured rather than monochrome, appreciating its historic roots but at the same time able to integrate a variety of elements from the wider evangelical tradition of which it was a part.

BIBLIOGRAPHY

ARCHIVE MATERIALS

Kõrgema Usuteadusliku Seminari arhiiv Tartus (KUSA) [Baptist Theological Seminary Archive, Tartu]

Eesti Baptisti Usuteaduse Seminari protokolliraamat 1920-1940 [Baptist Theological Seminary minute book 1920-1940].

Eesti Baptisti Usuühingu kirjavahetus 1945 (EBUKirj1945) [Estonian Baptist Union correspondence 1945].

Kalju Raidi kirjavahetus ja märkmed [Correspondence and notes of Kalju Raid].

Konsultatsioonide lindistusi 1981-1987. Nimistu. [Recordings of the consultation days 1981-1987. A list of topics.].

Olvik, Oskar, 'Koguduse siseseid ja -väliseid distsipliini küsimusi [Internal and Exernal Issues of Church Discipline] (11-13.05.1973), audiotape.

Tärk, Osvald, 'Abieluküsimusi: 1. Kor., 7. pt.' [Marriage Issues: 1. Cor., ch. 7), parts 1-3 (13.03.1981, 08.04.1981, 14.05.1981), audiotape.

Vanempresbüteri ja usuasjade voliniku kirjavahetus 1945-1966 (VpUvk1945-1966) [Correspondence of the Senior Presbyter and the Commissioner of the CARC 1945-1966].

Eesti Evangeeliumi Kristlaste ja Baptistide Koguduste Liidu arhiiv Tallinnas (EEKBLA) [The Archive of the Union of Evangelical Christian and Baptist Churches of Estonia, Tallinn, since 2004 in Tartu]

Aastakonverentsid 1989-1991 [Annual conferences 1989-1991].

EEKBL kirjavahetus usuasjade volinikuga 1966-1990 (KirjUv1966-1990) [The correspondence of the UECBE with the Commissioner of the CRA 1966-1990].

EKB vanempresbüteri aruanded (VpAruanded) [The UECBE Senior Presbyter's reports].

Evangeeliumi Kristlaste-Baptistide koguduste statistilised aruanded 1945-1963 [The UECBE statistical reports 1945-1963].

Evangeeliumi Kristlaste-Baptistide koguduste statistilised aruanded 1964-1990 [The UECBE statistical reports 1964-1990].

Evangeelsest tööst Maarjamaal (1988) [About Evangelistic Work in the Land of Mary (1988)].

Johannes Lipstoki raamatukogu kataloog (1958) [The list of books in Johannes Lipstok's library (1958)].

Juhatuse koosolekute protokollid (JKP) [Minutes of the Executive Board] (30.01.1981-12.12.1987).

Juhatuse koosolekute protokollid koos lisadega (JKPLis) [Minutes of the Executive Board, with attachments] (11.01.1988-02.03.1992).

Kaaskirjad koguduste 1976. a. aruandele [Explanatory letters attached to churches' 1976 reports].
Kirjavahetus EKBÜN-iga [Correspondence with the AUCECB].
Kirjavahetus ja dokumendid 1950-1974: 'Kalju' kogudus [Correspondence and documents 1950-1974: 'Kalju' Church].
Küsimused 1964. aasta aruande juurde [Questions attached to the 1964 report].
Osvald Tärgi materjalid [Materials of Osvald Tärk].
Presbüterite nõukogu protokollid 1969-1985 (PNProt1969-1985) [Minutes of the Presbyters' Council 1969-1985].
Revideerimisaktid 1956-1957 [Inspection reports 1956-1957].
Robert Võsu materjalid [Materials of Robert Võsu].

Nõukogude Sotsialistlike Vabariikide Liidu Ministrite Nõukogu juures asuva Usukultusasjade Nõukogu Voliniku ENSV-s arhiiv (1945-1990) Eesti Vabariigi Siseministeeriumis Tallinnas (UNVA) [The Archive of the Estonian Commissioner of the CRA at the Council of Ministers of the USSR (1945-1990), in the Ministry of Internal Affairs of the Estonian Republic]

Aruanded ja ülevaated kirikute tegevuse kohta ENSV-s 1971-1990 (AÜ1971-1990) [Reports and surveys about the activities of churches in the ESSR 1971-1990].
EKB Oleviste kogudus [The ECB Oleviste Church].
Kirjavahetus usukeskustega vabariigis 1977-1990 [Correspondence with religious centres in the republic 1977-1990].

Eesti Riigiarhiiv Tallinnas (ERA) [Estonian State Archives, Tallinn]

Usuasjade Volinik [The Commissioner of the CRA] R-1989.

Tartu 'Kolgata' Baptisti Koguduse arhiiv [Tartu 'Kolgata' Baptist Church Archive]

Tartu EKB koguduse sissetulnud kirjad 1945-1950 [Incoming correspondence of Tartu ECB church 1945-1950].

Toivo Pilli's personal archive

'Evangeeliumi Kristlaste Baptistide põhimõtted' [Principles of Evangelical Christians Baptists] (late 1980s?).
Dahl, Aita, interview notes (15.01.2001).
Jürma, Ermo, notes at Metsaküla retreat (07.02.1985).
Kahar, Marika, 'Muusikakursused Oleviste kirikus' [Music Courses at Oleviste Church] (n. p., n. d.).
Mäemets, Margus, private letter (12.04.2005).
Moskovskaja Bogoslovskaja Seminarija Evangel'skih Hristjan-Baptistov, leaflet (n. p., n. d.).
Peeter Võsu autobiograafia [Peeter Võsu's Autobiography], manuscript (1951), electronical version.
Puusaag, Jüri, private letter (16.08.2002).
Remmel, Aamo, private letter (26.01.2001).

Tuulik, Enno, private letter (20.02.2005).
Tammo, Joosep, e-mail message (09.10.2006).

Uudu Rips' personal archive

Lecture notes 1973-1978, notebook 1-3.

ORAL INFORMATION

Bychkov, Alexei, oral information (03.07.2000).
Lipping, Dimitri, oral information (21.03.2003).
Niilo, Aili, oral information (21.12.2003).
Meriloo, Ülo, telephone interview (08.06.2000).
Proos, Artur, oral information (20.08.2002).
Puusaag, Jüri, oral information (08.05.2003) .
Rips, Uudu, recorded interview (20.04.2000).
Roosimaa, Peeter, telephone interview (10.05.2003).
Roosimaa, Peeter, oral information (17.07.2002).
Tammo, Joosep, telephone intervew (25.05.2000).
Tammo, Joosep, oral information (10.07.2000).
Tammo, Raigo, oral information (13.05.2002).
Valk, Avo, telephone interview (18.05.2003).

THESES AND DISSERTATIONS

Bondareva, Irina, '"Separation or Cooperation?"': Moldavian Baptists, 1940-1965', MTh thesis (Prague: IBTS, 2004).
Kroll, Allan, 'Effataa ärkamine' [Effataa Revival], diploma thesis (Tallinn: EMKTS, 2006).
Mäemets, Margus, 'Kuressaare koguduse noortetöö 1970 kuni 2005 – ajalooline vaatenurk' [Youth Work in Kuressaare Church from 1970 to 2005: A Historical Perspective], diploma thesis (Tartu: Kõrgem Usuteaduslik Seminar, 2006).
Paldre, Ene, 'Ühislaulu areng ja tähendus EKB Liidu kogudustes' [Development and Meaning of Communal Singing in the UECBE Churches], BTh thesis (Tartu: Tartu University, 2001).
Pierson, Steven James, 'We Sang Ourselves Free: Developmental Uses of Music among Estonian Christians from Repression to Independence', PhD dissertation (Deerfield, Illinois: Trinity International University, 1998).
Pilli, Toivo, 'Eesti baptistid ja nende teoloogilise mõtte kajastumine ajakirjas *Teekäija* kuni 1940' [Estonian Baptists and their Theology as Reflected in *Teekäija* until 1940], ThM thesis (Tartu: Tartu University, 1996).
Rahkema, Eerik, 'Johannes Lipstok kui vaimulik juht' [Johannes Lipstok as a Spiritual Leader], diploma thesis (Tartu: Kõrgem Usuteaduslik Seminar, 2002).
Raitila, Jyrki, 'History of Evangelicalism and the Present Spiritual Situation in Estonia', MA thesis (Providence Theological Seminary, 1996).
Remmel, Atko, 'Ateismi ajaloost Eestis (XIX sajandi lõpust kuni aastani 1989)' [The History of Atheism in Estonia (From the End of the Nineteenth Century to 1989)],

.ThM thesis (Tartu: Tartu University, 2004).

Ritsbek, Heigo, 'The Mission of Methodism in Estonia', project thesis (Boston: Boston University, 1996).

Saard, Riho, 'Baptismi Viron ja Pohjois-Liivinmaan kuvernementeissa 1865-1920' [The Baptist Movement in the Provinces of Estonia and Northern-Livonia 1865-1920], pro gradu thesis (Helsinki: Helsinki University, 1994).

Steeves, Paul D., 'The Russian Baptist Union, 1917-1935: Evangelical Awakening in Russia', PhD dissertation (University of Kansas, 1976).

Tamm, Priit, 'Eesti Metodisti Kirik 1940-1980: Vaatlusi olulisematele arengut mõjutanud protsessidele ja probleemidele' [Estonian Methodist Church 1940-1980: Observations about Major Problems and Processes which Influenced its Development], BTh thesis (Tartu: Tartu University, 1998).

Valk, Tõnis, 'Eesti Evangeeliumi Kristlaste-Baptistide Liidu ja riigivõimu suhted aastatel 1953-1964' [The Relationship between the State Authorities and the Union of Evangelical Christians-Baptists of Estonia during 1953-1964], diploma thesis (Tartu: Kõrgem Usuteaduslik Seminar, 2003).

Vertšerkovskaja, Oksana, 'Vene baptisti koguduste teke ja areng Eesti Evangeeliumi Kristlaste ja Baptistide Koguduste Liidu ajaloo taustal' [The Beginnings and Development of Russian Baptist Churches in the Background of UECBE History], diploma thesis (Tartu: Kõrgem Usuteaduslik Seminar, 1999).

Viise, Michael, 'The Estonian Evangelical Lutheran Church During the Soviet Period 1940-1991', PhD dissertation (University of Virginia, 1995).

UNPUBLISHED PRIMARY SOURCES – BOOKS AND BOOKLETS

Ader, Ernst, *Eesti usuajalugu, VIII: Läänemaa ärkamine ja selle tagajärgi* [Estonian Faith History, VIII: West Coast Revival and its Consequences], typewritten manuscript (n. p., n. d.). TPL.

'Baptismi ajalugu' [History of Baptists], typewritten collection of articles [1984]. EEKBLA.

Cho, Yonggi, *Loov usk* [Creative Faith], Estonian translation, typewritten manuscript (n. p., n. d.). TPL.

Dahl, Efraim Joel, *Evangeeliumi kristlate-baptistide tõekspidamistest* [About the Principles of the Evangelical Christians-Baptists], typewritten manuscript (n. p., n. d.). TPL.

Dahl, Efraim Joel, *Evangeelse maailma radadel. Pühitsus Piiblis ja ajaloos* [On the Paths of the Evangelical World: Sanctification in the Bible and in History], typewritten manuscript (Tallinn, 1976). KUSA.

Dahl, Efraim Joel, *Usutervistamine Piiblis, algkristluses ja tänapäeval* [Healing through Faith: In the Bible, Early Christianity and Today], typewritten manuscript (1980?). KUSA.

Eesti EKB koguduste presbüterite konverents Tallinnas, 15.-18. veebruaril 1968. a. [The Estonian ECB Presbyters' Conference in Tallinn, 15-18 February 1968], typewritten manuscript [1968]. Ülo Meriloo's personal library.

Finney, Charles, *Kõned ärkamiste üle* [Lectures on Revivals of Religion], typewritten Estonian translation (n. p., n. d.). KUSA.

Graham, Billy, *Püha Vaim: Jumala väe virgutav jõud inimese elus* [The Holy Spirit:

Activating God's Power in Your Life], typewritten Estonian translation (n. p., n. d.). KUSA.

Jääger, Johannes, *Tema kutsus mind* [He Called Me], typewritten manuscript (1984). TPL.

'Kalju' koguduse karjase Robert Võsu jutlusi ajavahemikul 1944-1969 [Sermons of 'Kalju' Church Pastor, Robert Võsu, from 1944 to 1969], typewritten manuscript. KUSA.

King, Martin Luther, *Kõned ja jutlused* [Speeches and Sermons], typewritten Estonian translation (n. p., n. d.). KUSA.

Laks, Johannes, *Aleksander Sildos: elulugu* [Aleksander Sildos: A Biography] (Tallinn, 1967), typewritten manuscript. TPL.

Mangs, Frank, *Issanda tee* [The Lord's Way], typewritten Estonian translation (1970s?). KUSA.

McConkey, James H., *Püha Vaimu kolmekordne saladus* [Three-Fold Secret of the Holy Spirit], typewritten Estonian translation (n. p., n. d.). KUSA.

Murray, Andrew, *Alandus* [Humility], typewritten Estonian translation (n. p., n. d.). KUSA.

Olvik, Oskar, *Homileetika* [Homiletics], typewritten manuscript (1957). KUSA.

Olvik, Oskar, *Neli kõnet* [Four Sermons], typewritten manuscript (1964). EEKBLA.

Olvik, Oskar, *Palve: kaheksa kõnet palvest* [Eight Sermons on Prayer], typewritten manuscript (Tallinn, 1965). EEKBLA.

Olvik, Oskar, *Mälestused* [Memoirs], part 1-2, typewritten manuscript (Tallinn, 1966). Oleviste ECB Church library, Tallinn.

Olvik, Oskar, *Esimene Korintose kiri* [The First Epistle to the Corinthians], typewritten manuscript (1960). KUSA.

Palumäe, Elmar, comp., *Elusõnu mitmest suust: Eduard Lilienthal ja Aleksander Sildos,* [Words of Life from the Lips of Many: Eduard Lilienthal and Aleksander Sildos], book 6, typewritten manuscript (1977). KUSA.

Pederson, Duane, *Jeesus-rahvas* [Jesus People], typewritten Estonian translation (n. p., n. d.). TPL.

Rinker, Rosalind, *Te võite veendunult tunnistada* [You Can Witness with Confidence], typewritten Estonian translastion (n. p., n. d.). KUSA.

Roberts, Oral, *Kui tahad saada terveks, siis talita järgmiselt* [If You Need Healing, Do these Things], typewritten Estonian translation (n. p., n. d.). KUSA.

Sildos, Aleksander, *Elulugu* [A Biography] (1967), typewritten manuscript. TPL.

T[ärk], O[svald], *Teeviit* [Guidepost], typewritten manuscript (n. p., n. d.). KUSA.

Tärk, Osvald, *Usk ja haigused* [Faith and Illnesses] (n. p., n. d.), typewritten manuscript. KUSA.

Tärk, Osvald, *Efesose kiri* [The Epistle to the Ephesians], typewritten manuscript (1957). KUSA.

Tärk, Osvald, *Piibli teoloogia* [Biblical Theology], typewritten manuscript (1958). KUSA.

Tärk, Osvald, *Vaimulikud talitused EKB kogudustes* [Spiritual Ordinances in the ECB Churches], typewritten manuscript (1959). EEKBLA.

[Tärk, Osvald], *Püha õhtusöömaaeg. Viis kõnet pühast õhtusöömaajast* [The Lord's Supper. Five Sermons on the Lord's Supper], typewritten manuscript (1965). EEKBLA.

[Tärk, Osvald], *Märkmeid O. Tärgi jutlustest 1965. a.* [Notes from the Sermons of O.

Tärk, 1965], typewritten sermon collection (1966?). KUSA.

Tärk, Osvald, 'Märkmeid O. Tärgi jutlustest 1981-1982.a.' [Notes from the Sermons of O. Tärk from the years 1981-1982], typewritten sermon collection (n. p., n. d.). KUSA.

Veermets, H., *Albomi juurde. Haapsalu koguduse 100 aastapäev* [To the Album. The 100th Anniversary of the Haapsalu Church], typewritten manuscipt (1984). EEKBLA.

Vink, Johannes, comp., *Aleksander Sildose surm* [Death of Aleksander Sildos], typewritten manuscript ([Vancouver], 1977). TPL.

Võsu, Robert, 'Halle pietism Eestimaal XVIII sajandil' [Halle Pietism in Estonia in the 18th Century], handwritten manuscript (1943). Original manuscript at the Estonian Literary Museum in Tartu, a copy available at KUSA.

[Võsu, Robert,] *Baptistide arengust ja põhimõtetest* [About the Development and Principles of Baptists], typewritten manuscript [1966]. Merike Uudam's personal library.

Võsu, Robert, *Mäejutlus* [The Sermon on the Mount], typewritten manuscript (Tallinn, 1957). EEKBLA.

Võsu, Robert, *Kristluse ajalugu* [A History of Christianity], vol. 1-4, typewritten manuscript (Tallinn, 1957-1960). KUSA.

Võsu, Robert, *EKB koguduste ajalugu* [A History of ECB Churches], typewritten manuscript (1959). KUSA.

Võsu, Robert, *Armastusest* [About Love], typewritten manuscript (1965). KUSA.

Võsu, Robert, *Isiklik evangelism* [Personal Evangelism], typewritten manuscript (Tallinn, 1971). EEKBLA.

Yli-Vainio, Niilo, *Väe saladus* [Mystery of the Power], typewritten Estonian translation (n. p., n. d.). KUSA.

UNPUBLISHED PRIMARY SOURCES – ARTICLES, PAPERS, DOCUMENTS

(The pagination of articles in typewritten publication Logos *is according to the issues owned by Üllas Linder. The pagination of articles published in* Lectio, Jäljed, Evangelismikogumik I *and* Lugemisvihik *is according to the copies owned by the present author.)*

Arder, Arpad, 'Robert Võsu – 70. aastane' [Robert Võsu – 70 Years Old], *Logos*, no. 1 (1984), pp. 22-24.

Christenson, Larry, 'Palu, et Kristus valitseks' [Pray that Christ would Rule], *Lectio V* (1978), pp. 17-32.

'Filmikommentaar Moskvast' [Film Comments from Moscow], *Jäljed II* (1979), pp. 3-6.

Green, Michael, 'Algkristliku evangelisatsiooni meetod ja taktika' [The Method and Tactics of Evangelism in the Early Church], *Logos*, no. 3-4 (1987), pp. 8-17.

Grossmann, Siegfried, 'Harismaatiline integratsioon koguduses' [Charismatic Integration in the Church], *Lectio V* (1978), pp. 13-16.

'Informatsioon' [Information], *Logos*, no. 1 (1982), pp. 20-21.

'Johannes Jääger – in memoriam', *Logos*, no. 3 (1986), pp. 59-60.

Jürma, Ermo, 'Diakooniast' [About Diaconie-work], *Logos*, no. 1 (1986), pp. 28-30.

Kaasik, Voldemar, 'Tagasivaade Pärnu Immaanueli kogudusele' [Pärnu 'Immanuel'

Church in Retrospect], *Logos*, no. 4 (1984), pp. 12-14.

'Kui oodatu ei tule...' [When the One Who Has Been Waited for Does Not Come] *Jäljed II* (1979), pp. 27-40.

Kurg, Ingmar, 'Jõuludeks: Jumala Sõna lihakssaamine' [For Christmas: The Incarnation of God's Word], *Logos*, no. 6 (1983), pp. 9-14.

Kurg, Ingmar, 'Homileetilisi märkmeid' [Homiletical Notes], *Logos*, no. 1 (1986), pp. 22-27.

Lange, Anne, 'Ühest T.S. Elioti luuletajaisiksuse tahust' [About One Aspect of T.S. Eliot as a Poet], *Lugemisvihik* (1988), pp. 11-18.

'Lausanne'i leping: Kuulgu maailm tema häält!' [Lausanne Covenant: Let the Earth Hear His Voice], typewritten Estonian translation, in *Evangelismikogumik I* [A Collection of Articles on Evangelism I] (1980), pp. 4-19. TPL.

'Living Soundist' üldse... [About 'Living Sound'...], *Jäljed II* (1979), pp. 7-13.

Mäemets, Herman, 'Priikoguduste tekkimine Eestis ja nende evangeelse tegevuse algus' [Origins of the Revivalist Free Churches in Estonia and the Beginning of their Evangelistic Activity], *Logos*, no. 4 (1982), pp. 15-27.

Olvik, Oskar, 'Ülevaade evangeeliumi kristlaste ajaloost' [Overview of the History of Evangelical Christians], in *Eesti Evangeeliumi Kristlaste juubel 50: 1905-1955* [The 50th Jubilee of Estonian Evangelical Christians: 1905-1955] (1955), typewritten manuscript, pp. 43-53. KUSA.

Olvik, Oskar, 'Usulise ja kõlbelise elu probleeme meie kogudustes' [Problems of Religious and Moral Living in our Churches], in *Eesti EKB koguduste presbüterite konverents Tallinnas, 15.-18. veebruaril 1968. a.* [The Estonian ECB Presbyters' Conference in Tallinn, 15-18 February 1968], typewritten manuscript [1968], pp. 111-135. Ülo Meriloo's personal library.

Otto, Manfred, 'Harismaatilise liikumise pingeväli' [An Area of Tension in the Charismatic Movement], *Lectio V* (1978), pp. 6-12.

Pilli, Toivo, 'Albert Ruutsoo vabakogudslikust vaimulaadist' [Albert Ruutsoo on Free Church Spirituality], manuscript of an unpublished article based on an interview with Ruutsoo from the early 1990s. TPL.

Pohl, Adolf, 'Piibel ja sinu tänane Kristuse kogemus' [The Bible and Your Present Experience of Christ], *Logos*, no. 2 (1982), pp. 1-5.

Pohl, Adolf, 'Meie arusaam ristimisest' [Our Understanding of Baptism], *Logos*, no. 2 (1985), pp. 7-10.

'Presbüterite konverents 24.-26.04.1987 Tallinnas' [The Presbyters' Conference in Tallinn, 24.-26.04.1987], *Logos*, no. 1-2 (1987), pp. 3-4.

Puusaag, Jüri, 'Sajandivanune Tallinna 'Kalju' kogudus [A Century-Old Tallinn 'Kalju' Church], *Logos*, no. 3 (1984), pp. 5-8.

Puusaag, Jüri, 'Evangeelse töö mured ja rõõmud' [Joys and Sorrows of Evangelistic Work], *Logos*, no. 3 (1985), pp. 10-15.

Puusaag, Jüri, 'Inimeste püüdja või inimeste hirmutaja?' [Fishing for Men or Scaring Men?], *Logos*, no. 2 (1986), pp. 9-14.

Puusaag, Jüri, 'Kogudusekeskne evangelism' [Church-Centred Evangelism], *Logos*, no. 3 (1988), pp. 9-13.

Rahkema, Eerik, 'Süütult kannatades' [Suffering Innocently], *Logos*, no. 3-4 (1987), pp. 18-22.

Rebane, Ants, 'Piibellik pühitsus' [Biblical Sanctification], *Logos*, no. 1(1981) – no. 5 (1982).

Rebane, Ants, 'Kristuse koguduse ühtsus' [The Unity of Christ's Church], *Logos*, no. 1 (1985), pp. 8-11.

Rebane, Ants, 'Kristuse ihu ja Kristuse vaim II' [The Body of Christ and the Spirit of Christ II], *Logos*, no. 1 (1986), pp. 15-18.

Rebane, Ants, 'Üks lootus' [One Hope], *Logos*, no. 2 (1986), pp. 15-18.

Rebane, Ants, 'Üks ristimine' [One Baptism], *Logos*, no. 1-2 (1987), pp. 33-38.

Remmel, Meego, '"Ma lähen koju, ma lähen ära..." [I will go home, I will go away...]. In memoriam Robert Võsu', *Logos* (April 1994), p. 17.

Ridaliste, Imant, 'Ärkamise ettevalmistamine' [Preparing for Revival], *Logos*, no. 2 (1986), pp. 2-4.

Riistan, Ain, 'The Union of Estonian Evangelical Christian and Baptist Churches: Diversity in Unity or Issues Concerning Spirituality and Identity', a paper in Church History course (Prague: IBTS, 1997). TPL.

Riistan, Ain, 'Theological Education in Estonia – a Survival of the Fittest Game or an Opportunity for the Future?', unpublished paper (Pancrac Teologicky Forum, 12 July 2002, Siroky Dul, Czech Republic). TPL.

Roosimaa, Peeter, 'Apokalüpsis – Ilmutusraamatu eksegeetilisi probleeme' [Apocalypsis – Exegetical Problems of the Book of Revelation], *Logos*, no. 2 (1982) - no. 5 (1983).

Schaeffer, Francis, 'Uus religioosne laine' [A New Religious Wave], *Logos*, no. 4 (1982), pp. 28-32, no. 5 (1982), pp. 19-24.

Süld, Meelis, 'Ateistlik propaganda Nõukogude Eesti ajalehtedes aastail 1952 ja 1962' [Atheistic Propaganda in the Soviet Estonian Newspapers in 1952 and 1962], unpublished seminar paper (Tartu: Tartu University, 1998). TPL.

Talts, Marek, 'Albert Tammo elulugu' [A Biography of Albert Tammo], course paper (Kõrgem Usuteaduslik Seminar, 2005). TPL.

Tammo, Joosep, 'Kristlus ja maailmareligioonid' [Christianity and World Religions], *Logos*, no. 1 (1986), pp. 38-43.

Tammo, Joosep, 'Kogudused ja vendlus koondumise ja läkituse pingeväljas' [Local Churches and the Broherhood in the Tension Area of Being Gathered and Being Sent], *Logos*, no. 3 (1986), pp. 8-12.

Tammo, Joosep, 'Meil on suur ülempreester Jeesus' [We Have a Great High Priest Jesus], *Logos*, no. 1 (1988), pp. 4-8.

Tammo, Joosep, 'Nüüdisaegse evangeelse töö põhimõtted ja võimalused' [Principles and Opportunities for Present Day Evangelism], *Logos*, no. 3 (1988), pp. 4-9.

Tärk, Osvald, 'Evangeelium on Jumala vägi' [The Gospel is the Power of God], in *Eesti EKB koguduste presbüterite konverents Tallinnas, 15.-18. veebruaril 1968. a.* [The Estonian ECB Presbyters' Conference in Tallinn, 15-18 February 1968], typewritten manuscript [1968], pp. 151-164. Ülo Meriloo's personal library.

Tärk, Osvald, 'Jutlustaja kantslil' [A Preacher in the Pulpit], a presentation at the presbyters conference, 29.05.1976, typewritten manuscript. TPL.

Tärk, Osvald, '"Uus suund" ristimise õpetuses' ['A New Trend' in the Teaching of Baptism], *Logos*, no. 5 (1982), pp. 25-27.

Tärk, Osvald, 'Meie vendluse põhimõtted' [Principles of our Brotherhood], *Logos*, no. 1 (1981), no. 1-4 (1982), no. 1-2 (1983).

Tärk, Osvald, 'Tööraskuste õigest kasutamisest' [How to Use Difficulties in Ministry for Good], *Logos*, no. 6 (1982), pp. 12-15.

Tärk, Osvald, 'Jumalast antud meeleparanduse aeg' [A God-given Time for

Repentance], *Logos*, no. 1-2 (1987), pp. 5-9.

Valk, Daily, 'Eesti Evangeeliumi Kristlaste ja Baptistide Koguduste Liidu laste- ja noortetöö ülevaade' [A Survey of Children's and Youth Work in the Union of Evangelical Christian-Baptist Churches in Estonia], course paper (Tartu: Kõrgem Usuteaduslik Seminar, 2003). KUSA.

Võsu, Robert, 'Kristlase kohustused' [Responsibilities of a Christian], *Logos*, no. 1 (1982), pp. 1-3.

Võsu, Robert, 'Sada aastat priikoguduse algusest' [One Hundred Years from the Beginning of the Revivalist Free Church], *Logos*, no. 4 (1982), pp. 1-2.

Võsu, Robert, 'Püha Vaimu olemus' [The Nature of the Holy Spirit], *Logos*, no. 5 (1982), pp. 10-18.

Võsu, Robert, 'Külvakem rohkesti!' [Sow Abundantly!], *Logos*, no. 1 (1983), pp. 1-3.

Võsu, Robert, *Jeesus Kristus – koguduse alus* [Jesus Christ – A Foundation for Church], *Logos*, no. 2 (1984), pp. 4-9.

Võsu, Robert, 'Püha Vaim ja valevaimud' [The Holy Spirit and Wrong Spirits], *Logos*, no. 5 (1985), pp. 11-17.

Võsu, Robert, 'Armastuse tähendus apostel Johannese kirjades' [The Meaning of Love in the Epistles of the Apostle John], *Logos*, no. 3 (1986), pp. 27-34.

Võsu, Robert, 'Baptismist' [About the Baptist Movement], *Logos*, no. 4 (1986), pp. 19-23.

Võsu, Robert, 'Tasadus ja alandus Pauluse käsitluses' [Meekness and Humility in Paul], *Logos*, no. 1-2 (1987), pp. 28-32.

Wieske, Günther, 'Euroopa kristlased piibli ja kultuuri pingeväljas' [European Christians in the Tension Area of the Bible and Culture], *Logos*, no. 3-4 (1987), pp. 42-48.

'Üles, üles, järve uppunud kellad!' [Up, Up, You Bells That Are Drowned in the Lake], *Jäljed I* (1979), pp. 4-6.

Zhidkov, Mihail, and Jüri Puusaag, 'Billy Graham taas Nõukogude Liidus' [Billy Graham again in the Soviet Union], *Logos*, no. 4 (1984), pp. 28-30.

PUBLISHED PRIMARY SOURCES – BOOKS

Aastaraamat 2006: Eesti Evangeeliumi Kristlaste ja Baptistide Koguduste Liit [Yearbook 2006: The Union of Evangelical Christian and Baptist Churches in Estonia] (Tallinn, 2006).

Arder, Arpad, *Kus on Arpadi kuningas?* [Where is Arpad's King?] (Tallinn: [Logos,] 1992).

Busch, M., *Ridala ärkamise ajalugu* [A History of the Revival in Ridala] (Keila: K.-Ü. 'Külvaja' trükk, 1928).

Eesti Baptisti koguduste ajaloolik Album 25 Juubeli aasta mälestuseks [In Commemoration of the 25th Anniversary: An Historical Album of Estonian Baptist Churches] (Tallinn: J. Felsbergi ja A. Tetermanni trükk, 1911).

Evangeelsed laulud [Evangelical Hymns] (Tallinn, 1975).

Jumala teenistuses: Rein Uuemõis [In the Service of God: Rein Uuemõis] (Tallinn: Oleviste kogudus, 2001).

Kalmus, Ain [Evald Mänd], *Päästa meid ära kurjast* [Save Us from Evil] (Lund: Eesti Kirjanike Kooperatiiv, 1979).

Kaups, Karl, *Riigikirik ja vabakogudus* [State Church and Free Church] (Keila: Külvaja trükk ja kirjastus, 1934).

Kaups, Richard, *Hea Sõnum ja Eesti Baptisti Kogudused* [A Good Message and Estonian Baptist Churches] (Santa Barbara, California, 1974).

Kaups, Asta, *Pärija* [Inheritor] (Tallinn, 2000).

Kiil, Evald, *Issandast kutsutud viinamäe tööle* [Called by God for Work in the Vineyard] (Tallinn, 1993).

Kiil, Evald, *Meenutusi nelipühi ärkamisest Eestis* [Memories of the Pentecostal Revival in Estonia] (Tallinn: Logos, 1997).

Laks, Johannes, *Kakskümmendviis aastat vabakoguduslist liikumist Eestis 1905-1930* [Twenty-Five Years of a Free Church Movement in Estonia 1905-1930] (Tallinn, 1930).

Laks, Johannes, *Mälestusi eluteelt ja töömaalt* [Memoirs from Life and Work] (Toronto: Toronto Vabakoguduse Kirjastus, 1965).

Leinus, Ruudi, comp. and ed., *Osvald Tärk. Uskuge Jumalasse* [Osvald Tärk. Believe in God] (Tallinn: Eesti EKB Liit, 1999).

Liik, Viljo, *Meenutusi möödunust* [Memories from the Past] (Kärdla: Kärdla Baptistikogudus, 2005).

Meriloo, Ülo, *Ränduri päevik* [A Diary of a Pilgrim] (Tallinn, 2001).

Nee, Watchman, *Loomulik usuelu* [The Normal Christian Life], Estonian translation (Rakvere, 1993).

Parman, Alland, Merike Uudam and Norie Roeder, *Kui kristlik on Eestimaa?* [How Christian is Estonia?] (Tallinn: Estonian Evangelisation Alliance, 1997).

Piibli õpetus Eesti Evangeeliumi Kristlaste ja Baptistide Koguduste Liidu kogudustes [Biblical Teaching in the UECBCE Churches] (Tallinn: Eesti EKB Liit, 1998).

Proos, Taimi, *Südametunnistuse pärast: Henrik Kokamägi elust ja tööst* [For the Sake of Conscience: About the Life and Work of Henrik Kokamägi] (Tallinn: Eesti Piibliselts, 2002).

Raid, Lembit, *Vabamõtlejate ringidest massilise ateismini* [From the Circles of Freethinkers to Mass Atheism] (Tallinn: Eesti Raamat, 1978).

Rips, Uudu, comp., *Issanda aednik. Märkmeid Paul Himma elust* [A Gardener of the Lord. Notes from the Life of Paul Himma] (Tartu: Saalemi Baptisti Kogudus, 2000).

Roosimaa, Peeter, *Pöördumine ja uussünd* [Conversion and New Birth] (Tartu: EKB Liidu Kõrgem Usuteaduslik Seminar, 2003).

Rosenvald, Valdur, *Pühitsuselu* [Life of Sanctification] ([Tallinn?]: Vaimulik kirjavara, 1999).

Seppur, A[leksander], *Jees. Krist. Evg. Priikoguduse tekkimine ja levinemine Läänemaa ärkamises* [The Beginning and Development of Jesus Christ's Evangelical Free Church in the Revival of Western Estonia] (Toronto, 1970).

Tamm, Aare, comp., *Teel allikale* [On the Way to a Fountain], vols. 1-2 (Tallinn: Logos, 2002).

Tammo, Joosep, *Kesköö on päeva algus* [At Midnight the Day Begins] (Tallinn: Eesti EKB Liit, 1998).

Tuglas, Elo, *Elukiri* [A Print of Life] (Tallinn: Faatum, 1993).

Tärk, Osvald, *Kümme käsku* [Ten Commandments] (Tallinn: Eesti Kristlik Kirjastus, 1990).

Tärk, Osvald, *Markuse evangeeliumi seletus* [Explaining the Gospel of Mark] (Tallinn: Logos, 1993).

Tärk, Osvald, *Armastuse käsu all* [Under the Law of Love] (Tallinn: Eesti EKB Liit, 2004).

Tärk [Tjark], O.A., *Izbrannye trudy* [Selected Works], vols. 1-2 (Moskva: Izdanie Sojuza EHB Rossii, 2005).

Vanaselja, Taimi, *Kun sydän pelkää* [When the Heart is Frightened] (Hämeenlinna: Päivä Osakeyhtiö, 2000).

Võsu, Robert, *Evangeelne eetika* [Evangelical Ethics] (Tallinn: Logos, 1996).

PUBLISHED PRIMARY SOURCES – ARTICLES, ESSAYS, DOCUMENTS

Arder, Veronika, 'Muusikatöö' [Music Ministry], in *Oleviste 50. Oleviste koguduse juubelikogumik* [Oleviste 50. The Anniversary Collection of Oleviste Church] (Tallinn: Oleviste kogudus, 2000), pp. 15-18.

Bärenson, Jaan, 'Oleviste koguduse asutamine' [Formation of the Oleviste Church], in *Oleviste 50. Oleviste koguduse juubelikogumik* [Oleviste 50. The Anniversary Collection of Oleviste Church] (Tallinn: Oleviste kogudus, 2000), pp. 6-8.

Dahl, Harald Victor, 'Ülevaade Liidust' [A Survey of the Union], in R. Kaups, ed., *50 aastat apostlite radadel* [50 Years in the Ways of the Apostles] (Keila: E.B.K. Liidu Kirjastus, 1934), pp. 17-22.

'Eesti Vabariigi priiusk on kõige parem usk' [Revivalist Free Faith in the Estonian Republic is the Best Faith], interview with Astrid Teekel, *Teekäija* (March 1994), pp. 3-4.

Evangeeliumi Kristlaste Vabakoguduse Põhikiri [The Statute of The Evangelical Christian Free Church] (Keila: Külvaja trükk, 1926).

'Evangel'skie hristjane-baptisty v sovetskoi Pribaltike' [The Evangelical Christians-Baptists in the Soviet Baltics], *Bratskii Vestnik*, no. 6 (1947), pp. 36-38.

Johannson, August, 'Juubeli aasta Eesti Baptisti Ühenduses' [An Anniversary Year in the Estonian Baptist Union], *Teekäija*, no. 3 (1909), p. 18.

Kaups, Karl, 'Katsuge vaimud läbi' [Test the Spirits], *Teekäija*, no. 23 (1924), pp. 333-335.

Kaups, Karl, 'Protestantism' [Protestantism], *Teekäija*, no. 21 (1931) – no. 3 (1933).

Kaups, Karl, 'Eesti Baptismi ideelised põhialused' [The Principles of the Estonian Baptist Movement], in R. Kaups, ed., *50 aastat apostlite radadel* [50 Years in the Ways of the Apostles] (Keila: E.B.K. Liidu kirjastus, 1934), pp. 10-15.

Kaups, Karl, 'Kojuhüütud ustavaid sulaseid' [Faithful Servants Who Have Been Called Home], in R. Kaups, ed., *50 aastat apostlite radadel* [50 Years in the Ways of the Apostles] (Keila: E.B.K. Liidu kirjastus, 1934), pp. 100-116.

Kaups, Karl, 'Pilke tulevikku' [Visions for the Future], in R. Kaups, ed., *50 aastat apostlite radadel* [50 Years in the Ways of the Apostles] (Keila: E.B.K. Liidu kirjastus, 1934), pp. 203-207.

Kaups, Karl, 'Mineviku teedel' [On the Ways of the Past], in *Põllu Vagudel* [On the Furrows of the Fields], no. 28 (1965), pp. 71-96; no. 31 (1966), pp. 70-104.

Kaups, Richard, 'Evangelisatsioon' [Evangelisation], in R. Kaups, ed., *50 aastat apostlite radadel* [50 Years in the Ways of the Apostles] (Keila: E.B.K. Liidu kirjastus, 1934), pp. 22-26.

Kaups, Richard, 'Kogudused' [Churches], in R. Kaups, ed., *50 aastat apostlite radadel* [50 Years in the Ways of the Apostles] (Keila: E.B.K. Liidu kirjastus, 1934), pp. 26-

89.

Kibuspuu, Jüri-Valdur, '50 aastat tagasi toimus Hiiumaal suur ärkamine' [50 Years Ago a Large Revival Took Place in Hiiumaa Island], *Teekäija*, no. 9 (2006), p. 22.

Kurg, Ingmar, 'Üks mälestus Arpad Arderist' [One Reminiscence about Arpad Arder], *Teekäija* (November 1995), pp. 20-21.

Leven, Lars, 'Näide kasvavast kogudusest Rootsis' [An Example of a Growing Church in Sweden], *Teekäija* (September 1993), pp. 3-5.

Lige, Tarmo, 'Kogudus põlvkondade vahetusel' [Church on the Threshold of Generations], in *Oleviste 50. Oleviste koguduse juubelikogumik* (Tallinn: Oleviste kogudus, 2000), pp. 31-34.

Matson, Daniel H., 'Hingedevõitmine' [Winning Souls], *Teekäija*, no. 21/22 (1930), pp. 265-266.

Meriloo, Ülo, 'Ühistöö aastad' [Years of Cooperation], in *Oleviste 50. Oleviste koguduse juubelikogumik* [Oleviste 50. The Anniversary Collection of Oleviste Church] (Tallinn: Oleviste kogudus, 2000), pp. 8-10.

Meriloo, Ülo, 'Karjaste läkitamine' [Sending out the Pastors], in *Oleviste 50. Oleviste koguduse juubelikogumik* [Oleviste 50. The Anniversary Collection of Oleviste Church] (Tallinn: Oleviste kogudus, 2000), pp. 39-40.

Mänd, Evald, 'Mälumatk mineviku radadele' [A Journey of Memory in the Paths of the Past], *Usurändur*, no. 1 (1984), pp. 31-35.

Paldre, Ene, 'Lauluvaliku kujunemine Eesti vabakiriklikes kogudustes' [Shaping the Choice of Songs in Estonian Free Churches], *Usuteaduslik Ajakiri*, no. 2 (2003), pp. 55-73.

Passelmann, P., 'Ülevaade kirjandusest' [A Survey of Literature], in R. Kaups, ed., *50 aastat apostlite radadel* [50 Years in the Ways of the Apostles] (Keila: E.B.K. Liidu kirjastus, 1934), pp. 160-164.

Schmidt, Martin, 'Eesti baptisti jutlustajate usuteadusliku hariduse ajaloost' [About the History of Estonian Baptist Preachers' Theological Education], in R. Kaups, ed., *50 aastat apostlite radadel* [50 Years in the Ways of the Apostles] (Keila: E.B.K. Liidu kirjastus, 1934), pp. 174-184.

Tammo, Joosep, 'Evangeeliumi Kristlaste ja Baptistide Koguduste Liidu põhimõtted ja töösuunad' [Principles and Visions for the Work of the Union of the Churches of Evangelical Christians and Baptists], *Teekäija* (July-August 1994), pp. 12-15.

Toom, Tarmo, 'Järelsõna' [Epilogue], in Osvald Tärk, *Kümme käsku* [Ten Commandments] (Tallinn: Eesti Kristlik Kirjastus, 1990), pp. 91-94.

Toom, Tarmo, 'Ikka veel Pauluse vaiast' [Even More about Paul's Thorn], *Teekäija* (March 1994), p. 16.

Ugam, Milone, 'Laste- ja noortetöö' [Youth and Children's Work], in *Oleviste 50. Oleviste koguduse juubelikogumik* [Oleviste 50. The Anniversary Collection of Oleviste Church] (Tallinn: Oleviste kogudus, 2000), pp. 10-14.

Uuemõis, Haljand, 'Evangeeliumi kristlaste liikumisest' [About the Evangelical Christian Movement], *Teekäija* (June 1995), pp. 5-6.

Uuemõis, Haljand, 'Effataa-ärkamine' [Effataa Revival] in *Oleviste 50. Oleviste koguduse juubelikogumik* [Oleviste 50. The Anniversary Collection of Oleviste Church] (Tallinn: Oleviste kogudus, 2000), pp. 22-24.

Veevo, Udo, 'Veel Pauluse vaiast' [More about Paul's Thorn], *Teekäija* (January 1994), p. 16.

Võsu, Robert, 'Eesti EKB Liidu tegevusest 1991. a.' [About the Activities of the

UECBE in 1991], *Teekäija*, no. 10 (1992), pp. 16-18.

Võsu, Robert, 'Autobiograafia' [Autobiography], *Kalju Sõnum*, no. 1 (2004), pp. 8-9.

Zhidkov, Y., 'Na poljah raboty nashevo bratstva' [In the Fields of Our Brotherhood], *Bratskii Vestnik*, no. 4 (1946), pp. 31-41.

Zhidkov, Y., 'Vzgljad nazad' [A Look Behind], *Bratskii Vestnik*, no. 1 (1948), pp. 5-10

Zhidkov, Y., 'Nash otshet' [Our Report], *Bratskii Vestnik*, no. 1 (1947), pp. 13-18

PUBLISHED SECONDARY SOURCES – BOOKS

Allpere, Anne, *Estonian Cantometric Attempt II: The Sacred and the Profane – Can It Be Heard?* (Tallinn: Academy of Sciences of the Estonian SSR, 1989).

Altnurme, Riho, Eesti Evangeeliumi Luteriusu Kirik ja Nõukogude riik 1944-1949 [The Estonian Evangelical Lutheran Church and the Soviet State 1944-1949] (Tartu: Tartu Ülikooli Kirjastus, 2001).

Altnurme, Riho, ed., *Eesti teoloogilise mõtlemise ajaloost: sissejuhatavaid märkusi ja apokrüüfe* [History of Theological Thought in Estonia: Introductiory Remarks and Apocrypha] (Tartu: Tartu Ülikooli Kirjastus, 2006).

Anderson, Alan, *An Introduction to Pentecostalism: Global Charismatic Christianity* (Cambridge: Cambridge University Press, 2004).

Archer, Kenneth J., *A Pentecostal Hermeneutic for the Twenty-First Century: Spirit, Scripture and Community* (London, New York: T&T Clark, 2004).

Astley, Jeff, *Ordinary Theology: Looking, Listening and Learning in Theology* (Ashgate, 2002).

Atkinson, David J., and David H. Field, eds., *New Dictionary of Christian Ethics and Pastoral Theology* (Downers Grove, Illinois, and Leicester, England: InterVarsity Press, 1995).

Au, Ilmo, and Ringo Ringvee, *Kirikud ja kogudused Eestis* [Churches and Congregations in Estonia] (Tallinn: Ilo, 2000).

Bailey, J. Martin, *The Spring of Nations: Churches in the Rebirth of Central and Eastern Europe* (New York: Friendship Press, 1991).

Balders, Günther, *Theurer Bruder Oncken* (Wuppertal und Kassel: Oncken Verlag, 1984).

Bebbington, David W., *Evangelicalism in Modern Britain. A History from the 1730s to the 1980s* (Grand Rapids, Michigan: Baker Book House, 1992).

Bebbington, David W., ed., *The Gospel in the World: International Baptist Studies* (Carlisle: Paternoster, 2002).

Bebbington, David W., *The Dominance of Evangelicalism: The Age of Spurgeon and Moody* (Leicester: Inter-Varsity Press, 2005).

Beeson, Trevor, *Discretion and Valour. Religious Conditions in Russia and Eastern Europe* (Glasgow: Collins Fontana Books, 1974).

Benner, D., ed., *Baker Encyclopaedia of Psychology* (Grand Rapids, Michigan: Baker Book House, 1985).

Berkhof, Louis, *Systematic Theology* (Grand Rapids, Michigan: Eerdmans, 1949).

Boeve, Lieven, *Interrupting Tradition: An Essay on Christian Faith in a Postmodern Context* (Louvain-Dudley, MA: Peeters Press, 2003).

Bolshakoff, Serge, *Russian Nonconformity* (Westminster Press: Philadelphia, 1950).

Bosch, David J., *Transforming Mission: Paradigm Shifts in Theology of Missions*

(Maryknoll, New York: Orbis Books, 1997).

Bourdeaux, Michael, *Religious Ferment in Russia. Protestant Opposition to Soviet Religious Policy* (London and New York: Macmillan and St. Martin's Press, 1968).

Bourdeaux, Michael, *Patriarch and Prophets* (London: Macmillan, 1970).

Brandenburg, Hans, *The Meek and the Mighty: The Emergence of the Evangelical Movement in Russia* (New York: Oxford University Press, 1977).

Bray, Gerald, *Biblical Interpretation: Past and Present* (Downers Grove, Illinois: InterVarsity Press, 1996).

Brown, Callum G., *The Death of Christian Britain* (London: Routledge, 2001).

Burgess, Stanley M., and Gary B. McGee, eds., *Dictionary of Pentecostal and Charismatic Movements* (Grand Rapids, Michigan: Zondervan, 1988).

Busch, L. Russ, and Tom J. Nettles, *Baptists and the Bible* (Nashville, Tennessee: Broadman and Holman Publishers, 1999).

Cavanaugh, William T., *Torture and Eucharist* (Oxford: Blackwell Publishing, 1998).

Cessario, Romanus, *The Virtues or the Examined Life* (London and New York: Continuum, 2002).

Chan, Simon, *Pentecostal Theology and the Christian Spiritual Tradition* (Sheffield: Sheffield Academic Press, 2000).

Chumachenko, Tatiana A., *Church and State in Soviet Russia: Russian Orthodoxy from World War II to the Khrushchev Years* (New York and London: M.E. Sharpe, 2002).

Collins, Kenneth J., *The Evangelical Moment: The Promise of an American Religion* (Grand Rapids, Michigan: Baker Academic, 2005).

Corrado, Sharyl, and Toivo Pilli, eds., *Eastern European Baptist History: New Perspectives* (Prague: IBTS, 2007).

Cothen, Grady C., and James M. Dunn, *Soul Freedom: Baptist Battle Cry* (Macon, Georgia: Smyth and Helwys, 2000).

Crabb, Stanley, comp. and ed., *Our Favourite Memories. European Baptist Federation 1949-1999* (n. p., n. d.).

Cross, Anthony R., *Baptism and the Baptists* (Carlisle: Paternoster Press, 2000).

Davis, Ellen F., and Richard B. Hays, eds., *The Art of Reading Scripture* (Grand Rapids, Michigan: Eerdmans, 2003).

Davis, Nathaniel, *A Long Walk to Church: A Contemporary History of Russian Orthodoxy* (Boulder and Oxford: Westview Press, 1995).

Davies, Norman, *Europe. A History* (London: Pimlico, 1997).

Dillenberger, John, and Claude Welch, *Protestant Christianity: Interpreted Through its Development* (New York and Toronto: Macmillan Publishing Company, 1988).

Durasoff, Steve, *The Russian Protestants, Evangelicals in the Soviet Union: 1944-1964* (Rutherford: Farleigh Dickinson University Press, 1969).

Durnbaugh, Donald F., *The Believers' Church* (Scottdale, Pennsylvania: Herald Press, 1985).

Ellis, Jane, *The Russian Orthodox Church: A Contemporary History* (London and Sydney: Croom Helm, 1986).

Evangelicalism and the Orthodox Church: A Report by the Evangelical Alliance Commission on Unity and Truth among Evangelicals (London: ACUTE, 2001).

Fee, Gordon D., and Douglas Stuart, *How to Read the Bible for All Its Worth* (Grand Rapids, Michigan: Zondervan, 1993).

Ferguson, Sinclair B., and David F. Wright, eds., *New Dictionary of Theology* (Leicester, England, and Downers Grove, Illinois: Inter-Varsity Press, 1988).

Festschrift für Feier des 50 jahrigen Jubiläums des Predigerseminars der deutschen Baptisten zu Hamburg-Horn vom 1. Bis 3. Juni 1930 (s. a. [1930?]).

Fiddes, Paul, *Tracks and Traces: Baptist Identity in Church and Theology* (Carlisle: Paternoster, 2003).

Finney, Charles G., *The Autobiography, condensed and edited by Helen Wessel* (Minneapolis, Minnesota: Bethany House Publishers, 1977).

Fletcher, William C., *The Russian Orthodox Church Underground, 1917-1970* (London and New York: Oxford University Press, 1971).

Fowler, Stanley K., *More Than A Symbol: The British Baptist Recovery of Baptismal Sacramentalism* (Carlisle: Paternoster Press, 2002).

Gerner, Kristian, and Stefan Hedlund, *The Baltic States and the End of the Soviet Empire* (London and New York: Routledge, 1993).

Gilmore, Alec, ed., *Christian Baptism* (London: Lutterworth Press, 1959).

Gnadenteich, Jaan, *Kodumaa kirikulugu* [Church History of the Home Country] (Tallinn: Logos, 1995).

Green, Bernard, *Crossing the boundaries: A history of the European Baptist Federation* (Didcot: The Baptist Historical Society, 1999).

Green, Bernard, *Tomorrow's Man: A Biography of James Henry Rushbrooke* (Didcot: The Baptist Historical Society, 1997).

Grenz, Stanley, *Sexual Ethics: A Biblical Perspective* (Carlisle: Paternoster Press, 1998).

Grenz, Stanley, and John Francke, *Beyond Foundationalism: Shaping Theology in Postmodern Context* (Louisville, Kentucky: Westminster John Knox Press, 2001).

Guroian, Vigen, *Ethics After Christendom: Toward an Ecclesial Christian Ethic* (Grand Rapids, Michigan: Eerdmans, 1994).

Hardman, Keith J., *Charles Grandison Finney 1792-1875: Revivalist and Reformer* (Grand Rapids, Michigan: Baker Book House, 1990).

Heinilä, Pentti, *Erittäin salainen* [Top Secret] (Helsinki: Uusi Tie, 1995).

Hiiemaa, Karin, *Südame kutsel: Eesti misjonärid Aafrikas* [On the Call of the Heart: Estonian Missionaries in Africa] (Tallinn: Olion, 2000).

Hollenweger, Walter J., *The Pentecostals* (Peabody, Massachusetts: Hendrickson, 1988).

Ilja, Voldemar, *Vennastekoguduse (herrnhutluse) ajalugu Eestimaal (Põhja-Eesti) 1730-1743* [The History of the Fraternity of the Moravian Brethren (Herrnhuter) in Estonia (North-Estonia) 1730-1743], vol. 1 (Tallinn: Logos, 1995).

Ilja, Voldemar, *Vennastekoguduse (herrnhutluse) ajalugu Eestimaal (Põhja-Eesti) 1744-1764* [The History of the Fraternity of the Moravian Brethren (Herrnhuter) in Estonia (North-Estonia) 1744-1764], vol. 2 (Tallinn: Logos, 2000).

Ilja, Voldemar, *Vennastekoguduse (herrnhutluse) ajalugu Liivimaal (Lõuna-Eesti) 1729-1750* [The History of the Fraternity of the Moravian Brethren (Herrnhuter) in Livonia (South-Estonia) 1729-1750], vol. 3 (Tallinn: Logos, 2002).

Istorija evangel'skih hristjan-baptistov v SSSR [History of Evangelical Christians-Baptists in the USSR] (Moskva: Izdanije VSEHB, 1989).

Johnson, Paul, Modern Times. *A History of the World from the 1920s to the 1990s* (London: Orion Books, 1994).

Jones, Keith, *A Believing Church* (Didcot: The Baptist Union of Great Britain, 1998).

Jürjo, Indrek, *Pagulus ja Nõukogude Eesti* [Exile and the Soviet Estonia] (Tallinn: Umara, 1996).

Kahle, Wilhelm, *Evangelische Christen in Russland und der Sovetunion* (Wuppertal und

Kassel: Oncken Verlag, 1978).

Kay, William K., and Anne E. Dyer, eds., *Pentecostal and Charismatic Studies: A Reader* (London: SCM Press, 2004).

Kärkkäinen, Veli-Matti, *Pneumatology: The Holy Spirit in Ecumenical, International and Contextual Perspective* (Grand Rapids, Michigan: Baker Academic, 2002).

Kimbrough, S.T., ed., *Methodism in Russia and the Baltic States: History and Renewal* (Nashville, Tennessee: Abingdon Press, 1995).

Klein, William W., et. al., *Introduction to Biblical Interpretation* (Nashville: Thomas Nelson Publishers, 1993).

Kolarz, Walter, *Religion in the Soviet Union* (London and New York: Macmillan and St. Martin's Press, 1961).

Kupsch, Eduard, *Geschichte der Baptisten in Polen, 1852-1932* (Lodz: Im Selbstverlag des Verfassers, s.a. [1932?]).

Kyle, Richard, *Evangelicalism: An Americanized Christianity* (New Brunswick and London: Transactions Publishers, 2006).

Larsen, Timothy, ed., *Biographical Dictionary of Evangelicals* (Leicester, England: Inter-Varsity Press, 2003).

Laur, Mati, Tõnis Lukas, et al., *History of Estonia* (Tallinn: Avita, 2000).

Lauristin, Marju, Peeter Vihalemm, et al., eds., *Return to the Western World: Cultural and Political Perspectives on the Estonian Post-Communist Transition* (Tartu: Tartu University Press, 1997).

Liiman, Raigo, *Usklikkus muutuvas Eesti ühiskonnas* [Religiosity in the Changing Estonian Society] (Tartu: Tartu Ülikooli Kirjastus, 2001).

Lossky, Nicholas, et al., *Dictionary of the Ecumenical Movement* (Geneva and Grand Rapids: WCC Publications and Eerdmans, 1991).

Martin, William, *A Prophet with Honor: The Billy Graham Story* (New York: William Morrow and Company, 1991).

Matera, Frank J., *New Testament Ethics: The Legacies of Jesus and Paul* (Louisville, Kentucky: Westminster John Knox Press, 1996).

McBeth, Leon H., *The Baptist Heritage. Four Centuries of Baptist Witness* (Nashville, Tennessee: Broadman, 1987).

McClendon, James Wm., Jr., *Systematic Theology: Ethics, vol. 1* (Nashville: Abingdon Press, 1986).

McClendon, James Wm., Jr., *Systematic Theology: Doctrine, vol. 2* (Nashville: Abingdon Press, 1994).

Medvedev, Roy, and Zhores Medvedev, *Khrushchev: The Years in Power* (London and Oxford: Oxford University Press, 1977).

Messer, Donald E., *Calling Church and Seminary into the 21st Century* (Nashville: Abingdon Press, 1995).

Moltmann, Jürgen, *The Spirit of Life: A Universal Affirmation* (London: SCM Press, 1992).

Murphy, Nancey, *Theology in a Postmodern Age* (Prague: IBTS, 2003).

Murray, Stuart, *Biblical Interpretation in the Anabaptist Tradition* (Kitchener, Ontario: Pandora Press, 2000).

Murray, Stuart, *Church after Christendom* (Milton Keynes: Paternoster Press, 2004).

Nesdoly, Samuel, *Among the Soviet Evangelicals* (Edinburgh: The Banner of Truth Trust, 1986).

Noll, Mark, *American Evangelical Christianity: An Introduction* (Oxford: Blackwell

Publishers, 2001).

Noll, Mark, *The Rise of Evangelicalism: The Age of Edwards, Whitefield and the Wesleys* (Leicester: Inter-Varsity Press, 2004).

Norman, R. Stanton, *More Than Just a Name. Preserving our Baptist Identity* (Nashville, Tennessee: Broadman and Holman, 2001).

Ojamaa, Jüri and Jaak Hion, eds., *Aruanded Riikliku Julgeoleku Komitee 2. ja 4. osakonna tööst 1956. aastal* [Reports of the Work of the KGB 2. and 4. Department in 1956] (Tallinn: Rahvusarhiiv, 2000).

Okulov A., et al, *Teaduslik ateism* [Scientific Atheism] (Tallinn: Eesti Raamat, 1975).

Olson, Roger E., *The Westminster Handbook to Evangelical Theology* (Louisville and London: Westminster John Knox Press, 2004).

Ortberg, John, *God Is Closer Than You Think* (Grand Rapids, Michigan: Zondervan, 2005).

Oxford-rühmade liikumisest [About the Oxford-groups' Movement] (Tartu: Eesti Kristlik Üliõpilasühing, 1934).

Payne, Ernest A., *Out of Great Tribulation: Baptists in the U.S.S.R.* (London: Baptist Union of Great Britain and Ireland, 1974).

Pilli, Toivo, *Usu värvid ja varjundid: Eesti vabakoguduste ajaloost ja identiteedist* [Shades and Colours of Faith: About Estonian Free Church History and Identity] (Tallinn: Allika, 2007).

Plaat, Jaanus, *Usuliikumised, kirikud ja vabakogudused Lääne- ja Hiiumaal: usuühenduste muutumisprotsessid 18. sajandi keskpaigast kuni 20. sajandi lõpuni* [Religious Movements, Churches and Free Churches in West-Estonia and Hiiumaa Island: Transformational Processes of Religious Entities from the mid-18th Century to the End of the 20th Century] (Tartu: Eesti Rahva Muuseum, 2001).

Plaat, Jaanus, *Saaremaa kirikud, usuliikumised ja prohvetid 18.-20. sajandil* [Churches, Religious Movements and Prophets in Saaremaa Island in the 18th-20th Centuries] (Tartu: Eesti Rahva Muuseum, 2003).

Podberezkii, I. V., *Byt' Protestantom v Rossii* [To Be a Protestant in Russia] (Moskva: Institut religii i prava, 1996).

Poewe, Karla, ed., *Charismatic Christianity as a Global Culture* (Columbia, South Carolina: University of South Carolina Press, 1994).

Price, Charles, and Ian Randall, *Transforming Keswick* (Carlisle: OM Publishing, 2000).

Randall, Ian, *Evangelical Experiences: A Study in the Spirituality of English Evangelicalism 1918-1939* (Carlisle: Paternoster, 1999).

Randall, Ian, ed., *Baptists and the Orthodox Church: On the Way to Understanding* (Prague: International Baptist Theological Seminary, 2003).

Randall, Ian, Toivo Pilli and Anthony R. Cross, eds., *Baptist Identities: International Studies from the Seventeenth to the Twentieth Centuries* (Milton Keynes: Paternoster, 2006).

Raun, Toivo U., *Estonia and the Estonians* (Stanford, California: Hoover Institution Press, 1991).

Räisänen, Heikki, et al., *Reading the Bible in the Global Village* (Atlanta: Society of Biblical Literature, 2000).

Reconciliation Through Christ. Official report of the 12th Congress of BWA (Valley Forge: BWA and Judson Press, 1971).

Remmel, Meego, *The Role of Christian Ethics in Postmarxist and Postmodern Estonia*

(Bonn: Verlag für Kultur und Wissenschaft, 2002).

Rognlien, Bob, *Experiential Worship* (Navpress, 2005).

Rowe, Michael, *Russian Resurrection. Strength in Suffering – A History of Russia's Evangelical Church* (London: Marshall Pickering, 1994).

Ryman, Björn, et al., *Nordic Folk Churches: A Contemporary History* (Grand Rapids, Michigan, and Cambridge, UK: Eerdmans, 2005).

Saard, Riho, *Eesti rahvusest luterliku pastorkonna väljakujunemine ja vaba rahvakiriku projekti loomine, 1870-1917* [The Formation of a Lutheran Clergy of Estonian Descent and the Establishment of a Programme for a Free People's Church, 1870-1917] (Helsinki: Societas Historiae Ecclesiasticae Fennica, 2000).

Saard, Riho, *Eesti kirikute esivaimulikkond 1165-2006* [Estonian Church Leaders 1165-2006] (Tallinn: Argo, 2006).

Salo, Vello, *Riik ja kirikud 1940-1991* [The State and Churches 1940-1991] (Brampton, Ontario: Maarjamaa, 2000).

Sannikov, Sergei, *Dvadsat' vekov hristjanstva* [Two Thousand Years of Christianity], vol. 2 (Odessa and Sankt Peterburg: Bogomyslie, 2001).

Savinskii, Sergei, *Istorija evangel'skih hristjan-baptistov Ukrainy, Rossii, Belorussii, 1917-1967* [History of Evangelical Christians-Baptists in Ukraine, Russia and Byelorussia, 1917-1967], vol. 2 (Sankt Peterburg: Biblija dlja vseh, 2001).

Sawatsky, Walter, *Soviet Evangelicals Since World War II* (Kitchener, Ontario: Herald Press, 1981).

Seton-Watson, Hugh, *From Lenin to Khrushchev: The History of World Communism* (New York: Frederick A. Praeger Publications, 1960).

Shurden, Walter B., *The Baptist Identity. Four Fragile Freedoms* (Macon, Georgia: Smyth and Helwys, 1993).

Shurden Walter B., ed., *Proclaiming the Baptist Vision: Baptism and the Lord's Supper* (Macon, Georgia: Smyth and Helwys, 1999).

Sild, Olaf, and Vello Salo, *Lühike Eesti kirikulugu* [A Short Estonian Church History] (Tartu, 1995).

Snyder, Howard A., ed., *Global Good News: Mission in a New Context* (Nashville: Abingdon Press, 2001).

Snyder, C. Arnold, *Following in the Footsteps of Christ: The Anabaptist Tradition* (London: Darton, Longman and Todd, 2004).

Spilka, Bernard, et al., *The Psychology of Religion: An Empirical Approach* (New York, London: The Guilford Press, 2003).

Springer, Kevin, *Kolmas aalto* [Riding the Third Wave] (Hämeenlinna: Päivä OY, 1990).

Spurgeon, C.H., *Lectures to My Students: A Selection from Addresses Delivered to the Students of the Pastors' College, Metropolitan Tabernacle,* vol. 1 (London: Passmore and Alabaster, 1876).

Stacy, Wayne, ed., *A Baptist's Theology* (Macon, Georgia: Smyth and Helwys, 1999).

Stassen, Glen H. and David P. Gushee, *Kingdom Ethics: Following Jesus in Contemporary Context* (Downers Grove, Illinois: InterVarsity Press, 2003).

Stoffer, Dale R., *The Lord's Supper: Believers Church Perspectives* (Scottdale, Pennsylvania: Herald Press, 1997).

Sweet, Leonard, *Postmodern Pilgrims* (Nashville, Tennessee: Broadman and Holman Publishers, 2000).

Taagepera, Rein, *Estonia. Return to Independence* (San Francisco and Oxford:

Westview Press, 1993).

Tamm, Egle, *Moodsad kirikud: Eesti 1920.-1930. aastate sakraalarhitektuur* [Modern Churches: Church Architecture in Estonia in the 1920s and 1930s] (Tallinn: Eesti Arhitektuurimuuseum, 2001).

Tenth Baptist World Congress. Official Report (Nashville, Tennessee: BWA and Broadman Press, 1961).

Terry, John M., *Evangelism: A Concise History* (Nashville, Tennessee: Broadman and Holman, 1994).

Tidball, Derek J., *Who are the Evangelicals? Tracin the Roots of Today's Movements* (London: Marshall/Pickering, 1994).

Thompson, Philip E., and Anthony R. Cross, *Recycling the Past or Researching History? Studies in Baptist Historiography and Myths* (Milton Keynes: Paternoster, 2005).

Tomlin, Graham, *The Provocative Church* (London: SPCK, 2002).

The Truth That Makes Men Free. Official Report of the 11th Congress of BWA (Nashville, Tennessee: BWA and Broadman, 1966).

Tull, Joe E., and James E. Carter, *Ministerial Ethics: Moral Formation for Church Leaders* (Grand Rapids, Michigan: Baker Academic, 2004).

Urban, G. R., ed., *Stalinism, its Impact on Russia and the World* (Aldershot: Wildwood House, 1985).

Vahtre, Lauri, *Elu-olu viimasel vene ajal* [Living Conditions During the Last Russian Rule] (Tallinn: Kirjastuskeskus, 2002).

Viirsalu, V., *Loojangu eel/Hämarus laskub maale* [Before Sunset/Dusk Falls on the Earth] (n. p., n. d., 2001).

Walker, Andrew, and Kristin Aune, eds., *On Revival: A Critical Examination* (Carlisle: Paternoster, 2003).

Ward, W.R., *The Protestant Evangelical Awakening* (Cambridge: Cambridge University Press, 1992).

Wardin, Albert, ed., *Baptists Around the World* (Nashville, Tennessee: Broadman and Holman, 1995).

Welch, Claude, *Protestant Thought in the Nineteenth Century 1870-1914*, vol. 2 (New Haven and London: Yale University Press, 1985).

Westerhoff, John, *Will Our Children Have Faith?* (New York: The Seabury Press, 1976).

Witte, John, and Michael Bourdeaux, eds., *Proselytism and Orthodoxy in Russia. The New War for Souls* (Maryknoll, New York: Orbis Books, 1999).

Wolffe, John, ed., *Evangelical Faith and Public Zeal: Evangelicals and Society in Britain 1780-1980* (London: SPCK, 1995).

Wright, Nigel, *New Baptists, New Agenda* (Carlisle: Paternoster Press, 2002).

PUBLISHED SECONDARY SOURCES – ARTICLES AND ESSAYS

Altnurme, Riho, 'Die Estnische Evangelisch-Lutherische Kirche in der Sowjetunion (bis 1964)', in Siret Rutiku and Renhart Staats, eds., *Estland, Lettland und Westliches Christentum* (Kiel: Friedrich Wittig Verlag, 1998), pp. 233-246.

Bebbington, David W., 'Moody as a Transatlantic Evangelical', in Timothy George, ed., *Mr. Moody and the Evangelical Tradition* (London and New York: T. & T. Clark

International, 2004), pp. 75-92.

Bourdeaux, Michael, 'The Quality of Mercy: A Once-only Opportunity', in John Witte and Michael Bourdeaux, eds., *Proselytism and Orthodoxy in Russia. The New War for Souls* (Maryknoll, New York: Orbis Books, 1999), pp. 185-196.

Brackney, William H., 'Inroduction', in William H. Brackney, ed., *The Believers Church: A Voluntary Church* (Kitchener, Ontario: Pandora Press, 1998), pp. 1-7.

Brown, Cheryl and Wesley Brown, 'Progress and Challenge in Theological Education in Central and Eastern Europe', *Transformation*, vol. 20, no. 1 (January 2003), pp. 1-12.

Cross, Anthony R., 'Dispelling the myth of English Baptist Sacramentalism', *The Baptist Quarterly*, vol. 38, no. 8 (2000), pp. 367-91.

'Eesti Nõukogude Sotsialistlik Vabariik: majandus' [The Estonian Soviet Socialist Republic: economy], in *Eesti Nõukogude Entsüklopeedia* [Estonian Soviet Encyclopaedia], vol. 2 (Tallinn: Valgus, 1987), pp. 319-338.

Elliott, Mark, and Anita Deyneka, 'Protestant Missionaries in the Former Soviet Union', in John Witte and Michael Bourdeaux, eds., *Proselytism and Orthodoxy in Russia. The New War for Souls* (Maryknoll, New York: Orbis Books, 1999), pp. 197-223.

Ellis, Jane, 'Some reflections about religious policy under Kharchev', in Sabrina P. Ramet, ed., *Religious Policy in the Soviet Union* (Cambridge and New York: Cambridge University Press, 1993), pp. 84-104.

Fiddes, Paul, 'Baptism and the Process of Christian Initiation', *The Ecumenical Review*, no. 54 (2002), pp. 48-65.

Hauerwas, Stanley, 'On Keeping Theological Ethics Theological', in Stanley Hauerwas and Alasdair MacIntyre, eds., *Revisions: Changing Perspectives in Moral Philosophy* (Notre Dame: University of Notre Dame Press, 1983), pp. 16-42.

Heth, William A., 'Divorce, but No Remarriage', in H. Wayne House, ed., *Divorce and Remarriage: Four Christian Views* (Downers Grove, Illinois: InterVarsity Press, 1990), pp. 73-129.

Howe, Claude L., 'The Mission Impulse Propels the Baptist Experience', in Charles W. Deweese, ed., *Defining Baptist Convictions. Guidelines for the Twenty-First Century* (Franklin, Tennessee: Providence House Publishers, 1996), pp. 148-156.

Kiivit, Jaan, 'Eesti Evangeelne Luterlik Kirik pärast Teist maailmasõda' [The Estonian Evangelical Lutheran Church after the Second World War], in J. Gnadenteich, *Kodumaa kirikulugu* [Church History of the Home Country] (Logos: Tallinn, 1995), pp. 102-115.

Kliimask, Jaak, 'Economic Transformation in the Post-Socialist City. The Case of Tallinn', in Martin Aberg and Martin Peterson, eds., *Baltic Cities: Perspectives on Urban and Regional Change in the Baltic Sea Area* (Lund: Nordic Academic Press, 1997), pp. 151-167.

Kool, Anna-Marie, 'A Protestant Perspective on Mission in Eastern and Central Europe', *Religion in Eastern Europe*, vol. XX, no. 6 (December 2000), pp. 1-21.

Kurg, Ingmar, 'Kristlikud organisatsioonid ja oikumeeniline suhtlemine Eestis' [Christian Organisations and Ecumenical Interaction in Estonia], in *Evangeelne kuulutus ja antievangeelne maailm. Aastaraamat 2001* [Evangelical Message and Anti-Evangelical World. Yearbook 2001] (Tartu: Eesti Evangeelne Allianss, 2002), pp. 31-43.

Kurg, Ingmar, 'Kristlikud uskkonnad ja organisatsioonid tänapäeva Eestis' [Christian Denominations and Organisations in Present Day Estonia], in J. Gnadenteich, *Kodumaa kirikulugu* [Church History of the Home Country] (Tallinn: Logos, 1995), pp. 115-125.

Lewin, Moshe, 'Grappling with Stalinism', in David L. Hoffmann, ed., *Stalinism* (Oxford: Blackwell Publishing, 2003), pp. 42-61.

Luchterhandt, Otto, 'The Council for Religious Affairs', in Sabrina P. Ramet, ed., *Religious Policy in the Soviet Union* (Cambridge and New York: Cambridge University Press, 1993), pp. 55-83.

Miller, Richard B., 'Rules', in Gilbert Meilaender and William Werpehowski, eds., *The Oxford Handbook of Theological Ethics* (New York: Oxford University Press, 2005), pp. 220-236.

Paul, Toomas, 'Eesti kirik 1980. aastatel' [The Estonian Church in the 1980s], *Vikerkaar*, no. 6 (1991), pp. 59-64.

Pearse, Meic, 'Revivals as Historically Situated Events: Lessons for the Future', in Andrew Walker and Kristin Aune, eds., *On Revival: A Critical Examination* (Carlisle: Paternoster, 2003), pp. 157-168.

Penner, Peter, 'Critical evaluation of recent developments in the Commonwealth of Independent States', *Transformation*, vol. 20, no. 1 (January 2003), pp. 13-29.

Pilli, Einike, and Daily Valk, 'Eesti EKB Liidu haridustöö evangeliseerimise ja eluaegse õppimise dünaamikas' [The UECBE Educational Work in the Dynamics of Evangelism and Lifelong Learning], in Toivo Pilli, ed., *Teekond teisenevas ajas: peatükke Eesti vabakoguduste ajaloost* [A Journey in Changing Time: Chapters from the History of Estonian Free Churches] (Tartu: Kõrgem Usuteaduslik Seminar ja Sõnasepp OÜ, 2005), pp. 51-88.

Pilli, Toivo, 'The Role of the Monthly Publication "Teekäija" in the Estonian Baptist Church 1904-1940', in Siret Rutiku and Reinhart Staats, eds., *Estland, Lettland und Westliches Christentum* (Kiel: Friedrich Wittig Verlag, 1998), pp. 211-218.

Pilli, Toivo, 'Baptists in Estonia 1884-1940', *The Baptist Quarterly*, vol. XXXIX, no. 1 (January 2001), pp. 27-34.

Pilli, Toivo, 'Union of Evangelical Christians-Baptists of Estonia 1945-1989: Survival Techniques, Outreach Efforts, Search for Identity', *Baptist History and Heritage*, vol. XXXVI, nos. 1 and 2 (Winter/Spring 2001), pp. 113-135.

Pilli, Toivo, 'The Forced Blessing of Unity: Formation of the Union of Evangelical Christians-Baptists in Estonia', *Teologinen Aikakauskirja* [Finnish Journal of Theology], no. 6 (2003), pp. 548-562.

Pilli, Toivo, 'Eesti baptistide eklesioloogiast *Teekäija* vaatepeeglis: 1904-1940' [About Estonian Baptist Ecclesiology in the Mirror of *Teekäija*: 1904-1940], in Toivo Pilli, ed., *Teekond teisenevas ajas: peatükke Eesti vabakoguduste ajaloost* [A Journey in Changing Time: Chapters from the History of Estonian Free Churches] (Tartu: Kõrgem Usuteaduslik Seminar ja Sõnasepp OÜ, 2005), pp. 29-50.

Pilli, Toivo, and Tõnis Valk, 'Ühest ateistliku töö meetodist: evangeeliumi kristlaste-baptistide palvemajade sulgemine Eestis 1945-1965' [A Method of Atheistic Work: Closures of Evangelical Christian-Baptist Prayer Houses in Estonia, 1945-1965], in Toivo Pilli, ed., *Teekond teisenevas ajas: peatükke Eesti vabakoguduste ajaloost* [A Journey in Changing Time: Chapters from the History of Estonian Free Churches] (Tartu: Kõrgem Usuteaduslik Seminar ja Sõnasepp OÜ, 2005), pp. 89-127.

Pilli, Toivo, 'From a Thunderstorm to a Settled Still Life, Estonian Baptists 1959-1972', part 1, *The Baptist Quarterly*, vol. 41, no. 3 (July 2005), pp. 158-174; part 2, *The Baptist Quarterly*, vol. 41, no. 4 (October 2005), pp. 206-223.

Pilli, Toivo, 'Christians as Citizens of a Persecuting State: A Theological and Ethical

Reflection from a Historical Perspective', *Journal of European Baptist Studies*, no. 1 (September 2006), pp. 5-22.

Pilli, Toivo, 'Finding a Balance between Church and Academia: Baptist Theological Education in Estonia', *Religion in Eastern Europe*, vol. XXVI, no. 3 (August 2006), pp. 17-43.

Plaat, Jaanus, 'Eesti vabakoguduste vastupanu nõukogude religioonipoliitikale võrreldes luterliku ja õigeusu kirikuga (1944-1987)' [The Resistance of Estonian Free Churches to Soviet Religious Policies, in Comparison with Lutheran and Orthodox Churches (1944-1987)], in Toivo Pilli, ed., *Teekond teisenevas ajas: peatükke Eesti baptismi ajaloost* [A Journey in Changing Time: Chapters from the History of Estonian Free Churches] (Tartu: Kõrgem Usuteaduslik Seminar ja Sõnasepp OÜ, 2005), pp. 128-159.

Porter, Jean, 'Virtue', in Gilbert Meilaender and William Werpehowski, eds., *The Oxford Handbook of Theological Ethics* (New York: Oxford University Press, 2005), pp. 205-219.

Ramet, Sabrina P., 'Religious Policy in the era of Gorbachev', in Sabrina P. Ramet, ed., *Religious Policy in the Soviet Union* (Cambridge and New York: Cambridge University Press, 1993), pp. 31-52.

Randall, Ian, '"Arresting People for Christ": Baptists and the Oxford Group in the 1930s', *The Baptist Quarterly*, vol. 38, no. 1 (1999), pp. 3-18.

Randall, Ian, 'Every Apostolic Church a Mission Society: European Baptist Origins and Identity', in Anthony R. Cross, ed., *Ecumenism and History, Studies in Honour of John H.Y. Briggs* (Carlisle: Paternoster, 2002), pp. 281-301.

Saard, Riho, 'Eesti kirikute juhtivvaimulikkond läbi aegade' [Estonian Church Leaders through the Centuries], part 2, *Akadeemia*, no. 3 (1998), pp. 604-625.

Saard, Riho, 'Uskonnollisen ja teologisen kirjallisuuden lähettäminen Suomesta Neuvosto-Viroon 1950-1980-luvuilla' [Sending Religious and Theological Literature from Finland to Soviet Estonia in the 1950s-1980s], *Teologinen Aikakauskirja* [Finnish Journal of Theology], no. 6 (2003), pp. 538-547.

Saard, Riho, 'Eesti varase baptismi eneserefleksioonist' [About the Self-Reflection of Early Estonian Baptists], in Toivo Pilli, ed., *Teekond teisenevas ajas: peatükke Eesti vabakoguduste ajaloost* [A Journey in Changing Time: Some Chapters from History of Estonian Free Churches] (Tartu: Kõrgem Usuteaduslik Seminar ja Sõnasepp OÜ, 2005), pp. 9-28.

Sawatsky, Walter, 'Protestantism in the USSR', in Sabrina P. Ramet, ed., *Religious Policy in the Soviet Union* (Cambridge: Cambridge University Press, 1993), pp. 319-349.

Scarot, M., 'Counterfactuals and the Invention of Religious Traditions', in Jan W. van Henten and Anton Houtepen, eds., *Religious Identity and the Invention of Tradition* (Assen: Van Grocum, 2001), pp. 21-40.

Teraudkalns, Valdis, 'Socialist Ideas among Latvian Baptists in the First Half of the Twentieth Century', in Sharyl Corrado and Toivo Pilli, eds., *Eastern European Baptist History: New Perspectives* (Prague: IBTS, 2007), pp. 102-118.

Turner, Max, 'Revival in the New Testament', in Andrew Walker and Kristin Aune, eds., *On Revival: A Critical Examination* (Carlisle: Paternoster, 2003), pp. 3-21.

Vahermägi, Mari, 'Vooruslikkusest pühitsuselus Osvald Tärgi ja Robert Võsu kirjapärandi valgel' [About Virtues in Sanctification in the Light of the Literary Heritage of Osvald Tärk and Robert Võsu], in Toivo Pilli, ed., *Teekond teisenevas ajas: Peatükke Eesti vabakoguduste ajaloost* [A Journey in Changing Time: Chapters from the History of Estonian Free Churches] (Tartu: Kõrgem Usuteaduslik Seminar ja Sõnasepp OÜ, 2005), pp. 160-180.

Volf, Miroslav, 'Fishing in the Neighbor's Pond: Mission and Proselytism as Challenge to Theology and Church Life in Eastern Europe', *Religion in Eastern Europe*, vol. XVI, no. 1 (February 1996), pp. 34-47.

Walter, Karl Heinz, 'The Future of Theological Education Within the European Baptist Federation', *Religion in Eastern Europe*, vol. XXI, no. 3 (June 2001), pp. 20-33.

Walters, Philip, 'A survey of Soviet religious policy', in Sabrina P. Ramet, ed., *Religious Policy in the Soviet Union* (Cambridge and New York: Cambridge University Press, 1993), pp. 3-30.

Watson, David L., 'The Mystery of Evangelism: Mission in an Age of Cosmic Discovery', in Howard A. Snyder, ed., *Global Good News: Mission in a New Context* (Nashville: Abingdon Press, 2001), pp. 26-40.

Williams, George H., 'The Believers' Church and the Given Church', in Paul Basden and David S. Dockery, eds., *The People of God: Essays on the Believers' Church* (Nashville: Broadman, 1991), pp. 325-332.

Zubkova, Elena, 'Russia after the War: Hopes, Illusions and Disappointments', in David L. Hoffmann, ed., *Stalinism* (Oxford: Blackwell Publishing, 2003), pp. 280-301.

General Index

Studies in Baptist History and Thought

(All titles uniform with this volume)
Dates in bold are of projected publication
Volumes in this series are not always published in sequence

David Bebbington and Anthony R. Cross (eds)
Global Baptist History
(SBHT vol. 14)

This book brings together studies from the Second International Conference on Baptist Studies which explore different facets of Baptist life and work especially during the twentieth century.

2006 / 1-84227-214-4 / approx. 350pp

David Bebbington (ed.)
The Gospel in the World
International Baptist Studies
(SBHT vol. 1)

This volume of essays from the First International Conference on Baptist Studies deals with a range of subjects spanning Britain, North America, Europe, Asia and the Antipodes. Topics include studies on religious tolerance, the communion controversy and the development of the international Baptist community, and concludes with two important essays on the future of Baptist life that pay special attention to the United States.

2002 / 1-84227-118-0 / xiv + 362pp

John H.Y. Briggs (ed.)
Pulpit and People
Studies in Eighteenth-Century English Baptist Life and Thought
(SBHT vol. 28)

The eighteenth century was a crucial time in Baptist history. The denomination had its roots in seventeenth-century English Puritanism and Separatism and the persecution of the Stuart kings with only a limited measure of freedom after 1689. Worse, however, was to follow for with toleration came doctrinal conflict, a move away from central Christian understandings and a loss of evangelistic urgency. Both spiritual and numerical decline ensued, to the extent that the denomination was virtually reborn as rather belatedly it came to benefit from the Evangelical Revival which brought new life to both Arminian and Calvinistic Baptists. The papers in this volume study a denomination in transition, and relate to theology, their views of the church and its mission, Baptist spirituality, and engagements with radical politics.

2007 / 1-84227-403-1 / approx. 350pp

July 2005

Damian Brot
Church of the Baptized or Church of Believers?
A Contribution to the Dialogue between the Catholic Church and the Free Churches with Special Reference to Baptists
(SBHT vol. 26)

The dialogue between the Catholic Church and the Free Churches in Europe has hardly taken place. This book pleads for a commencement of such a conversation. It offers, among other things, an introduction to the American and the international dialogues between Baptists and the Catholic Church and strives to allow these conversations to become fruitful in the European context as well.

2006 / 1-84227-334-5 / approx. 364pp

Dennis Bustin
Paradox and Perseverence
Hanserd Knollys, Particular Baptist Pioneer in Seventeenth-Century England
(SBHT vol. 23)

The seventeenth century was a significant period in English history during which the people of England experienced unprecedented change and tumult in all spheres of life. At the same time, the importance of order and the traditional institutions of society were being reinforced. Hanserd Knollys, born during this pivotal period, personified in his life the ambiguity, tension and paradox of it, openly seeking change while at the same time cautiously embracing order. As a founder and leader of the Particular Baptists in London and despite persecution and personal hardship, he played a pivotal role in helping shape their identity externally in society and, internally, as they moved toward becoming more formalised by the end of the century.

2006 / 1-84227-259-4 / approx. 324pp

Anthony R. Cross
Baptism and the Baptists
Theology and Practice in Twentieth-Century Britain
(SBHT vol. 3)

At a time of renewed interest in baptism, *Baptism and the Baptists* is a detailed study of twentieth-century baptismal theology and practice and the factors which have influenced its development.

2000 / 0-85364-959-6 / xx + 530pp

Anthony R. Cross and Philip E. Thompson (eds)
Baptist Sacramentalism
(SBHT vol. 5)
This collection of essays includes biblical, historical and theological studies in the theology of the sacraments from a Baptist perspective. Subjects explored include the physical side of being spiritual, baptism, the Lord's supper, the church, ordination, preaching, worship, religious liberty and the issue of disestablishment.
2003 / 1-84227-119-9 / xvi + 278pp

Anthony R. Cross and Philip E. Thompson (eds)
Baptist Sacramentalism 2
(SBHT vol. 25)
This second collection of essays exploring various dimensions of sacramental theology from a Baptist perspective includes biblical, historical and theological studies from scholars from around the world.
***2006** / 1-84227-325-6 / approx. 350pp*

Paul S. Fiddes
Tracks and Traces
Baptist Identity in Church and Theology
(SBHT vol. 13)
This is a comprehensive, yet unusual, book on the faith and life of Baptist Christians. It explores the understanding of the church, ministry, sacraments and mission from a thoroughly theological perspective. In a series of interlinked essays, the author relates Baptist identity consistently to a theology of covenant and to participation in the triune communion of God.
2003 / 1-84227-120-2 / xvi + 304pp

Stanley K. Fowler
More Than a Symbol
The British Baptist Recovery of Baptismal Sacramentalism
(SBHT vol. 2)
Fowler surveys the entire scope of British Baptist literature from the seventeenth-century pioneers onwards. He shows that in the twentieth century leading British Baptist pastors and theologians recovered an understanding of baptism that connected experience with soteriology and that in doing so they were recovering what many of their forebears had taught.
2002 / 1-84227-052-4 / xvi + 276pp

Steven R. Harmon
Towards Baptist Catholicity
Essays on Tradition and the Baptist Vision
(SBHT vol. 27)
This series of essays contends that the reconstruction of the Baptist vision in the wake of modernity's dissolution requires a retrieval of the ancient ecumenical tradition that forms Christian identity through rehearsal and practice. Themes explored include catholic identity as an emerging trend in Baptist theology, tradition as a theological category in Baptist perspective, Baptist confessions and the patristic tradition, worship as a principal bearer of tradition, and the role of Baptist higher education in shaping the Christian vision.
2006 / 1-84227-362-0 / approx. 210pp

Michael A.G. Haykin (ed.)
'At the Pure Fountain of Thy Word'
Andrew Fuller as an Apologist
(SBHT vol. 6)
One of the greatest Baptist theologians of the eighteenth and early nineteenth centuries, Andrew Fuller has not had justice done to him. There is little doubt that Fuller's theology lay behind the revitalization of the Baptists in the late eighteenth century and the first few decades of the nineteenth. This collection of essays fills a much needed gap by examining a major area of Fuller's thought, his work as an apologist.
2004 / 1-84227-171-7 / xxii + 276pp

Michael A.G. Haykin
Studies in Calvinistic Baptist Spirituality
(SBHT vol. 15)
In a day when spirituality is in vogue and Christian communities are looking for guidance in this whole area, there is wisdom in looking to the past to find untapped wells. The Calvinistic Baptists, heirs of the rich ecclesial experience in the Puritan era of the seventeenth century, but, by the end of the eighteenth century, also passionately engaged in the catholicity of the Evangelical Revivals, are such a well. This collection of essays, covering such things as the Lord's Supper, friendship and hymnody, seeks to draw out the spiritual riches of this community for reflection and imitation in the present day.
2006 / 1-84227-149-0 / approx. 350pp

Brian Haymes, Anthony R. Cross and Ruth Gouldbourne
On Being the Church
Revisioning Baptist Identity
(SBHT vol. 21)

The aim of the book is to re-examine Baptist theology and practice in the light of the contemporary biblical, theological, ecumenical and missiological context drawing on historical and contemporary writings and issues. It is not a study in denominationalism but rather seeks to revision historical insights from the believers' church tradition for the sake of Baptists and other Christians in the context of the modern–postmodern context.

2006 / 1-84227-121-0 / approx. 350pp

Ken R. Manley
From Woolloomooloo to 'Eternity': A History of Australian Baptists
Volume 1: Growing an Australian Church (1831–1914)
Volume 2: A National Church in a Global Community (1914–2005)
(SBHT vols 16.1 and 16.2)

From their beginnings in Australia in 1831 with the first baptisms in Woolloomoolloo Bay in 1832, this pioneering study describes the quest of Baptists in the different colonies (states) to discover their identity as Australians and Baptists. Although institutional developments are analyzed and the roles of significant individuals traced, the major focus is on the social and theological dimensions of the Baptist movement.

2 vol. set 2006 / 1-84227-405-8 / approx. 900pp

Ken R. Manley
'Redeeming Love Proclaim'
John Rippon and the Baptists
(SBHT vol. 12)

A leading exponent of the new moderate Calvinism which brought new life to many Baptists, John Rippon (1751–1836) helped unite the Baptists at this significant time. His many writings expressed the denomination's growing maturity and mutual awareness of Baptists in Britain and America, and exerted a long-lasting influence on Baptist worship and devotion. In his various activities, Rippon helped conserve the heritage of Old Dissent and promoted the evangelicalism of the New Dissent

2004 / 1-84227-193-8 / xviii + 340pp

Peter J. Morden
Offering Christ to the World
Andrew Fuller and the Revival of English Particular Baptist Life
(SBHT vol. 8)
Andrew Fuller (1754–1815) was one of the foremost English Baptist ministers of his day. His career as an Evangelical Baptist pastor, theologian, apologist and missionary statesman coincided with the profound revitalization of the Particular Baptist denomination to which he belonged. This study examines the key aspects of the life and thought of this hugely significant figure, and gives insights into the revival in which he played such a central part.
2003 / 1-84227-141-5 / xx + 202pp

Peter Naylor
Calvinism, Communion and the Baptists
A Study of English Calvinistic Baptists from the Late 1600s to the Early 1800s
(SBHT vol. 7)
Dr Naylor argues that the traditional link between 'high-Calvinism' and 'restricted communion' is in need of revision. He examines Baptist communion controversies from the late 1600s to the early 1800s and also the theologies of John Gill and Andrew Fuller.
2003 / 1-84227-142-3 / xx + 266pp

Ian M. Randall, Toivo Pilli and Anthony R. Cross (eds)
Baptist Identities
International Studies from the Seventeenth to the Twentieth Centuries
(SBHT vol. 19)
These papers represent the contributions of scholars from various parts of the world as they consider the factors that have contributed to Baptist distinctiveness in different countries and at different times. The volume includes specific case studies as well as broader examinations of Baptist life in a particular country or region. Together they represent an outstanding resource for understanding Baptist identities.
2005 / 1-84227-215-2 / approx. 350pp

James M. Renihan
Edification and Beauty
The Practical Ecclesiology of the English Particular Baptists, 1675–1705
(SBHT vol. 17)
Edification and Beauty describes the practices of the Particular Baptist churches at the end of the seventeenth century in terms of three concentric circles: at the centre is the ecclesiological material in the Second London Confession, which is then fleshed out in the various published writings of the men associated with these churches, and, finally, expressed in the church books of the era.
2005 / 1-84227-251-9 / approx. 230pp

Frank Rinaldi
'The Tribe of Dan'
A Study of the New Connexion of General Baptists 1770–1891
(SBHT vol. 10)
'The Tribe of Dan' is a thematic study which explores the theology, organizational structure, evangelistic strategy, ministry and leadership of the New Connexion of General Baptists as it experienced the process of institutionalization in the transition from a revival movement to an established denomination.
2006 / 1-84227-143-1 / approx. 350pp

Peter Shepherd
The Making of a Modern Denomination
John Howard Shakespeare and the English Baptists 1898–1924
(SBHT vol. 4)
John Howard Shakespeare introduced revolutionary change to the Baptist denomination. The Baptist Union was transformed into a strong central institution and Baptist ministers were brought under its control. Further, Shakespeare's pursuit of church unity reveals him as one of the pioneering ecumenists of the twentieth century.
2001 / 1-84227-046-X / xviii + 220pp

Karen Smith
The Community and the Believers
A Study of Calvinistic Baptist Spirituality in Some Towns and Villages of
Hampshire and the Borders of Wiltshire, c.1730–1830
(SBHT vol. 22)
The period from 1730 to 1830 was one of transition for Calvinistic Baptists.
Confronted by the enthusiasm of the Evangelical Revival, congregations within
the denomination as a whole were challenged to find a way to take account of
the revival experience. This study examines the life and devotion of Calvinistic
Baptists in Hampshire and Wiltshire during this period. Among this group of
Baptists was the hymn writer, Anne Steele.
2005 / 1-84227-326-4 / approx. 280pp

Martin Sutherland
Dissenters in a 'Free Land'
Baptist Thought in New Zealand 1850–2000
(SBHT vol. 24)
Baptists in New Zealand were forced to recast their identity. Conventions of
communication and association, state and ecumenical relations, even historical
divisions and controversies had to be revised in the face of new topographies
and constraints. As Baptists formed themselves in a fluid society they drew
heavily on both international movements and local dynamics. This book traces
the development of ideas which shaped institutions and styles in sometimes
surprising ways.
2006 / 1-84227-327-2 / approx. 230pp

Brian Talbot
The Search for a Common Identity
The Origins of the Baptist Union of Scotland 1800–1870
(SBHT vol. 9)
In the period 1800 to 1827 there were three streams of Baptists in Scotland:
Scotch, Haldaneite and 'English' Baptist. A strong commitment to home
evangelization brought these three bodies closer together, leading to a merger of
their home missionary societies in 1827. However, the first three attempts to
form a union of churches failed, but by the 1860s a common understanding of
their corporate identity was attained leading to the establishment of the Baptist
Union of Scotland.
2003 / 1-84227-123-7 / xviii + 402pp

Philip E. Thompson
The Freedom of God
Towards Baptist Theology in Pneumatological Perspective
(SBHT vol. 20)
This study contends that the range of theological commitments of the early Baptists are best understood in relation to their distinctive emphasis on the freedom of God. Thompson traces how this was recast anthropocentrically, leading to an emphasis upon human freedom from the nineteenth century onwards. He seeks to recover the dynamism of the early vision via a pneumatologically-oriented ecclesiology defining the church in terms of the memory of God.
2006 / 1-84227-125-3 / approx. 350pp

Philip E. Thompson and Anthony R. Cross (eds)
Recycling the Past or Researching History?
Studies in Baptist Historiography and Myths
(SBHT vol. 11)
In this volume an international group of Baptist scholars examine and re-examine areas of Baptist life and thought about which little is known or the received wisdom is in need of revision. Historiographical studies include the date Oxford Baptists joined the Abingdon Association, the death of the Fifth Monarchist John Pendarves, eighteenth-century Calvinistic Baptists and the political realm, confessional identity and denominational institutions, Baptist community, ecclesiology, the priesthood of all believers, soteriology, Baptist spirituality, Strict and Reformed Baptists, the role of women among British Baptists, while various 'myths' challenged include the nature of high-Calvinism in eighteenth-century England, baptismal anti-sacramentalism, episcopacy, and Baptists and change.
2005 / 1-84227-122-9 / approx. 330pp

Linda Wilson
Marianne Farningham
A Plain Working Woman
(SBHT vol. 18)
Marianne Farningham, of College Street Baptist Chapel, Northampton, was a household name in evangelical circles in the later nineteenth century. For over fifty years she produced comment, poetry, biography and fiction for the popular Christian press. This investigation uses her writings to explore the beliefs and behaviour of evangelical Nonconformists, including Baptists, during these years.
2006 / 1-84227-124-5 / approx. 250pp

Other Paternoster titles
relating to Baptist history and thought

George R. Beasley-Murray
Baptism in the New Testament
(Paternoster Digital Library)

This is a welcome reprint of a classic text on baptism originally published in 1962 by one of the leading Baptist New Testament scholars of the twentieth century. Dr Beasley-Murray's comprehensive study begins by investigating the antecedents of Christian baptism. It then surveys the foundation of Christian baptism in the Gospels, its emergence in the Acts of the Apostles and development in the apostolic writings. Following a section relating baptism to New Testament doctrine, a substantial discussion of the origin and significance of infant baptism leads to a briefer consideration of baptismal reform and ecumenism.

2005 / 1-84227-300-0 / x + 422pp

Paul Beasley-Murray
Fearless for Truth
A Personal Portrait of the Life of George Beasley-Murray

Without a doubt George Beasley-Murray was one of the greatest Baptists of the twentieth century. A long-standing Principal of Spurgeon's College, he wrote more than twenty books and made significant contributions in the study of areas as diverse as baptism and eschatology, as well as writing highly respected commentaries on the Book of Revelation and John's Gospel.

2002 / 1-84227-134-2 / xii + 244pp

David Bebbington
Holiness in Nineteenth-Century England
(Studies in Christian History and Thought)

David Bebbington stresses the relationship of movements of spirituality to changes in their cultural setting, especially the legacies of the Enlightenment and Romanticism. He shows that these broad shifts in ideological mood had a profound effect on the ways in which piety was conceptualized and practised. Holiness was intimately bound up with the spirit of the age.

2000 / 0-85364-981-2 / viii + 98pp

Clyde Binfield
Victorian Nonconformity in Eastern England 1840–1885
(Studies in Evangelical History and Thought)
Studies of Victorian religion and society often concentrate on cities, suburbs, and industrialisation. This study provides a contrast. Victorian Eastern England—Essex, Suffolk, Norfolk, Cambridgeshire, and Huntingdonshire—was rural, traditional, relatively unchanging. That is nonetheless a caricature which discounts the industry in Norwich and Ipswich (as well as in Haverhill, Stowmarket and Leiston) and ignores the impact of London on Essex, of railways throughout the region, and of an ancient but changing university (Cambridge) on the county town which housed it. It also entirely ignores the political implications of such changes in a region noted for the variety of its religious Dissent since the seventeenth century. This book explores Victorian Eastern England and its Nonconformity. It brings to a wider readership a pioneering thesis which has made a major contribution to a fresh evolution of English religion and society.
2006 / 1-84227-216-0 / approx. 274pp

Edward W. Burrows
'To Me To Live Is Christ'
A Biography of Peter H. Barber
This book is about a remarkably gifted and energetic man of God. Peter H. Barber was born into a Brethren family in Edinburgh in 1930. In his youth he joined Charlotte Baptist Chapel and followed the call into Baptist ministry. For eighteen years he was the pioneer minister of the new congregation in the New Town of East Kilbride, which planted two further congregations. At the age of thirty-nine he served as Centenary President of the Baptist Union of Scotland and then exercised an influential ministry for over seven years in the well-known Upton Vale Baptist Church, Torquay. From 1980 until his death in 1994 he was General Secretary of the Baptist Union of Scotland. Through his work for the European Baptist Federation and the Baptist World Alliance he became a world Baptist statesman. He was President of the EBF during the upheaval that followed the collapse of Communism.
2005 / 1-84227-324-8 / xxii + 236pp

Christopher J. Clement
Religious Radicalism in England 1535–1565
(Rutherford Studies in Historical Theology)
In this valuable study Christopher Clement draws our attention to a varied assemblage of people who sought Christian faithfulness in the underworld of mid-Tudor England. Sympathetically and yet critically he assess their place in the history of English Protestantism, and by attentive listening he gives them a voice.
1997 / 0-946068-44-5 / xxii + 426pp

Anthony R. Cross (ed.)
Ecumenism and History
Studies in Honour of John H.Y. Briggs
(Studies in Christian History and Thought)
This collection of essays examines the inter-relationships between the two fields in which Professor Briggs has contributed so much: history—particularly Baptist and Nonconformist—and the ecumenical movement. With contributions from colleagues and former research students from Britain, Europe and North America, *Ecumenism and History* provides wide-ranging studies in important aspects of Christian history, theology and ecumenical studies.
2002 / 1-84227-135-0 / xx + 362pp

Keith E. Eitel
Paradigm Wars
*The Southern Baptist International Mission Board
Faces the Third Millennium*
(Regnum Studies in Mission)
The International Mission Board of the Southern Baptist Convention is the largest denominational mission agency in North America. This volume chronicles the historic and contemporary forces that led to the IMB's recent extensive reorganization, providing the most comprehensive case study to date of a historic mission agency restructuring to continue its mission purpose into the twenty-first century more effectively.
2000 / 1-870345-12-6 / x + 140pp

Ruth Gouldbourne
The Flesh and the Feminine
Gender and Theology in the Writings of Caspar Schwenckfeld
(Studies in Christian History and Thought)
Caspar Schwenckfeld and his movement exemplify one of the radical communities of the sixteenth century. Challenging theological and liturgical norms, they also found themselves challenging social and particularly gender assumptions. In this book, the issues of the relationship between radical theology and the understanding of gender are considered.
2005 */ 1-84227-048-6 / approx. 304pp*

David Hilborn
The Words of our Lips
Language-Use in Free Church Worship
(Paternoster Theological Monographs)
Studies of liturgical language have tended to focus on the written canons of Roman Catholic and Anglican communities. By contrast, David Hilborn analyses the more extemporary approach of English Nonconformity. Drawing on recent developments in linguistic pragmatics, he explores similarities and differences between 'fixed' and 'free' worship, and argues for the interdependence of each.

2006 / 0-85364-977-4

Stephen R. Holmes
Listening to the Past
The Place of Tradition in Theology
Beginning with the question 'Why can't we just read the Bible?' Stephen Holmes considers the place of tradition in theology, showing how the doctrine of creation leads to an account of historical location and creaturely limitations as essential aspects of our existence. For we cannot claim unmediated access to the Scriptures without acknowledging the place of tradition: theology is an irreducibly communal task. *Listening to the Past* is a sustained attempt to show what listening to tradition involves, and how it can be used to aid theological work today.

2002 / 1-84227-155-5 / xiv + 168pp

Mark Hopkins
Nonconformity's Romantic Generation
Evangelical and Liberal Theologies in Victorian England
(Studies in Evangelical History and Thought)
A study of the theological development of key leaders of the Baptist and Congregational denominations at their period of greatest influence, including C.H. Spurgeon and R.W. Dale, and of the controversies in which those among them who embraced and rejected the liberal transformation of their evangelical heritage opposed each other.

2004 / 1-84227-150-4 / xvi + 284pp

Galen K. Johnson
Prisoner of Conscience
John Bunyan on Self, Community and Christian Faith
(Studies in Christian History and Thought)
This is an interdisciplinary study of John Bunyan's understanding of conscience across his autobiographical, theological and fictional writings, investigating whether conscience always deserves fidelity, and how Bunyan's view of conscience affects his relationship both to modern Western individualism and historic Christianity.

2003 / 1-84227- 151-2 / xvi + 236pp

R.T. Kendall
Calvin and English Calvinism to 1649
(Studies in Christian History and Thought)
The author's thesis is that those who formed the Westminster Confession of Faith, which is regarded as Calvinism, in fact departed from John Calvin on two points: (1) the extent of the atonement and (2) the ground of assurance of salvation.

1997 / 0-85364-827-1 / xii + 264pp

Timothy Larsen
Friends of Religious Equality
Nonconformist Politics in Mid-Victorian England
During the middle decades of the nineteenth century the English Nonconformist community developed a coherent political philosophy of its own, of which a central tenet was the principle of religious equality (in contrast to the stereotype of Evangelical Dissenters). The Dissenting community fought for the civil rights of Roman Catholics, non-Christians and even atheists, on an issue of principle which had its flowering in the enthusiastic and undivided support which Nonconformity gave to the campaign for Jewish emancipation. This reissued study examines the political efforts and ideas of English Nonconformists during the period, covering the whole range of national issues raised, from state education to the Crimean War. It offers a case study of a theologically conservative group defending religious pluralism in the civic sphere, showing that the concept of religious equality was a grand vision at the centre of the political philosophy of the Dissenters.

2007 / 1-84227-402-3 / x + 300pp

Donald M. Lewis
Lighten Their Darkness
The Evangelical Mission to Working-Class London, 1828–1860
(Studies in Evangelical History and Thought)
This is a comprehensive and compelling study of the Church and the complexities of nineteenth-century London. Challenging our understanding of the culture in working London at this time, Lewis presents a well-structured and illustrated work that contributes substantially to the study of evangelicalism and mission in nineteenth-century Britain.
2001 / 1-84227-074-5 / xviii + 372pp

Stanley E. Porter and Anthony R. Cross (eds)
Semper Reformandum
Studies in Honour of Clark H. Pinnock
Clark Pinnock has clearly been one of the most important evangelical theologians of the last forty years in North America. Always provocative, especially in the wide range of opinions he has held and considered, Pinnock, himself a Baptist, has recently retired after twenty-five years of teaching at McMaster Divinity College. His colleagues and associates honour him in this volume by responding to his important theological work which has dealt with the essential topics of evangelical theology. These include Christian apologetics, biblical inspiration, the Holy Spirit and, perhaps most importantly in recent years, openness theology.
2003 / 1-84227-206-3 / xiv + 414pp

Meic Pearse
The Great Restoration
The Religious Radicals of the 16th and 17th Centuries
Pearse charts the rise and progress of continental Anabaptism – both evangelical and heretical – through the sixteenth century. He then follows the story of those English people who became impatient with Puritanism and separated – first from the Church of England and then from one another – to form the antecedents of later Congregationalists, Baptists and Quakers.
1998 / 0-85364-800-X / xii + 320pp

Charles Price and Ian M. Randall
Transforming Keswick
Transforming Keswick is a thorough, readable and detailed history of the convention. It will be of interest to those who know and love Keswick, those who are only just discovering it, and serious scholars eager to learn more about the history of God's dealings with his people.
2000 / 1-85078-350-0 / 288pp

Jim Purves
The Triune God and the Charismatic Movement
A Critical Appraisal from a Scottish Perspective
(Paternoster Theological Monographs)
All emotion and no theology? Or a fundamental challenge to reappraise and realign our trinitarian theology in the light of Christian experience? This study of charismatic renewal as it found expression within Scotland at the end of the twentieth century evaluates the use of Patristic, Reformed and contemporary models (including those of the Baptist Union of Scotland) of the Trinity in explaining the workings of the Holy Spirit.
2004 / 1-84227-321-3 / xxiv + 246pp

Ian M. Randall
Evangelical Experiences
A Study in the Spirituality of English Evangelicalism 1918–1939
(Studies in Evangelical History and Thought)
This book makes a detailed historical examination of evangelical spirituality between the First and Second World Wars. It shows how patterns of devotion led to tensions and divisions. In a wide-ranging study, Anglican, Wesleyan, Reformed and Pentecostal-charismatic spiritualities are analysed.
1999 / 0-85364-919-7 / xii + 310pp

Ian M. Randall
One Body in Christ
The History and Significance of the Evangelical Alliance
In 1846 the Evangelical Alliance was founded with the aim of bringing together evangelicals for common action. This book uses material not previously utilized to examine the history and significance of the Evangelical Alliance, a movement which has remained a powerful force for unity. At a time when evangelicals are growing world-wide, this book offers insights into the past which are relevant to contemporary issues.
2001 / 1-84227-089-3 / xii + 394pp

Ian M. Randall
Spirituality and Social Change
The Contribution of F.B. Meyer (1847–1929)
(Studies in Evangelical History and Thought)
This is a fresh appraisal of F.B. Meyer (1847–1929), a leading Free Church minister. Having been deeply affected by holiness spirituality, Meyer became the Keswick Convention's foremost international speaker. He combined spirituality with effective evangelism and socio-political activity. This study shows Meyer's significant contribution to spiritual renewal and social change.
2003 / 1-84227-195-4 / xx + 184pp

Geoffrey Robson
Dark Satanic Mills?
Religion and Irreligion in Birmingham and the Black Country
(Studies in Evangelical History and Thought)
This book analyses and interprets the nature and extent of popular Christian belief and practice in Birmingham and the Black Country during the first half of the nineteenth century, with particular reference to the impact of cholera epidemics and evangelism on church extension programmes.
2002 / 1-84227-102-4 / xiv + 294pp

Alan P.F. Sell
Enlightenment, Ecumenism, Evangel
Theological Themes and Thinkers 1550–2000
(Studies in Christian History and Thought)
This book consists of papers in which such interlocking topics as the Enlightenment, the problem of authority, the development of doctrine, spirituality, ecumenism, theological method and the heart of the gospel are discussed. Issues of significance to the church at large are explored with special reference to writers from the Reformed and Dissenting traditions.
2005 / 1-84227330-2 / xviii + 422pp

Alan P.F. Sell
Hinterland Theology
Some Reformed and Dissenting Adjustments
(Studies in Christian History and Thought)
Many books have been written on theology's 'giants' and significant trends, but what of those lesser-known writers who adjusted to them? In this book some hinterland theologians of the British Reformed and Dissenting traditions, who followed in the wake of toleration, the Evangelical Revival, the rise of modern biblical criticism and Karl Barth, are allowed to have their say. They include Thomas Ridgley, Ralph Wardlaw, T.V. Tymms and N.H.G. Robinson.
2006 / 1-84227-331-0

Alan P.F. Sell and Anthony R. Cross (eds)
Protestant Nonconformity in the Twentieth Century
(Studies in Christian History and Thought)
In this collection of essays scholars representative of a number of Nonconformist traditions reflect thematically on Nonconformists' life and witness during the twentieth century. Among the subjects reviewed are biblical studies, theology, worship, evangelism and spirituality, and ecumenism. Over and above its immediate interest, this collection provides a marker to future scholars and others wishing to know how some of their forebears assessed Nonconformity's contribution to a variety of fields during the century leading up to Christianity's third millennium.

2003 / 1-84227-221-7 / x + 398pp

Mark Smith
Religion in Industrial Society
Oldham and Saddleworth 1740–1865
(Studies in Christian History and Thought)
This book analyses the way British churches sought to meet the challenge of industrialization and urbanization during the period 1740–1865. Working from a case-study of Oldham and Saddleworth, Mark Smith challenges the received view that the Anglican Church in the eighteenth century was characterized by complacency and inertia, and reveals Anglicanism's vigorous and creative response to the new conditions. He reassesses the significance of the centrally directed church reforms of the mid-nineteenth century, and emphasizes the importance of local energy and enthusiasm. Charting the growth of denominational pluralism in Oldham and Saddleworth, Dr Smith compares the strengths and weaknesses of the various Anglican and Nonconformist approaches to promoting church growth. He also demonstrates the extent to which all the churches participated in a common culture shaped by the influence of evangelicalism, and shows that active co-operation between the churches rather than denominational conflict dominated. This revised and updated edition of Dr Smith's challenging and original study makes an important contribution both to the social history of religion and to urban studies.

2006 / 1-84227-335-3 / approx. 300pp

David M. Thompson
Baptism, Church and Society in Britain from the Evangelical Revival to
Baptism, Eucharist and Ministry
The theology and practice of baptism have not received the attention they deserve. How important is faith? What does baptismal regeneration mean? Is baptism a bond of unity between Christians? This book discusses the theology of baptism and popular belief and practice in England and Wales from the Evangelical Revival to the publication of the World Council of Churches' consensus statement on *Baptism, Eucharist and Ministry* (1982).
2005 / 1-84227-393-0 / approx. 224pp

Martin Sutherland
Peace, Toleration and Decay
The Ecclesiology of Later Stuart Dissent
(Studies in Christian History and Thought)
This fresh analysis brings to light the complexity and fragility of the later Stuart Nonconformist consensus. Recent findings on wider seventeenth-century thought are incorporated into a new picture of the dynamics of Dissent and the roots of evangelicalism.
2003 / 1-84227-152-0 / xxii + 216pp

Haddon Willmer
Evangelicalism 1785–1835: An Essay (1962) and Reflections (2004)
(Studies in Evangelical History and Thought)
Awarded the Hulsean Prize in the University of Cambridge in 1962, this interpretation of a classic period of English Evangelicalism, by a young church historian, is now supplemented by reflections on Evangelicalism from the vantage point of a retired Professor of Theology.
2006 / 1-84227-219-5

Linda Wilson
Constrained by Zeal
Female Spirituality amongst Nonconformists 1825–1875
(Studies in Evangelical History and Thought)
Constrained by Zeal investigates the neglected area of Nonconformist female spirituality. Against the background of separate spheres, it analyses the experience of women from four denominations, and argues that the churches provided a 'third sphere' in which they could find opportunities for participation.
2000 / 0-85364-972-3 / xvi + 294pp

Nigel G. Wright
Disavowing Constantine
Mission, Church and the Social Order in the Theologies of
John Howard Yoder and Jürgen Moltmann
(Paternoster Theological Monographs)

This book is a timely restatement of a radical theology of church and state in the Anabaptist and Baptist tradition. Dr Wright constructs his argument in dialogue and debate with Yoder and Moltmann, major contributors to a free church perspective.

2000 / 0-85364-978-2 / xvi + 252pp

Nigel G. Wright
Free Church, Free State
The Positive Baptist Vision

Free Church, Free State is a textbook on baptist ways of being church and a proposal for the future of baptist churches in an ecumenical context. Nigel Wright argues that both baptist (small 'b') and catholic (small 'c') church traditions should seek to enrich and support each other as valid expressions of the body of Christ without sacrificing what they hold dear. Written for pastors, church planters, evangelists and preachers, Nigel Wright offers frameworks of thought for baptists and non-baptists in their journey together following Christ.

2005 / 1-84227-353-1 / xxviii + 292

Nigel G. Wright
New Baptists, New Agenda

New Baptists, New Agenda is a timely contribution to the growing debate about the health, shape and future of the Baptists. It considers the steady changes that have taken place among Baptists in the last decade – changes of mood, style, practice and structure – and encourages us to align these current movements and questions with God's upward and future call. He contends that the true church has yet to come: the church that currently exists is an anticipation of the joyful gathering of all who have been called by the Spirit through Christ to the Father.

2002 / 1-84227-157-1 / x + 162pp

Po **Paternoster:**
thinking faith

Paternoster
9 Holdom Avenue,
Bletchley,
Milton Keynes MK1 1QR,
United Kingdom
Web: www.authenticmedia.co.uk/paternoster

July 2005